D1570717

A Wilderness of Possibilities

In honour of Professor C.M. Naim

A Wilderness of Possibilities

Urdu Studies in Transnational Perspective

edited by

KATHRYN HANSEN AND DAVID LELYVELD

OXFORD
UNIVERSITY PRESS

OXFORD
UNIVERSITY PRESS

YMCA Library Building, Jai Singh Road, New Delhi 110 001

Oxford University Press is a department of the University of Oxford.
It furthers the University's objective of excellence in research, scholarship and education by publishing worldwide in

Oxford New York
Auckland Cape Town Dar es Salaam Hong Kong Karachi
Kuala Lumpur Madrid Melbourne Mexico City Nairobi
New Delhi Shanghai Taipei Toronto

With offices in
Argentina Austria Brazil Chile Czech Republic France Greece
Guatemala Hungary Italy Japan Poland Portugal Singapore
South Korea Switzerland Thailand Turkey Ukraine Vietnam

Oxford is a registered trademark of Oxford University Press
in the UK and in certain other countries.

Published in India
by Oxford University Press, New Delhi

First published 2005

ISBN-13: 978-0-19-567020-2
ISBN-10: 0-19-567020-5

Typeset in Goudy 10/12.5
by Eleven Arts, Keshav Puram, Delhi 110 035
Printed in India by De Unique, New Delhi 110 018
Published by Manzar Khan, Oxford University Press
YMCA Library Building, Jai Singh Road, New Delhi 110 001

Contents

Part 2: The Critical Project and Its Revision

Acknowledgements

This volume, and the conference that gave rise to it, would not have been possible without the moral and financial support of numerous individuals and institutions. The editors wish to thank Carlo Coppola, Steven Poulos, and Frances Pritchett for their encouragement when the idea of a conference to honour Naim Sahib was just getting off the ground. The lively workshops on focused topics in Urdu literature organized by Fran and Carla Petievich at Columbia University provided the model for the kind of interaction we sought to replicate. Eventually, a plan for a collaborative international conference took shape. The South Asia centres of five universities contributed to this endeavour: the University of California at Berkeley, the University of Chicago, Columbia University, Cornell University, and most importantly, the University of Texas at Austin. All these institutions are grantees of the Title VI programme of the US Department of Education, without whose assistance over decades we would barely exist.

For their tireless efforts in conference coordination at Columbia, particular thanks are due to Philip Oldenburg, then Associate Director of the Southern Asian Institute, and Ezra Kover, his most patient assistant, along with their team of student volunteers. Others who assisted at critical junctures with fund raising, conceptualization, and logistical support include the late Norman Cutler, Sally Noble, Richard Cohen, Patrick Olivelle, Saeed Shafqat, and Omar Qureshi, along with Phil, Fran, Steve, and Carla. Veena Oldenburg organized the sumptuous meals which did so much to generate an atmosphere of conviviality during the three-day fête.

Special mention is owed to the American Institute of Pakistan Studies, another sponsor, whose unique contribution was to bring three distinguished senior Urdu scholars from Pakistan to add to the lustre of the conference. Brian Spooner and Wilma Heston worked on this initiative on the US side, while Nadeem Akbar made arrangements in Islamabad. Unfortunately, after itineraries were fully formed and tickets booked, each of these scholars felt compelled to cancel their visits to the US in the wake of the 11 September tragedy. Their presence at the meeting was sorely missed.

In converting the conference proceedings into a book, we first wish to thank Naim Sahib and all the contributors, whose cooperation and goodwill extended well beyond the ebullience of the meeting through tiresome rounds of revision. The Committee on Southern Asian Studies at Chicago generously provided financial support towards the publication costs. Karline McLain assisted with editing the first draft for the publishers, and two anonymous readers offered valuable corrections and advice. The bibliography of Naim's writing was initially compiled by Fran Pritchett, although the format has been changed somewhat for this publication.

KATHRYN HANSEN
DAVID LELYVELD

Note on Transliteration

The use of diacritics in this work is limited to passages and words in Urdu, Persian, and Hindi, and to references to book titles and their authors and editors in these languages. Well-known proper names and words are exempted from transliteration, e.g., Ghalib, Mir, Iqbal, ghazal, etc.

The transliteration scheme closely follows that used in Platts' *Dictionary of Urdu, Classical Hindi, and English* (1884), with the exception of the following letters:

چ ch	چھ chh	ش sh	ش gh

The *iẓāfat* is indicated by –i.

Readers should take note that variations in spelling are common in Urdu texts of all periods. The object of transliteration in this volume is to enable the reader to identify accurately the written forms of expressions in Urdu as they appear in the texts under discussion.

Contributors

MUZAFFAR ALAM is Professor in the Department of South Asian Languages and Civilizations at the University of Chicago, after having earlier taught for three decades at the Centre for Historical Studies, Jawaharlal Nehru University, New Delhi. His works include *The Crisis of Empire in Mughal North India: Awadh and the Punjab, 1707–48* (1986), and *The Languages of Political Islam: India, c. 1200–1800* (2004).

ADITYA BEHL teaches Hindi and Urdu literature and Indian cultural history in the Department of South Asia Studies at the University of Pennsylvania. His interests are in literary theory and comparative religions, and he writes on Sufi narrative poetry and religious ideology in Mughal India. His monograph on Hindavi Sufi romances, *Shadows of Paradise: An Indian Islamic Literary Tradition, 1379–1545*, is forthcoming. He has translated fiction and poetry from Hindi, Urdu, and Punjabi into English, notably Shaikh Manjhan's *Madhumālatī: An Indian Sufi Romance* (2000). He is also the co-editor of *The Penguin New Writing in India* (1994).

SHAMSUR RAHMAN FARUQI was for many years an adjunct professor at the University of Pennsylvania. He also held the Khan Abdul Ghaffar Khan Chair in the Faculty of Humanities at Jamia Millia Islamia University, New Delhi. A poet, critic, fiction writer and translator, his recent publications are *Early Urdu Literary Culture and History* (2001), and *Lug͟hāt-i Rozmarrah* (a dictionary of modern Urdu usage, 2003). His other works include *Tanqīdī Afkār* (essays on poetic theory and criticism, 1983); *Tafhīm-i G͟hālib* (close readings of poems from the *Dīvān-i G͟hālib*, 1989); *The Shadow of a Bird in Flight* (English translations of Persian poetry, 1994); and *Shiʿr-i Shor Angez* in four volumes (ghazals of Mir Taqi Mir with commentary, 1996). He retired from the Indian Post Office in 1994 and lives in Allahabad, where he edits his Urdu monthly journal, *Shabkhūn*.

MICHAEL H. FISHER is Danforth Professor of History at Oberlin College. He has published extensively about interactions between Indians and Britons in India and Britain during the pre-colonial and early colonial periods. His most recent book, *Counterflows to Colonialism: Indian Travellers and Settlers in Britain, 1600–1857* (2004), analyses how concepts of ethnicity, race, and gender changed for the tens of thousands of Indians who ventured to Britain.

KATHRYN HANSEN is Professor of South Asian Studies and past director of the Center for Asian Studies at the University of Texas at Austin. She teaches courses in Hiṇdi and Urdu literature, theatre, folklore, and gender studies. Her book *Grounds for Play: The Nautanki Theatre of North India* (1992) received the A.K. Coomaraswamy Book Prize. Recently she has published a number of articles on Parsi theatre.

SYED AKBAR HYDER is Assistant Professor of Asian Studies and Islamic Studies at the University of Texas at Austin. His research interests include Islam in South Asia, Sufism, Indo-Persian studies and Urdu literature. He has published in *Cultural Dynamics* and *Sufi Illuminations*. He received his PhD from Harvard University in 2000.

DAVID LELYVELD is Associate Dean of Humanities and Social Sciences and Professor of History at William Paterson University in Wayne, New Jersey. He is the author of *Aligarh's First Generation: Muslim Solidarity in British India* (1978, reprinted 2003). He has held faculty and administrative positions at the University of Minnesota, Columbia University, and Cornell University. His most recent publications deal with the social and political history of Urdu and its differentiation from Hindi. His current project, *Sir Syed and Macaulay's Curse*, is a study of Sir Sayyid Ahmad Khan, Justice Sayyid Mahmud, and Sir Sayyid Ross Masud.

BARBARA METCALF is the Alice Freeman Palmer Professor of History at the University of Michigan. A specialist in the history of South Asian Muslims, she is the co-author of *A Concise History of India* (2002), author of *Islamic Revival in British India: Deoband, 1860–1900* (1982, 2nd edition 2002); translator and commentator on *Perfecting Women: Maulana Ashraf 'Alī Thanavi's Bihishti Zewar* (1990); and editor and contributor to *Making Muslim Space in North America and Europe* (1996).

GAIL MINAULT is Professor of History at the University of Texas at Austin. She is the author of *The Khilafat Movement* (1982) and *Secluded Scholars: Women's*

Education and Muslim Social Reform in Colonial India (1998). She is currently doing research on the intellectual history of Delhi between the 1820s and 1857.

CARLA PETIEVICH is Associate Professor of History and Director of Women's Studies at Montclair State University in New Jersey, and has taught Urdu at several universities in North America. In addition to *Assembly of Rivals: Delhi, Lucknow, and the Urdu Ghazal* (1992) and *The Expanding Landscape: South Asians and the Diaspora* (1999), she has published articles on various topics in the field of Urdu literature. She is currently at work on a book of translations from Dakani Urdu, Lakhnavi *Rek͟htī* and Punjabi Sufi poetry.

FRANCES W. PRITCHETT is Professor of Modern Indic Languages, Department of Middle East and Asian Languages and Cultures, Columbia University. Her research interests include traditional Urdu and Hindi poetry and prose, especially classical ghazal. Her books include *The Romance Tradition in Urdu: Adventures from the Dastan of Amir Hamzah* (1991); *Nets of Awareness: Urdu Poetry and Its Critics* (1994); and *Āb-e ḥayāt: Shaping the Canon of Urdu Poetry* (2001), translated in association with S.R. Faruqi.

KUMKUM SANGARI is a professorial fellow at the Centre for Contemporary Studies, Nehru Memorial Museum and Library, New Delhi. She has written on nineteenth- and twentieth-century north Indian, British, American, and Latin American literature, critical theory, religious conversion, medieval devotional traditions, and contemporary women's issues. She is the author of *Politics of the Possible: Essays in Gender, History, Narratives, Colonial English* (1999). Among her co-edited volumes are *Recasting Women: Essays in Colonial History* (1989) and *From Myths to Markets: Essays on Gender* (1999).

RAMYA SREENIVASAN is Assistant Professor of History at the State University of New York at Buffalo. She obtained her PhD from Jawaharlal Nehru University in 2002 for her research on the history of the Padmini legend between the sixteenth and twentieth centuries. Her interests include the social history of South Asian literatures, historiography and patriarchies, and transitions from the pre-colonial period to colonialism. Her articles have appeared in the *Journal of Medieval History* and in *Unfamiliar Relations: Family and History in South Asia*, edited by Indrani Chatterjee.

SANJAY SUBRAHMANYAM is Professor of Indian History and Culture at Oxford University. He has written on diverse aspects of South Asian and Indian Ocean history, and has published several books including *The Career and Legend of Vasco da Gama* (1997), and *Penumbral Visions: Making Politics in Early Modern South India* (2001).

Introduction

Kathryn Hansen and David Lelyveld

Not much was known of Urdu language and literature in the United States when Chaudhri Muhammad Naim started teaching at the University [illegible] Durrani, the [illegible] called Mu[illegible] of his [illegible] Ghalib [illegible] institution. [illegible] but very [illegible] *New York Times* [illegible] hard pressed [illegible] were. The [illegible] him that the [illegible] spoke in India [illegible] The [illegible] consulate in New York [illegible] information. The [illegible] Columbia [illegible] that Mir and [illegible]

The [illegible] the Mir-Durrani [illegible] goals by [illegible] established [illegible] Harvard [illegible] announced that [illegible] South Asia was not one of them, nevertheless recruited a [illegible] scholar of Islamic religious literature [illegible] published [illegible] study of Iqbal [illegible] the bequest. The [illegible] Fund also supported the [illegible] Russell and Khurshidul Islam's *Three Mughal Poets* in 196[illegible] prepared in the United States [illegible]

Introduction

KATHRYN HANSEN AND DAVID LELYVELD

Not much was known of Urdu language and literature in the United States when Choudhri Mohammed Naim started teaching at the University of Chicago in the fall of 1962. When Ataullah Khan Ozai-Durrani, the Afghan-American inventor of a pre-cooked rice concoction called 'Minute Rice' died in May 1964, he directed that half a million dollars of his considerable fortune be devoted to translating the poetry of Mir and Ghalib under the auspices of Harvard University or another 'such non-profit institution'. This bequest created a good deal of confusion. A conscientious but very junior reporter at the *New York Times*, assigned to the story, was hard pressed to find out who Mir (spelled Meer Taqui Meer) and Ghalib were. The attorneys charged with administering Ozai-Durrani's bequest told him that the two poets had written in Persian 'or whatever language they spoke in India in the nineteenth century'. The librarian at the Indian consulate in New York said that only the Pakistanis could provide information. The professor of Iranian studies at Columbia University said that Mir and Ghalib were of little significance except, again, to Pakistanis.[1]

The executors of the Ozai-Durrani legacy determined to achieve its goals by interpreting them loosely and reaching beyond the US to the established sites of Orientalist scholarship. Harvard, which had recently announced that it could only support the study of some parts of the world and South Asia was not one of them, nevertheless recruited a learned German scholar of Islamic religious literatures, Annemarie Schimmel, who had just published her study of Iqbal, to oversee studies that were broadly related to the bequest. The Ozai-Durrani Fund also supported the publication of Ralph Russell and Khurshidul Islam's *Three Mughal Poets* in 1968, which had been prepared in the United Kingdom.[2]

At the same time, however, the 1960s witnessed the expansion of 'area studies' in the US. American study of the Indian subcontinent had begun long before with the advent of missionaries and the establishment of university chairs of Sanskrit studies, the first being set up at Yale in 1841. During the nineteenth century, Indologists trained in classical studies created institutional homes for research on India at a number of elite universities. Meanwhile, scholar-missionaries eager to learn more of Indian languages, history, and culture established a field-based style of knowledge and interest in contemporary affairs that held sway through the middle of the twentieth century.[3] It was the experience of World War II that pushed the American academy towards international studies, bringing new methods of intensive language learning and a relationship of cooperation between universities and the government.[4] When the colonial empires of Europe collapsed and British rule ended in South Asia, US policy makers attempted to fill the power vacuum before Communist or anti-American forces could gain a foothold.[5]

In 1958, the US Congress passed the National Defense Education Act (NDEA), earmarking federal funds for foreign language centres and setting up scholarships for the study of neglected languages such as Hindi and Urdu. In 1965, this legislation was replaced by the famed Title VI of the Higher Education Act, which continues to underwrite South Asian language and area instruction. The National Resource Centers, as they are now called, were established as early as 1959, and presently there are some ten devoted to South Asia that receive federal funding.[6] Another important federal initiative was the Fulbright Program in India, begun in 1950, and its counterpart in Pakistan dating to 1953. The study of South Asian languages received a major boost when the Rockefeller Foundation set up the linguistics programme at Deccan College in 1954. Veterans of its courses, such as C. M. Naim, began to teach Indian languages at the new South Asia centres, broadening the curriculum and offering an entirely new level of expertise.[7]

Against this background, it is safe to say that Professor Naim played a major role in establishing Urdu studies in the US. Naim's influence has touched anyone interested in Urdu literature and the wider contexts of cultural history associated with Urdu. Although he did not set out to be an institution builder, virtually every American student of Urdu has built from the foundations that he set down over more than forty years. Throughout this period, Naim stretched the conventional expectations of an academic career. His work has been personal, idiosyncratic, experimental, and widely various in its interests, grounded in the integrity of a continual curiosity, open-mindedness, and generosity of spirit.

'Urdu Scholarship in Transnational Perspective: An International

Conference in Honor of Professor C.M. Naim' took place at Columbia University on the island of Manhattan during 28–30 September 2001. The conference was a tribute to the respect and gratitude that so many scholars of literature and history wanted to express for Naim's personal achievement. Even more, the conference signified the substantial transformation of the location of Urdu studies over the previous decades. Coming just two weeks after the terrorist destruction of the World Trade Center, the conference unexpectedly affirmed an international solidarity of humanistic scholarship in the face of forces of fanaticism and division.[8] In a succession of felicitations, presentation of scholarly papers, reports on the status of Urdu in North America, and a final panel on the future of Urdu studies, the conference marked Naim's manifold contributions to the world of Urdu. The essays gathered in this volume proceed from that conference and extend its substance to a broad public.

Captured herein are themes and approaches that resonate with some of the major turns of Naim's research and writing. In the early days when so little was known of the Urdu literary landscape in North America, Naim translated the pillars of Urdu poetry, Ghalib and Faiz, and then ranged widely over the terrain of modern prose and poetry, often publishing his translations in the journals he founded and edited: *Mahfil* (later *Journal of South Asian Literature*) and the *Annual of Urdu Studies*. A number of contributors to this collection bring forth lucid new translations of texts not yet available to English readers (Alam and Subrahmanyam, Behl, Petievich), and several return to the 'giants'—Ghalib, Iqbal, Mir—with fresh perspectives (Pritchett, Metcalf, Faruqi).

Naim was particularly mindful of the achievements of women writers like Parvin Shakir and Qurratulain Hyder, and attuned to the social constraints imposed upon women by gender norms. He used both translation and the expository essay ('How Bibi Ashraf Learned to Read and Write') as remedies. But it was his bold engagement with sexuality in literary representation that pioneered a new frontier of Urdu scholarship ('The Theme of Homosexual [Pederastic] Love in Pre-modern Urdu Poetry', 'Transvestic Words? The Rekhtī in Urdu'). Whereas Behl and Petievich tackle sexuality through the recovery of previously censored voices, Sreenivasan and, to an extent, Alam and Subrahmanyam consider the interplay among gender, genre, and history via narratives that naturalize sexuality in the romantic encounter. The latter essays also reveal a receptiveness to what might be called the 'little traditions' of Urdu, contained within folklore, *qiṣṣas*, popular plays, and the like, another legacy of Naim ('Popular Jokes and Political History').

Yet it is perhaps Naim's stature as a reflective Indian Muslim, caught within 'the ambiguities of heritage', that appears most frequently, refracted in the multiple strands of scholarship in this volume. While exploring the depth of the past, most recently in his translation from Persian of Mir's 'autobiography' and his excavation of the milieu of Delhi College in the early nineteenth century, Naim also writes as a public intellectual very much rooted in the present. He comes back again and again to education, to human rights, to the struggle of minorities, and to his deep disquiet at recent political and cultural developments in South Asia. The threatened status of Urdu in India recurs as a central motif in these pieces. As counterpoint, several essays here signal the ways in which Urdu writers have reshaped their chosen forms of expression to serve larger constituencies and engage with public affairs. Hyder's contribution on Premchand's drama *Karbalā* overtly demonstrates the literary fashioning of communal harmony. Minault explores the evolution of Urdu journalism from Persian court chronicles, a development often linked to the emergence of the modern nation. Others too show a generative role for Urdu, as it connects Europe and India through the travel diary (Fisher) or through poetic discourses of geography and civilization (Metcalf).

Choudhri Mohammed Naim was born into a zamindar family in the town of Bara Banki, about 27 kilometres from Lucknow. The official year of his birth is 1936, but his mother later told him that in fact he was born two years before that; the date had been altered at the time of his admission to school. The youngest son, he remained with his mother and sisters in Bara Banki after the death of his father, due to the absence of his three brothers who worked in other parts of the country. He completed his schooling at the local Government High School, then lived at home while commuting by train to the University of Lucknow, where he studied Urdu literature for his BA and MA under the guidance of Sayyid Masud Hasan Rizvi Adib, Al-e Ahmad Suroor, and Ehtisham Husain Rizvi.

After completing his MA in 1955, Naim was selected for a six-week programme in linguistics at Deccan College, Poona (now Pune), funded by the Rockefeller Foundation and led by Indian and American scholars of linguistics and literature, including Henry A. Gleason, Jr, Sukumar Sen, Masud Husain Khan, Murray Emeneau, Gordon Fairbanks, and Edward C. Dimock. He was chosen for the full-year programme the following year, 1956–7, and then for a summer programme in Dehra Dun, where he worked with the sociolinguist, John Gumperz. Gumperz recruited him, on very short notice, to teach Hindi-Urdu while pursuing further graduate studies in Linguistics at the University of California, Berkeley, starting in the fall term of 1957.

At Berkeley, Naim taught classes and joined with others, under Gumperz's direction, in preparing teaching materials, a project funded by the US Office of Education. The first batch was a set of conversations in Hindi-Urdu, taught as one language in a newly devised Roman script, accompanied by photographic slides and language tapes for individual study. Naim wrote the texts and drills for the two volumes of Part I. The voice on the tapes was usually Naim's. The situations ranged from a conversation with a fruit seller in Aligarh to chatter among friends on Hazratganj in Lucknow. This was followed by behaviourist sentence pattern drills, the prevailing orthodoxy in American second-language teaching. After the first year of Hindi-Urdu, students could take Hindi, or Urdu, or both.

Naim completed a second MA in Linguistics at Berkeley in 1961 but could not continue for a PhD due to his deficiency in German and French. By then he was also married and was about to become a father. In the meantime, Ed Dimock invited him to the University of Chicago. There was no organized South Asia programme there at the time, so he worked initially in Oriental Studies, then in Linguistics, and in 1968 became a member of the Department of South Asian Languages and Civilizations. Chicago proved to be an ideal place, for it allowed him the freedom to work in his own way and benefit from the friendship and wisdom of colleagues such as Dimock, Colin P. Masica, and A. K. Ramanujan.

There was nothing new, of course, in teaching Urdu to foreigners, but in recruiting people like Naim and Ramanujan to the regular faculty, the University of Chicago broke the mould of sahibs and munshis that had existed since Gilchrist's day from the beginning of the nineteenth century at Fort William College.[9] Other American universities, such as the University of Pennsylvania and Cornell University, as well as Berkeley and Harvard, continued the pattern of employing American or European professors, often qualified by their purported expertise in linguistics rather than in any particular language, to supervise native speaker informants, graduate students, or their spouses, in language instruction. This system was considered sufficient to prepare students, usually in the social sciences, for the linguistic demands of fieldwork. In the case of Naim and Ramanujan, professorial status freed them to shift their teaching and scholarship from linguistics and language pedagogy to more advanced literary studies. They were also able to train students at a higher level, so that the students could actually do research in literary or historical texts, a feature of American area studies that was notably absent from the training of students of modern South Asian history, for example, in places like Oxford or Cambridge.

Until the 1960s, and in many cases well beyond that, most scholarship in modern South Asian history and social sciences, even in South Asia itself, was based primarily on English language sources. As a result, British rulers and a relatively small population of English-educated Indian males were assumed to be the sole agents of change. Models of history closely followed European lines with themes of change from medieval to renaissance, the role of printing and the voluntary associations, and the rise of nationalism. History was history of the nation state. Even when the Cambridge historians turned to pre-colonial mentalities, they had to do so by relying on English sources. In this respect, places like the University of Chicago played an important role in opening up academic inquiry to new and deeper levels of contact with indigenous knowledge. Massive collection building under the US Library of Congress supported by Public Law 480 meant that books in many South Asian languages became available in university libraries. Scholars began to concentrate on linguistically defined regions of South Asia, and in order to receive federal funding, young scholars were expected to study the languages of those regions. The dominant expectation as South Asian area studies expanded in the 1960s was that research projects would have a regional emphasis with documentary basis in Indian-language materials.[10]

Another transformation that took place on the American scene during the early stages of Naim's career was the liberalization of immigration and citizenship laws in 1965 to enable increasing numbers of people from places other than Europe to settle in the United States.[11] Like many Indians coming to the US, Naim had for a long time every intention to return to India. In 1971–2, in fact, he packed up all his books and took his two American-born children with him to accept a readership in Comparative Literature at Aligarh Muslim University. It was not a good experience. He returned to the University of Chicago, and there in 1976 was promoted to Associate Professor with tenure. Several years later he became an American citizen.[12]

The creation of a South Asian diaspora in the United States and Canada, as well as, of course, the United Kingdom, has played a significant role in the transformation of Urdu and South Asian studies. Coming in the wake of the birth of Pakistan and the diminution of Urdu within India as a language of official use or practical advantage, the study of Urdu literature has come to be a way of calling into question fixed categories of history and identity that are the stuff of nationalist projects. Ralph Russell of the School of Oriental and African Studies, University of London, was among the first to realize that there was now a new constituency for the study of Urdu among the children of immigrants.[13] Naim's project, on the other hand, was directed to a smaller, but nonetheless growing constituency: 'Urduwallahs' in the West. This was the audience he identified for the *Annual of Urdu Studies*, which he first brought out in 1981.[14] For fifteen years before that, from 1963 to 1978, he had co-edited with Carlo Coppola the journal *Mahfil* (in 1973 renamed *Journal of South Asian Literature*), devoted to a wider selection of literatures from South Asia, including English. Now, however, there was a large enough community interested specifically in Urdu. Personally typed by the editor on his Kaypro computer, the *Annual of Urdu Studies* included articles, translations, book reviews, documents, news, and bibliography. Over the following ten years, Naim brought out seven finely crafted issues, then called a halt. After a hiatus of three years, the journal revived in expanded form under the editorship of Muhammad Umar Memon and associate editor, G. A. Chaussée.

Urdu studies continued to gain strength in institutional terms throughout the span of Naim's career. For students lacking the diasporic connection, programmes of language study abroad proved an integral part of building competence in Urdu. In 1974, the Berkeley Urdu Language Program in Pakistan (BULPIP) was begun to provide advanced training in Urdu in an immersion situation. A substantial percentage of American academics who work on Urdu, South Asian Islam, and Pakistan have over the years been alumni of BULPIP, and the programme can rightly take credit for enabling scholars to pursue more sophisticated research both in Pakistan and India.[15] The American Institute of Indian Studies supported language training as early as 1969, but only in 1998 began offering an advanced programme for Urdu students in Lucknow, largely because of the success of BULPIP. Urdu also has received special support since the establishment of the American Institute of Pakistan Studies in 1973. AIPS has worked more closely with BULPIP in recent years and has assisted with funding for the Urdu conference at Columbia in 2001.

In the last decade, the powerful resources of the Internet have been placed at the service of Urdu. The Digital South Asia Library project of the Center for Research Libraries, Chicago, has made dictionaries, textbooks, photographs, maps, and other reference materials available online. Most valuable for Urdu scholars are the two searchable dictionaries, Platt's *Dictionary of Urdu, Classical Hindi, and English* (1884) and Shakespear's *Dictionary, Hindustani and English* (1834). Selected issues of *Mahfil/Journal of South Asian Literature* and the *Annual of Urdu Studies* have been digitized and added to the site, and three Urdu textbooks written by C. M. Naim are available in their entirety. Individual scholars like Frances Pritchett have also set up their own websites where a wealth of information is readily accessible to Urdu lovers. A plethora of private efforts, for example, the websites *www.eurdubazaar.com* and *www.jadeedadab.com*, add to the promotion of Urdu letters, making it impossible for the identities of a Mir or Ghalib to remain in question today.

This brief account of Naim's career and the history of Urdu studies would be incomplete without mention of the tragic events of 11 September 2001 and the ensuing media spotlight on terrorists claiming to act in the name of Islam. Pakistan played a strategic role in the American-led overthrow of the Taliban in Afghanistan and continues to assist the US in confronting Al Qaeda. With Pakistan's vital position as an ally reconfirmed, the irony is that due to security concerns American scholars have often been denied permission to travel there for research. Yet as funding in the United States for the study of Islamic societies and cultures has been increasing, more universities than ever now offer Urdu as a separate course of instruction from Hindi. According to the most recent survey by the Modern Languages Association, enrolments in Urdu have more than quadrupled since 1998, although the numbers remain modest.[16] Two new entities, the South Asia Summer Language Institute and the South Asia Language Resource Center, have been formed to buttress the teaching of modern languages including Urdu. Whether global events with their peculiar spin in American higher education circles will strengthen humanistic Urdu scholarship is another matter. It is certainly not the case that Urdu scholarship, even in the United States, is bound up with American political agendas. The history of Urdu studies is strewn with unanticipated consequences.

The conference at Columbia in September 2001, which was the basis for all but one of the papers in the present volume, exemplified the international reach of Urdu studies and the ways in which Urdu partakes of and contributes to contemporary discourses about culture and history. Seeing Urdu from a transnational perspective highlights all the more the hybrid, borderless nature of language and literature. Even as many of its literary champions have sought to shore up the embankments of a <u>*kh*</u>*āliṣ* or 'chaste' Urdu free of supposed intrusions, Urdu, more visibly than most standardized or literary languages, draws from wide-ranging migrations and encounters within South Asia and beyond. The continued dominance of Arabic and Persian diction, images and genres, the persistence of local linguistic varieties, the colonial encounter with English, the competition with Hindi, and now the voice of an Urdu diaspora, all reveal that Urdu has always lived in juxtaposition to other languages and literatures, has never been a monolingual thing unto itself.

In the first group of essays, scholars grounded for the most part in the discipline of history demonstrate the rewards of reading Urdu texts within a changing pattern of speech forms, written languages, genres, patronage systems, and audiences. These discussions not only locate Urdu literary works within their historical and cultural contexts, but also bring out the ambiguities of those contexts, their overlapping and shifting boundaries, and the different resonances contained within the texts as a result. What emerges is a notion of the divergent social and political spaces that Urdu literature has occupied through the centuries, and the ways in which Urdu writers have deftly woven their works within them.

Kumkum Sangari's reading of Qurratulain Hyder's novel (or novels), *Āg kā Daryā/River of Fire*, exemplifies the spirit of receptivity to a work of multiple voices and perspectives. Sangari sees Hyder as drawing upon a number of genres, from ancient Buddhist Jataka tales, to the oral *dāstān* tradition, to the modernism of the twentieth-century novel, in a narrative structure that contests the boundaries of time and space. She compares Hyder's treatment of genre to a performance of Hindustani music, in which the musician 'shows' one raga as inherent in another. The novel draws on the historical stereotypes and reconstructions that appeared in romances, poetry, and school textbooks, but only to reveal their intertextuality as multiple perspectives. By carrying characters forward from one historical era to another, splitting and combining them in new contexts, Hyder creates multiple 'modes of affiliation' that reach beyond standard categories such as family lineage or religion. The recurring theme of travel and mobility puts characters in unexpected geographical locations and creates a 'centrifugal nationalism' that ultimately celebrates India as a civilization over its identity as a nation state. By tracking generations over time, the novel sees the rise and fall of elites and subordinate classes, so that what the civilization ultimately celebrates is transience itself, as well as love as 'elective affinity', free of prescribed solidarities.

Sangari's analysis of Hyder's novel provides a meta-historical frame for the contribution of Muzaffar Alam and Sanjay Subrahmanyam, who trace the literary lineage of the Nal and Daman story from the Persian poem by Faiẓī, commissioned by the emperor Akbar for his private entertainment, to its later Urdu retellings. This essay raises the question of the salience of British colonial dominance in the cultural history of modern India and the probable extent of continuities from pre-colonial time. The Nal-Daman story has its origins in the Mahabharata and has been rendered in many languages of South Asia, but its expression in Persian represents a deliberate effort to cross conventional boundaries and bring an Indian story as a celebration of India itself into the cosmopolitan, 'transnational' field of Islamicate culture. Faiẓī speaks of playing an Indian melody on an Irani instrument. Indian love themes are now cast in Sufi terms of divine union, exemplified in a celebration of sati as a metaphor—not, presumably, an actual practice.

To the extent that Faiẓī's poem documents a sense of belonging to India in the Mughal court, later Urdu versions, based largely on Faiẓī, replicate this tendency but express less interest in reaching to audiences beyond India. Aḥmad Sarāwī's *Nal Daman* is an example of a more localized *qaṣba* culture, characteristic of the decentralization of Mughal dominance. Freely drawing upon the local Bangdu of the Meerut area and the literary structure of an Awadhi version of the story, it also draws extensively on Faiẓī's Persian text. Munshī Lāl Bhagwant Rāi 'Rāḥat' Kakorwī's *Nal-Daman Hindī*, published in 1859, is significantly more explicit both about sex and about the Hindu character of the story, but it still closely parallels Faiẓī's Persian poem and its Sufi treatment of love. Rāḥat's work, however, was printed commercially and subsidized by several merchants. Carrying with it sediments of Faiẓī's text, Rāḥat's work reaches a somewhat different, more popular audience, particularly as fewer people are able to read Persian. At the same time, another version of the story in Braj, attributed to Ṭoḍarmal, Akbar's revenue minister, becomes increasingly popular. Although it is Vaishnava rather than Sufi, its supposed authorship also bears the authority of the Mughal court.

Ramya Sreenivasan also traces the literary genealogy of an Indian story as a mark of cross-fertilization as well as cultural conflict over time. Although Malik Muḥammad Jāyasī's Awadhi *Padmāvat*, written about 1540 in Persian script and immersed in Sufism, has not been included in the canon of Urdu literature, scholars of Hindi literature have been happy to claim it. Nevertheless, Jāyasī served as an inspiration for subsequent Persian and Urdu versions, first in the *maṣnavī* and later as prose *qiṣṣa* literature. The change in language and genre coincided with the shift from a Sufi text, transmitted in Sufi networks, to courtly culture, to commercial Urdu printing for a popular audience. The theme of love is similarly transformed from mystical to secular.

In the course of the nineteenth and early twentieth centuries, however, a counter-tradition emerges in Urdu founded, according to Sreenivasan, on James Tod's *Annals and Antiquities of Rajasthan* (1829–32). Tod of course adapted his story from a variety of prior sources, mostly in Braj, but it is likely that later writers, such as Bankimchandra in Bengali, drew upon Tod's English text. '*Aẓamat-i Chitor* by Rudar and Dev Datt (1914) and Kishan Chand Zebā's historical drama *Padminī* (1926) may have drawn on authors like Bankim, presumably in translation, or Tod, or both, but certainly not directly on the literary tradition based on Jāyasī's *Padmāvat.* These later Urdu versions by Hindu authors are characterized by marked Sanskritic vocabulary associated with Hindu heroes and Arabic or Persian vocabulary with Muslim villains. Rajputs are defined as standing for all Hindus and Alauddin Khalji for all Muslims.

Gail Minault similarly crosses the Mughal-British divide to ask, 'Did an expanded readership for print signal an emerging colonial hybrid culture, or a vernacular discourse with links to traditional cultures, or both?' She addresses this question by comparing the system of *akhbār nawīsī*, the official or private networks of news writing associated with the Mughal court and successor states, with the rise of printed Urdu newspapers, particularly in Delhi. Arguing against press censorship, Ram Mohan Roy, a pioneer in newspaper publishing in Calcutta, made the point forcefully that the Mughal rulers, for all their shortcomings, were better informed than the British were, but the question of a public space for news is different from private or official networks. Minault alludes in passing to the native newspaper reports that the British introduced for official circulation, drawn on a selected reading of the vernacular press. But her chief interest is the literary ferment in early nineteenth-century Delhi, notably associated with Delhi College. The press, despite an infinitesimal circulation, was a participant in this new culture of 'print capitalism'. Her conclusion with respect to the question of whether colonial rule marked a sharp cultural break is that, at least in Delhi, 'literate Indians maintained continuities with their own ways of transmitting information and engaged in selective responses to Western influence'.

Michael Fisher turns the tables on who gets to study whom by calling attention to the Urdu writings of two travellers to Britain at the very outset of the Victorian era. As part of a larger study of the prehistory of the South Asian community in Britain, Fisher calls attention to the independent, self-confident perspectives of Yūsuf Khān 'Kambalposh' and Karīm Khān who, again, crossed the border between Mughal and British culture by going right to the heart of the beast. Kambalposh travelled to Europe (1836–8) purely out of curiosity, *dekhne kā shauq*. The Urdu account of his travels, written in the tradition of *riḥlat* literature, was ultimately published in several editions. Karīm Khān's journey (1839–41) had practical business to attend to on behalf of the Nawab of Jhajjar and was perhaps less adventurous. His work was a manuscript diary, not intended for public circulation. Both of them noted the difference between official and personal relations with the British and, even more, the greater access they had to the British in Britain than to their colonial rulers in India. In the case of Karīm Khān's mission, his encounters with the British only reinforced the lack of access to power that characterizes the colonial situation, but both travellers exemplify the sustaining power of Mughal culture even on foreign territory.

Barbara Metcalf addresses the theme of travel and agency as it crosses into the twentieth century in the writing of Muhammad Iqbal. In Metcalf's reading, Iqbal directly questioned the boundaries of language, national identity, historical periodization and conventional geographic categories that had come to the foreground in the final decades of colonial rule. A native speaker of Punjabi, Iqbal wrote poetry in Urdu and Persian; he wrote discursive prose in English. His use of Persian, like Faiẓī's in the late sixteenth century, was a transnational gesture to a wider public. The same could be said of his English. Along with Faiẓī and the literary tradition that followed him, Iqbal wanted the rest of the world to appreciate the beauty and cultural richness of India. To the extent that Iqbal appropriated colonial categories, like 'East' and 'West', it was to undermine their authority. This included the assumption, not unknown among South Asian Muslims, that the Arabic Middle East had a superior claim to authentic Islam. As a *kāfir-i hindī*, an Indian infidel, proud of his Hindu ancestors, Iqbal claimed a more universal perspective on the meaning of Islam.

According to Metcalf, Iqbal represented a 'counter-modernity', most particularly in his major poem written in Persian, the *Jāvednāma*, which, a quarter-century before and even more boldly than Qurratulain Hyder's *Āg kā Daryā*, intercut periods and persons from different times and places. Although he sometimes lapsed into a narrower communal chauvinism, Iqbal at his best was an embodiment of an open mind, always ready to cross borders to other worlds. Metcalf quotes Iqbal's famous lines about nationalism in his poem 'Vataniyyat': *hijra: hai tark-i vaṯn, sunnat-i maḥbūb-i ilāhī* (to depart the homeland is the example of God's Beloved). At the same time, Iqbal believed that the power of language, *sirr-i ādam* (Adam's secret), enabled humanity to create new worlds of justice and beauty.

If in this first set of essays temporal and spatial boundaries are questioned and remapped, the second group of contributors, all literature scholars, tackle some of the critical paradigms that have informed Urdu literary history. These authors examine both the theoretical limitations of accepted criteria of literary judgement and the omissions that result from applying them. Excluded or marginalized classes of writers receive attention here, women and popular poets, as well as anomalous texts like Premchand's *Karbalā* that defy communal (and generic) categories. By expanding the field of Urdu literature and gesturing towards new methodologies of reading, these essays enable the pleasure of the text to come to the fore.

Shamsur Rahman Faruqi, in his discussion of Mir Taqi Mir's 'autobiography', *Ẕikr-i Mīr*, confronts and then dismantles the familiar 'reflection' thesis of Urdu criticism. According to this credo, a poet's verse is assumed to mirror his life and times and provide insights into them. Beginning from the observation that Mir's *Ẕikr* seems to dissemble rather than reveal the facts about the author, Faruqi finds that Urdu critics expect poetry, especially the ghazal, to express the poet's personality and present the reader with his true feelings. This axiom has a long history, which Faruqi traces to the English Romantics, although this is less his concern than the ways in which it has distorted literary judgement. Mir, the 'poet of sorrow' according to Majnun Gorakhpuri, lived in a quintessential 'age of sorrow', yet his *oeuvre* contains many light-hearted, humorous verses that cannot be squared with his doleful image. For the pre-modern poet like Mir, Faruqi maintains, self-expression was not the objective of poetic utterance. The poet's business, rather, was the creation of a new theme (*maẓmūn āfirīnī*), an exercise of invention in which artistry resided in disguising the familiar in novel ways. Looking within Mir's own verse, Faruqi finds the key to his poetic practice when he asserts, 'I used *Rekẖta* (Urdu poetry) as a veil over my true utterance.' Dissembling thus returns, not as a distraction or deviation, but as the true art of the poet.

Aditya Behl articulates the search for new ways of enjoying Urdu poetry in his discussion of Naẕīr Akbarābādī, the eighteenth-century poet who celebrated the street life of Agra. Although Naẕīr has enjoyed sustained popularity, his work stands outside the canon. Behl identifies strands of Naẕīr's poetry that show his knowledge of the classics, his macaronic verse for example, but largely he gives access through translation to Naẕīr's colourful depictions of marketplace activity, sensual experience, and social commentary. For an appreciation of Naẕīr, Behl argues, the critic must reclaim his service-class background and the bazaar culture of the eighteenth century, a devalued historical period; both can be used to unlock his literary spirit. Behl points to the intertwinings of desire, consumption, and economic gain in Naẕīr's verse that render concrete the usually idealized emotion of Urdu poetry, placing it within public spaces. Further, he illustrates how Naẕīr, for all his gusto and frank acceptance of sexuality, holds to a decided morality. His poetic satires exude an anti-aristocratic sentiment, but beyond that he presents the reader with a humanistic vision that levels all distinction. Behl concludes that in stretching canonical boundaries, Naẕīr not only enriched Urdu literature but added to the dynamism of cultural life in the eighteenth and early nineteenth centuries.

Carla Petievich too questions the exclusions written into the poetic canon, in this instance with reference to women's voices. She juxtaposes two *tazkiras* or poetic genealogies, which she characterizes as the earliest form of critical writing on Urdu poetry. The first, *Bahāristān-i Nāz*, provides a rare record of historical women who are known to have written verse in Urdu. The poets documented, such as Māh Laqā Chandā and Munnī Bāī Hijāb, adhere to standard conventions of ghazal composition, at least in the few examples of their work cited by Ranj, the compiler. Yet legends associated with the women cluster around their poetic personae and almost usurp the place of the poetry in the text. Petievich contends that the *tazkira* is meant to promote the notoriety of courtesan poets as much as (or more than) to preserve their poetry. Titillating details of the women's lives take centre stage, allaying male anxiety about female authorship.

The second anthology, *Tazkira-i Rekhtī*, equally addresses the reader as voyeur, this time in relation to *rekhtī*, the specialized genre in which male poets write as if they were secluded women. Domestic activities and minor affairs of the heart, some with lesbian overtones, dominate the *rekhtī* of Lucknow, often narrated with a teasing or petulant tone. In contrast the Dakani poet Hāshmī, also represented in this *tazkira*, speaks plaintively of the pangs of love in separation. Petievich argues that *rekhtī* texts in general depict secluded women banding together to exclude men from their own realm of pleasure. Male anxiety about purdah, and fantasies about what goes on behind it, are at their core. Noting the absence of historical women writing *rekhtī*, Petievich finds that *rekhtī* is a male invention that once more seems intended to exoticize women rather than convey the realities of their lives and experience.

As counterpoint to Petievich's discussion of the limits of *tazkira* as indigenous criticism, Frances Pritchett subjects to scrutiny another tool of Urdu literary analysis, the *sharḥ* or poetic commentary. Choosing a single *she'r*, the enigmatic couplet that opens Ghalib's Urdu Divan, and the voluminous body of explication that surrounds it, Pritchett reconstructs a conversation about the meaning (or lack of meaning) of a dense cluster of images. Ghalib himself was the first to gloss his allusion to obscure sartorial practices of plaintiffs in Iran. Thereafter, commentators argued for and against the meaningfulness of the verse, as well as the adequacy of Ghalib's own précis. What they did not do, Pritchett argues, is avail of the helpful analytical categories of Persian-Urdu poetics found in handbooks of rhetoric. In search of the reasons for the commentators' focus on prose paraphrase of meaning and their lack of interest in poetic devices and affinities of sound, Pritchett shows how Ghalib was beset by critics who attacked his poetry as devoid of meaning. Ghalib, the master of 'meaning creation', often failed to find readers who could appreciate his clever juxtapositions. The commentators, in consequence, sought to rescue his poetry by providing 'solutions' to the riddles it posed. Had they looked beyond the polemic of meaningfulness, they would have found resources within the tradition for a more expansive practice of poetic interpretation.

The utilitarian ethics of Progressivism, which supplanted the older aesthetics of beauty, provide the starting point for Syed Akbar Hyder's discussion of Premchand's drama, *Karbalā*, published in the 1920s. Hyder asserts that Premchand sought to restore communal harmony through his writing as part of a larger project of nation building. In publishing the play originally in the medium of Hindi, he addressed it primarily to Hindu readers, albeit his objective in retelling the popular story of Husayn's martyrdom was to undermine communal antagonism by 'ideologically fracturing religious communities'. Premchand borrows heavily from the *marṡiya* narratives of Karbala, overlaying them with nationalist characterizations of resilient women. His most striking innovation is the inclusion of 'Dutt Brahmans' who come to Husayn's aid. These dedicated Hindus 'metamorphosed into ideal Muslims' serve as models for Premchand's readership, exemplars of inter-communal respect. When Premchand brought out the Urdu version, he was accused of trivializing the hallowed narrative by ensconcing it in dramatic format, long demeaned as mere entertainment. Honouring Muslim sentiments, Premchand indicated that the drama should only be read, not performed. Hyder finds in *Karbalā* a reconceptualization of both the nation and religious identity, valid as much today as in Premchand's time.

The historical and literary range of these studies exemplifies, once again, the complex interweaving of perspectives on space and time that one encounters in the study of Urdu. One might say that this complexity is reflected in the ghazal itself, a form whose genius lies in its restless power to draw the reader into unexpected juxtapositions and ways of understanding. Alluding to the boundless potential of the field of Urdu, perhaps, Naim when he founded the *Annual of Urdu Studies* inscribed on its cover a favourite *she'r* of Mirza Ghalib:

ہے کہاں تمنا کا دوسرا قدم یا رب

ہم نے دشتِ امکاں کو ایک نقشِ پا پایا

غالب

hai kahāṇ tamannā kā dūsrā qadam, yā rab
ham ne dasht-i imkān ko ek naqsh-i pā pāyā
What is the second step of my longing, Oh Lord?
In this wilderness of possibilities, I have only found one footprint.

As Naim himself explained: 'The craving within the human heart is boundless; it is always reaching out for newer horizons.... The world is only one footprint.... Many more worlds are still behind the veil.'[17]

Notes

[1] Joseph Lelyveld, 'Inventor Leaves Half Million for Translation of 2 Persian Poets', *New York Times*, 19 June 1964; reprinted in *Annual of Urdu Studies* 4 (1984), 97–9; available at *http: //dsal.uchicago.edu/books/annualofurdustudies.*

[2] Editor's Note, by C.M. Naim, in *AUS* 4 (1984), 99. Annemarie Schimmel, *Gabriel's Wing: A Study into the Religious Ideas of Sir Muhammad Iqbal*, Leiden: E. J. Brill, 1963; Ralph Russell and Khurshidul Islam, *Three Mughal Poets: Mir, Sauda, Mir Hasan*, Cambridge, MA: Harvard University Press, 1968.

[3] Scholar-missionaries developed a deep attachment to India and often passed their affection for India to their children. W. Norman Brown, the founding figure in South Asian academic studies in the US, grew up in India and learned Hindi as a child, while accompanying his missionary father who served as principal of a school in Jabalpur. Maureen L. P. Patterson, 'Institutional Base for the Study of South Asia in the United States and the Role of the American Institute of Indian Studies', in Joseph W. Elder *et al.* (eds), *India's Worlds and U.S. Scholars, 1947–1997*, New Delhi: Manohar/American Institute of Indian Studies, 1998, 19–23.

[4] During the war, institutions such as the University of Chicago housed intensive language programmes run by the US government, which proved highly effective. *See* Susan Seizer *et al.*, 'South Asia at Chicago', available at *http:// www.lib.uchicago.edu/e/su/southasia/50yrs1.html.*

[5] Richard Davis, *South Asia at Chicago*, cited in Seizer, 'South Asia'.

[6] Patterson, 'Institutional Base', 33–4.

[7] Ibid., 31.

[8] 'Held on the fifteenth floor of the School of International and Public Affairs, the walls of windows gave a sweeping, uninterrupted view of the Manhattan skyline; the obvious gap in the southern horizon was a constant reminder of the tumultuous events that preceded the conference.' Mubena Khanum, 'Landmark Conference on Urdu Studies', *Southern Asian Institute Newsletter*, Columbia University, 26: 1, Fall 2001, 1.

[9] Sisir Kumar Das, *Sahibs and Munshis: An Account of the College of Fort William*, New Delhi: Orion, 1978; Bernard S. Cohn, 'The Command of Language and the

Language of Command', in Ranajit Guha (ed.), *Subaltern Studies IV*, New Delhi: Oxford University Press, 1985, 276–329.

[10] Frank Conlon, 'History (Colonial and Post-Colonial)', in *India's Worlds and U.S. Scholars*, 288.

[11] *See* Carla Petievich (ed.), *The Expanding Landscape: South Asians and the Diaspora*, New Delhi: Manohar, 1999.

[12] C.M. Naim, 'On Becoming an American', *Toronto South Asian Review*, 1: 1, 1982, reprinted in C. M. Naim, *Ambiguities of Heritage*, Karachi: City Press, 1999, 169–74.

[13] Ralph Russell, *A New Course in Hindustani for Learners in Britain*, Part 1, London: Extramural Division, School of Oriental and African Studies, University of London, 1980.

[14] 'A Letter from the Editor', *Annual of Urdu Studies*, 1, (1981), 124; *http://dsal.uchicago.edu/books/annualofurdustudies/*

[15] Steven Poulos, 'Urdu in America: The Last Forty Years', oral presentation at the conference 'Urdu Studies in Transnational Perspective', 29 September 2001.

[16] Surendra Gambhir, private communication, December 2003; statistics from a pre-publication copy of the Modern Languages Association survey of Higher Education Foreign Language Enrolments.

[17] *Twenty-five Verses of Ghalib*, trans. C. M. Naim, Calcutta: Writers Workshop, 1970, 26–7.

PART 1

Urdu Literature and the Political Imaginary

The Configural Mode:
Āg kā Daryā

Kumkum Sangari*

When it appeared in 1959, Qurratulain Hyder's *Āg kā Daryā* created a sensation. It received a Sahitya Akademi Award and was translated into fourteen Indian languages within a decade. Yet this enthusiastic and somewhat astonished reception, the general acknowledgement of Hyder's stature (compared to Garcia Marquez), her 'historical sweep' and invocation of an inclusive syncretic culture, did not result in serious critical attention to the way the novel had cast the pain and promise of a secular-nationalist *imaginaire* into a unique literary-historical form.

The structural innovation of *Āg kā Daryā* lay in the staging of four historical periods: the fourth century BC and the inception of the Mauryan empire by Chandragupta, the end of the Lodi dynasty and the beginning of Mughal rule in the late fifteeenth and early sixteenth centuries, the late eighteenth-century beginnings of East India Company rule up till its consolidation in the 1870s, and the two decades ending in the 1950s that encompassed nationalist struggle, partition, and independence. These constitute four sequential yet discrete experiential moments that can neither be made amenable to a causal and teleological reading, nor slotted as the discontinuous fragments characteristic of a high modernism. They are more readily grasped as a single constellation, as an individual attempt to apprehend a 'civilization', and as a doubled gesture repeated in a different conjuncture when Hyder's own English version, *River of Fire*, appeared in 1998. This was a fifth moment,

*Author's note: I am deeply grateful to C. M. Naim for encouraging me to work on *Āg kā Daryā*, to Shama Futehally for her generous help with the Urdu text, and to Ahmer Nadeem Anwer for his invaluable comments on the first draft of this essay.

rendered invisible by labels of mistranslation or transliteration, yet so powerful that I was compelled to reread *Āg kā Daryā* backwards from *River of Fire*, very much in the manner of the eponymous 'river' which, in the author's own words, is a metaphor for time that flows forward and backward.[1]

River of Fire is a novel recomposed by the author (she calls it transcreation). *Āg kā Daryā* carried multiple generic possibilities that span much of the history of the Indian novel: a 'researched' historical novel, a 'mutiny' novel (an antidote to Raj fantasies), a regional novel in the *shahr-āshob* tradition (lamenting the repeated decline and destruction of Awadh), a political 'discussion' novel (which evolved from the dialogues in reformist polemical treatises), a historical romance, an inter-racial romance (an ironic replay of Anglo-Indian fiction), a courtesan novel, an urban Lucknow-centred 'college' story, a fictionalized female autobiography, a cosmopolitan novel (on émigrés and expatriates). Some of these become less vivid in *River of Fire*; some narrative sequences and narrative voices also change; each revision or reorganization remodulates it in intention and effect, in motif, theme, and reference; there is an overall abridgement that clips character and dialogue. This abbreviating process began in the author-approved translation into Hindi in 1968; it may have been a consequence of editorial interventions, yet it indicates that some concerns had gradually receded or become less pressing. Though the basic spatial and temporal structure remains unchanged, this 'final' version interferes so substantively with the earlier that it blocks any unproblematic return to the 'original'. The two novels have now to be read against each other and grasped together as part of a single configuration (to which I shall return), rather than in the banalities of mistranslation or of the authorial hubris of recreation.

Since I cannot do justice to even one of these novels here nor undertake a comparative study, I shall, working backwards from *River of Fire*, try to convey how the four moments remain linked to each other through succession, sedimentation and retrieval, and discuss some of the literary and historical coordinates of Hyder's chosen form.

The Emplotment of Character

In each of these moments, a central set of characters reappear with partly altered names, either as different persons or in recognizably similar situations. Scholars, historians, travellers, seekers, (potential) artists and writers, they relive individual trajectories of mutilation, desertion, uprooting, exile, wandering, and settlement, often repeating a 'cycle' of withdrawal into personal and/or spiritual resolution in the face of gross political violence.

Champak in the first story is deserted by her fiancé Hari Shankar who becomes a Buddhist *bhikshu*; she rejects the same option for herself and shifts her affection to Gautam Nilambar; captured in war, she is forced to join the harem of an old *mantri* but still desires Gautam. Champavati in the second story, the sister of a learned Brahmin in Ayodhya, agrees to wed Syed Abul Mansur Kamaluddin and seems ready to convert to Islam, but Kamal, a travelling scholar, never returns; she searches for him, then joins a band of Vaishnav *sannyasins* and retires to Brindaban. Champa Jan in the third story is a rich, intelligent courtesan in Lucknow who dallies with a British nabob and members of the landowning elite, but falls in love with the *bhadra* Gautam Nilambar Dutt and waits for him to return from Calcutta. Her middle age is spent as a *chowdhrain* of *tawaifs*; she eventually becomes an old beggar who lurks at the railway station, still in love with an ultimately indifferent man. Champa Ahmed in the fourth story, daughter of a genteel lawyer who supports the Muslim League, is a petit bourgeois, self-fictionalizing social climber, who plays out a series of relationships with various men including Gautam Nilambar, does not marry any of them, works in England for some years and returns to set up a legal practice with her father in her home town, Benares.

Nirmala in the first story is a princess who, captured in war, escapes from her captor's harem and becomes a Buddhist nun. In the second story, Nirmala's renunciation seems to be re-enacted by Champavati; Nirmala also lingers in Ruqqaiya Bano Begum, the aristocratic woman scholar, who is captured in war and never gets to marry Kamaluddin, the man she loves. In the third story, Nirmala can be glimpsed in the nun Annabella, the illegitimate daughter of Maria Theresa and Cyril Ashley. In the fourth story, Nirmala reappears as a bright, educated girl from Lucknow who enrols in Cambridge. In love with Gautam, who is also attracted to Champa Ahmed, Nirmala refuses to marry him; she dies of tuberculosis in England.

The parallel men are the Gautam Nilambars, Hari Shankars, Kamaluddins and Cyril Ashleys. Gautam Nilambar in the first story, a student at Shravasti, is the son of a rich Brahmin but not inclined to priesthood; his home destroyed, his hand mutilated in war, he is forced to give up sculpture and becomes an actor. He searches for the lost Champak, but when he does find her, he rejects her; he dies a wanderer. Gautam Nilambar Dutt in the third story is an English-educated Bengali in British service. Though fascinated with the Lakhnavi *tawaif*, Champa Jan, Dutt rejects her; he leaves his government job to teach in a Brahmo school, and eventually becomes a prosperous publisher. Gautam Nilambar in the fourth story, son of an Allahabad High Court judge, is a bohemian artist at Shantiniketan who travels abroad, joins the Indian Foreign

Service, settles restlessly into a bureaucratic job, and participates in the museumization of 'culture'.

Hari Shankar in the first story is a prince who, disguised as a Greek, travels widely over Central Asia, then renounces his kingdom and his fiancée to become a Buddhist monk. Hari Shankar appears in the second story of *Āg kā Daryā* as a soldier who fights alongside Kamaluddin to defend Jaunpur from the Afghans, but he disappears from the second story of *River of Fire*. Munshi Hari Shankar in the third story is a native clerk who introduces Gautam Nilambar Dutt to Lucknow, upholds both purdah as a status symbol and the *Manusmṛti*'s strictures against freedom for women. Hari Shankar Raizada in the fourth story, son of a Congress barrister who writes Urdu poetry, the childhood friend and professed alter-ego of the scientist Kamal Reza, works in the USA for a while and returns to a government job in India.

Abul Mansur Kamaluddin of Nishapur appears for the first time in the second story. The son of a Persian mother and an Arab father, he comes to 'Hindustan' in 1476 in search of fortune on the advice of a Phoenician Jew and becomes a court translator in Jaunpur. He passes through an 'intellectual' romance with the learned Ruqqaiya, a kinswoman of his patron Sultan Hussain Shah 'Nayak', then falls in love with Champavati. Separated by war, he makes no concerted attempt to find her until it is too late. When Jaunpur is destroyed by Sikandar Lodi, he deserts the sultan he serves, encounters Chistiya Sufis, Buddhist *bhikshus*, and Kabir, and finally settles down in Bengal, tills the land, and marries the Shudra Sujata Debi. His elder son enters Mughal service, and because of this Kamaluddin is dubbed a traitor, beaten, and left to die by Sher Shah's soldiers. In the third story, he is symbolically split between two characters who may or may not be his descendants: the impoverished Bengali ferryman Abdul Mansur, and Abul Mansur Kamaluddin Ali Reza Bahadur (known as Nawab Kamman), a hereditary landowner in Awadh. Nawab Kamman, though married, is an admirer of Champa Jan. He goes to England with Malika Kishwar's party to plead against her deposition. When he returns two years later, after the revolt, he finds his city, Lucknow, in ruins. In the fourth story, Kamaluddin is split between two cousins: the Switzerland-returned Amir Reza who does not marry Champa Ahmed, and the ardently socialist and nationalist Kamal Reza who studies in Cambridge, returns to a derelict Lucknow but cannot find a job; the land reforms impoverish Kamal's parents, their ancestral property is unfairly confiscated as evacuee property, and dispossessed, they are compelled to emigrate to Pakistan.

Cyril Ashley appears in the third story. The son of an indigent clergyman, he makes his fortune in India, becomes a hookah-smoking nabob, seduces the Eurasian Maria Theresa and then deserts her. He takes Sujata for his *bibi*, makes a fortune, gets a knighthood, marries a British woman, dies lonely but founds a colonial 'dynasty'. His great-grandson, Cyril Ashley of the fourth story, is a member of the fashionable left in Cambridge who dabbles in socialism, researches Anglo-French relations in India, and falls in love with Champa Ahmed. He joins the family tea plantations in Sylhet, East Pakistan, leaves socialism behind, and renovates the 'traditional' white burra-sahib hierarchy into a neocolonial enterprise that once again exploits the labour of the poor.

In each story the characters become more complex as they are inflected by their previous persona: they are distant from yet related to the earlier characters. For instance, in the second story, Kamaluddin is a travel writer, scholar of comparative religions, translator, and composer of popular Bengali devotional poetry. As a historian, exile, wanderer, seeker, and (ironically) in the male privilege of deferral, he is a counterpart of Gautam of the first story; as a multilingual cosmopolite and a potential renunciate, Kamaluddin also bears traces of the Buddhist prince, Hari Shankar of the first story. The novels, then, become a 'family' history without, necessarily, blood descent. Caught in political calamities, connected to each other through relations of love and friendship, the characters exist in the fullness of each historical moment as well as across the stretch of time.

The Champa, Gautam, and Kamal characters remain central; the Nirmalas and Hari Shankars are adjuncts or 'weak' characters. In *River of Fire*, Hari Shankar disappears from the second story; Margaret Teasdale, the great-granddaughter of the first Cyril Ashley's liaison with Shunila, is dropped in the fourth. The relationship of Kamaluddin with Ruqqaiya is more detailed in the second story but Talat (an author-surrogate figure), an irreverent journalist and self-appointed *dāstān-go*, is attenuated in the fourth. Yet in *River of Fire*, even as the characters become less full-bodied and somewhat enigmatic, the connections between them become sharper. This reshuffling of narrative arrogates the familiar liberty of the *dāstān-go*: characters, situations, episodes can disappear, change or be reinflected, details can be dropped or added, some sequences abbreviated and others expanded depending on the mood and context of narration. The narrative grid is stable, the embellishments alter: it has a fixed core and a floating text of elaboration. Such performative restructuring, which rehearses the interplay between orality and writing, was not only common in oral narrative but resembles musical improvisation as well. The possibility of housing many narrative variants in the same structure is analogous to setting a different raga to the same *bandish* or the same *bandish* to a different raga.

The serving classes are more individualized in their relationships, hybridities, migrations, and politics in *Āg kā Daryā*. They acquire a somewhat choric and static character in *River of Fire*, returning more often as a set of functions—maids, innkeepers, ferrymen—and as generic or metaphoric names that, however, do indicate a set of recurring and massified social relationships. Gungadin the coachman appears in the third and fourth story while the equally typified Abdul appears as a ferryman and as a servant of Cyril. A milkmaid, Sujata, helps the injured Gautam in the first story; in the second, Sujata Debi is the Shudra girl whom Kamaluddin marries; in the third, Sujata, the daughter of impoverished gentility till now in the service of Awadh rulers, becomes the *bibi* of Cyril Ashley; in the fourth story, a beautiful Purbi Champa labours on Cyril Ashley's tea plantation. The Shunilas of the second and third story of *Āg kā Daryā* are renamed Sujata in *River of Fire* (Bimal Roy's famous film *Sujata* may have fixed it as a generic name for disprivilege.) The persistent inequality of the serving classes is perhaps the latent but unarticulated bedrock of the river of fire, that place of recurring human labour which creates the very soil of temporal concurrence, that gives, ironically, a resilience to the 'civilization' (a term I shall annotate later) that seldom dignified this labour.

The Spread of Time

Āg kā Daryā lacks that tight 'organic' form to which the late nineteenth-century bourgeois novel self-consciously aspired, and acquires its coherence as a narrative not in its episodes or content—the four stories are not of equal length, they can be contracted or enlarged, episodes can be dropped or replaced, as indeed they were in *River of Fire*—but in its structure: the spatializing of four moments. Even as it occupies the linear time of recorded history, the novel also unfolds it as spatial concurrence. This structure, shorn of some of the laboured elaborations of 1959, protrudes more in *River of Fire*; the sense of concurrence too is sharper, as if Hyder grasped her original conception and its significance with more precision.

The spatial concurrence of different temporal periods in *Āg kā Daryā* is distinct from a simple cultural continuity; it involves continuities of transmission as well as retrievals of the past, and more broadly, an idea of history that is itself infused with forms of concurrence. The objective historical coordinates and semantic analogues for this metaphor spread across the late nineteenth and early twentieth centuries in historiography, theatre, early cinema, music, narrative, and literary modernism. The modalities of transmission and retrieval were oral, aural, visual, and written.

One form of concurrence was generated by the ideologically varied historical reconstructions that appeared not merely in historical writing but in high and popular literature—romances, poetry, plays, historical novels, school books, prescriptive pamphlets, political treatises, orientalist tracts—throughout the colonial and nationalist period. This concurrence was distinct from revival; rather it was that pervasive phenomenon from which sectarian 'Hindu' or 'Muslim' revivals made their myopic recuperations of the past. Analogues for the millenial span and leaping time structure of *Āg kā Daryā* can be found as much in the 'histories' of India by the British which compressed 'ancient', 'medieval' and colonial India into manageable maps, as in emergent anthological modes, such as the compendious canons of 'great women' assembled by the Indian mofussil intelligentsia which opened the past to a single and telescopic, if often tendentious, thematic gaze.[2]

If print culture had naturalized the synchronic spread of disparate historical moments within the covers of a book, shifting between historical periods had been naturalized in theatre and cinema. The languages of performance and theatricality, which re-enacted historically discrete affective grammars and reabsorbed them into contemporaneous modes, slid from print and performance into early cinema, which by the 1950s had reproduced and reinvented a vast historical repertoire. The concurrent times in *Āg kā Daryā* not only replay these processes of retrieval, but are themselves unimaginable without them. Each historical moment unabashedly fades or 'cuts' into a new time on the same space in cinematic fashion, while each mutated character could be the same film 'star' in a new role, costume, and time.

The other history of retrieval and concurrence, which was at once historical and stylistic, is that of oral and literary intertextuality. This is a history of the persistence and permutation of orality in music and narrative, the concurrence of narratives where originals and variants (ancient, medieval, colonial) flowed side by side into the twentieth century, the repetition of old *oeuvres* in many forms, the entry and absorption for centuries of new grammars, and finally with colonialism, an acceleration of the entry, the absorption and the reinvention, which found new stylistic coordinates in literary modernism for both concurrence and the transformations of time into space. If realism had instituted the law of omniscience, and modernism was read as 'spatial form' that liberated a narrative from realism's naturalization of linear temporality, Hyder makes no exclusive choice. Authorial omniscience coexists with complex narration in shifting voices and registers, a modernist structure, and self-conscious modernist devices such as the flashback or the photograph as a visual mnemonic device. This unproblematic occupation of realism and modernism rolled both into a capacious secular *imaginaire*. The incorporation of other genres (discussed below) stretches the boundaries of realism, authorial irony destabilizes conventions of reproduction through imitation, while the palimpsest of forms evokes, with some verisimilitude, the modalities of layering, silting, and other cumulative processes that compose a cultural geography. Indeed, Hyder's fulsome use of love stories is not surprising, since (at least in the north) these stories continued to live new lives and old lives, went from genre to genre, from orality and manuscript to print and performance, from print to orality, and were reframed by colonial and bourgeois ideologies in high and popular literature.

In literary-historical terms, not only did the uneven march of Indian literary forms display a degree of synchrony, but the several centuries of European and English literary forms which arrived en bloc (at least notionally, in practice in piecemeal, idiosyncratic, and regional variations), also came to rest on the level plane of print with Indian literary forms. 'English' as a social, literary, and ideological ensemble mediated the Urdu novel as much as any other. *Āg kā Daryā* presented related, intersecting, and bifurcating histories of Indian and British culture long before they were theorized in critical discourse, and inaugurated a cosmopolitan gaze that could take in Britain with ease and authority. What the English version could more readily demonstrate were the concurrences produced by colonization and the imbrication of colonialism in systems of representation—as in the artifices of colonial history, Anglo-Indian fiction, travel or missionary accounts, Indological and anthropological evaluations of Indian religions or customs.[3] The language itself made available another layer of intertextuality and certain cross-referential clusters. Some of the chapter titles introduced in *River of Fire* exhibit the pleasures and seductions of orientalism, travelogues, and English literature, as well as the absorption, translation, and adaptation of literary English by Indian elites with a degree of irony: 'The Abominable Customs of the Gentoos and Mussalmans', 'The Forest of Arden', 'Miss Champa Ahmed (Graduation Portrait by C. Mull, Hazrat Ganj, Lucknow)'.

Some other valences of literary cross-referentiality change in *River of Fire*. *Āg kā Daryā* carried a more intricate and text-derived exposition of ancient India (from the *Ṛgveda* and *Arthashāstra* to the *Nāṭyashāstra*), a theory of religious change (the conflicts, unification, and relocation of ancient and medieval sects), and an inventory of music (classical, devotional, popular, and filmic); it had more memorative aspects (Walter Benjamin's term), and transmitted more orality: *śloka*, *dohā*, song, poem, *shā'irī*. *River of Fire* connotes more the making of reflexive intertextualities, colonial and medieval, as in Kamaluddin's first person travelogue, *The Marvels and Strange Tales of Hindustan*. It is not for this reason more 'anglicized' (surely a multilingual subcontinent permits the freedom to re-inflect!). In fact, the heavy mediation of T.S. Eliot in *Āg kā Daryā* (the epigraph, the section on the Vedas in the first story, the descriptions of London, the consciousness, and conversation of characters in the fourth story), diminishes considerably. When I asked Qurratulain Hyder why the epigraph from *Four Quartets* had been dropped, she shrugged and said casually '*chhūṭ gayā hogā*' as if it were a minor and unimportant matter.[4]

Āg kā Daryā also presents concurrence as a recurring experience of 'over-accumulation' or cultural compression that is not peculiar to or even restricted to modernity though it may be compounded by modernity. The cacophony of the dead sediments, layer upon layer, like the ancient Persian and new American coins that collect in the Saryu river in *River of Fire*. A contesting diversity assails each age, and this is too much for any single individual to carry or assimilate.

The weight of the past as embodied in literature, religion, philosophy, music, and popular culture mediates each present; it also fastens each character into a web of relationships and a grid of gendered textualities that compel him/her to move both backward and forward. The conflicting pressure of the Vedas and the Buddha's teachings, of sixty-two schools of philosophy, already burdens Gautam in the first story. (In *Āg kā Daryā* he has a theatricalized mythological vision of Aryans travelling into the subcontinent along with Indra, Parvati, Saraswati, and other gods and goddesses.) In the second story, Kamaluddin is beset in a dream by taunting spectres from fifteen centuries that include the emperors Chandragupta and Ashoka, Bharat Muni, Raja Bhoja, Gangu Teli, Kalidasa, Bhavabhuti, Bhartrihari, Harsha, Shudraka, Alha, Udal, sundry queens, and Rajput clans who all remind him of his mortality. Significantly, many of these featured in print, theatric, cinematic, and orientalist retrieval from the nineteenth century, and could just as well be spectres for the novels' colonial and contemporary protagonists. In the fourth story, the Lucknow gang conjure and converse with historical figures from Awadh. The experience of concurrence in moments of crisis for the characters comes encased as spectrality: as signs of a thickly populated archive, spectres both literalize textuality and assert a grim performativity.

The authorial persona is also besieged by this multitudinous past. There is, however, a subtle distinction between what the characters read, their textual apprehension of India, and the authorial inscription of literary-cultural density through a combination of narrative excess, and a selective 'placement' of character, emplotment, and author, that together suggest a notion of elective affinity.

The author labours under the varying pressure of diverse configural narrative forms and temporalities. Many earlier notions of recurrence and concurrent time were circulating in the century that preceded *Āg kā Daryā*, and these hover beneath the structure of the novels. They are variously acknowledged, incorporated, or displaced, and each pushes towards the *longue durée*. There are traces of several structured notions of continuity, such as cyclicity and reincarnation, not only in the beliefs of characters in *yugas*, rebirth, and karma (especially in the first and second story), but in a larger rhythmic ebb and flow of characters, kingdoms, epochs. There is an insistent reminder of the Jatakas' retrospective unfolding cycle of the rebirth of the Buddha as he accumulated good deeds and his 'placement' of himself through parable into numerous situations and identities. The Jatakas enumerate the Buddha's manifold previous existences as an animal (elephant, wise partridge, quail, antelope, lion), as prince, as Brahmin trader, dice player, and his good deeds in every birth. These were often seemingly concurrent births (so very many took place 'when Brahmadatta ruled at Benaras'!), and the stories were simultaneously, if retrospectively, recounted by the Buddha to his pupils. Other conserving genealogical forms such as the feudal pieties of the bardic *vanshāvalī*, the bourgeois longings of the Victorian dynastic novel and family saga also lurk in the structure of reference.

Hyder has insisted that her novel is not, as many readers believe, about reincarnation.[5] If both the claims and disclaimers of 'reincarnation' are bracketed, another meaning can be elicited: the novels evoke earlier modes of affiliation. For instance, when Champavati in the second story speaks to Kamaluddin of their bond established in previous births, this gently affines Kamal with Gautam of the first story, resituates the stranger as a familiar, the traveller as an insider. Karma and rebirth can be read as metaphors of the long civilizational time of belonging.[6]

The novels also re-enact the *longue durée* of the narrative structures of curiosity that persisted until the nineteeth century in the heroic quest cycles of the *dāstān*, with its double access to fictional time and contemporary time, its episodic structure, its syncretizing encounters with *pīrs*, *jogīs*, Sufis, and mystics, its irrepressible desire to find the stories, and the women, hidden behind the mysterious wonders that filled the world. Though the desires of the protagonists of Hyder's novels are seldom fulfilled, they are stirred by similar, non-parochial, cognitive aspirations. The constant repetition of seasons in nature and in song (*bārahmāsas* are sung throughout) mark another sort of recurrence and continuous transmission that is tied to structures of feeling and desire.

Rather than cut, juxtapose, and paste earlier temporalities in a collage, Hyder seems to travel through earlier genres, or to borrow a term from music, 'shows' other forms in the novels just as the *ṭhumrī* 'shows' one raga in another (*ek rāg meṅ dūsre rāg ko dikhānā*). Thus, the Sufi genre of *malfūẓāt* or the recorded conversations of spiritual masters surface in *Āg kā Daryā* when Kamaluddin becomes a disciple of Kabir in the second story, and is submerged in *River of Fire* where it lingers only as a strong 'quality' in Kamal's dialogues with several persons.

If all these notations of concurrent time 'speak' to each other, they are also unsettled by each other or by an intense, if troubled, historicity. The conservative potentials of some of the genealogical forms that Hyder 'shows' are curtailed by a conscious self-positioning in chosen 'lineages' that can relegate feudal ties or class bonds, and loosen religious identities. In one sense, earlier collations of 'tradition' in the compendium, inventory, digest, bhakti-Sufi hagiography, or romance narrative had built up not only a sense of textual 'weight' but also a precedent for non-family lineages. The medieval *taẕkira* or biographical compendium often traced Sufi lineages, the lineage of *ṭarīqas*, or the wider network of allegiances. The spatial catholicity of compendious medieval hagiologies implied being born into webs of narrative and interlocution rather than being born into ascriptive primordiality, and so suggested modes of non-familial bonding or elective affinity.[7] The social production of *allegiance*, the activity of making a constellation by tracing the confluence of lines that intersect in an individual life (as biography), informs the emplotment and embedment of character in both novels. An 'elected' past (as opposed to a merely wilful or falsely constructed one), as expression of choice and affinity, is indispensable to a secular *imaginaire*. The cross-generic notations in the novels reproduce and ground this both formally and historically. At one level, even the epistemic difficulty of interpreting history is resolved on the plane of elective affinity. In *Āg kā Daryā*, left and liberal South Asian students make a new elective community, an island of self-respect that defies partition; they reconsolidate their composite heritage in a moment of breakdown despite tensions on the borders between India and East and West Pakistan.

At another level, a sociology of mobility threatens to depreciate the transformative potential suggested by elective affinities. Though it is the subject of political discussion and affiliation in the fourth story, the novels do not bother overmuch with India's transition to capitalism, a dominant preoccupation of twentieth-century social realism. Perhaps shifts in the mode of production were too drastic to accomodate in a *longue durée* or into the reiterative narrative structure. The profoundest changes come with war, conquest, rebellion and partition: downward mobility and upward mobility seem to pivot on cataclysmic political events. There is an abiding fascination with the parvenu, the *déclassé*, the reversal of fortune: Chandragupta Maurya, many sultanate slave dynasties, the nabob Cyril Ashley, and Champa Ahmed are upstarts. If the downward class mobility and upward spiritual mobility of Kamaluddin in the second story is more marked in *Āg kā Daryā* (as a courtier who becomes a farmer, and who commingles low and high culture by writing local folktales in Arabic and Bengali), then the upward mobility of Champa Ahmed is more emphatic in *River of Fire*. The related problematic of travel, the self-remaking it can enforce, and the parvenu, continues when Indians go to England.

If encyclopaedic narrative cycles (*Kathāsaritsāgara*, Jatakas) that could absorb or even regroup around new narrative forms and string diverse stories together lurk inside *Āg kā Daryā*, it departs from the way in which they nested narratives within narratives, and suggests a deliberated outward narrative movement. This intertextuality pushes towards a socially inflected literary history, especially a history of the changing reception of texts. It is not self-referential but leads out into other contexts, evades the closures of religious or national identity. The implied reader (one who follows the cues), a reader of Indian and English classic and popular literature, besieged by a plethora of generic codes and narratives from Sanskrit drama to French existentialism, is positioned to pursue the openness of this referential structure.

In both novels, narratives bind together the visual, literary, oral, and performative—they are a form of concurrence, definitionally multiple, compulsively recycled, and synonymous with the spread of time, the *longue durée*. Narrative *saturation* becomes a *figure* for civilizational density while the narrative matrix corresponds to its mobile, migrant, and sedimenting history.

Secular Nationalism and Its Affects

The colonial period spawned many cyclic theories of decline. These ranged from theosophy which propagated an attenuated set of reincarnations based on karmic law, to T.S. Eliot's conservative notion of the decay and fall of a monumentalized Europe and his vision of history as debris that had to be spatially reassembled, to the imperious and eurocentric Spenglerian world view of cyclic decline. Though images from Eliot's circular past-animated present do float in *Āg kā Daryā*, along with other conserving genealogical homologies, the end of a period is not synonymous with decay. These theories of 'decline' are noted and startlingly inverted in the novels, in which becoming modern is both old and new, heart-breaking but still promising.

Āg kā Daryā belongs to, and *River of Fire* records, a particular moment when popular culture and popular-colonial-national retrievals were yet not-quite-archive, not-yet-retro or postmodern pastiche, but a sedimented, over-flowing and paradoxically contemporaneous archive, which gave a sense of fullness, a fullness that was destroyed by partition but remembered and experienced as loss and as pressure. In *Āg kā Daryā*, the fullness disrupted by partition is not that of culture but of its sharing: the rupture of individual, affective, and conjunctural webs of connection and reconnection. There is only one qualitative shift: after 1947, transmissibility is poised to become more the gesture of the scholar, the Indologist, the anthropologist, the state and its museums; and paradoxically, also that gesture of political protest against the artificial separation of 'national' heritages which indicts the new politics of recollection and recuperation (and the aporia of alienation that lies in-between). The notations of concurrence in *River of Fire*, however, suggest a recollected constellation that remains the inalienable experience of the generations in transition but may well disappear with them.

Though concurrence had become a modernist device (as with T.S. Eliot), here concurrence is still affective, a historical sediment, that was secured, temporarily, by a secular nationalism. Both novels propose a secular nationalism imaged as a civilizational strength with still retrievable potentials, that is, nationalism in itself is a source of and a support for concurrence. This is borne out by the structure of the novels: a series of historical tableaux (as the *jhānkī* of Parsi theatre and as filmic device) that position the characters and stretch across time through repetition, affinity, and inflection; 'familial' lineages of disposition and vocation without, necessarily, blood descent; a dialogic arrangement of sections and characters in the river of fire that (as metaphor) flows backwards and forwards; a topographic stability in which the same space is crossed and recrossed in different times by different persons. (The novels are circular only in that they begin and end in the monsoon, in the forest of Shravasti, on the banks of the Saryu.) The affinities across time, character, and religious belief make 'religious' divisions unsustainable: true nationalism (regardless of its origin) becomes a recession of parochial identities.

The narratives are dotted with polyglot and cosmopolitan cameos, for instance, the 'temporary' student formations sketched in the fourth story. The Hindu, Muslim, and Christian students of Tattarwalla School in Lucknow (run by a Gandhian Congressi Kayasth) sing bhajans and qawwalis. The Jewish, Buddhist, Hindu, Muslim, Sikh and Christian students of Isabella Thoburn College come from most regions in India, from America, Europe, Burma, and Sri Lanka; they learn Urdu, Persian, Hindi, and Sanskrit; girls from different religions celebrate every festival and 'exchange' religious customs as much as clothes. A socialist internationalism grounded in a progressive nationalism (more detailed in *Āg kā Daryā* but fading, with some historical veracity, in *River of Fire*), is lived out by Indian and Pakistani students who travel to eastern Europe and interact with the British left in post-war England.

Evidently, this was a particular sort of nationalism, one that was closely linked in its images and affects to Jawaharlal Nehru's vision. Nehru described his 25,000–mile electoral tour in 1951–2 to Edwina Mountbatten thus:

> Vast multitudes gather at my meetings and I love to compare them, their faces, their dresses, their reactions to me and what I say. *Scenes from the past history of that very part of India rise up before me and my mind becomes a picture gallery of past events.* But more than the past, the present fills my mind and I try to probe into the minds and hearts of these multitudes.... As I wander about, *the past and the present merge into one another* and this merger leads me to think of *the future. Time becomes like a flowing river in continuous motion with events connected with one another.*[8]

This spectrality, naturalized as a historiographic reflex, this concurrent past, the identification of this past with an irrevocably connected 'multitude', and the river image are somewhat unilinear yet remarkably close to *Āg kā Daryā*. Nehru too had seen India as an 'ancient palimpsest on which layer upon layer of thought and reverie had been inscribed.... All these existed together in our conscious or subconscious selves...and they had gone to build up the complex and mysterious personality of India'. The unity of India was more than 'an intellectual conception': 'it was an emotional experience' that 'overpowered' him (Nehru 1959: 272). Nehru's problematic, however, was that of binding a vast tract of event-filled time into a *moment*, a demarcating, eventful, transformative moment into which a modern and independent India could crystallize.

The Problematic of Civilization

Āg kā Daryā marked a significant moment. For the first time a woman writer (as far as I can ascertain) annexed over twenty-five centuries of Indian history as subject matter. The grand nationalist vision of a pluralist civilization had till then been a male domain (Nehru was one among others), while women had been for almost two centuries the subjects of colonial, nationalist, or sectarian histories, often invented and usually patriarchal. In the 1930s and 1940s, the discourse of antiquity and civilization (now a questionable term) also carried the ambivalent Hindu chauvinist or anti-colonial and nationalist resonances of the 'already civilized': old civilizations like India did not need to be civilized by new nations like England. However, the more significant meaning, that of a civilization having a greater binding force than a nation, carried the anguish of partition and emerged from the compulsion to defeat the two-nation/two-culture theory and defend a cultural space larger than a nation. Civilizations were not divisible into nations, national boundaries came and went, civilizations endured.

In Hyder's novels, civilization became a category extending beyond national, religious, and state boundaries; it included not just literature,[9] music, philosophy, myth, or art but also affective structures, which in turn produced many of the coherences of that civilization. Ancient and medieval 'culture' for Hyder, whether Arab, European, or Indian, was a cross-regional traffic, always conflict-riven, yet always familiar with, affected or influenced by, and aware of 'other' cultures, and at times almost cosmopolitan. Hyder's preface to the 1968 translation makes, on the lines of Nehru's *Discovery of India*, a creative relation between in-migration (Aryan, Arab, Turk) and cultural diversity, and also celebrates the civilizational capacity to synthesize and develop a varied and mixed culture. For her too, the Indic civilization is unique: in the lability of its 'traditions' which were adapted, changed, and invented, as a complex of linkages and differences that defines the entire subcontinent, and in its unity that encompasses but does not regiment diversity. Contemporary Indians are products of this Indic civilization rather than of its nations. As in Nehru's text, in *Āg kā Daryā* the syncretic is not just secular and multi-religious, it is also the dynamic of constant change, always poised on the new that surrenders neither to an insider's hegemonic assimilation nor to an outsider's imperious hegemony. For Hyder, as for Nehru, the modern adventure is not limited by national boundaries, and it is neither a repetition nor a denial of the past. The first story displays the ancient commingling of Greek, Vedic, Buddhist, Persian; the second, the peak of religious syncretisms in which currents from many countries converged; while the third and the fourth demonstrate the hybridization of both the British—from nabob to innkeeper—and the Indian—from feudal aristocracy to the colonial middle classes.

In each period there is an interplay of different epistemologies, languages, and literatures. (Ancient and medieval 'India' was a part of a large Asian or more accurately Eurasian constellation stretching to the Middle East, parts of Europe, and China, a geographical universe that persisted till the nineteenth century, as is evident in *dāstāns* which encompassed Central and South Asia and China.) In such a continuously reconstellating view, 'India' is never an insular or ingrown entity, rather it becomes a point of convergence and reconvergence. The novels seem to bear out Irfan Habib's contention that the 'idea' of India as a cultural unity was not a modern secular invention but a much older one, one that was a product of conquest (Mauryan emperor Ashoka's inscriptions in circa 250 BC), and travellers' visions or a view from outside (Alberuni's *Kitāb-ul-Hind* in the eleventh century), while the affect-laden idea of India as a distinctive composite culture emerged from immigrants and converts, such as Amir Khusrau's *Nuh Sipir* in 1318 (Habib 1999). *Āg kā Daryā* poignantly extends this view to South Asian students in England who continue to represent a 'panoramic' and 'united India' in their cultural activities after partition, and to those, like Kamal Reza, who leave India for Pakistan. (Hyder herself was based in Pakistan when she wrote the novel.) 'India', then, has never existed in a settled and authoritative source culture, a culture of origin, but has 'lived' always in the form of encounters, surprises, conversations, transitions, translocations, and reimagings.[10]

The History Lesson and the Stereotype

Indeed, the basic problematic of the novel, in which much revolves around love, seems to be a classic secular one: how was the subcontinent to be defined as a historical community shaped by ancient, medieval, colonial, and ongoing interactions and intertwining of languages, settlements, and religions, and how was the line between diversity and systemic inequality, between religion and culture, to be drawn and navigated? How was historical evidence to be used to refute stereotypes, how was religious difference to be understood in ways that were at once historical and experiential, how could this complexity be narrated to reclothe the denuded stereotypes of communal propaganda and the stark evacuation of partition?

At one level, of course, each character makes his or her 'India'. If civilization is a dynamic and changing entity, it is also an inevitably contested one. The most poignant is Kamal Reza's newly severed India. The so-called 'imperfection' of both novels—the uneven pace of narration, the occasional stilted or prolix passage, the awkwardnesses in translation—can perhaps be read in the same way. These rough edges are what make them subjective individual apprehensions of 'India': gestures governed by contingency, immediate concerns, and shifting preoccupations. The fluidity of the intersection between history, 'civilization', and individual lives may well be another name for such 'imperfection'.

However, the troubled problematic of history, especially sectarian and nationalist history mired in anachronism, cannot be resolved only through individual Indias, and here the novels make a quixotic, even paradoxical use of the history lesson and the stereotype.

The novels directly and unabashedly introject discrete chunks of textbook political history, freely mix school book with romance, annotating the significance of historical narratives even as they display the quandaries of lovers. The one anchors the other, yet they are dissimilar in that the history lesson is too hard-edged to be recuperated into fiction, and the fiction too individuated to be absorbed into the 'representative' claims of history.

Unlike colonial historical novelists, Hyder did not need a chauvinist chronicle of self-respect to explain the subjection of Hindus by Muslims or Indians by the British. She needed a narrative to navigate the division and remaking of nations. *Āg kā Daryā* relocated the late nineteenth-century school textbook's characteristic interleaving of history, as well as the school book's own imbrication in the history of novelization, into a purposive secular politics.[11]

The history lessons are multi-accented. As cacophonous as the spectres, they are delivered, dialogically, in many voices other than that of the authorial persona: a Sufi, a peasant, a prince turned *jogī*, an old zamindar, a nawab, a coachman, a Calcutta Baboo, a student. In *River of Fire*, Nawab Kamman, an aristocratic nationalist, recounts the events of 1857 to his *bhadra* friend, Gautam, as a sign of Hindu-Muslim unity, a tale of British atrocity, and a proof of the valour of militant women—young and old, royal women and courtesans. Gautam cannot fully share the trauma of 1857 with Nawab Kamman because he is a loyalist who perceives the British as harbingers of modernity.

Hyder projects the persona of a scholar-novelist, and annexes what had largely been the provenance of male writers of the historical novel (few women wrote historical novels). The persona harks back to the tutelary woman of nineteenth-century popular writing (though here the novelist does not encash her gender in a female voice), and usurps the pedagogic authority that had been bestowed on dutiful women in the past century,[12] but with a new confidence that exploits the authority of history as the collective enterprise of a new nation, as well as the social, political, and nationalist legitimacy of the teacher in the 1940s and 50s. One may well ask, as I have done elsewhere, if the Indian novel itself began as a teaching text, could women enter it save as teachers (Sangari 2002: 35–6)? However, by the 1950s, social realism as well as women writers had acquired a stable narrative authority (for instance, Ismat Chughtai and Rashid Jehan). The pedagogy too enters a new register. The authorial persona suggests a learned woman, a *vidūshī*, who displays her erudition and ability to read subcontinental history and world history as a mode of narrative authority, who puts herself in a lineage of ancient and medieval learned women, but who subverts the exclusive 'Vedic-Hindu' model of the learned woman. Indeed, as a woman learned in *multiple* traditions, she puts this nineteenth-century stereotype to secular use.

Yet the four stories are dotted with learned women! Hyder holds up this and other textual and oral stereotypes—communal, regional, colonial, patriarchal, orientalist—with a bold frontality, allows them to be reread. The stereotype is a 'preconstructed piece' (Bromley 1988: 101) from which memories, narratives and history can be fashioned. It is also an end product of both the historical process and of historiography, one that calcifies those wider typicalities which historians construct to represent period, class, or region. The stereotype is too pervasive to displace entirely, too often transmitted, too much the *mise-en-scène*, the still, the stuff of the historical and mythological film, the colonial narrative, the romance; it lurks in stock images, formulaic themes, narrative conventions. Conducive to amnesia, the stereotype is, paradoxically, also a 'code' by which a period or genre is 'recognized'—it resists the complexity of history, but is also carried by it, and clings to any grand *récit* of a 'civilization'.

The novels show how inexorably typicality mediates a retrieval of the past, how heavily retrieval involves the construction and replication of stereotypes, how even thick historical contexts do not entirely displace them. Stereotypes are a part of the baggage that civilizations carry. 'History' and the 'stereotype' stand in relations of cooperation, friction, and antagonism: if history as available through narratives comes replete with stereotypes, the history lesson has to neutralize them.

The novels work through a narrative strategy of accumulation. Stereo-types are not disbanded, they are sometimes smudged by juxtaposition, or under-mined by their sheer heterogeneity. This is partly because they are crucial to intertextuality, one of the ways in which it is made, as well as to the repeated textual apprehension of India. For instance, characters learn their world through them. In the third story, Gautam is perceived as the stereo-typical, provincial Bengali *babu* and *bhadra* reformer (*à la* Sarat Chandra) whose sympathy for women does not go beyond a passive ambivalence. He in turn, unable to understand the language of servile coquetry in an Awadh *tawaif*'s salon, filters Champa Jan through the complementary lens of English literature and ancient Indian literature, mixes Shakespeare, Keats, Bhartrihari, and Damodar Gupt. At least six nodes of intertextuality in the third story are also stereotypes: the nawab, the *bhadra babu*, the nabob, the *tawaif*, the *bibi*, the Eurasian vamp. The narrative unwinds them from common spools and lets them loose without 're-binding' them to a single ideological axis: it both absorbs and contends with the (stereo)typicality, the interchangeability of character in popular representational modes.

In this sense, the novels work at once through a grid of familiarity and through the 'estrangement' of over-typification. The essentialization of stereotypes is frequently displaced by, paradoxically, intensifying an only-too-familiar descriptive grammar. The encounters with courtesans and *bibis* are distanced by a theatricalized stylization, and are almost typical enough to evoke the *mise-en-scènes* of legend, early theatre, and cinema. In sum, they are almost typical enough to be a repertoire: maids who behave like stage *kuṭnīs* or go-betweens, sophisticated courtesans who fall in love with 'innocent' men, the 'good' prostitute who is a 'wife' at heart and desires marriage, a *bibi*-but-not-wife who uses *jādū-ṭonā* to get rid of her rivals, gallant young men enlisted to detach courtesans or 'modern vamps' from unfaithful husbands, naïve and forsaken 'native' girls.

This use of repetition and intertextuality begins to assemble a history of misogyny, begins to frame a question: why do the terms and tropes of misogyny change so little across time and cultural differences? Civilization, the novels suggest, may have come at a price.

Ex-centric Nationalism and the Traveller

The 'answers' in the novel move from the Nehruvian problematic to arrive at what can only be called an 'ex-centric' or centrifugal nationalism, as opposed to an insular, inward-turning or sectarian nationalism, a plural culture constituted by travel, worked out through love troped as travel. In other words, a diffuse civilizational identity that is as much a matter of political modes of discovery and retrieval as of direct lines of inheritance, an ex-centric nationalism that can equally productively look backwards and turn outwards, and is presented through an epic range that can anchor the diverse 'Indias' that have travelled in and out of the subcontinent.[13] In this context, intertextuality becomes analogous to an ex-centric nationalism: a narrative that directs attention outwards to other narratives, genres, and reading communities, that does not assimilate or appropriate but marks their space.

The novels are densely populated with travellers. They travel because of the dislocation of war, famine, poverty, economic need; travel for conquest, profit, pleasure, education, (Buddhist) proselytism, curiosity, spiritual quest. The exigencies of wandering, settlement, and uprooting structure families and relationships, bonding and desertion. Travel within India is as important as from without, in-migration is as important as out-migration. No one is seen as an insider everywhere: the Bengali Gautam is perceived as an outsider in Lucknow, the refugee Nawab Kamman as an outsider in Calcutta, Champa Ahmed as an outsider in upper-class Lucknow and in England, the *muhājir* as an outsider in West Pakistan. The stories are located in places that were cultural crossroads—Magadhan Pataliputra, Jaunpur under the Sharqi sultans, Awadh under princely rule, colonial Calcutta, Lucknow, and London. The characters travel to several other cities; transitional or transnational spaces—rivers, borders, ships, trains—recur in each story. Few travellers can carry everything: what they leave behind is transmuted into emotional structures and carried as unarticulated 'depth'.

The proper history of the subcontinent seems to be a history of travellers from time immemorial: the overlap of 'separate' historical periods, the way they shade into one another, the way narratives, artefacts, and ideas travel across time and space, and come to be linked through life histories, through the continuations of poverty, domestic service, the caste order, social hierarchy, and instrumental modes of legitimation. This entire complex is gained through 'repeating' a set of protagonists over twenty-five centuries. The episteme of travel permits the traversal of two millenia and also suggests, as in the metaphor of the river, at once a sedimenting and a linear historicity.

Nehru wrote that 'some kind of dream of unity has occupied the mind of India since the dawn of civilization', and there is a 'distinctively Indian' 'national heritage' (Nehru 1959: 61–2). If Nehru looked for an essence, a unifying principle for modern India, for Hyder the persistent preoccupation and anxiety about mortality and transience defined the distinctive character and heritage of the subcontinent. If travel notches into the individuality of cosmopolitanism and the collectivity of a Nehruvian nationalism on the one side, on the other side it notches into transience: there are many travelling students of mortality in *Āg kā Daryā*. The diagnosis of transience that lies at the heart of the impulse to believe in something permanent and unchangeable has more continuity than religious sects. Transience is the overarching trope that both defines and subsumes travel. The understanding that all things pass holds together all transient phenomena including love.

Love too is a form of elective affinity. It insistently, even if casually or briefly, lifts the barriers of caste, class, religion, region, and nation. Mediated by settled vocabularies of desire and alterity, it too produces a concurrent repertoire: generic repetition clings to love, and the narrative enacts this in its structure. Love, cohabitation, and marriage across borders are not only part of the episteme of travel but subject to the exigencies of travel, each story circles around desertion and separation. The way men love women they cannot, will not, do not marry, the way they hover but never come up to scratch, these notations of male desire, male indifference, and male self-division pluck out the similarity between the patriarchal assumptions of men from different religions: Brahmin, Buddhist, Muslim, Sufi, Brahmo, Christian. Common patriarchal ideologies and practices can hardly be hailed as signs of secular unity, but they do cut across religious identities with more tenacity than love.

The deserted and waiting women who dot each narrative also suggest that in the episteme of travel women may have signified 'home'. Women may have been deserted more often because they travelled less. Women who nativize male travellers are in this sense merely counterparts of the women who lose them. If the civilizational episteme is to be located in travel and transience, waiting women are a harsh but inevitable corollary, because beneath the varied trajectories of peripatetic men lies the continuity of patriarchies and the serving classes. The plot of female renunciation and/or sublimation is broken only when women travel, when they cease to wait for men (like Champa Ahmed), and more strongly, by the single working woman (like Talat) who rejects the bourgeois love plot altogether.

Āg kā Daryā carries some traces of the concern with the low status of women that was common in male reformist and nationalist discourses. Apart from a critique of double standards, these tend to recede in *River of Fire*. Broadly speaking, the novels do not occupy the prescriptive space of the uplift and reform of women, or engage the progressive critique of tradition: the condition of widows, choice of marriage partner, enforced domestic labour, ill-treatment, issues related to property, divorce, *mehar*, or dowry. Again, unlike Hindi and Urdu women's journals till the 1940s, they do not directly approach the issue of 'modernizing' women, whether in their domestic comportment, proper education, or future professions. It may be this that led to Hyder being labelled bourgeois. However, it is likely that her civilizational problematic inhibited this discourse not only as a discourse of social transformation but also as a gendered discourse of communal prejudice. It may have been difficult to broach the condition of women without repeating the clichés of a civilizational rupture or a 'fall' from a golden past. Her narrative resolution is to instantiate and individuate the women characters as intensely as possible. The Champa women have lucid and complex agencies, and belong in the tradition of Tagore's and Chughtai's heroines. Hyder does not reserve punitive fates for transgressive or overweening women characters as did the reformist novel. Rather, the (usually) desolate denouements stem from the conjunction of stereotypicality, intertextuality, political events, and patriarchies. For instance, the courtesan Champa Jan is not placed inside the 'social problem' tradition; her destitution results from the annexation of Awadh and the 1857 revolt. She is not a candidate for social reform. Though Hyder may not be a declared feminist, the novels show the centrality of textual, oral, and visual representation in the construction of gender. Their discourse of civilization is not triumphal: it is visibly congealed with stereotypes, tempered with misogyny, disrupted by violence.

Configuring the Secular

The configural mode of 'grasping together' the diversity and dense affiliations of a multi-religious subcontinent is more crucial to the secular *imaginaire* of *Āg kā Daryā* than the politically correct history lessons within it.[14] It stands as a full analogue of the secular in the sense that historical periods were held together concurrently (over and above the embedded precapitalist subject) in a vast temporal and spatial spread that asked now for a loyalty that was different from older loyalties of region, religion, or language, loyalty to the idea of a civilization that was wider, deeper, and more compelling than its division into separate nations.

River of Fire, by implicitly re-grasping the original moment of its own composition, completes a configural process, resituates the first moment of composition now as itself a part of a wider configuration, at the cost of some dis-identification, and with occasional irony. This original moment is separated by that gap of four decades in which communalism resurfaced and escalated, the self-aggrandizing discourse of Hindu civilization sharpened, altered the ideological location of Vedic India, and created new vulnerabilities (which may well account for the abridgement of the first story).

If *Āg kā Daryā* was a way of winning a certain poise and distance from 1947, a way of reclaiming the subcontinent from the violence that had torn it apart by pulling it into a consoling civilizational *longue durée* in which repeated destruction could be accommodated to the recurrent rise and fall of kingdoms (reminiscent of the fourteenth-century Ibn Khaldun's philosophy of history), in the four decades which mediated *River of Fire*, the borders that had partitioned Bengal and Punjab began to criss-cross India as expanding spaces of insecurity and communal violence. If in the relative calm of the Nehruvian period (now itself a past), Hyder had written briefly on pre-partition violence and essayed only a stark one-line chapter on partition in *Āg kā Daryā*, in *River of Fire* she gives even less space to its atrocity and grief—perhaps because 'partition' lives within the nation, still needs to be distanced, and 'civilization' still has to be reclaimed.

Āg kā Daryā marked a moment in Indian literary modernism. The nature of this modernism speaks of its own contingency. If in omniscient narration, sight can extend infinitely in a temporality that can be aligned into a single horizon (as in the modern notion of history) and string together a whole series of moments into one act of attention, *Āg kā Daryā*'s modernism advances rather than fractures this realist 'consensus'.[15] If imagining a nation meant holding together the anonymous, simultaneous actions of all its members in a calendrical clocked time (as imaged in reading the daily newpaper or in the omniscient narrator[16]), imagining a civilization implied a simultaneity across differential and multiple temporalities, a holding together of past and present 'multitudes'. In *Āg kā Daryā*, a modernism emerges not from the need to supersede realism, but from the pressure to exceed the nation and its formal limits.

European modernism, according to Perry Anderson, redeemed and released the classic stocks of high culture against the ravages of the market as the organizing principle of culture and society (P. Anderson 1984: 105). If I were to adapt his conjunctural explanation, the modernism of *Āg kā Daryā* set out to redeem the stock of a mixed culture, its complex affective-literary-historical resources, and released it, not against the market but against monolithic religious identities and political violence. The surrealist image brought differing commodity forms into collision, and as Fredric Jameson demonstrates, the objects in these images, as products of a not yet fully industrialized and systemized economy, still show the traces of an artisanal organization of labour, and a resonant depth that invites libidinal investment (Jameson 1971: 96–105). *Āg kā Daryā* brought, not commodity forms, but the plenitude of a mixed culture into collision with the reduction of xenophobic ideologies. However, in this too it carries (like the objects in surrealist images) an uneffaced mark of artisanal labour: that resonant and affective depth of a not-yet-remote orality in which a storyteller could sign and transmit many given narratives, worked into, but not worked over or fully transformed by, literary modernism. In this respect, it remains bound to the 1950s, a decade in which it was still possible to circumvent the full ideological consequences and contradictions of the commodity forms which were to change irrevocably the very problematic of simultaneity and concurrence.

Notes

[1] Author's Preface, Hyder 1968: 9 (Hindi). The other versions I have used are Hyder 1959 (Urdu); Hyder 1998 (English), and Hyder 2000 (Hindi).

[2] For one such late nineteenth-century canon, *see* Sangari 1999: 241–2.

[3] For the concurrences and related histories produced by colonization, and the secular implications of cultural mixing in India, *see* Sangari 1999: xxvi–xxviii, xxxvi–xlii.

[4] Conversation with Qurratulain Hyder, 2002.

[5] Author's Preface, 1988, in Hyder 2000: 7.

[6] On karma as an ambivalent genealogizing device that gave souls a multi-religious trajectory in some medieval hagiologies, *see* Sangari 2000: 90–2.

[7] On non-family or elective communities in medieval hagiographies that created synchronic and composite communities across historical time and space, *see* Sangari 2000: 79–80.

[8] Quoted in Guha 2002: 2. My emphasis.

[9] For a discussion of literature transcending the boundaries of India and Pakistan, *see* Hina 1997: 38.

[10] I owe this formulation to Ahmer Nadeem Anwer.

[11] On the relationship between school textbooks and early novelization, *see* Sangari 1999: xliv–xlv, 196–220.

[12] On the pedagogic authority bestowed on dutiful and reformist women, through the use of female voices in textbooks, tracts, and other nineteenth-century narratives, *see* Sangari 1999: 197–201, 238–9, 247, 341–3.

[13] Though he discusses only contemporary travel, Clifford (1997) has been suggestive for my formulations here.

[14] Paul Ricoeur makes a useful but generalized distinction between the episodic (following Louis O. Mink) and the configural dimensions of narrative that I have bent to my own purposes. He sees the configural act, the act of 'grasping together', as central to all narrative (Ricoeur 1984: 67), whereas I have used it to indicate a conscious and modernist device.

[15] On the realist consensus and the single perspective, *see* Ermarth 1992: 27–8.

[16] For a discussion of the relationship between the concept of the nation and omniscient narration, *see* B. Anderson 1983: 17–40.

Bibliography

Anderson, Benedict, *Imagined Communities: Reflections on the Origin and Spread of Nationalism*, London: Verso, 1983.

Anderson, Perry, 'Modernity and Revolution', *New Left Review*, no. 44 (1984), 96–113.

Bromley, Roger, *Lost Narratives*, London: Routledge, 1988.

Clifford, James, *Routes: Travel and Translation in the Late Twentieth Century*, Cambridge, MA: Harvard University Press, 1997.

Ermarth, Elizabeth, *Sequel to History*, Princeton: Princeton University Press, 1992.

Guha, Ram, 'The Biggest Gamble in History', *The Hindu*, 3 February 2002, 1–2.

Habib, Irfan, 'The Envisioning of a Nation: A Defence of the Idea of India', *Social Scientist* 27: 9–10, September–October 1999, 1–12.

Hina, Zahida, 'Urdu Literature and the Patriarchal Family', in Neelam Hussain, Samiya Mumtaz, Rubina Saigol (eds.), *Engendering the Nation State*, vol. 2, Lahore: Simorgh, 1997, 33–42.

Hyder, Qurratulain, *Āg kā Daryā*, Delhi: n.p., 1959 (Urdu).

______, *Āg kā Daryā*, Delhi: Sahitya Akademi, 1968 (Hindi).

______, *River of Fire*, Delhi: Kali for Women, 1998 (English).

______, *Āg kā Daryā*, trans. N.K. Vikram, Delhi: Indraprastha Prakashan, 2000 (Hindi).

Jameson, Fredric, *Marxism and Form*, Princeton: Princeton University Press, 1971.

Nehru, Jawaharlal, *Discovery of India*, New York: Doubleday, 1959 [1945].

Ricoeur, Paul, *Time and Narrative*, vol. 1, Chicago: University of Chicago Press, 1984.

Sangari, Kumkum, *Politics of the Possible: Essays on Gender, History, Narratives, Colonial English*, Delhi: Tulika, 1999.

______, 'Tracing Akbar: Hagiographies, Popular Narrative Traditions and the Subject of Conversion', in N. Chandoke (ed.), *Mapping Histories: Essays Presented to Ravinder Kumar*, Delhi: Tulika, 2000, 61–103.

______, 'Feminist Criticism and Indian Literary History', *Hindi: Language, Discourse, Writing*, 2: 4 (January–March 2002), 35–50.

The Afterlife of a Mughal *Maṣnavī*: The Tale of Nal and Daman in Urdu and Persian

MUZAFFAR ALAM AND SANJAY SUBRAHMANYAM*

Introduction

The debate on the degree of 'continuity' or 'rupture' in the history of northern India during the transition between the Mughal successor states and the rule of the East India Company has often been posed exclusively in political or economic terms, so as to ask whether the transition to colonialism was smooth or disruptive. The cultural and literary aspects of this transition have thus not received their due share of attention, and we have some difficulty in understanding, on the basis of extant literature, what the nature of the relationship between Mughal literary production and that in the nineteenth century really was, beyond such general observations as that 'flowery Persian was already giving way in north India to the fluid and demotic Urdu' (Bayly 1988: 122–3). To be sure, careful studies of the major literary figures of the period allow us some significant clues, and in this respect the work of C.M. Naim has been exemplary, in providing a framework for understanding the transition between the period of, say, Mir Taqi 'Mir', in the latter half of the eighteenth century, and Ghalib's Delhi in the next century (Naim 1999).

We could begin, however, with a slightly different question. What were the major published texts in the mid-nineteenth century in Urdu, which have subsequently fallen into oblivion, where both literary scholars and the general public are concerned? What was the relationship between these texts and the production of the eighteenth century, or even of the high Mughal period? Did these writings draw inspiration primarily from a 'folk' milieu, or

*We are grateful to Kathryn Hansen, David Lelyveld, Velcheru Narayana Rao, and David Shulman for their comments on an earlier draft of this paper.

were they also influenced by court literature? One of the texts that come to mind in this context is the so-called *Nal Daman Hindī*, also mentioned as *Dāstān-i Rāḥat Afzā*, written in the middle years of the nineteenth century by a certain Bhagwant Rāi Kākorwī, whose pen-name was 'Rāḥat'. The poet was still alive at the time of the deposition of the ruler of Awadh, Wajid Ali Shah in 1856, and Aloys Sprenger listed Rāḥat's *Nal-Daman* in his catalogue of the Awadh royal library. But it was not only with royal patrons that Bhagwant Rāi was successful. In fact, his *Nal-Daman* text went into several scores of editions published by Munshi Nawal Kishor of Lucknow and others, even though it was sometimes wrongly attributed to a certain Tāj Bahādur. Several of the major *tazkiras* of Urdu poets have noted Rāḥat's text, amongst them 'Abdul Ghafūr Nassākh's *Sukhan-i Shu'arā*. Though he was still clearly very popular into the 1930s, the author has today fallen into relative oblivion (Farmān Fateḥpurī 1971: 420–9).

To be sure, Rāḥat was not the first author in Urdu to attempt to present the story of Nal and Daman, or Nala and Damayantī, either in verse or in prose. His text is often compared to that of his near contemporary, Mīr Niyāz 'Alī Dehlawī 'Nikhat', of which an incomplete version survives in the Rampur Reza Library (and which is dated to about AH 1256), a text that however never attained a similar popularity to that of Rāḥat. Still another text is mentioned by Garcin de Tassy in the following terms: 'The Saiyid Nûr-i Alî Bangâlî (i.e. from Bengal) is the author of a prose romance in Urdu about Nal, and Daman entitled *Bahâr-i ishc*, i.e. (the Springtime of Love). A copy of this work may be found in the library of the Asiatic Society in Calcutta. This copy originates from the library of Fort William College' (Garcin de Tassy 1839: 398). Other versions are also known to historians of the *maṣnavī* form. Gopī Chand Nārang cites a number of these, including a first Urdu prose version (of which a manuscript may be found in the British Library), by Ilāhī Bakhsh 'Shauq' written in AH 1217/1802; the author, 'Shauq', is known to have worked for the Mughal prince Mirza Mazhar Bakht, son of Mirza Jawan Bakht. Other prose Urdu versions include one by a certain Raghunāth, as well as the 1885 play by Ṭālib Banārasī, which was again printed by the omnipresent Munshi Nawal Kishor. Among versified versions, the first we have access to is by Aḥmad Sarāwī (on which more later); a second is by 'Nikhat' mentioned above; a third is the *Nal-Daman* of Aḥmad 'Alī from Lucknow, also written before 1854; and a fourth is Kālī Prashād's 1869 text, printed from Lucknow (Nārang 1962: 17–38).

In the present essay, we shall not attempt a comprehensive analysis of all these texts, but instead confine ourselves to two major examples from the

Urdu tradition, namely the texts of Aḥmad Sarāwī and Rāḥat. Our justification for choosing these two texts should be clear, the former because it is the earliest available example, and the latter because it was far and away the most popular. An analysis of the other texts too is no doubt justified, but must await another occasion. But before analysing these two Urdu texts, we must begin with some reference to the work that seems fundamentally to have been their inspiration, namely the Persian *maṣnavī* of *Nal-Daman* by the Mughal poet-laureate of the time of Akbar, Abu'l Faiẓ ibn Mubārak, better known as 'Faiẓī' or 'Fayyāẓī'.

A First Telling: Faiẓī's Original

The story of Nal and Daman or Nala and Damayanti is known to us from the classical tradition that dates to the version from the Mahabharata, known generally as the *Nalopākhyāna*. Within the Sanskrit and vernacular traditions, a number of later retellings exist, from the *Naiṣadhīyacarita* of Śrīharṣa, to versions in almost all the Indian regional languages, including Tamil and Telugu.[1] These stories seem, in almost all versions, to revolve around the following plot. A king called Nal (or Nala) falls in love with a princess called Damayanti (or Daman) without ever having seen her. She in turn falls in love with him through the mediation of a messenger bird. The two are united after a first test in the form of a *svayamvara*, a bridegroom contest, in which the princess must choose Nal not only from amongst a variety of other suitors, but from a few gods who have transformed themselves into identical versions of Nal. This feat accomplished, the two lovers return to Nal's residence, where they spend some time in marital bliss. But Nal is an inveterate gambler who is also not very good at gambling. He is hence tricked by his brother into a game, wherein he loses his kingdom. (The similarity between this incident and the loss of his kingdom by Yudhishthira is what prompts the telling of the Mahabharata version.) The couple are forced into exile in the forest, where Nal eventually abandons his wife, and is also transformed into his own antithesis, a short, dark, and ugly man. He wanders off and finds menial employment in another kingdom, while Daman, after many travails returns to her parents' home. But she still hopes to reunite with him, and manages to discover his whereabouts through spies. To motivate him to return, she announces a second (false) *svayamvara*. Nal arrives there accompanying his new master, and is presently obliged to reveal his true identity after Daman subjects him to a test in the form of a series of conundrums. The couple are reunited, and Nal also acquires a set of new skills including gambling. So armed, he defeats his brother in a fresh dice game and recovers his kingdom. The couple are thus reinstalled in their rightful place.

This, in a very bald summary, represents the core plot that reappears in almost all versions, whether in Telugu or Braj Bhasha. However, as we shall see, it is atop this very bare infrastructural skeleton that individual poets can create a far more elaborate superstructure. The great Mughal poet Faiẓī's telling of the Nal-Daman story comes framed in a narrative of the circumstances of its composition, which runs as follows. One night, in the late sixteenth century, the Mughal emperor Akbar (1556–1605) is said to have summoned his poet-laureate, Faiẓī, to his presence. Faiẓī had been at his own residence, sitting in a meditative frame of mind; and when the summons arrived, he naturally rushed to the court. But there was no great political or spiritual crisis afoot. Instead, the emperor asked Faiẓī why, as the poet-magician of the court, the flute of his pen did not produce a poetic fire, and cast a new magic spell? In short, why, instead of addressing the staple question of love in general, did the poet not turn to the specifics of love as it happened in India (*dar hind za 'ishq sar guzashtī ast*)? (Faiẓī 1987) Since Faiẓī knew about love, the emperor stated, as well as the art of weaving tales, this should really be no problem for him. The words of instruction that are put in Akbar's mouth by the poet are as follows, with not only the general theme, but the very specific example of a story that already had wide currency at that time, being clearly set out by the patron:

Nau sāz fasāna-i kuhan rā
'ishq-i nal-o-khūbī-i daman rā.
Tell that old tale anew,
Of the love of Nal and the beauty of Daman.
(...)
Ṣad naghma-i dard dar sukhan rīz
Dar sāghar-i nau mai-i kuhan rīz.
Make a hundred songs of pain into poetry,
Fill the fresh goblet with an old wine.[2]

Akbar suggested to the poet, moreover, that he should place all his arts at the service of this enterprise of bringing alive a story in which love had reduced the lovers themselves into a burnt offering at the temple.

Of the two lovers' coquetry and submission (*nāz-o-niyāz*),
carry lessons to the lovers' assembly.
See what love once was like in India (*dar hind*),
the dagger-thrusts that drowned their hearts in blood.

How those who've played with love in this land,
passed on with their hearts and livers shattered.
How they burnt themselves in fire,
how they became ashes in love's temple.

The text in question was naturally to be written in Persian, in the verse-narrative form known as the *maṣnavī*, and it soon acquired great popularity among readers of Indian Persian, as we see from the numerous manuscripts that are available of it, in major collections both in India and abroad.[3]

Ranked first among the poets of his age by an admittedly prejudiced observer, his own brother, Shaikh Abu'l Fazl, Faiẓī was equally praised for his technical skills by Mullā 'Abdul Qādir Badāyūnī, otherwise not necessarily a great admirer of his. Badāyūnī wrote: 'In many separate branches of knowledge, such as poetry, the composition of enigmas, prosody, rhyme, history, philology, medicine and prose composition, Shaikh Faiẓī had no equal in his time' (Badāyūnī 1925, iii: 411–12). But we also possess the other side of Badāyūnī's judgement of Faiẓī: 'All Jews, Christians, Hindus, and fire-worshippers, not to speak of Nizārīs and Sabāhīs [Ismā'ilīs], held him in the very highest honour for his heresy, his enmity to the followers of Islam, his reviling of the very fundamental doctrines of our faith, his contemptuous abuse of the noble companions [of the Prophet] and those who came after them...'. This is a view that must undoubtedly be taken with a very large pinch of salt, but the text of the *maṣnavī* of *Nal-Daman* does confirm that Faiẓī was religiously liberal and tolerant, and particularly open to Chishti Sufi ideals and vocabulary.

When Faiẓī was commissioned to present a Persian version of the Indian story of Nal and Daman, the resources before him were thus both ample, and somewhat restrictive. The poet was soon to conceive of the story as one of five *maṣnavī*s that he planned to write, but of which he completed only two before his premature death, namely the *Nal-Daman* text (completed in Safar AH 1003, a year before his death), and the *Markaz-i Adwār*, which he was finishing in his last weeks. The three other texts were never completed, though the first had certainly been begun as early as AH 996 (Desai 1963: 25–7). In embarking on this vast programme, Faiẓī's ambition was quite clearly to make a statement that would extend beyond India to Iran, and to the Persian-speaking world more generally, of which he believed himself to be a part. It is thus no coincidence that the formal model for *Nal-Daman* comes from Niẓāmī's *Laylā-Majnūn*, in terms of the metrical scheme utilized as well as a number of other features. But Faiẓī also departed from received models, whether in his choice of metaphors, in his capacity to draw on Indian cultural resources, and his own particular predilections which took him in directions that separate him both from his Indian and Iranian forebears.

It has often been supposed by writers that this is the first 'Indian' story that one finds in the Persian *maṡnavī* tradition. But this is not strictly true, with the misunderstanding perhaps arising from Badāyūnī's description of the *maṡnavī*. Amongst earlier texts, there is a short *maṡnavī* on an Indian theme by Ḥasan Sijzī Dehlawī, in the fourteenth century (Ṣiddīqī 1979); and to an extent even Amīr Khusrau's *Dewal Rānī Khiẓr Khānī* can be classified as a predecessor to Faiẓī's text. But the major difference may be that Amīr Khusrau was not drawing upon a major existing tradition; he was practically the first to write the Dewal Rānī story, and thus had neither the same sorts of constraints nor the same framework of options before him.

Faiẓī naturally opens his text with the praise of God (*ḥamd*), followed by a very long two-part praise of the Prophet (*na'‘t*), and then praise of the emperor Akbar (Faiẓī 1987). The story proper begins only after this very extensive set of prefatory remarks, and we enter into the *mise-en-scène* that we have already rehearsed: Akbar's summoning of Faiẓī, his suggestion of the theme, the poet's mix of interest and trepidation at the enterprise that was before him. His model was clear from the start, namely the great Persian poet Niẓāmī Ganjawī (ca. 1141–1209):

When the ebb and flow of this verse reach Layla,
she'll transform her clothes into chains.
When this magic is heard by Majnun,
he'll even forget Layla herself.
Let me arrange the fire-temple anew.
Let me tell of the love of idol and Brahmin (*but-o-barahman*).

This is a key set of terms that will recur time and again in the text, and which perhaps require some explanation. The role of the 'idol' (*but*, from Buddha, but also *ṣanam*) is a complex one in the Persian poetry of the time. The lover is usually portrayed in terms of this metaphor as the worshipper of the idol, in a powerful device that plays with the idea of infidelity; an alternative mode is to present the beloved as kafir, that is as an infidel. Once the metaphor of the 'idol' has been worked into the structure of a poem, a series of other possibilities open up, namely the references to the beloved's residence as a temple or idol house, the reference to rivalry in terms of iconoclasm (the smashing of other idols, etc.). The drive is very clearly to turn what is an eminently negative lexical item in an orthodox vocabulary on its head, and the role of the poet is both to provoke and to invert. In his own use of metaphors impregnated with 'Indian' local colour, Faiẓī does not stop at *but* and *ṣanam*, but goes much further. The play between the Indian world of the Brahmin and his sacred thread (*zunnār*), and the classical Persian world of Layla and Majnun is thus clear from the start, as indeed is the relationship between the linguistic worlds and registers that are to be played with:

Let me combine the melody (*āhang*) of the Indian voice,
with the sound of instruments from Pahlawi and Dari.
Let me take my suffering's candle
and ignite it at the fire-temples of Fars.
We shall take our thoughts to the Iranians,
and offer this fire to them in gift.

This is an integral part of Faiẓī's conception of matters, for his audience is not only within India, but embraces the larger Persian-speaking world, including Safavid Iran. At the very end of the poem, he returns to this theme, speaking of how he has brought together the patterns of Ganja (native place of Niẓāmī), with the ideas of Delhi, and erected an idol house which is still accessible to the intelligent reader who is not immersed in matters Indian. This is his idea then of a new style, where the best of India and Iran will be combined to fresh effect. A verse from the introductory section may be cited in support of Faiẓī's contention that he delicately combines elements from different cultures.

This breath is not for petty people,
and this flask too dear for bargain-hunters.
This liquor will go to the head,
for it's distilled from Indian sugar.[4]

On Aḥmad Sarāwī's 'Nal Daman'

Poets who adapted this story in Mughal northern India were several, including a certain Sūrdās, whose version in Awadhi verse has come down to us in more than one manuscript (Sūrdās 1961; Chandra 1938). Sūrdās describes himself in the text as the son of Govardhandas of the Kambu *gotra*, from a family originally from Kalanur in the Punjab, which had then settled in Lucknow, where Sūrdās was born. The text, written in an Avadhi that is located between the relatively bucolic register of Jāyasī and the more Sanskritized one of Tulsīdās, was clearly composed in the last years of the reign of the Mughal emperor Shah Jahan in 1714 Samvat, or AH 1068, which is to say, 1656–7 CE. Emperor Shah Jahan is mentioned by name in the text, and the oldest manuscript is one held in the Prince of Wales Museum (Mumbai), written in the Persian script, with a colophon in Persian, stating that it was copied on 4 Shawwal AH 1110. The colophon makes it amply clear that the patron of the copy is a certain Diler Khan (perhaps a Bijapuri Afghan noble in Mughal service), and the scribe states that his own rather elaborate name is Bābullāh ibn Sayyid Muḥammad Zāhid Ḥasanī al-Ḥusainī al-Bukhārī al-Najafī.[5] The form of the text is of sequences of nine lines in *chaupāi*, followed by a *dohā*. Garcin de Tassy, who apparently possessed 'a lovely copy of this work in Persian characters', made at Delhi in 1752–3, was convinced (perhaps because he had not read the work fully) that its author was the celebrated blind poet of the sixteenth century, 'son of Bābā Rāmdās, also a musician'. The French savant equally informs us that the text was known both as the *Bhākha Nal Daman* and the *Qiṣṣa-i Nal Daman* (Garcin de Tassy 1839: 486–8). Based on his somewhat incorrect chronology, Garcin also asked the following question, which is in the event, of no great relevance: 'Was it from this text that Faïzî, brother of Akbar's minister, Abû Fazl, translated the Persian romance on the same subject? For it is said in the *Ayeen-i Akbery* that this work was translated from the *hindouî*'.

Sūrdās's text certainly could not have influenced Faiẓī, but it may have had some influence on the *Nal Daman* of Aḥmad Sarāwī probably dating from the mid-eighteenth century.[6] The extant edition of the text, by the well-known scholar Sayyid 'Abdullah, contains an extensive introduction published earlier in the *Oriental College Magazine* from Lahore, which is primarily concerned with features of the language used in Sarāwī's text. Since this introduction is the only serious discussion to date of the text, we may begin by briefly noting its central arguments. The text was written in the Meerut area, in Sarawa district, and 'Abdullah opines that it is in 'Haryanawi' or 'Haryani', a language earlier discussed at length by Ḥāfiẓ Maḥmūd Sherānī, who had argued moreover that the Haryanawi literature was not confined to the strict domain of Haryana.[7] Sayyid 'Abdullah attempts to follow this line of reasoning. He traces Persian literature on Indian themes to Mas'ūd Sa'd Salmān and his use of *bārahmāsa*, and notes that it gained further ground under Akbar, to continue until the last days of the Mughals. This *hindustāniyat* of Persian is demonstrated—so he argues—by Faiẓī's *Nal-Daman*, though we can also count the Persian translation of the Ramayana, *Singhāsan Batīsī*, *Kāmrūp wa Kāmalatā*, and other texts on Indian 'folk' themes, among the major 'bridge stories' that passed from the Indic to the Persian.[8]

For Sayyid 'Abdullah, there is no doubt whatsoever that Aḥmad Sarāwī derived his text primarily from Faiẓī's version of the Nal-Daman story. But was

Sarāwī's version superior to that of Faiẓī? Here, he notes that views of Faiẓī's *maṣnavī* were somewhat mixed. Thus, the celebrated eighteenth-century savant Khān-i 'Ārzū was not a great fan of Faiẓī's *Nal-Daman*, which he described as 'not particularly extraordinary' (*chandān khūb na gufta*), but to this one may counterpose 'Abdul Qādir Badāyūnī's view of the text, according to which Faiẓī's was one of the best *maṣnavīs* ever in Persian. No wonder then that Akbar had the text copied by a special calligrapher, and used to have it read out to him at night. It is noted by 'Abdullah that though Sarāwī's text is based on Faiẓī, it represents a considerable shortening of the source text.

As for the author, he would seem to be Sayyid Aḥmad 'Alī Sarāwī, from Sarawa in tahsil Hapur, some 14 miles from Meerut, on the banks of a branch of the Kali Nadi. Sarawa, it is noted, was earlier known as Fath Garh, and it had been founded by the Ghurids. In 1737, the town became the political and revenue centre of Raja Dala Ram; but his son left Sarawa for Bulandshahr during the end of the reign of Muhammad Shah, and Sarawa fell into decline. The town was otherwise known for its sizeable population of Shaikhs, and a large congregational mosque dated to the late seventeenth century (that is AH 1112). If Aḥmad Sarāwī wrote when the town still flourished, he probably did so in the middle decades of the eighteenth century. The text of his *Nal-Daman* can thus be seen in the context of the later Mughal life in *qaṣba* towns like Barnawa and Sardhana, with their share of intellectuals who existed with some degree of autonomy from the life and patronage of the imperial centre or even the great provincial centres.

Sayyid 'Abdullah is struck by the difference in dialects between the Meerut area (where the form is called *pachharī bolī*) and Delhi. The differences, he argues, are based on the balance of elements between Haryani (Bangdu), Braj Bhasha, Deccani, Punjabi, and Rajasthani. Following Maḥmūd Sherānī, he too argues, based on reading texts from the later Mughal period such as 'Abdī's *Fiqh-i Hindī* and several ranging from the end of Aurangzeb's reign to that of Muhammad Shah, that Sarāwī's text is in 'Haryani', even if not in its mainstream. Rather, he feels that the Deccani influence on the text, while present, is relatively limited. He also notes the formal structure of the text, namely, the punctuation at the end of every sixteen-line passage (*band*) with a two-line counter-verse (*sorṭhā*), which is generally far less influenced by Persian than the main text. We may also notice the similarity to the *chaupāi-dohā* alternation in the Sūrdās text. The dialectal differences are also marked orthographically, as we see from the treatment of the retroflex 'd', and the exchangeable nature of 'l' and 'r' in words like *ḍārī* for *ḍālī*, or *tarwār* for *talwār*. There are also effects in terms of exaggerated use of long vowels. 'Abdullah's is thus a discussion that is mostly focused on questions of language and dialect, relating to the identity within this very specific region of the language used. On the use of Persian in the text, he opines that it actually is overdone at times, and produces an unseemly effect. There is thus a point of view espoused by the introduction with regard to what is the 'proper' place of Persian in such texts. To combine the vernacular *champā kī kalī* with *nāf* (Persian, navel) in a description of Daman thus sounds wrong to Sayyid 'Abdullah (his condemnatory term for such a mixture is *bhaddāpan*). But at other times, he admits that Sarāwī does manage to introduce Persian proverbs into his text, without overly straining it. 'Abdullah compares Sarāwī's early eighteenth-century text with passages from Muḥammad Afẓal's *Bārah Māsa*, and Maḥbūb 'Ālam's *Dard Nāma* and *Maḥshar Nāma*, as well as Quṭbī's *Terah Māsa*, and argues that we can discern similarities in style, and even in metre in some cases. Since these are largely earlier examples, we thus see that Sarāwī has precursors on whom to draw from at least in the seventeenth century.

So much for the learned editor's introduction. In the text of Aḥmad Sarāwī, we begin with a rather understated *ḥamd* that does not lay the emphasis on the theme of *'ishq* (love) that we will find in the other *Nal-Daman* texts. This is followed by praise-verses, a *na't* to the Prophet, and a *manqabat* for the companions of the Prophet, in which both Sunnis and Shi'as are accommodated, with even the twelve imams of the latter finding mention. But once into the text proper, Aḥmad Sarāwī does not tell us why he writes his text, nor does he explicitly mention his indebtedness to Faiẓī's Persian version. Instead he begins in mixed Persian and vernacular:

Hāṅ ai qalam subuk kharāmam
Barkash raqamī tū az maqāmam
Ta man kiyam wa kujā maqām ast
Kū mamlikat wa marā che nām ast
O my smooth-running pen!
Trace a line concerning my place,
that it may be clear who I am and where my place is,
Which country I come from and what my name is.

Hai kishwar-i hind dil kusha tar
Barr-u-baḥrash farḥ faẓā tar
There's a country called Hind that pleases the heart,
Whose land and waters increase pleasure.

The text then continues in an explicitly patriotic mode, exalting the land not in a narrow sense (say Sarawa, or the Meerut region), but looking to a wider identity:

Hai hind bihisht kī nishānī
Har chashma āb-i zindagānī
Hind is the sign of Paradise,
And each stream is the Elixir of Life.

In the passages that follow, we shall give the verses in translation alone, while pointing the rigorous philologist reader to the published text. So, Sarāwī continues:

Each town and village of this land,
is as if Paradise has been spread out everywhere.
Each garden has flowers of every sort
And every flower-bed is like the firmament.
The land of Hind is full of love
And each pebble is like a pearl.
Nay, what is the value of a mere pearl?
Each brick of this land is dearer than my body's clay.

Aḥmad Sarāwī continues in this vein for some more lines, praising love in Hind and the beauty of the women there in order to conclude:

O Ahmad! Continue your praise no longer.
The virtues of Hind are no matter of play.
In Hind, there's a famous place called Sarawa
Which can compare with Paradise itself.
Where each child is a master in love and science,
May God keep it ever flourishing.

The counter-verse (or *sorṭhā*) then runs:

Both king and beggar are happy there,
there's music and play day and night,
one can find no trace of sorrow,
everybody is ever blissful.

This piece of strictly local patriotism being taken care of, the poet then takes us southwards to the great city of Ujjain, where Raja Nal is reigning in all his glory. As is the usual sequence in most versions of the story, he falls ill for no apparent reason, and we have a description of his mysterious sickness, as well as the attempts to cure him. They are bound to fail, of course, since what ails him is a malady beyond any physician's grasp. Thus, we have Nal reproach one of the doctors:

Nal said: 'O foolish doctor,
Don't fret unduly at my pulse.
My real pain is within my heart,[9]
as if my vein of frenzy had been sliced open.
This heart of mine, that is stained with blood,
recognize it, if you really have understanding.'

So, the king even in this state has some degree of lucidity. But it does not produce a solution, and when the doctors have consistently failed to produce a remedy, storytellers gather to tell him tales in order to give him solace. One of these storytellers states:

'Why do you want to hear stories and tales
Of old affairs that have long gone?
I shall tell you a respectable tale,
Listen, O King, hear it all.
In the land of the Deccan, creator of turmoil (*fitna-kheẓī*),
is a shop which is busy spreading trouble,
a beloved who is the life of the whole Deccan,
whose beauty is manifest in the whole world.
She is the crowning beauty of the world,
and in the Deccan she has maddened everyone.
The Brahmins have forgotten their *pūjā*,
nor do they remember any other thing.'

An extensive description follows of Daman's beauty, spread out over two long verses or *bands*. These are the conventional phrases, a moon-like face, eyes that cut like swords, hair as black as snakes, on a body like a sandalwood tree. The metaphors are largely Indian rather than from the vocabulary of Persian poetry, as when the parting in Daman's hair is compared to a line of white cranes in the midst of black clouds. As for her forehead, it is like the moon of the fourteenth night of the cycle. This is all set down, however, in a tone that is discreet and metaphorical, not the explicit description that we shall find in the later Urdu poet Rāḥat. The face, mouth, teeth, and neck having been described, we move briefly to the arms and hands, with golden rings on her fingers. The *sorṭhā* counter-verse breaks the description, with a description of hair falling down Daman's back, returning to the metaphor of the snake and the sandal tree:

The breasts on her body sit proudly,
They would put oranges to shame.

Her belly as soft as a lotus-leaf,
And her feet are firm on the ground.
The navel like a *champā* bud,
Her waist slim, and her buttocks like the Qaf mountain.
Her thighs like two tall trees,
And her stature like an erect cypress.

Thus, we see that the eighteenth-century poet remains more or less the epitome of sobriety, following his sixteenth-century predecessor Faiẓī in this respect. The same sobriety may be found in the passages that follow, detailing first their love-in-separation, then the exchange of messages, until we come to the *svayamvar* when Daman manages to choose Nal over his rivals. It can equally be seen in the description of the wedding night, after the *svayamvar*, with the metaphors being of their union as a battle between the Sun and the Moon. Daman's beauty is described once more, and Nal approaches her, intoxicated as if he had been bitten by a snake.

The beauty threw a rose at his face,
And the prince came back to his senses.
Now it's a battle of the Sun and the Moon,
And an invasion by the armies of beauty.
Let's see which of the two loses,
And who's the first to strike with the sword.
(...)
Nal, the king, Rustam of his time,
Quickly bent over his target,
The prince gathered himself together,
conquered the fort, and drove separation away.

Soon the night is over, and dawn breaks; the time has come for them to leave Daman's parents and return to Nal's kingdom of Ujjain with his goods and beautiful slave girls. Here he rules for some years, until frenzy (*junūn* or *saudā*) raises its head again. Nal is ill, and the doctors cannot cure him. It is in this enfeebled state that the ungrateful brother strikes, and wins the game against him. Nal and Daman are soon exiled, as they must be in every version of their story. There follows an incident in which a bird the couple are trying to capture flies off with Nal's clothes, and then that of the fish that escape while Daman tries to cook them. Relations between the two lovers begin to sour. Nal now tries to persuade her to return home to her parents, and she reproaches him for making this suggestion. The pair spends some more days together in the forest when Nal, again in a fit of frenzy, leaves her. Daman is in despair in the forest, and here Aḥmad Sarāwī recounts an incident involving a python (*azhdahā*) that attacks Daman in the forest, until she is saved by a traveller. The princess will now pass through a series of small episodes, including a meeting with some other-worldly white-robed creatures on the water, who reassure her that all will turn out well; her rescue by a passing army commander, and the sad destruction of his army; and finally, Daman's chance arrival in the city of her aunt and uncle. As for Nal, he too goes through his transformation into his alter ego 'Bāhang' (on account of a snakebite), and arrives for his part in the city of King Rutbaran, who employs him in his stables. The particularity of the text in this entire section lies in its capacity to mix marked Persian words into a Hindi context, and its play of levels and vocabularies is at times highly complex.

Aḥmad Sarāwī thus produces a racy narrative, one in which the philosophizing on statecraft that characterizes Faiẓī has no place worth the mention. It is thus that he manages to reduce the narrative considerably in size, while keeping each of the major incidents and landmarks of the Faiẓī text in place. An example of this is Aḥmad Sarāwī's rapid treatment of the section on Daman's birth that plays a prominent part in Faiẓī. Instead, we get a rather summary view, as follows:

> There was a queen in the house of the king,
> With a bud-like mouth, and a beautiful voice,
> She was barren, and had no children,
> And the king was unhappy on this account.
> He looked for a remedy from everyone,
> In search of the child he did not have.[10]

The relationship between Sarāwī's text and that of Faiẓī is not that of a faithful translation to an original, though at times Sarāwī borrows entire phrases from his predecessor, and most of the central ideas are clearly those of the late sixteenth-century poet. In general, if one compares the two, one can see that even where he follows Faiẓī, Sarāwī tends to economize, dropping some lines which he no doubt considered secondary or inappropriate. Sayyid 'Abdullah finds that even if Sarāwī follows Faiẓī (and it is clear that he usually does, in opposition to the Sanskrit versions), he has in some ways made the narrative better and 'more interesting' (*ziyāda dilchasp*); in fact 'Abdullah's contention is that Sarāwī is a good poet who would have been even better if he were not so in awe of Faiẓī.[11] Certainly, the plot of Sarāwī holds no surprises for the reader of Faiẓī; after the separation, we have the riddles that Daman poses to Nal to establish his identity, his recovery of his original form, the lovers' reconciliation, the return to Ujjain, and the recovery of the kingdom through the repetition of the dice game.

The last lines of Sarāwī's *maṣnavī* end with winter in the garden, with crows cawing instead of nightingales, but there is no explicit description of the death of Nal and Daman, as we find in the other versions. Indeed, this may be because it seems the text is incomplete in the manuscript, with only the beginning of the last section. Thus, the closing lines of Sarāwī run:

> The 'springtime' of winter had begun,
> Frost fell, and people began to shiver.
> The autumn wind began to blow,
> and the woods resounded with falling leaves.
> All flowers and gardens were desolate,
> In place of the nightingale, crows began to caw.
> All trees came to be denuded,
> And leaves turned pale everywhere.
> No green was to be seen anywhere,
> And the garden became a fearsome sight.
> The world's flowering plants were all dried up,
> as if a hot black wind (*lū*) had blown there.
> Nal was saddened in his mind,
> He came and sat forlorn in the garden.
> No flowers or nightingales were in sight,
> And instead the crows made their harsh sound.
> (...)

Commentators have noted that Aḥmad Sarāwī was also the author of other texts in Urdu, namely a version of *Yūsuf-Zulaikhā*, and a *maṣnavī* called *Gul Ṣanaubar*, as well as two prose texts, *Mor Pankhī* and *Rashk-i Parī*; he was thus clearly practised at these adaptations from the Persian. Yet, some doubt remains as to the precise extent of his indebtedness to Faiẓī. For instance, the noted critic Gopī Chand Nārang has surmised that Sarāwī may also have had a text in the vernacular Bhakha in front of him, linking this to the relative absence of eroticism in the text, as well as to the heavy presence of Indic metaphors. In our next version, the first of these characteristics would have changed, perhaps on account of the growing influence of poets such as Mīr Aṣar and Mīr Ḥasan, who it is usually admitted, were those who introduced heavier doses of eroticism into Urdu texts.

The Retelling by Rāḥat

Aḥmad Sarāwī's text is a clear indication of the fascination that Faiẓī's *Nal-Daman*, with its powerful innovations and mastery of technique, seems to have exercised already in the seventeenth and eighteenth centuries. The hallmarks of Faiẓī's treatment came to be his insistence on the delicate line that had to be trod between love and excess (or frenzy), with the intellect being the only means of preventing the one from degenerating into the other. All this was tied up with a brilliant closing section, in which the Indo-Persian poet's fascination with the theme of sati was combined with the earlier themes, to allow a closure where a return to an explicitly Sufi flavour was possible. In this section, we pursue the continuing afterlife of Faiẓī's *Nal-Daman*, through a reading of Munshī Lāl Bhagwant Rāi Rāḥat Kākorwī's *Nal-Daman Hindī*, written in northern India and published in 1859, thus immediately after the important political events of 1857–8 (Rāḥat 1869). Bhagwant Rāi was the son of Munshī Dīn Dayāl, and a student of the celebrated Āg͟hā Ḥasan 'Amānat' Lakhnawī, author of the *Indar Sabhā*. A quite prolific writer, Rāḥat is also known for *Nigāristān-i Rāḥat*, his Urdu translation of the *maṡnavī* entitled *Nairang-i 'Ishq* of Muḥammad Akram G͟hanīmat Kunjāhī, a poet of Aurangzeb's period. The text recounts the tumultuous love story of a merchant 'Aziz and a boy called Shahid in the Punjab (G͟hanīmat Kunjāhī 1962). Rāḥat also authored at least two other *maṡnavī* texts, *Maṡnavī Zohra-o-Bahrām* and *Soz-i 'Āshiqāna*.

Bhagwant Rāi actually starts his *maṡnavī* with a *ḥamd* of some twenty lines in which the orienting theme of love (*muḥabbat* and *'ishq*) is developed at some length. But, the author being a Hindu Kayastha, there is no *na't* in this text, the Prophet thus not being the object of praise. The text then continues:

> *Jo dekhā āj kal hindī kā charchā*
> *Huā dil ek din mushtāq iskā*
> *Ke 'ishq-i nal jo thā 'ālam meṅ mashhūr*
> *Kare hindī zabāṅ meṅ usko maskūr*
> *Agar che fārsī meṅ sab bayāṅ hai*
> *Magar ṭūl uskī har ek dāstāṅ hai*
> *Kare tu mukhtaṣar aisā bayāṅ sab*
> *Khule har ek pe jo rāz-i nihāṅ sab.*
> Seeing the demand for Hindi in our times,
> the desire came upon me one day,
> that Nal's love which was famous in this world
> should be brought into the Hindi tongue.
> Though it has all been told in Persian
> yet it's been done at tedious length.
> Why not recount it all in brief,
> that each reader might grasp the point?

'Hindi' in his version really means 'Urdu', as was often the case at this time, not only in terms of its script but in its heavily Persianized diction, and

Rāḥat seems to be ignorant of earlier versions such as that of Aḥmad Sarāwī. The Urdu version does indeed 'recount it all in brief', reducing the 4000 verses of Faiẓī's original to less than half that number. As in the case of Sarāwī, the influence of Faiẓī on Bhagwant Rāi is evident, both in terms of the organization of the story and the presence of some key episodes that were Faiẓī's own innovations. For instance, three or four lines after the beginning there are some verses on *muḥabbat*, the Urdu equivalent of Faiẓī's praise of *'ishq*. Bhagwant Rāi, however, does not utilize Faiẓī's development of the idea of two stages of love, one within the bounds of reason, and another where love is transformed into an uncontrollable passion. Nor does he dilate on another distinction clear to Faiẓī, and which appears both at the beginning and in the concluding sections of the Persian *Nal-Daman*, namely that between bodily love and real love, which is approximated to the Sufic idea of union. In the Urdu text, we pass without clear distinctions between the rather concrete love of the deer, which seeks its companion in the forest, to the execution of Mansur because of his declaring: *ana al-ḥaqq* ('I am God').

Bhagwant Rāi perhaps logically reduces the initial sections of Faiẓī's text drastically, passing very quickly to a brief description of Hindustan, and thence to Ujjain, where Nal rules as the king:

> The land of Hindustan is pleasing,
> each town a colourful garden.
> Its idols are so free and easy
> that they rob the ascetic's heart.
> God gave them such beauty and grace
> that China dolls cannot reach the dust of their feet.
> These infidels have tresses to their waist,
> to entrap in them the heart of Islam.
> Where such idols rule with ease,
> shouldn't everyone prostrate before them?
> (...)
> This is a land of wonders upon this earth,
> no other foreign land can match it.

This small passing reference to the inferiority of foreign lands (*wilāyat*) before the wonders of Hindustan was presumably inspired by the recent British annexation of Avadh and the suppression of the 1857 revolt; such comparative references are absent from Sarāwī's version. The verse then continues:

> It seems to be a part of Paradise,
> for the status of this land is towering.

If we were to describe its beauty in detail,
our paper would be transformed into a painting.
In terms of beauty, it has such a name,
that Canaan would do well to be its slave.

These verses suggest an even more highly developed sense of 'patriotism' on the part of our nineteenth-century author than one finds in Faiẓī or Sarāwī, who—we have noted—are not entirely lacking in these sentiments either. From this discussion of Hindustan, we pass on to Ujjain, where Nal rules in typical Mughal style, assuring such peace that the wolf and the lamb (*gurg aur mesh*) drink from the same waters.

As in the other versions, Nal falls ill of a mysterious sickness here too. Once more, the doctors are called in to diagnose him. But the doctors function differently now, for they are, above all, preoccupied with taking the patient's pulse (*nabẓ*). Nal declares thereupon that he is in love; the only question that remains is one of identifying whom he is in love with. Stories of love are hence told in his court, and soon enough the figure of Daman appears. The beauty of Daman is, however, somewhat differently described here, when compared to the other texts. The emphasis on the appellation 'Hindu', in the double sense of 'dark', and as a religious category (in opposition to 'Musalman') is quite clear when one reads the text of Rāḥat. We should also emphasize that this Urdu text is rather explicit in developing a series of detailed physical descriptions. We may cite some examples. The description of Daman by the storyteller inside the story runs as follows:

The Deccan is a place of wondrous beauty
a colourful garden, full of rose-like faces.
Each of them has a special style,
that drives even the sane mad with love.
But there is one moon-faced one there,
who the whole world desires to acquire,
If that idol were seen by a pious Muslim,
he would desire her like any Brahmin.
The net (*dām*) she has made with her tresses
has produced her name itself—Daman.
Thousands of Brahmins are mad about her,
and want somehow to approach that silvery idol.
What can I say of the love she inspires,
that black-eyed, black-haired Hindu.
(...)
Not only will the Hindu die for her tresses,
the Musalman too would sacrifice his faith for it.

A further long passage illustrates the innovations the Urdu poet has introduced for his part, for if on the one hand he prefers brevity, on the other hand he dilates on aspects that would probably have made the earlier poets blush.

On her chest lie two fresh apples,
which no hand has besmirched so far.
Her whole belly is so soft and silky
that it would put ermine itself to shame.
And her waist, as thin as a flower-stalk,
has the greatest connoisseurs rapt in wonder.
Her gliding walk undulates
as if she bears her tresses as a weight.
In the belly's river lies a whirlpool,
her navel, that has drowned a thousand hearts.
Beyond this lies the place of shame,
where the pen can find no real place.
That secret place cannot be drawn,
so how can Rāḥat write of it subtly?
If the poet exercises all his craft
he may give a mere glimpse of it.
The morning's air cannot reach it,
so the flower-bud is yet to open.
Her hips are so very wondrous,
as if the bottom were higher than the top.
What shall I tell you of her thighs?
for they glisten with a delicate light.
When the mirror looks upon their beauty
despairing, he throws his own shine in the dust.
Whoever looks upon the calves of that fairy,
will never again find peace from his unrest.
The henna on the edges of her feet,
has watchers all rubbing their hands in envy.

The story moves on to the second episode, where the circumstances of the birth of Daman are explained. Here, once more, we can see that the Urdu poet in fact follows Faiẓī very closely. The king's wife, we know, is barren, and he is despondent as a result. But he cannot marry again, for he does not dare to share his bed with two women, something that would be like having two kings on a throne or two moons in the sky. Bhagwant Rāi treats the theme in exactly the same terms, and using very nearly the same words as Faiẓī:

He had no son before him,
and was imprisoned in the cage of grief,
For he had no pearl before him,
and in his desire shed tears without end.
Nor could he have another wife
for fear that this might cause discord,
For how can two kings sit on one throne,
or two moons co-exist in the same constellation?

Faiẓī's lines run:

Yak takht dū shāh bar natābad
Yak burj dū māh bar nayāyad

Those of Bhagwant Rāi parallel them extremely closely.

Sambhāleṅ takht ek do shāh kyon kar
Raheṅ ek burj meṅ do māh kyon kar.

Such examples can be easily multiplied, showing the close dependence of the Urdu poet on his Persian forebear, but also rendering the points of departure all the more significant when they do occur. In Bhagwant Rāi's version, the episode of the holy man in the desert who grants the king a boon is followed very closely, and after the birth of Daman, he is once more consulted so far as her horoscope and future are concerned. The long advice given by the holy man to the king also appears in a similar form to that in the Persian poem (and unlike that of Sarāwī).

It would be tedious to enter into a detailed comparison of the different versions of the poems, and we shall content ourselves in the paragraphs that follow to noting some of the main deviations and innovations in the text of Rāḥat compared to that of Faiẓī. For example, in the episode of the exchanged letters between the lovers, the Urdu text notes that they were put inside envelopes (*lifāfā*), something that Faiẓī does not of course mention. Where Faiẓī gives minute details of how Daman ties up her letter, in Bhagwant Rāi she rather summarily takes a hair from her head to tie it. In the episode where Daman and the messenger bird converse in a corner, the Urdu text has her making rather lame excuses to her friends for why she needs to speak with this messenger. A new morality seems to have set in, making crude concealment necessary. When Daman's father finds out about her secret passion, Bhagwant Rāi's version has it that he is afraid of his reputation because his daughter is still too young. The nineteenth-century preoccupation with an appropriate age for marriage has thus invaded the text, something that does not bother the Mughal poet.

Perhaps the most significant deviation takes place in the description of the union of Nal and Daman after the *svayamvar*. While Sarāwī, like Faiẓī, skirts metaphorically around the issue, the later Urdu poet takes us much further down the track of sexual love, seen from an explicitly and rather aggressively male viewpoint:

> Daman was then brought to his side,
> the curtain between them was raised.
> When the rituals had been performed,
> the place came to be deserted.
> When they were alone at last in the palace,
> Desire put his foot forward boldly.
> The lover was now growing impatient,
> the wait had been too long for him.
> As his hand moved with speed and hope,
> it first touched the fresh pomegranate.
> Having caressed it a while in lust,
> he then bent over the grape-like lips,
> to chew upon the pistachio in her mouth,
> to taste the pleasure of her apple-like cleft chin.
> Having tasted each fruit turn by turn,
> he placed his hand at length around her waist.
> If she showed some signs of shyness,
> he scarcely hesitated.
> The silvery branch he drew to his waist,
> and joined it to the soaked-through date.
> Seeing these two fresh flower-like bodies so,
> the candle kept burning there in shame.
> When the raindrop approached the oyster's mouth,
> the jeweller could not pierce the shell.
> The hard diamond which stood in the way
> of a sudden became soft, and yielded.
> The body that was as flushed as vermilion,
> grew pale from the flash of lightning.
> The face turned as pale as the moon,
> for desire had now at last subsided.
> Still he clasped his beloved to his body,
> For in his heart, passion still was beating.

The consummation complete, the lovers can now return to Ujjain, where Nal rules. The disaster that follows is described in terms that are similar to those in Faiẓī, indeed perhaps even more explicit. For Nal neglects the affairs of state totally, so lost is he in his excessive passion for Daman:

Ever since Nal returned with Daman,
he attended to nothing except her.
The affairs of the Sultanate were abandoned,
and he cared for her, and her alone.
When this went on for some time,
one thing after the other went to ruin.

Nal falls ill, and both his people and the courtiers gradually become angry with him. This allows the evil brother to take advantage of the situation by inviting him to play both chess (*shatranj*) and dice (*chausar*), the latter an innovation of Rāḥat's text. Exile and the travails of the jungle follow, and Nal eventually abandons Daman in the middle of the night. Here again, Bhagwant Rāi introduces a minor new element into Daman's reflection. Can he have fallen in love with another woman, she wonders ? The episode follows in which Daman comes under the protection of the army commander. To his questions in the earlier versions, the nineteenth-century Urdu text adds a new one: Is she from Hindustan or from abroad (*wilāyat*), the army commander asks Daman.

The Urdu text also deviates somewhat from that of Faiẓī in bringing back the theme of the ill effect of Kali into the text, with Kali concretely being the snake that bites Nal and transforms him into his alter ego Bahuk.[12] This is not a full-fledged rehabilitation of the Kali theme into the poem, for Bhagwant Rāi still remains faithful to Faiẓī's conception of love and excess as the principal axis around which to organize the narrative. The sudden introduction of Kali here suggests that the Urdu poet was aware of other versions, and sought in his own way to effect some minor reconciliations. A few other elements from popular Islam also feature in the Urdu text: for example, Daman is said to have met the legendary Khwaja Khizr on her wanderings before finding her way to the kingdom of her aunt and uncle. The rediscovery of Nal, disguised as Bahuk, now follows the same pattern as in the other versions, as does the invitation that brings him and Rutbaran to the town of Bidar or Bandar. The identification of Bahuk as Nal is completed here, and the usual significant scene follows where Daman questions Nal, albeit in far greater detail than in the other texts.

The reconciliation of Nal and Daman, their return to Ujjain, and his victory over his brother, all these follow the familiar pattern. The Urdu text also follows Faiẓī closely in the last episode, where Nal grows old, and prepares to give up his throne and retire from the world. This is the moment when

Nal also summons Daman, and seeks to take leave from her, he being now reduced to mere skin and bones. As in Faiẓī's Persian text, she states that she would gladly go along with him, and a Sufic discussion follows between the two of them concerning love on earth, and its relationship to union with the divine. Nal even goes so far as to state that his love for her has really been a means for him to reach a higher love. Nal dies, and Daman laments. Gathering flowers and sandalwood, she makes a pyre for him. Then, wearing colourful clothes, she goes smiling to his body and washes it with rose water. When everything is ready, Daman takes Nal's head in her lap, and she is declared to have become a sati; unlike Faiẓī's version, sati is presented here as a matter of duty (*dastūr*). As in Faiẓī's text, there is no need for fire to be brought, for Daman's body here too begins to burn on its own (*k͟hud ba k͟hud*). The people around start to lament and create a clamour, but nothing can be done. Her body burns like a camphor candle, as brightly as the sun. Bhagwant Rāi then concludes the story:

> This silver-bodied one had pure love,
> dying with her idol she became dust.
> O cup-bearer, pour me some fine red wine
> that my heart may flower with happiness.

The colophon of the Urdu text is once again far more modest, and far less abstract than that of Faiẓī:

> Now I should thank the Creator,
> who from nothing brought forth all creation,
> This work has been done thanks to Him,
> and carried through from beginning to end.
> When the *mas̤navī* was made ready,
> I thought someone should examine it.
> I took it to a benefactor Kali Prashad,
> who heard it and grew very glad.[13]
> [....]
> So long as the sun shines in the sky,
> may this story remain famous in the world.
> O cup-bearer! Pour me such a wine
> that I may not be intoxicated again.

The Urdu poet has thus apparently produced the text on his own inspiration, and then taken it to a series of patrons. Besides Kālī Prashād mentioned above, we know that the text's printing was subsidized by at least two other such individuals: Lala Jai Narayan and Lala Bakhtawar Singh.

The patronage of the Mughal court has passed in symbolic fashion to that of the merchant (*saudāgar*), but at least one part of Faiẓī's message still retains an interest for nineteenth-century readers.

Conclusion

There has been much debate over the years on the translation of texts from Sanskrit into Persian at the court of Muslim sultans, whether the *Ṭūṭī-Nāma* and other cycles of stories, or esoteric and philosophical texts (Phukan 2001). It is certain that in the late sixteenth and seventeenth centuries, such projects of 'translation' (with the word being used in the widest possible meaning) gained a massive momentum under the Mughals, for reasons that are of a complex nature. The major Sanskrit epic texts were rendered into Persian now, and were at times also drawn upon by chroniclers to provide a history of India in the period before Muslim rule. In some instances, it would appear that these Persian versions enjoyed a great deal of legitimacy even amongst Hindu readers (this is the case with the translation of the Mahabharata), while in others, the Persian versions languished for long in obscurity (Qazwīnī Sh. 1358). Within this broad context, the case of *Nal-Daman* is a particular one. The text did not have any particularly weighty religious connotation, and seems to have been absorbed into the Persian tradition by Faiẓī as a relatively secular theme upon which he could develop a series of reflections and arguments of his own, concerning royal power, the nature of love, and the place of the intellect in managing the affairs of the world. What is of interest is the power of the poet's intervention, which—if it is partly related to his prestige and that of the Mughal court—is also largely the consequence of the literary and thematic appeal that his text carried. For many of the literati of northern India then, the story of Nal and Daman (or Nala and Damayanti), would never be the same again after Faiẓī had remoulded it to his own ends. This was clearly the case both with Aḥmad Sarāwī and with Bhagwant Rāi, though each of them drew in a selective fashion on Faiẓī, emphasizing some elements and downplaying others.

The elements that we have drawn upon here seem clearly to support the view that a strong line of continuity can be drawn from the Mughal court culture of the late sixteenth century and the cultural and literary world of the smaller towns of northern India (such as Sarawa, Barnawa, Sardhana, Jayas, or Bilgram) in the eighteenth century.[14] While it may be possible that Aḥmad Sarāwī knew of some vernacular telling of the Nal-Daman story (even if not that of Sūrdās), it is nevertheless clear that he was influenced above all by Faiẓī's version. The same was true for Bhagwant Rāi, who both transmitted and transformed Faiẓī's text, reducing its emphasis on political reflection and statecraft and increasing the explicitly erotic content of the tale. The story as it was told by Bhagwant Rāi continued to hold its own then until the end of the nineteenth century, though one can imagine that by then the number of readers of Faiẓī's original text had dwindled somewhat. But Bhagwant Rāi would eventually have to face other competitors too, who told the story of Nal and Daman in Braj Bhasha, and whose works gained popularity in print from the 1870s onwards. Amongst these was a text attributed, ironically enough, to another prominent member of Akbar's court, his Khatri financial intendant Ṭoḍarmal, and entitled *Nalcharitāmrit* ('Nectar of the Life of Nal') (Ṭoḍarmal 1882; Varmā 1883; Wadley 1999). In texts like these, written with an explicitly Vaishnav flavour, we sense that the story has taken a quite different direction from that in the hands of Faiẓī and his heirs, where the story remains—whether it is primarily political or erotic—a robustly 'secular' tale. It is perhaps in this sense that the destiny of stories such as these can point to both the continuities and the profound cultural changes that swept northern Indian culture between the times of the Mughals and the end of the nineteenth century. For even if the stories ostensibly remained the same, their divergent treatment at the hands of rival traditions points to the trends that eventually led to a growing gulf between the worlds of 'Hindi' and 'Urdu'. But this is a theme that we must leave for another occasion.

Notes

[1] There are also a number of illustrated versions, for example in Eastman (1959).

[2] Faiẓī's text merits comparison with that of a (slightly later) contemporary, namely Nau'ī Khabūshānī, for whom *see* Dawud and Coomaraswamy (1912); for more recent discussions, *see* 'Ābidī (1984), as also Sharma (forthcoming).

[3] Thus, eleven manuscripts are reported in the Khuda Bakhsh Library (Patna) alone, thirteen manuscripts at the Aligarh Muslim University Library, besides several in the India Office Library (including the oldest extant MSS dating to AH 1069). For printed editions, see *Nal Daman-i Fārsī az Rashḥāt-i Qalam-i Abu'l Faiẓ Faiẓī* (Lucknow: Nawal Kishor, 1877; reprinted 1889 and 1930); Tamīzuddīn Arzāṅ (ed.), *Nal Daman* (Calcutta: the author, 1831); the edition from Kanpur of the Nizami Press (AH 1294), and the more recent Iranian edition entitled *Dāstān-i Nal-o-Daman* (Tehran, 1335 Shamsi [1956]). One may also consult the facsimile Moscow edition: Abul Faiz Fajzi, *Nal'i Daman* (Moscow: Chudoz. Lit., 1982).

[4] We have discussed Faiẓī's *Nal-Daman* in far greater detail in a companion essay, for which, *see* Alam and Subrahmanyam (forthcoming).

[5] The last page of the manuscript appears in photographic reproduction in the Agravāl and Juyāl edition; *see* Sūrdās (1961).

[6] Sarāwī (1978). The edition is based on the text of Sarāwī in the possession of Punjab University, Lahore (U.I. VI. 328/2730). 'Abdullah notes that no other manuscript is known, though Sprenger and Garcin de Tassy have mentioned Sarāwī's text without specifying which manuscript they saw. The Lahore manuscript is bound together with some others; it has forty-five folios, with each page containing sixteen lines. Several scribes seem to have participated in setting it down. The last pages are in *shikast* and half-*shikast*, and after folio 8b, one folio seems to be missing. The main scribe is Jān Muḥammad, but his place of residence is illegible; the manuscript date is 11 Ramazan 40 (probably 1240), and it seems to be based on an earlier autograph version. The original text is probably dated in the eighteenth century, though the exact dating by the editor (c. 1142 or soon after) is debatable, being based almost solely on orthographic considerations (*imlā*).

[7] Sherānī (1987), reprinted from the original in two parts in the *Oriental College Magazine*, November 1931 and February 1932; also Sherānī (1982).

[8] For a discussion of some of these themes, *also see* the editors' introduction to Manjhan (2000).

[9] The literal term is of course 'liver' (*jigar*).

[10] There is a small gap in Sarāwī's text here, but even so it is clear that the development is considerably shorter than in Faiẓī.

[11] Sarāwī (1978), Editor's Introduction, p. 11.

[12] Kali plays a significant role in most of the Sanskrit versions, as well as a number of other vernacular versions.

[13] Is this the same Kālī Prashād to whom a slightly later version of the story, also in Urdu, is also attributed ?

[14] This issue has already been analysed in Alam (1996). Further work clearly needs to be done on literary aspects of the question.

Bibliography

'Ābidī, S.A.H., 'Nau'ī Khabūshānī', in *Hindustānī Fārsī Adab: Research and Literary Articles of S.A.H. Abidi*, Sharīf Ḥusain Qāsemī (ed.), Delhi: Indo-Persian Society, 1984, 105–20.

Alam, Muzaffar, 'Assimilation from a Distance: Confrontation and Sufi Accommodation in Awadh Society', in R. Champakalakshmi and S. Gopal (eds.), *Tradition, Dissent and Ideology: Essays in Honour of Romila Thapar*, Delhi: Oxford University Press, 1996.

Alam, Muzaffar and Sanjay Subrahmanyam, 'Love, Passion and Reason in Faiẓī's *Nal-Daman*', in *Studies on Persianate Societies*, forthcoming.

Badāyūnī, 'Abdul Qādir, *Muntakhab ut-Tawārīkh*, trans. G.S.A. Ranking, W.H. Lowe, and Wolseley Haig, 3 vols, Calcutta: Asiatic Society of Bengal, 1925.

Bayly, C.A., 'Indian Society and the Making of the British Empire', *The New Cambridge History of India*, vol. II.1, Cambridge: Cambridge University Press, 1988.

Chandra, Motī, 'Kavi Sūrdās kṛt "Naldaman" Kāvya', *Nāgarīprachārinī Patrikā*, 43 (2), 1938 [1995 VS], 121–38.

Dawud, Mirza Y., and Ananda K. Coomaraswamy (trans.), *Burning and Melting: Being the Suz-u-Gudaz of Muhammad Riza Nau'i of Khabushan*, London: Luzac, 1912.

Desai, Z.A., 'Life and Works of Faidi', *Indo-Iranica*, 16 (3), 1963, 1–35.

Eastman, Alvan Clark, *The Nala-Damayanti Drawings: A study of a portfolio of drawings made for Samsar Cand of Kangra (1774–1823), illustrating an early Indian romance*, Boston: Museum of Fine Arts, 1959.

Faiẓī, Abu'l Faiẓ ibn Mubārak, *Mathnavī Nal-Daman Faiẓī*, Md. Taiyab Siddiqui (ed.), Patna: Book Emporium, 1987.

Farmān Fateḥpurī, *Urdū kī Manẓūm Dāstāneṅ*, Karachi: Anjuman-i Taraqqi-i Urdu, 1971.

Garcin de Tassy, J.H.S.V., *Histoire de la Littérature Hindoui et Hindoustani*, Tome I, Paris: Oriental Translation Fund, 1839.

G͟hanīmat Kunjāhī, Muḥammad Akram, *Nairang-i 'Ishq*, Maqbūl ud-Daulā Mirzā Muḥammad Mahdī 'Alī K͟hān 'Qabūl' (ed.), Kalan Kothi: Matba' Shaikh Nisar 'Ali, AH 1268.

G͟hanīmat Kunjāhī, Muḥammad Akram, *Nairang-i 'Ishq: Mas̱navī G͟hanīmat*, G͟hulām Rabbānī 'Azīz (ed.), Lahore: Punjabi Adabi Akademi, 1962.

Manjhan, Mīr Sayyid Manjhan Shaṯṯārī Rājgīrī, *Madhumālatī: An Indian Sufi Romance*, Aditya Behl, Simon Weightman, and Shyam Manohar Pandey (eds. and trans.), Oxford: Oxford University Press, 2000.

Naim, C.M., (trans. and ed.) *Zikr-i Mir: The Autobiography of the Eighteenth Century Mughal Poet: Mir Muhammad Taqi 'Mir'*, Delhi: Oxford University Press, 1999.

Nārang, Gopī Chand, *Hindustānī Qiṣṣoṅ se Māk͟hūz Urdū Mas̱nawiyāṅ*, New Delhi: Maktaba-i Jami'a, 1962.

Phukan, Shantanu, '"Through Throats Where Many Rivers Meet": The Ecology of Hindi in the World of Persian', *The Indian Economic and Social History Review*, 38 (1), 2001, 33–58.

Qazwīnī, Mīr Ghiyās-ud-Dīn 'Alī Naqīb K͟hān, *Mahābhārat*, S. M. Rezā Jalālī Nainī and N.S. Shukla (eds.), Tehran: Kitabkhana-i Tahuri, 1358 Shamsi.

Rāḥat, Bhagwant Rāi Kākorwī, *Nal-Daman Hindī*, Delhi: Kālī Prashād (lithograph), 1859 (reprinted 1869).

Sarāwī, Aḥmad, *Nal Daman*, Sayyid Muḥammad 'Abdullah (ed.), Karachi: Anjuman-i Taraqqi-i Urdu, 1978.

Sharma, Sunil, 'Novelty, Tradition and Mughal Politics in Nau'i's *Sūz-o-Godāz*', in *Professor Hashmat Moayyad Festschrift*, forthcoming.

Sherānī, Ḥāfiẕ Maḥmūd, *Panjāb meṅ Urdū*, Lucknow: Uttar Pradesh Urdu Academy, 1982 [1928].

Sherānī, Ḥāfiẓ Maḥmūd, 'Urdū kī Shākh Haryānī Zabāṅ meṅ Tālifāt', in *Maqālāt-i Ḥāfiẓ Maḥmūd Sherānī*, Maẓhar Maḥmūd Sherānī (ed.), vol. II, Lahore: Majlis-i Taraqqi-i Adab, 1987, 351–418.

Ṣiddīqī, Muḥammad Shakīl Aḥmad, *Amīr Ḥasan Sijzī Dehlavī: Ḥayāt aur Adabī Khidmat*, Lucknow: Siddiqi, 1979.

Sūrdās, *Nal Daman*, Vāsudev Sharaṇ Agravāl and Daulatrām Juyāl (eds.), Agra: Agra University, 1961.

Ṭoḍarmal, *Nalcharitāmrit arthāt Ḍholāmārū*, 2nd ed., Mathura: Munshi Kanhaiyalal, 1882 [1879].

Varmā, Ṭhākur Jāharsingh, *Naladamayantī kī Kathā*, Agra: n.p., 1883.

Wadley, Susan S., 'A *Bhakti* Rendition of Nala-Damayanti: Todarmal's "Nectar of Nal's Life"', *International Journal of Hindu Studies*, 3 (1), 1999, 26–56.

Genre, Politics, History: Urdu Traditions of Padmini

RAMYA SREENIVASAN

Padmini is believed to have been a queen in the ruling lineage of Chitor (modern Rajasthan) at the turn of the fourteenth century, when the kingdom was conquered by Sultan Alauddin Khalji. In modern India, a particular version of this queen's story has become one of the most widely known narratives about the medieval past. This dominant modern version narrates the story of a Hindu queen immolating herself to defend her chastity from the Muslim invader, and constructs a 'glorious' past within a nationalist 'history'.

The first available narrative of the Padmini legend tells a very different story, however. Malik Muḥammad Jāyasī's *Padmāvat* was composed in Avadhi (a dialect of Hindi prevalent in what is now central Uttar Pradesh) and probably written in the Persian script, around 1540 (de Bruijn 1996: 9–23). Heroic romances—in which a prince embarked on a dangerous quest to woo and wed a princess of fabled beauty and riches—were common to many literary traditions in medieval north India. The *Padmāvat* is a Sufi mystical appropriation of this formula that celebrates the transcendent love between the king Ratansen and his queen Padmavati. Jāyasī's poem became the model for a series of translations and adaptations into Persian and Dakkhini. Urdu versions between the eighteenth and early twentieth centuries continue this tradition, as they retell Padmini's story within the received conventions of Indo-Persian love poetry.

Meanwhile, James Tod, resident of the East India Company to the princely states of Rajasthan in the early nineteenth century, published his *Annals and Antiquities of Rajasthan* in 1829–32. Tod's monumental work on the history and sociology of the Rajputs of Rajasthan was based on his compilation and interpretation of medieval Rajput traditions. The *Annals* soon achieved canonical status in colonial India among Rajput groups as well as Indian nationalists. This influence is perceptible in a different version of the Padmini legend that began to emerge in new Urdu genres such as popular drama. For these Urdu writers, the story of Padmini no longer signified the transcendent love between a king and his queen. Instead, the legend came to exemplify a newly reinterpreted pattern of medieval Indian history in which 'patriotic Hindu' resisted 'Muslim invader'.

The contemporary Amīr Khusro's eyewitness account of the siege of Chitor by his patron and sultan, Alauddin Khalji, does not mention a queen Padmini. Modern historians have differed in their interpretations of Khusro's Quranic allusion to the *hudhud* (hoopoe) that brought news of the beautiful Queen of Sheba to Hazrat Suleman Nabi.[1] Historians have also questioned the credibility of Abu'l Faẓl's and Ferishta's accounts of Alauddin's conquest of Chitor, given the three centuries separating the events themselves from these reconstructions (Qanungo 1969: 5–6). In short, modern historians in India have been concerned primarily with the problem of determining whether Padmini was a historical figure.

The terms of this debate are set by the fact that Jāyasī's poem, the first narrative of Padmini, makes abundant use of fantastic elements, including supernatural intervention. Thus, modern historians read the *Padmāvat* as stitching together two kinds of stories. The first half of the poem is regarded as Sufi allegory, and the second as historical reconstruction—and faulty, because of fantastical reconstruction. Such readings of the poem are based upon twentieth-century assumptions—of the separation between 'literary' and 'historical' narratives, and of Sufism's transcendence of politics and history. This essay is concerned not with the historicity of the episode itself, but with exploring the persistence of the narrative and the avenues through which it was transmitted, reshaped, and transformed. Such shifts in narrative can best be understood as occurring at the intersection of genre and patronage.

It is important to recognize that the local elite patronizing regional Avadhi literature was heterogeneous in its ethnic origins and religious practices. Further, medieval Sufi practices did not constitute an autonomous terrain, but were constantly negotiating with the many practices and cultural forms of the historical world in which they were carving out a space for themselves. A historicizing of the *Padmāvat* and its location in local politics and history is warranted particularly because the *Padmāvat* reinterprets historical personages and events selectively. Further, its normative moral order engages with and re-articulates the political and patriarchal practices of the specific social groups that constituted the target audience for such poems. Thus reread, the *Padmāvat* and its adaptations suggest the boundaries of engagement, negotiation, and conflict within the evolving political imagery of late medieval and modern north India.

This essay begins by exploring the transmission and reception of Jāyasī's narrative and its adaptations. The passing of the *Padmāvat* into different languages between the seventeenth and twentieth centuries—from Avadhi into Persian, Dakkhini, Urdu—suggests transitions within the contexts of patronage for such narratives. At the same time, all these adaptations follow the plot of Jāyasī's poem at least in its bare details. Such continuities point to the resonance of this master narrative for successive generations of poets, patrons, and audiences. The poets who adapted the *Padmāvat* narrative into Persian, Dakkhini, and Urdu were aware of predecessors who had engaged in a similar enterprise. Many of these poets acknowledge their debt to earlier writers, thus locating themselves within a distinct Indo-Persian literary tradition of narratives about Padmini.

Strikingly, the authors of the later 'nationalist' narratives of Padmini do not acknowledge this tradition, and their versions break avowedly with the *Padmāvat* tradition. However, residual similarities of plot and narrative persist. A reading of these nationalist narratives of Padmini reveals two processes at once: first, the generic transmutations by which the nationalist 'history' of Padmini emerged; and second, the pressures of negotiating between the divergent pulls of generic conventions and the target audience for this new 'nationalist' narrative.

Transmission, Patronage, and Reception

Medieval accounts of the reception of Avadhi narratives such as the *Padmāvat* suggest that they were read both as 'tales of love' and as Sufi mystical narratives. The available evidence suggests three broad contexts of patronage: courtly, mercantile elite, and the Sufi institutional network. One group of manuscripts reveals the *Padmāvat*'s circulation in the region of Uttar Pradesh and Bihar between the seventeenth and early nineteenth centuries, in a variety of literate, text-oriented, and apparently lay contexts (Gupt 1952: 3–7). The patrons for whom such manuscripts were commissioned would have included merchants such as Banārasīdās in seventeenth-century Agra; local chiefs such as the Raja of Amethi (as can be inferred from the apocryphal stories of encounters between him and Jāyasī); and members of the local service gentry such as the Kayasths, in the Mughal heartland of the Gangetic plains.

On the other hand, a 1675 manuscript by Muḥammad Shākir, a Sufi shaikh from Amroha, takes great care in transcribing the Avadhi text of the *Padmāvat* into Persian script. It also provides Persian translations inserted between the lines of Avadhi text. Shākir adds a prefatory paragraph to the manuscript about an incident from the life of Nizamuddin Auliya. He cites as his source for this incident the *A<u>kh</u>bār al-A<u>kh</u>yār*, the well-known seventeenth-century compendium of the lives of Sufi shaikhs (Phukan 1996: 41–54). Shākir's manuscript thus indicates the significance of the Sufi network in interpreting and transmitting the *Padmāvat*. Jāyasī himself enters the Sufi *taẕkirat* (hagiographical) tradition in the seventeenth century, when he is celebrated as *muḥaqqiq-i hindī*, knower of the truths of al-Hind (Rizvi 1997, 1: 370).

The process of transmission and reinterpretation is continued by translations and adaptations of the *Padmāvat* in various languages. The first known adaptation was composed by Hans in Dakkhini in 1592, at the court of Ibrahim Shah in Bijapur (de Bruijn 1996: 26). Such adaptations include 'Abdul Shukūr Bazmī's *Rat-o-Padam*, composed in Gujarat in 1618–19, and 'Āqil <u>Kh</u>ān Rāzī's *Sham'-o-Parvāna*, composed in Delhi in 1658 (Abidi 1962: 1–12). Little is known about Bazmī himself; his narrative follows the *Padmāvat* closely but does not ascribe any deeper symbolism to the characters and events (Abidi 1962: 4). 'Āqil <u>Kh</u>ān Rāzī rose to become the governor of the *ṣūba* of Delhi under Aurangzeb, and was remembered by his biographers for his erudition in Sufi doctrine and his association with the contemporary Shattari Shaikh Burhanuddin Raz-i Ilahi. Unlike Bazmī's narrative, Rāzī's adaptation reinserts the *Padmāvat* narrative within a frame of Sufi symbolism (Phukan 1996: 47–51).

Both manuscript traditions and adaptations indicate that medieval audiences interpreted the poem in both mystical as well as lay contexts. Hans and Rāzī's retellings also point to a continuing tradition of courtly patronage for the *Padmāvat* narrative. Stray comments are also available from medieval readers such as 'Abdul Qādir Badāyūnī and Banārasīdās on other Avadhi narratives read as belonging to the same genre. All the evidence suggests dual contexts of interpretation for the *Padmāvat*: it was read for lay entertainment as well as for mystical instruction and experience. However, these parallel networks of interpretation, lay and mystical, do not necessarily imply two mutually exclusive social contexts of reception. It is to be expected that the Sufi network of *<u>kh</u>ānaqāhs* and *dargāhs* would generate mystical interpretations, and transmit these poems as the bearers of a spiritual message. But the lay contexts of patronage and transmission did not always imply non-mystical interpretations. One of the most influential Sufi adaptations of Jāyasī's poem was produced by a Mughal courtier under Aurangzeb, 'Āqil Khān Rāzī. In other words, Sufi modes of transmission implied Sufi modes of interpretation, but lay contexts of patronage did not always generate non-mystical interpretations.

Further, it is important to recognize the heterogeneity of patrons and audiences among the regional elite. As Muzaffar Alam shows, in the early seventeenth century a very large portion of land in the Mughal province of Avadh was in the control of Hindu Rajputs. The districts in their control often formed contiguous blocks, adding to their power and strength in the countryside (Alam 1996: 164–6). Muslims such as Afghans, *shaikhzādas*, and some local Rajput converts also occupied a high position in the province, and provided patronage for local poetic traditions.

Nor did medieval Sufi practices constitute an autonomous terrain: Sufis engaged with the politics and culture of the historical world in which they were carving out a space for themselves. Thus, Sufi centres in Avadh were involved in the relations between local communities of lay patrons and their relationship with the state. This is indicated even in the history of Jayas itself. In 1714, a revenue grant for the maintenance of the *khānaqāh* of Saiyid Jahangir Ashraf Simnani, one of Jāyasī's pīrs, had to be shifted to a safe area from a village where the keepers of the *khānaqāh* had begun to encounter serious trouble from 'the infidels' of the surrounding habitats (Alam 1996: 167). The apocryphal stories of Jāyasī's encounters with several local Hindu chiefs, such as the Raja of Amethi, suggest that Sufi institutions were engaged in this process of negotiation with local Hindu elites throughout this period.

A recent study of the *Padmāvat* has suggested a relationship between these distinct audience constituencies and the multiple layers of signification within the poem. Thomas de Bruijn argues that poems such as the *Padmāvat* were meant to function both in the surroundings of the local Sufi centres and in the circuit of patronage from regional rulers and nobles. He argues that this is why the poem illustrates both devotion and sacrifice to God and the heroic bravery of the prince, 'thus connect[ing] the two spheres of the poet's allegiance: the Sufi centre and the local court' (de Bruijn 1996: 63).

From the late eighteenth century, Urdu poets produced several adaptations and translations of the *Padmāvat*. The best-known of these is the *Mudallil-i Sham'-o-Parvāna*, begun by 'Ibrat and completed by 'Ishrat in the last decade of the eighteenth century. Known as the *Qiṣṣa-i Padmāvat* and also as the *Padmāvat Urdū*, this poem was reprinted several times through the course of the nineteenth and early twentieth centuries. The poets who adapted the

Padmāvat narrative into Urdu belonged to a comparable context of patronage. They were patronized by regional courts in Uttar Pradesh and Bihar such as Rampur and Balrampur, known for their encouragement of Urdu poets and poetry. Mīr Ẓiyāuddīn Ghulām 'Alī, who wrote under the penname 'Ibrat, was born in Shahjahanabad in the second half of the eighteenth century and grew up in Rampur. He joined the service of Mustafa Khan in the Rampur court. As he indicates in the *Sham'-o-Parvāna*, he was instructed in the art of poetry by Nawab Muhabbat Khan 'Muhabbat'. 'Ibrat died in 1789–90, before completing his adaptation of the *Padmāvat*. Mīr Ghulām 'Alī 'Ishrat similarly entered the service of the nawab of Rampur. He was instructed in the art of poetry by Mirza 'Ali Lutf who in turn had been instructed by Mirza Muhammad Rafi Sauda. 'Ishrat used to participate in the weekly *mushā'ira* at the house of a friend, Mirza Qudratullah Shauq, and completed 'Ibrat's incomplete poem at his friend's suggestion (Jalīl 1994: 33–4).

The author of an early twentieth-century *masnavī* adaptation, Ḥāfiẓ Khalīl Ḥasan 'Khalīl' was born in Manikpur and became the court poet in Balrampur state, whose ruler was again a reputed patron of Urdu poetry. Khalīl was known as a writer of *masnavīs* such as *Dushyant-Shakuntalā* and *Meghdūt*, as well as two original creations, *Butkada-i Khalīl* and *Firoz-Salma* (Jalīl 1994: 39).

The late eighteenth century marks the beginning of the emergence of Urdu adaptations of the *Padmāvat*, and the end of fresh Persian adaptations. This shift in the language of the *Padmāvat* adaptations is indicative of the rise of Urdu in the regional courts of north India. However, the patrons for the new Urdu adaptations are comparable to the patrons for the earlier Persian and Dakkhini adaptations: the *Padmāvat* narrative continues to resonate in these regional courtly cultures of Delhi, Rampur, and Avadh. By the second half of the nineteenth century, 'Ibrat's adaptation in particular was reprinted numerous times. The *Padmāvat* narrative thus reached a much wider readership through mass printing.

The switch from Persian to Urdu also seems to mark new limits to interpretation. In the absence of more specific evidence at this point, it is difficult to ascertain if the recitation of excerpts from the *Padmāvat* (or the transmission of manuscript copies) continued within the Sufi institutional network in this period. As the narrative enters Urdu, however, its generic classification seems to shift in significant ways. 'Ibrat's version is told and retold as *qiṣṣa*. As Frances Pritchett has shown, the entry of the *qiṣṣa* into the social world of mass printing in the nineteenth century was marked by a shift in generic boundaries to accommodate more popular as well as 'folk' narrative traditions (Pritchett 1985: 29–30). In the instance of the *Padmāvat*, its adaptations in Urdu and their subsequent publishing history suggest the marginalization of distinctly Sufi interpretations. Shifts in language and in patronage thus seem to be linked to shifts in both genre and interpretation, in ways that will be explored in the next section of this essay.

Genres of the *Padmāvat* Narrative

This section describes the typical narrative of the *Padmāvat* material that evolved within the Urdu *maṣnavī* tradition. These adaptations reveal the influence of 'Āqil Khān Rāzī's Sufi rereading of the *Padmāvat* narrative, the *Sham'-o-Parvāna* (composed in 1658). However, the Urdu adaptations reveal a shift towards the generic horizons of secular romance. This shift in interpretation is aided by the presence of elements from other contiguous medieval genres in the *Padmāvat* material.

'Ibrat and 'Ishrat's *Sham'-o-Parvāna* follows the *Padmāvat* closely in its plot. The poem begins with the praise of God (*ḥamd*), praise of the Prophet (*na't*), prayer (*munājāt*) and praise of the patron that were typical of the *maṣnavī* tradition. The narrative then begins by describing the young Rani Padmavat, and her friendship with a learned parrot. One day, a jealous enemy frees the bird from its cage. The parrot flies away into the forest, is trapped by a hunter, and is sold to a Brahmin trader from Chitor who takes the bird back to his land. There, Raja Ratansen of Chitorgarh buys the parrot and befriends it. The king learns of Padmavat's beauty from the parrot, and becomes a lover of the absent princess. The bird tells him that he must renounce the world and its wealth to embark on the difficult path of love (*ṭarīqa-i 'ishqbāzī*). Disregarding the pleas of his mother and his first wife Nagmat, Ratansen gives up his kingly robes (*libās-i bādshāhī*) for the garb of an ascetic (*jogī*). As Ratansen embarks for the beautiful city of Serendip, sixteen thousand companions join him. In the temple (*butkhāna*) at Serendip the parrot brings news of Padmavat to Ratansen and sows the seeds of love in his heart all over again.[2]

Padmavat learns of the ascetic stranger Ratansen from a friend. When she comes face to face with the disguised king, both are struck insensate (*'ālam-i behoshī aur bekhudī*). When Ratansen comes to his senses in the temple, he narrates his plight to the god Sadashiv. The goddess Gaura-Parvati suggests a scheme by which Ratansen can attain his beloved. Following her advice, Ratansen arrives in the court of Gandhrapsen and declares his desire to marry Padmavat. Meanwhile, Ratansen meets his beloved, is captured in her chamber, and is sentenced to be executed by the king. The god Sadashiv reappears in the guise of a Brahmin and reveals Ratansen's true identity to Gandhrapsen. Ratansen marries Padmavat, and finds happiness with her as 'she serves him wine'.

Nagmat sends a message to Ratansen, expressing her anguish at being separated from him. Ratansen now embarks with Padmavat on the return journey to Chitor. As they sail back, the sea appears before Ratansen in the guise of a Brahmin. The king ignores the Brahmin and is punished by being shipwrecked and separated from Padmavat, who is marooned on an island. The daughter of the sea takes pity on them and reunites them. Ratansen reaches Chitor with Padmavat. The co-wives quarrel and Ratansen brings about a rapprochement between them.

Ratansen is offended with the Brahmin Raghav Chetan and exiles him. As the Brahmin leaves, Padmavat gives him her anklet to appease his anger. He ingratiates himself with the Sultan Alauddin, and arouses the sultan's ardour for Padmavat by showing him the anklet and describing her beauty.

The sultan promptly lays siege to Chitor and asks Ratansen to surrender the beautiful Padmavat of Singhaldip. An insulted Ratansen refuses and war breaks out. Alauddin offers truce and beholds Padmavat's reflection in a mirror. On his way back, he tricks Ratansen, captures him, and takes him back to Delhi. The emperor sends a female emissary disguised as an ascetic (*jogan*) to Padmavat, but is unsuccessful in inducing Padmavat to surrender herself. Padmavat goes to Gora and Badal, the sons of Ratansen's sister, and rouses them to rescue Ratansen from Delhi. They disguise themselves as women in an entourage of palanquins and free Ratansen.

When the king returns to Chitor, he hears of another insult to his honour. Devpal, the king of Kumbhalmer, has tried to woo Padmavat in his absence. Ratansen now sets off to avenge this second insult. He is challenged to single combat by Devpal and kills the latter, but is mortally wounded himself. He dies on his return to Chitor, and his wives Padmavat and Nagmat commit sati.

Sultan Alauddin returns to attack Chitor, and the Rajputs led by Gora are defeated and killed in battle. Meanwhile Kanvalsen, Padmavat's son, has been anointed king. When the sultan enters the fort he finds that Padmavat is already dead. Stricken with grief, the sultan recognizes Kanvalsen as the new king of Chitor, and returns to Delhi.

I have narrated the outline of the *Sham'-o-Parvāna* in some detail, to demonstrate how closely the poem follows the *Padmāvat*. 'Ibrat describes the subject of his poem thus:

... Junūṅ sarmāya-i ratan hai
Ratan ke ‘ishq kā sho‘la thā sarkas̱‘ī / Padam ke bhī lagā dī dil ko ātash
Vo donoṅ ‘āshiq-o-m‘āshūq ho jam‘ / Jale ik bār jūṅ parvāna sham‘
Aur unkā likh ke maiṅ ne qiṣṣa-i tām / Mudallil Sham‘-o-Parvāna rakkhā nām.[3]

(The madness of love is Ratan’s wealth; the burning ember of Ratan’s love was rebellious / It set a spark in Padam’s heart as well; the two of them, lover and beloved / burnt at the same time like the moth and the flame; and I wrote their entire story / and called it the Testimony of the Flame and the Moth.)

‘Ishrat shares ‘Ibrat’s interpretation of the *Padmāvat* narrative, and describes himself as taking up the task of completing the poem after drinking ‘a draught of love’ (*ulfat kā ik jām*) (PU: 32). Further, they locate such exemplary love in the fitting landscape of ‘Hindustan’. In fact, Hindustan gains its distinct identity from providing the environment in which love reaches its pinnacle. The poet depicts himself as a nightingale, singing not only of an ideal love but also of his own garden (*chaman*) and his own land (*vaṭan*). Hindustan is paradise on earth (*jannat nishāṅ*), whose fame resounds even in Arabia and Persia. Hindustani love (*‘ishq-i hindī*) is more passionate than Arabian love (*‘ishq-i ‘arab*). The embers of Hindustani love emit brighter sparks, as even the sun (*āftāb*) burns more brightly here (PU: 10–11).

The influence of Rāzī here is striking. In his introduction, Rāzī claimed that in Hindustan ‘the fire of manifestation [of love] crackles the louder, and the reason for this is that the sun is stronger’ here.[4] ‘The proof of this increased heat of love in the Indian landscape’ is Padmavat, who literally burned to death for her love. For Rāzī, Hindustan is a land full of idols, the Persian word *but* also signifying the beloved. Hindustan is the land of idol worship (*but parastī*), and also, ‘by verbal similitude’, of devotion to the beloved. It is in Hindustan that love (*‘ishq*) finds its fullest expression (Phukan 1996: 50). ‘Ibrat appropriates this characterization of Hindustan, reiterating its status as the appropriate landscape for an exemplary love. Thus, the Urdu poetic adaptations of the *Padmāvat* material reiterate Rāzī’s Persian narrative of an ideal love that flourishes in the land of Hindustan.

Further, the borrowings from Rāzī illuminate the generic boundaries within which ‘Ibrat and ‘Ishrat locate their poem. The *Sham‘-o-Parvāna* belongs to the genre of the love story in the tradition of medieval Persian, Dakkhini, and Urdu *maṡ̤navī* on the subcontinent. In this context, it must be remembered that Rāzī (the acknowledged predecessor of ‘Ibrat, ‘Ishrat and Khalīl) had already recast the *Padmāvat* narrative to conform to ‘the grid of conventions and expectations that form the terrain’ of late medieval love poetry across a range of poetic forms, from ghazal to *maṡnavī*. Rāzī achieved this by invoking the stock trope of the moth as the paradigmatic lover, pursuing its impossible love of the flame and enduring the pain of that love (Phukan 1996: 47–8).

As indicated above, Rāzī himself was a practising Sufi and his adaptation of the *Padmāvat* clearly interprets Jāyasī's poem as a Sufi allegory. However, none of the available evidence suggests Sufi affiliations for 'Ibrat, 'Ishrat or Khalīl. And yet, as is well known, as forms such as the ghazal in Persian and Urdu were gradually secularized, they retained much of the poetics of love inherited from idioms of Sufi mysticism. 'Ibrat and 'Ishrat thus deploy the same poetics of love in a *maṡnavī* without any overt Sufi allegorical content.

The shift away from Sufi symbolism in 'Ibrat and 'Ishrat's poem is suggested by the absence of the well-known allegorical key to the *Padmāvat* narrative. This stanza provided allegorical equivalences for the characters in the poem. According to this key, Chitor stood for the body, Singhala for the heart, Padmini for wisdom, the parrot for the guru who shows the way, Nagmati for the concerns of this world, the messenger Raghav Chetan for the devil, and Alauddin for *māyā*, illusion. This allegorical interpretation, which was a persistent feature of the *Padmāvat* manuscripts through the centuries (de Bruijn 1996: 14–23), does not appear in the *Sham'-o-Parvāna*. Its absence indicates that the Sufi mystical frame of interpretation recedes in 'Ibrat and 'Ishrat's poem, to be replaced by the horizons of secular romance.[5]

Further, Jāyasī's *Padmāvat* appropriated tropes from other secular genres of medieval literature such as the *dāstān*: 'tales of heroic romance and adventure—stories about gallant princes and their encounters with evil kings, enemy champions, demons, magicians, Jinns, divine emissaries, tricky secret agents and beautiful princesses who might be human or of the *Parī* [fairy] race' (Pritchett 1991: 1). The idealization of Hindustan as the fitting landscape for a perfected love is also a trope that occurs in other medieval *maṡnavī*s like Faiẓī's *Nal-Daman*.[6] Talking birds, jealous queens, adventures at sea, shipwrecks, the appearance of supernatural creatures in human disguise and journeys of quest to the island of Singhaldvip—these elements were common to an entire range of medieval literary genres from the Indic *kathā* traditions to the Persian *dāstān* (de Bruijn 1996: 80; Gupt 1994, 1: 310). The presence of such features in 'Ibrat and 'Ishrat's *Sham'-o-Parvāna* would have further aided their reception within the secular horizons of popular nineteenth-century Urdu genres such as the *qiṣṣa* and *dāstān*.

In its own period, 'Ibrat and 'Ishrat's poem could still be reinserted into a religio-didactic frame of interpretation. An indication of this is an eighteenth-century manuscript that includes an incomplete account of 'Ibrat's poem, along with a Quranic account of the Virgin Mary and the birth and miracles of Christ. This manuscript compilation also includes a didactical retelling of the *Qiṣṣa-i Fīrozshāh* (a favourite *dāstān* theme), a story on the life of the Prophet Muhammad, and a miracle story connected with Fatima. Such a compilation does not necessarily suggest a specifically Sufi horizon of reception. It does suggest, however, that the *Padmāvat* adaptations, like the *Padmāvat* itself, could continue to be read within the broad horizons of Islamic moralist and religious poetry in the eighteenth century (de Bruijn 1996: 29). It is the numerous print editions of 'Ibrat and 'Ishrat's poem in the nineteenth century, issued by publishers such as the Nawal Kishor Press, that point to a more sustained secularization of the *Padmāvat* narrative within the horizons of Urdu *masṉavī* and *qiṣṣa*.

The Nation's 'History' and Its Sources

Rudar and Dev Datt's *'Aẓamat-i Chitor urf Qaumī Ān* was published from Lahore in 1914 by Bhai Daya Singh Bookseller, and priced inexpensively at eight annas.[7] Conversations between characters are interrupted and framed by the narrator's prose commentary. The mode of publication and the combination of prose and dialogue both suggest that the narrative straddled the fluid border between print narrative and oral performance.

Kishan Chand Zebā's historical drama (*tavārīk͟hī ḍrāma*) *Padminī* narrates a similar version of the Padmini legend; a second edition of a thousand copies was published from New Delhi in 1926. Zebā's play makes abundant use of songs, and contains several song-and-dance sequences depicting lavish court scenes. In these and other features, *Padminī* identifies itself as belonging to the genre of plays in Urdu/Hindustani of the kind staged by the 'Parsi' theatrical companies (Hansen 2001: 76–114). A second edition of the play was published in 1926 with a print run of a thousand copies. This indicates that the play was circulated as a printed text independently of its production on the stage. Zebā's own practice also points in the same direction. At many points in the play, he provides Urdu/ Hindustani translations in parentheses for the highly Sanskritized Hindi that he uses as linguistic standard.[8]

Zebā seems to have been a successful playwright in the 1920s. Besides *Padminī*, his plays included *Āftāb-i 'Iṣmat* (about Savitri), *Dānvīr Karan* (on Karna from the Mahabharata) and *Sarvan Kumār* (adapted from the Ramayana). He also wrote plays about historical personages such as *Laṅgoṭī-vālā* (on the Buddha), and about leading contemporary figures: *Shahīd Sanyāsī* on Swami Shraddhanand and *Shahīd-i Vaṭan* on Motilal Nehru; and plays about social reform issues such as *Kāyā Palaṭ urf Achhūt Uddhār* and *Bīvī aur Bevā*.[9] The playwright's *oeuvre* suggests a distinct range of concerns and a distinct target audience: inspirational narratives about dharmic exempla, social reform including widow remarriage and untouchability, and eulogies to contemporary leaders including Swami Shraddhanand, point to Zebā's Arya Samaj affiliations. This is borne out by internal evidence within his play *Padminī*.

These narratives represent a complete break from the Urdu *maṡnavī* adaptations of the *Padmāvat* narrative, and indicate the emergence of an alternative version of Padmini's story in Urdu. The shape of this new narrative suggests that these authors knew Tod's version of Padmini's legend, either directly, or as it was mediated through the accounts of early nationalists in colonial Bengal.

Both texts begin with Alauddin's intention of attacking Chitor because he covets its Rajput queen Padmini. He disregards the advice of one sagacious minister who tries to dissuade him. Zebā begins his preface by emphasizing Padmini's Rajput identity: *Rājpūt mahilā Padminī* (Zebā 1926: 3). She is the wife of the Rajput Rana Bhimsingh, the uncle of Rana Lakshmansingh who became king of Chitor in 1275 (Zebā 1926: 6). As the king is young, Bhimsingh rules on his behalf. Zebā states that Padmini was the daughter of Hamir Singh Chauhan of Ceylon. Datt and Datt mention that the Khalji sultan first laid siege to Chitor in 1300 (Datt 1914: 8). Alauddin's military commander is Malik Kafur, who conquered Gujarat earlier and brought back its queen Kamla Devi as prize for the sultan (Datt and Datt 1914: 3).

The 'Rajput warrior' of Chitor, however, is prepared to die in defence of his 'dignity, honour and faith' (*ān-shān 'izzat aur dharam*) (Datt and Datt 1914: 7). Moreover, the chaste Rajput woman would never tolerate being with a Musalman. Therefore, Bhimsingh refuses to surrender Padmini to Alauddin. Confronted with this resistance, Alauddin offers to lift the siege if he is allowed to glimpse Padmini's reflection in a mirror. The king reluctantly agrees for the sake of his country and his people (*jātī*) (Zebā 1926: 70). Alauddin beholds the beautiful queen and is smitten with desire for her. In order to win the queen, he tricks Bhimsingh, captures him, and takes him away to Delhi. He forces the captive king to write a letter to Padmini, asking her to surrender herself to the sultan (Zebā 1926: 82–3). Padmini, enraged by this letter, devises the palanquin scheme and sends the king's trusted warriors to rescue him; they free Bhimsingh at the cost of their own lives.

An enraged Alauddin returns to Chitor to raze it to the ground and capture Padmini. Bhimsingh is now certain that he and his Rajput followers will die defending their land and honour. He is concerned about Padmini's future. Padmini is quick to assure him that the Rajput women are equally eager to give up their lives defending their chastity and honour. She declares their intention to follow Rajput custom and immolate themselves (*jauhar*) before the men leave for their last battle. The women adorn themselves and the mass immolation takes place in the presence of the grieving Rajput men, desolate and even more determined to die fighting.

As Alauddin enters the fort over the dead body of Bhimsingh, he seeks Padmini, only to discover a pile of ashes. He realizes the value of his wise minister's advice that he had earlier disregarded: indeed, the Rajputs gave up their lives defending their honour and their land. He has failed to obtain Padmini. He also realizes that he has besmirched his reputation forever in the annals of history by pursuing a chaste, married, Rajput woman (Zebā 1926: 7; Datt and Datt 1914: 49).

This narrative reveals close parallels with the version of the Padmini story narrated by James Tod in his *Annals and Antiquities of Rajasthan* (1829–32). The names of the chief characters, the shape of the plot, and secondary details such as dates of events, all point to a striking consistency between these Urdu accounts and Tod's version (Tod 1995, 1: 307–14). Thus, like Tod, Zebā and the Datts make Padmini the wife of Bhimsingh, not Ratansen as in the *Padmāvat* tradition. In Tod's account, Bhimsingh is not the king of Chitor but the uncle and regent of the young king. The Datts and Zebā begin their accounts of the story at the same point as Tod's version: with Alauddin's determination to obtain Padmini. The salient points of their narratives again reveal the influence of Tod's account. These include the first siege, Alauddin's vision of Padmini's reflection in a mirror, and the capture of Bhimsingh by treachery. Zebā's and the Datts' descriptions of the palanquin scheme, Alauddin's return, the *jauhar* of the women, the final defeat of the Rajputs, and Alauddin's final conquest of Chitor, are also modelled on Tod's account.

However, it is the inclusion and exclusion of details secondary to the plot in Zebā's and the Datts' accounts that provide the most telling indication of Tod's influence. Thus, it is Tod's account in the *Annals* which mentions the date of Lakshmansingh's accession as king of Chitor (AD 1275), the name of Padmini's father as Hamir Sank (*sic*) Chauhan of Ceylon, the role of Malik Kafur in the conquest of Gujarat, and his capture of its queen, Kamla Devi. These are details absent from the *Padmāvat* tradition. Equally, the *Padmāvat* tradition's treatment of the Chitor king's journey to Singhaldip to win his bride is absent from the *Annals* account. Like Tod, Zebā and the Datts omit along with this trope the figure of Raghav Chetan, the Brahmin astrologer/

magician who instigated Alauddin to pursue Padmini in the *Padmāvat* narrative.

Tod's narrative of Rajput history in the *Annals and Antiquities of Rajasthan* was intended to provide the East India Company with a historical justification for its policy towards the regional princely states. At the same time, the *Annals* provided the Rajputs themselves with an account of the past that could be used to assert their political claims before the Company. Tod's *Annals* was thus comparable in its imperatives with the Rajputs' historical traditions that it compiled, collated, and reshaped. Between the sixteenth and eighteenth centuries, ruling Rajput lineages in the kingdoms of Rajasthan had used narratives of their past to assert rank amongst themselves and before their Mughal overlords. Rajput historical traditions (including the narrative of Ratansen and Padmini) thus became instrumental in consolidating Rajput power in the region.

James Tod came to the study of Rajput history with intellectual equipment acquired in late eighteenth-century Europe and politics shaped by his East India Company employment. Meanwhile, the Rajput kingdoms of Rajasthan were grappling with crisis in post-Mughal polities in the early nineteenth century. The intervention of the Marathas had intensified the contradictions in the Rajput political order. Eighteenth-century Rajput interpretations of their past had already begun to show the effect of these new pressures. Tod shaped and implemented Company policy in these changed local conditions. His readings and reinterpretations of Rajput history emerged out of his collaboration with local Jain and bardic informants. In his recasting of kingship, feminine virtue, and threats to the Rajput order, Tod rearticulated and reaffirmed the perspectives of the Mewar ruling lineage.

By the second half of the nineteenth century, Tod's *Annals* had become the authoritative account of Rajput history throughout the subcontinent. In a host of Indian languages, Tod's narratives of Rajput heroism became the subject for historical novels, tracts, and even school history textbooks. New nationalist imperatives for an idealized Rajput history shaped these colonial Indian adaptations of the Rajput traditions in Tod's *Annals*. Among the most influential of these colonial Indian narratives about the nation's glorious past were the Bengali novels of Bankimchandra Chattopadhyay, which were translated in turn into other Indian languages. Thus, Urdu translations of Bankim were available by the turn of the twentieth century.[10] Zebā and the Datts could have been aware of Tod's account either directly or through an intermediary account.

The shift to Tod's version of the legend of Padmini is most visible in the significance that Zebā and the Datts ascribe to the story and their insistence on its historicity. Thus, Zebā's preface asserts the historical veracity of the story; the 'history' of Padmini is then placed within a newly constructed 'ancient history' (*prāchīn itihās*) of India. The *Hindustān* of the *maṡnavī* tradition is replaced by *Bhāratvarsh*. Valiant women such as Padmini are the honour (*'izzat*) of this country (*desh*) and its people (*jātī*). Zebā's intention in writing this play is to make widely known this blessed history (*pavitra itihās*) of valiant women to the people of *Bhāratvarsh*, to inspire the people of *Bhāratvarsh* with this exemplary 'history' (Zebā 1926: 5–6). To this end, the play about Padmini is merely the first in a 'series of plays (*nāṭakmālā*) about chaste (*pativratā*) women'.[11] For Zebā, Padmini is a 'chaste, virtuous woman [who] is a shining jewel adorning Rajputana and an unrivalled treasure of the Rajput *jātī*; no, in fact, a precious ornament to the Hindu *jātī*' (Zebā 1926: 6).

Zebā reveals here the same metonymic slide between 'Rajput' and 'Hindu' that was so typical of nationalist historiography in the late nineteenth century (Chatterjee 1999: 95–134). Other elements in Zebā's *Padminī* strengthen this 'Hindu' and nationalistic frame of reference. The play opens with the figure of the nation personified as a goddess, *Bhārat Mātā*, upon whose face the map of India is superimposed (Zebā 1926: 9). The goddess addresses the *sūtradhār* as *Āryānandan*. Later in the play, when the people of Chitor plan to rescue Bhimsingh from the clutches of the sultan, they wave banners and chant slogans of *Bande Mātāram* (Zebā 1926: 106). The country is now depicted as the land of 'Hindus'. Reinforcing this construction is the depiction of the country as *Bhāratvarsh*, known in 'ancient' times as *Āryāvart*. Here the Rajput is the descendant of the Kshatriya. In this capacity the Rajput will uphold 'truth and righteousness' (*sat dharam*) by defending the cow, the Brahmin, and 'the lustre of the Vedic faith' (*vaidik dharam kā tej*) (Zebā 1926: 39).

Further, in Zebā's *Padminī*, the people of *Bhāratvarsh* aspire to 're-draw the map (*naqsha*) of *Āryāvart* in their beloved, ancient country'. In order to do so, they must 'create an abode of the gods (*dev maṇḍal*) once again in this demonic society (*rākshasa samāj*)'. Not only must they forsake their vices and love their country and their people (*jātī*), they must also conduct sacrifices as dictated by the shastra (Zebā 1926: 12). The *sūtradhār* indicates that these are the wishes of the goddess Bhārat Mātā herself. Further, he refers to a 'movement' (*āndolan*) at the present moment, in which 'elevated, virtuous souls are uplifting fallen Bhārat' through their strength of character and virtue. 'Disregarding the new and fake ways, they are rebuilding the ancient civilization (*sabhyatā*, *tahẓīb*) of the Aryans on the basis of their virtuous conduct' (Zebā 1926: 13). Again, such elements as the emphasis on rebuilding 'Aryan' culture through reformed conduct and customs and the concern for cow protection reveal Zebā's Arya Samaj affiliation.[12]

This is the burden that the Padmini story now carries: it offers a fallen country the potential for redemption. This narrative does so by teaching the series of exemplary virtues needed to reform society: 'love of country, loyalty to friend, loyalty to king, loyalty to God, and loyalty to husband' (Zebā 1926: 14).

Love, Conquest, and the Politics of Genre

As discussed above, the Urdu adaptations of the *Padmāvat* narrative celebrate the ideal love between Ratansen and Padmavat that flourishes in the land of Hindustan. The death of Padmavat and Ratansen marks the triumph of such love and the defeat of Alauddin's lesser desire. In contrast, in the narratives of Zebā and the Datts, feminine devotion is made to carry a new symbolic burden: the woman's voluntary self-sacrifice in the preservation of her honour is the ground on which the nation's honour can be recovered.

'Āqil Khān Rāzī's comparison of the love between Padmavat and Ratansen to the paradigmatic attraction between the moth and the flame has been discussed above. The Urdu *Padmāvat* narratives appropriate this interpretation of Padmavat's death. Thus the *Sham'-o-Parvāna* begins by comparing Ratansen to the moth, attracted to the flame that is Padmavat. At the end of the poem, though, 'Ishrat inverts the conventional image and compares the dead body of Ratansen to a silent flame (*sham' khāmosh*). He is also the moth, however, who has lost his life for his love (*ki ākhir 'ishq ne usko jalāyā*). Padmavat was earlier the luminous flame that attracted Ratansen. In immolating herself along with Ratansen, she metamorphoses into the moth herself. Both queens, Padmavat and Nagmat, burn themselves for Ratansen, like eager moths (*parvāna pur josh*) (PU: 94–5). Throughout, neither the king nor his queens are depicted as Rajput. These poets do not perceive the self-immolation of the queens as a peculiarly Rajput custom. While the self-immolation is seen as defining and confirming the exalted status of Hindustani love, that love is not associated with any single social group.

The definition of a 'Rajput' identity was one of the impulses governing Ratansen's career in Jāyasī's *Padmāvat*. The king's quest to win his bride accompanied by sixteen thousand followers, their threatened assault upon the fort of Singhala, and their being rewarded ultimately with a wife each—these are tropes that would have encoded the aspirations and trajectories of pastoral and semi-tribal groups in medieval north India, seeking upward mobility and ultimately Rajput status in the service of a warlord.[13] Equally, Ratansen's resisting the surrender of his wife either to the sultan or to the rival king Devpal was an action comprehensible within the ethics of medieval warrior and landholding elites, Rajput and non-Rajput. Jāyasī's narrative of Ratansen and Padmavati can be read as embodying this ethic for his target audience of patrons among the regional elites in sixteenth-century Avadh.

As indicated above, the Urdu *maṡnavīs* continued to be patronized by members of this regional elite until the early twentieth century. However, their social profile was transformed under colonial authority. In the medieval period, such groups had formed part of a Mughal and regional ruling elite of 'administrators, warriors, scribes and courtiers'. After the 1857 revolt, British authority destroyed some of the old landed gentry (Rajput, Jat, and Muslim), and created other, new landlords through grants. The old ruling elite was 'transmuted into a landlord bureaucrat class' (Sangari 1999: 192). Thus, earlier avenues for upward mobility through military or bureaucratic service with rival regional powers no longer existed.

This transformation of historical context helps to explain many of the differences between the later Urdu *maṡnavī* adaptations and the *Padmāvat*. The elements in Jāyasī's *Padmāvat* that had embodied the aspirations of his patrons among the regional elite become redundant to the Urdu *maṡnavī* narrative. Thus, Ratansen's 'Rajput' identity becomes an irrelevant detail for poets such as 'Ibrat, 'Ishrat and Khalīl. Ratansen's resistance to the sultan was seen in the *Padmāvat* as a defence of his Rajput valour. In contrast, 'Ishrat explains Ratansen's resistance as the natural response of any self-respecting man.

The Rajput identity that is denuded of any significance in the *maṡnavīs* is re-invested with enormous symbolic power and transformed in the new 'nationalist' accounts of Zebā and the Datts. As discussed above, Tod's *Annals* was located in the specific context of Rajput politics in nineteenth-century Rajasthan. For writers like the Datts and Zebā, writing in Lahore and Delhi respectively for the mass-publishing marketplace, that specific context of elite politics in the Rajput kingdoms was irrelevant, just as much as for nationalist writers in the Bengali *bhadralok*. In this altered historical context, the significance of Bhimsingh's 'Rajput' identity is transformed to portray an essentially 'Hindu' identity. Zebā and the Datts thus make the devotion of king and queen to each other an embodiment of ideal 'Hindu' love and virtue.

Zebā also relocates the Padmini story within a new 'Hindi' literary tradition through his distinctive use of language. He uses Urdu couplets to describe Alauddin's desire for Padmini and the sultan's distress at being unable to obtain her. In contrast, Bhimsingh's anguish at being separated from his beloved, while held captive by the emperor, is expressed in Hindavi couplets.

As argued below, Zebā's play makes it clear that Alauddin's desire is illicit. In this context, the distinction between Alauddin's *hijr*, *'ishq*, and *dīvāngī* on the one hand, and Bhimsingh's *birhā kī agnī* on the other, tilts the linguistic and cultural scales against Urdu. Thus, Zebā's play also turns away from the Urdu *maṣnavī* tradition in reconfiguring the bounds of desire and refashioning the language of love. In this context, it is interesting that both these accounts depict the relationship between Bhimsingh and Padmini as mutually monogamous. This 'Hindu' monogamy is then contrasted with repeated references to the 'Muslim' sultan's harem.

As a quintessentially 'Hindu' virtue, Padmini's devotion is entrusted with the burden of upholding the sanctity of the land and the virtue of its people. The 'Hindu' woman achieves this by her absolute loyalty to her husband, even at the cost of her own life.

Ye har ḥālat meṅ apne shoharoṅ ko mān detī haiṅ
Ye hindū aurateṅ apnī patī par jān detī haiṅ (Zebā 1926: 109).
(They respect their husbands in every eventuality/These Hindu women give up their lives for their husbands.)

In keeping with the tendency of Hindu nationalism in the late nineteenth and early twentieth centuries, Zebā's play makes this figure of the chaste 'Hindu' woman symbolic of the glory of ancient Indian history.[14]

Zebā demonstrates that Padmini's loyalty is capable of bearing this heavy burden by subjecting it to a test, when the captive Bhimsingh asks her to surrender to the sultan. Even as Bhimsingh regrets contemplating the surrender of 'a goddess' (*devī*) to a demon (*ek rākshas*), he is not certain whether Padmini will obey his order or defy it. The episode becomes a test of Padmini's virtue:

Yadī driḍh dharam par hai to vo bigḍī banā legī
Maiṅ apnā dharam to pālūṅ vo apnā dharam pālegī (Zebā 1926: 83).

By having her imprisoned husband rescued instead of surrendering herself, Padmini passes the test with flying colours. In fact, Zebā argues that in her refusal to surrender to the sultan, Padmini surpasses even Sita. The latter allowed herself to be abducted by Ravana, whereas Padmini declares that she would rather kill herself than surrender to the Musalman. It is on the strength of such exemplary virtue that Padmini rules not merely over her own land (*bhūmī*) but over the hearts of all 'Hindus' (*samast hindū janatā*) (Zebā 1926: 89). The same reinterpretation is evident in the title given by the Datts to their account. The story of Padmini no longer signifies the ideal love between a lover and his beloved, as it did in the Urdu *masnavīs*. Instead it signifies the honour of the 'people' as vested in the chastity of their women (*'azamat-i chitor urf qaumī ān*).

These divergent interpretations of feminine devotion differentiate the resolutions of the *masnavī* and the 'nationalist' narratives. In the *masnavī* tradition, Ratansen's death avenging the insult to his honour, and Padmavat's self-immolation, together proved the supreme value of their love. In contrast, in Zebā's and the Datts' texts Padmini's self-immolation proves the supreme virtue of Rajput and 'Hindu' women in upholding the honour of Bhārat, a nation of 'Hindus'(Datt and Datt 1914: 47). That honour, both of the woman and of the nation, is under threat from the 'Muslim' conqueror, Alauddin Khalji.

Given the shifts in patronage and audience constituencies between the Urdu *masnavīs* and the new 'nationalist' narratives, it is to be expected that the divergences between the two genres of narrative would be most visible in the depiction of Alauddin Khalji. To examine the *masnavī* versions first, the *Sham'-o-Parvāna* depicts Alauddin as the emperor of Hind and the refuge of the world (*'ālampanāh*). The sultan is so generous, merciful, and wise that the poet is hard-pressed to find words fit enough to describe him (PU: 80). It is Raghav Chetan who is instrumental in instigating the emperor to march upon Chitor, by showing him Padmavat's anklet and describing her beauty. The narrative's assessment of Alauddin's desire for Padmavat is conveyed indirectly. As a courtier of the emperor points out, not even a mean and lowly man will surrender his honour by surrendering his women (PU: 81). Alauddin persists however, and besieges Chitor.

It is significant that in these *masnavī* narratives, it is not Alauddin who is responsible for the death of the lovers Ratansen and Padmavat, but Devpal (the king of Kumbhalmer). Moreover, Padmavat and Nagmat commit sati upon the death of the king, not mass immolation (*jauhar*) as in the accounts of Zebā and the Datts. In these details, 'Ishrat follows the *Padmāvat* narrative faithfully. The lovers thus face repeated obstacles to their love and finally lose their lives defending that love.

Alauddin ultimately conquers Chitor, only to find Padmavat's ashes. He heaps her ashes on his head in recognition of his own mortality and the limits of his imperial power (PU: 96). Having lost Padmavat, he is not interested in retaining control over Chitor. He accepts Padmavat's son Kanvalsen as the new king of Chitor, anoints him with a robe of honour, and returns to Delhi.

In 'Ibrat and 'Ishrat's *masnavī*, therefore, Alauddin is not an ambitious emperor driven to territorial conquest. Nor is his Muslim identity particularly significant. Alauddin is merely a misguided lover who ultimately accepts the folly of his love, mourns the death of his desire, and accepts the bounds of mortality.

In contrast, the *'Aẓamat-i Chitor* of the Datts depicts Alauddin as the emperor who has conquered the world by the force of the sword. He desires to wipe out the kafir from Hind and spread the true faith of Islam. He wishes to conquer Chitor and see the flag of Islam fluttering from its ramparts. It is only after he has already expressed his intention to conquer Chitor that he hears of Padmini's beauty. He now wishes to obtain her for his harem as well, but the text has established that his primary motive was territorial conquest and the spread of Islam (Datt and Datt 1914: 2–4).

The implications of this conquest for the Rajputs are spelt out graphically. Padmini sees the battle against Alauddin as a battle for the faith, describing Bhimsingh as a *g͟hāzī* (Datt and Datt 1914: 13). (The irony of using this Islamic terminology to describe the 'Hindu' Rajput's battle is lost upon the authors.) Padmini also reminds Bhimsingh of his predecessors, Prithviraj, Jaipal, and Anangpal—earlier 'Rajput' rulers who had resisted the 'Muslim' conquest of their kingdoms. Not only is the (religious) faith of the Rajputs at stake, the honour of their women is also threatened. Bhimsingh recognizes that after his own death in defence of his land and his faith, 'the Musalman oppressor' will destroy Padmini's chastity and honour (Datt and Datt 1914: 15). It is at this point that Padmini declares that she would rather give up her life than surrender herself to the 'Musalman oppressor'.

Just as the exclusion of Nagmat from these narratives enables the construction of an idealized, 'Hindu' monogamous conjugality, the absence of Devpal serves to render the 'Muslim conqueror' as the sole threat to this Rajput, 'Hindu' order. As Bhimsingh and his men prepare for their last battle in defence of Chitor, Padmini leads the Rajput women to mass immolation (*jauhar*), a custom identified as distinctively Rajput. The Rajputs die in battle and Alauddin enters the fort victorious. At this point, however, when he finds that Padmini is dead, he is regretful that he has wasted so many lives and still failed in his pursuit of the queen. He returns to Delhi defeated even in victory, having learned his lesson about Rajput 'national pride, their love of their land and their honour' (Datt and Datt 1914: 47). The 'Muslim' conqueror who oppresses the women of his defeated rivals is finally vanquished by the valiant Rajput defence of their 'national pride' and the honour of their women.

Zebā's *Padminī* similarly depicts Alauddin as the 'Muslim' conqueror. Apprehensions about this 'Musḷim' conqueror are expressed by the personified cow (*gau mātā*). She addresses Bhimsingh as her Kshatriya protector and expresses her fears about the *yavans* who perversely torment cows in their conquered domains. The Brahmin expresses his own fears about the extermination of the Vedic faith from the land of Bhārat, if the *yavan* succeeds in conquering Chitor (Zebā 1926: 39). For her part, Padmini refuses to surrender herself to a *yavan* and is wary of treachery as she contemplates revealing herself to Alauddin's gaze in a mirror (Zebā 1926: 69, 71).

And yet, Zebā tempers his representation of Alauddin. Alauddin's 'Muslim' subjects tell him that they do not see the battle against Chitor as a battle for 'the Islamic faith'. Instead, they warn the emperor that 'all this battle is for a beautiful, married woman, which is forbidden to you by the faith'. As these 'Muslim' subjects clarify, 'To make one's wife a woman whose husband is alive, is against Islamic law (*shar*')' (Zebā 1926: 58–9). Zebā offers further clarification in his preface that Alauddin's sole motive in attacking Chitor was his desire to obtain Padmini: whether she was Hindu or Musalman was irrelevant to the emperor.

Thus, Zebā rescues Alauddin from the charge of personal bigotry that is imputed to him in the Datts' account. As Zebā is at pains to point out, 'Alauddin had no hatred for the Hindus.... Whatever else he may have been, Alauddin was not bigoted (*muta'aṣṣib*)' (Zebā 1926: 8). Thus, Bhimsingh reassures the cow (*gau mātā*) and the Brahmin that every 'virtuous Musalman' believes in the 'holy Quran', and the Quran 'forbids its believers from inflicting pain on any living thing'. Hence, he fears no insult from the *yavan* to the cow and the Brahmin, though the motherland will be ruined and its wealth destroyed (Zebā 1926: 39–40).

One can only speculate about the reasons for Zebā's relatively more moderate depiction of the figure of the 'Muslim' conqueror. On the one hand, his possible Arya Samaj affiliations explain his glorification of the 'ancient', 'Aryan' past and his anxiety to recover that past and its 'virtue'. On the other hand, though, the pressures of commercial success may have forced some sensitivity on his part to the expectations of his audience. In a period when the separation of Urdu and Hindi was increasingly marked and the former was increasingly associated with Muslim audiences, Zebā may well have been aware of the pressures of writing for an Urdu audience that was increasingly being identified as Muslim. These intangible pressures may account for his relatively mild treatment of the figure of the 'Muslim' conqueror.

It is clear from the above discussion that these refashioned 'nationalist' narratives of Padmini shift the emphasis away from the *maṣnavīs*' celebration of ideal love, to the Rajput identity of Padmini and the threat to the nation posed by the 'Muslim invader'. For all their divergences, though, several elements in the narrative of Alauddin's pursuit of Padmini are common to the two sets of versions. Most striking is the close relationship between love, sacrifice, and honour, shared by both the *masnavī* tradition and these 'nationalist' versions. In the former tradition, originating with the *Padmāvat*, a Sufi mystical trajectory determined that love had to be preceded by sacrifice. Further, such intense love for a principle of the divine, as glimpsed in the beloved, could only be fleeting. It was followed by and culminated in the literal obliteration of the protagonists through immolation, itself loosely symbolizing the flames of desire. In the process, Alauddin's desire is delegitimized and Ratansen defends his honour in preserving his love.

The same narrative tropes are ascribed radically different significance in the 'nationalist' versions of Zebā and the Datts. Here, the love of Padmini for Bhimsingh embodies a conjugal norm rather than an idealized, mystical love. This norm is made the symbolic centre of the moral order of the nation. Padmini's surrender is a surrender of the national honour itself. The threat posed by Alauddin thus extends far beyond the domain of love; it extends to the very identity of the nation, as a realm where such normative conjugality will be defended along with other such symbolic markers as the cow and the Brahmin. The love between a king and a queen and the threat to it from a conqueror are thus reworked radically in the transition from the *masnavī* tradition to 'nationalist' versions of the Padmini legend.[15]

Conclusion

This essay has explored the shifts within and between two Urdu traditions about Padmini—paradigmatic love story derived ultimately from Malik Muḥammad Jāyasī's *Padmāvat*, and nationalist 'history' derived from James Tod's *Annals and Antiquities of Rajasthan*—between the seventeenth and early twentieth centuries. The history of circulation and transmission of these narratives points to shifts in patronage that are articulated as shifts within the narrative itself. Thus, as the *Padmāvat* narrative moves from Persian to Urdu, and from the courts to mass publication, an earlier tradition of interpretation that read the narrative for its Sufi mystical symbolism seems to get marginalized. The presence of other, contiguous narrative forms within Jāyasī's *Padmāvat* aids in this ultimate secularization of its narrative in nineteenth-century *masnavīs*. With the advent of print and the circulation of narratives among a much larger audience and across a much wider geographical spread, a new 'nationalist' narrative of Padmini emerges in Urdu in the early twentieth century. Internal evidence reveals its proximity to the version that originated in James Tod's *Annals and Antiquities of Rajasthan*. This 'nationalist' narrative in Urdu breaks dramatically with the earlier *maṡnavī* tradition, as it transforms the significance of the queen, her exemplary love, and the nature of the threat posed by the conquering sultan.

Notes

[1] Mohammad Habib reads the reference to the Queen of Sheba as a veiled allusion to the queen Padmini. Habib 1981, 2: 188–90.

[2] It is at this point that 'Ibrat's narrative breaks off and 'Ishrat picks up the thread.

[3] 'Ibrat-o-'Ishrat 1928 (hereafter PU): 11.

[4] Shantanu Phukan's translation. Discussion of Rāzī's *maṡnavī* here is based on Phukan 1996.

[5] This bears out Christopher Shackle's characterization of the Urdu *maṡnavī* in north India as 'religiously neutral' for the most part. Shackle 2000: 59.

[6] See Muzaffar Alam and Sanjay Subrahmanyam's essay in this volume.

[7] I am grateful to Carla Petievich for providing me with a copy of this text.

[8] For instance, he translates *sabhyatā* in parentheses as *tahẕīb*, and *svatantratā* as *āzādī*. Zebā 1926: 13, 118.

[9] For a list of Zebā's plays and brief plot summaries, *see* Nāmī 1962, 3: 204–11. For reports of Zebā's popularity all over north India, *see* Faridi 1966: 10.

[10] *See* H.P. Bagchi, 'Contribution of Bengali Hindus to Urdu', Appendix in Faridi 1966: 114. Many of Bankim's novels had earlier been translated into 'Hindi' (in Nagari script) by Bharatendu Harischandra and other members of his circle. Tod's *Annals* was also known to 'Hindi' audiences from at least 1874 onwards, when it was reviewed in *Harischandra's Magazine* (Dalmia 1999: 292, 329).

[11] The *Āftāb-i 'Iṣmat* about Savitri clearly belonged to the same series.

[12] Shrīkrishna Khatrī Pahalvān of Kanpur, who came under the influence of the Arya Samaj, composed a Sāṅgīt called *Mahārānī Padminī* (1919), with similar emphasis on the preservation of the Hindu faith, following the example of 'goddesses like this one, who burned themselves on the pyre and saved their honor' (Hansen 1993: 110).

[13] For the typical trajectory and ethics of such 'Rajputizing' groups, *see* Kolff 1990: 71–116.

[14] *See* Sangari and Vaid (1989) for the pervasiveness of this phenomenon.

[15] I am grateful to Kathryn Hansen for encouraging me to explore the relationship between these two traditions in terms of shared narrative tropes.

Bibliography

Abidi, S.A.H., 'The Story of Padmavat in Indo-Persian Literature', *Indo-Iranica*, 15 (2), 1962, 1–12.

Alam, Muzaffar, 'Assimilation from a Distance: Confrontation and Sufi Accommodation in Avadh Society', in R. Champakalakshmi and S. Gopal (eds.), *Tradition, Dissent and Ideology: Essays in Honour of Romila Thapar*, New Delhi: Oxford University Press, 1996.

Chatterjee, Partha, *The Nation and its Fragments: Colonial and Postcolonial Histories*, New Delhi: Oxford University Press, 1999 [1993].

Dalmia, Vasudha, *The Nationalization of Hindu Traditions: Bharatendu Harischandra and Nineteenth-century Banaras*, New Delhi: Oxford University Press, 1999 [1997].

Datt, Rudar and Dev Datt, *'Aẕamat-i Chitor urf Qaumi Ān*, Lahore: Bhai Daya Singh Bookseller, 1914.

de Bruijn, Thomas, 'The Ruby Hidden in the Dust: A Study of the Poetics of Malik Muḥammad Jāyasī's Padmāvat', PhD dissertation, Leiden: University of Leiden, 1996.

Faridi, S.N., *Hindu History of Urdu Literature*, Agra: Ram Prasad & Sons, 1966.

Gupt, Ganapati Chandra, *Hindī Sāhitya kā Vaigyānik Itihās*, 5th revised edn., 2 vols, Allahabad: Lokbharati Prakashan, 1994.

Gupt, Mātāprasād (ed.), *Jāyasī Granthāvalī*, Allahabad: Hindustani Akademi, 1952.

Habib, Mohammad, 'The Campaigns of Alauddin Khalji Being the English Translation of "The Khaza'inul Futuh"', in K.A. Nizami (ed.), *Politics and Society during the Early Medieval Period: Collected Works of Professor Mohammad Habib*, 2 vols, Delhi: People's Publishing House, 1981.

Ḥāfiẕ Khalīl Ḥasan Mānikpurī, *Butkhāna-i Khalīl*, 'Alī Aḥmad Jalīl (ed. and introd.), Hyderabad: Aijaz Press, 1994.

Hansen, Kathryn, *Grounds for Play: The Nautanki Theatre of North India*, New Delhi: Manohar Books, 1993.

———, 'The *Indar Sabha* Phenomenon: Public Theatre and Consumption in Greater India (1853–1956),' in Rachel Dwyer and Christopher Pinney (eds.), *Pleasure and the Nation: The History, Politics and Consumption of Public Culture in India*, New Delhi: Oxford University Press, 2001.

'Ibrat-o-'Ishrat, *Padmāvat Urdū*, Lucknow: Khwaja Qutbaldin Ahmad Nami Press, 1928.

Kolff, Dirk H. A., *Naukar, Rajput and Sepoy: The Ethnohistory of the Military Labour Market in Hindustan 1450–1850*, Cambridge: Cambridge University Press, 1990.

Nāmī, 'Abdul 'Alīm, *Urdū Theṭar*, vol. 3, Karachi: Anjuman Taraqqi-i Urdu, 1962.

Phukan, Shantanu, 'None Mad as a Hindu Woman: Contesting Communal Readings of *Padmāvat*', *Comparative Studies of South Asia, Africa and the Middle East*, 16 (1), 1996, 41–54.

Pritchett, Frances, *Marvellous Encounters: Folk Romances in Urdu and Hindi*, New Delhi: Manohar, 1985.

———, *The Romance Tradition in Urdu: Adventures from the Dāstān of Amīr Hamza*, New York: Columbia University Press, 1991.

Qanungo, K.R., *Studies in Rajput History*, New Delhi: S. Chand & Co., 1969.

Rizvi, S.A.A., *A History of Sufism in India*, 2 vols, New Delhi: Munshiram Manoharlal, 1997 [1975].

Sangari, Kumkum, *Politics of the Possible: Essays on Gender, History, Narrative, Colonial English*, New Delhi: Tulika, 1999.

Sangari, Kumkum and Sudesh Vaid (eds.), *Recasting Women: Essays in Colonial History*, New Delhi: Kali for Women, 1989.

Shackle, Christopher, 'Beyond Turk and Hindu: Crossing the Boundaries in Indo-Muslim Romance', in David Gilmartin and Bruce B. Lawrence (eds.), *Beyond Turk and Hindu: Rethinking Religious Identities in Islamicate South Asia*, Gainesville: University Press of Florida, 2000.

Tod, James, *Annals and Antiquities of Rajasthan or the Central and Western Rajput States of India*, William Crooke (ed.), 3 vols, Delhi: Low Price Publications, 1995 [1920].

Zebā, Kishan Chand, *Padminī: Tavārīkhī Ḍrāma*, 2nd edn., Delhi: National Book Depot, 1926.

Appendix: List of known versions/manuscripts/editions of the Padmini legend in the nineteenth and twentieth centuries

1. 'Ibrat-o-'Ishrat, *Mudallil-i Sham'-o-Parvāna*, also known as *Qiṣṣa-i Padmāvat* or *Padmāvat Urdū*, 1797.
2. *Mudallil-i Sham'-o-Parvāna*, MS Copy, 1828, scribe unknown.
3. Ẕiyāuddīn 'Ibrat and Ghulām 'Alī 'Ishrat, *Padmāvat*, Lucknow, 1858.
4. Malik Muḥammad Jāyasī, *Padmāvat*, Lucknow, 1865 (in Persian characters, with commentary in Urdu by 'Alī Ḥasan; lith.).
5. Malik Muḥammad Jāyasī, *Padmāvat*, Lucknow, 1870 (with marginal notes in Hindustani by 'Alī Ḥasan of Amethi).
6. Maulvī Muḥammad Qāsim 'Alī Barelvī, title unknown, Nawal Kishor Press, 1871.
7. Muḥammad Qāsim 'Alī, *Padmāvat*, Kanpur: Nawal Kishor Press, 1873.
8. Ẕiyāuddīn 'Ibrat and Ghulām 'Alī 'Ishrat, *Padmāvat*, Kanpur, 1874.
9. Ẕiyāuddīn 'Ibrat and Ghulām 'Alī 'Ishrat, *Padmāvat*, Delhi, 1879.
10. Malik Muḥammad Jāyasī, *Padmāvat*, Lucknow, 1880 (in Devanagari characters, with meanings of difficult words).
11. *Padmāvat*, Lucknow: Munshi Nawal Kishor, 1881 (rendered into Devanagari script by Lālā Raghubardayāl, with notes on difficult words).
12. *Padmāvat... / murattab Mīr Ẕiyāuddīn 'Ibrat aur Ghulām 'Alī 'Ishrat*, Kanpur: Nawal Kishor Press, 1885.
13. Vihārī Lāl Bedil, *Padam Samāj*, Bijnaur: Matba-i Samar-i Hind, 1885.
14. Ẕiyāuddīn 'Ibrat and Ghulām 'Alī 'Ishrat, *Padmāvat*, Delhi, 1889.
15. Malik Muḥammad Jāyasī, *Padmāvat*, Farrukhabad, 1892 (selections; accompanied by explanations of each couplet and notes by Munshi Chintamani; lith.).
16. Malik Muḥammad Jāyasī, *Padmāvat*, Calcutta, 1896 (in Persian characters, with interlinear Hindustani translation by Aḥmad 'Alī Rāsī; lith.).
17. Malik Muḥammad Jāyasī, *Padmāvat*, Calcutta: Steam Machine Press, 1896 (in Hindi).
18. Malik Muḥammad Jāyasī, *Padmāvat*, Kanpur, 1899 (in Persian characters, with interlinear Hindustani translation and marginal notes by Aḥmad 'Alī Rāsī; lith.).
19. Ḥāfiẕ Khalīl Ḥasan 'Khalīl' Mānikpūrī, *Butkhāna-i Khalīl*, Agra, 1914.
20. Rudar Datt and Dev Datt, *'Aẕamat-i Chitor urf Qaumī Ān*, Lahore: Bhai Daya Singh Bookseller, 1914.*
21. Ustād Indraman, *Sāṅgīt Vīr Bahādur*, or *Rājā Ratan Siṁha kā Sākhā*, Hathras: 1915.

22. *Padmāvat Bhāshā Malik Muḥammad Jāyasī*, Nawal Kishor Press, 1920.
23. Pahalvān Shrīkrishna Khatrī, *Sāṅgīt Mahārānī Padminī*, Kanpur: Umadatta Vajpeyee, 1919.*
24. Rādhākrishna Dās, *Mahārānī Padmāvatī*, 2nd edn., Banaras: Durga Prasad Khatri, 1923.*
25. Rāmchandra Shukl, *Jāyasī Granthāvalī*, Kashi: Nagari Pracharini Sabha, 1924 (Hindi, in Nagari script).
26. Paṇḍit Bhagavatī Prasād Pāṇḍey 'Anuj', *Padmāvat Bhākhā matarjum.*
27. Kishan Chand Zebā, *Padminī: Tavārīkhī Ḍrāma*, 2nd edition, New Delhi: National Book Depot, 1926.*
28. *Padmāvat Urdū / Mīr Ẕiyāuddīn 'Ibrat aur Ghulām 'Alī 'Ishrat*, Lucknow: Nami Press, 1928.
29. *Padmāvat Bhāshā: Rājā Ratansen aur Padmāvat Rānī kī Prasiddh Kahānī*, Nawal Kishor Press, 1960.

(Asterisks indicate the nationalist versions of the legend.)

From *Akhbār* to News: The Development of the Urdu Press in Early Nineteenth-Century Delhi

GAIL MINAULT

The printing press has been related to rapid social and cultural change in early modern Europe (Eisenstein 1979), and Benedict Anderson, for one, ties the development of 'print capitalism' and vernacularization to the emergence of nationalism in Europe and its colonial empires (Anderson 1983: 33–46, 67–82). My purpose in this paper is to speculate on the role of print and the development of the Urdu periodical press in early nineteenth-century north India as these relate to emerging political consciousness in the colonial context. What did the expanding availability of newspapers and periodicals reveal about the market for the information they contained and its impact? Did an expanded readership for print signal an emerging colonial hybrid culture, or a vernacular discourse with links to traditional cultures, or both? These questions address, at least indirectly, the overall interpretive question of the source of social and political change in the period of the early colonial encounter. Did agents of change come exclusively from the West, or was 'native' agency also essential?

As I have been engaged in research over the past few years on the intellectual history of the city of Delhi in the early nineteenth century, I have come across old newspapers, early periodicals, and examples of some of the earliest books printed in the Mughal capital city.[1] In attempting to generalize from such fragmentary evidence, I have found it helpful to relate these materials to work on the transmission of knowledge and information in pre-colonial and colonial India.[2] In the immediate pre-colonial period, the transmission of knowledge, in the sense of formal learning, was organized around long-established practices of teacher-student (*gurū-shishya, ustād-shāgird*) relations and highly dependent on oral transmission, via dictation and recitation, in the absence of printed texts. Texts were important repositories of knowledge, wisdom, and sacredness, but the average student did not have access to copies, beyond what he had transcribed and memorized (Robinson 1993: 234–7). Similarly, poetry was composed for recitation—sometimes extemporaneously—and its written version often transcribed only after it had been heard in company. The oral tradition, therefore, dominated learning and literature; how much more so was it part of the transmission of social information: current affairs, news, rumour, gossip, and hearsay?

Counter to the expectation raised by such a question, in the Mughal empire and its successor states there was an elaborate system of written news reports, first established by the emperor Akbar, though patterned on earlier sultanate espionage systems. The Ghaznavids had their *barid*, or post and intelligence service, and the literature of Muslim statecraft is full of advice to kings on the need to be well informed, both about neighbouring states and about affairs at home. The *Qābūs Nāma* advises the king:

> ... in the same measure as you are informed of affairs in the world generally and of the doings of its princes, it is your duty to be acquainted with your own country and the conditions prevailing amongst your people and bodyguard. If you are ignorant of conditions in your own State, you will be even more ignorant of conditions in foreign States. (Kai-Kā'ūs 1951: 234)

Sanskrit literature on statecraft similarly counsels the king to listen to reports pertaining to the affairs of the population, and to be informed about the secret reports brought by spies.[3]

'Native Newspaper Reports'—*Akhbār* and *Akhbār Nawīs*[4]

Akbar was thus following an already established pattern of royal information gathering, though improving upon it, when he instituted a regular pattern of reporting, both at his own court and in the courts of his provincial governors and regional commanders. The *vāqi'a nawīs* (recorder of events) at the court was a chronicler who maintained a written record of the emperor's daily displacements, his rulings, appointments, promotions, ritual observances, and so on, and transmitted this information to the emperor's subordinates in the provinces who needed to know that he was still alive and well, and in charge. The emperor also had an army of other news writers who reported on the doings of those regional lieutenants, as a way of assuring himself that they were still on the job, administering justice, and neither oppressing the population nor rebelling against central authority. These *akhbār nawīs* or news writers were known to those on whom they reported, who could presumably threaten, collude with, or bribe them. As a precaution, therefore, there was a second tier of secret reporters, *sawāniḥ nigār* (surveyors of events) or *khufia nawīs* (secret writers). Public reports were dispatched to the court to be read aloud, but the emperor read the secret reports in private. The messenger or *harkāra* (lit., factotum) was also a spy who could report on events and on the other ranks of reporters. Consequently, if an officer was able to evade one form of surveillance, his actions would nevertheless reach the attention of the emperor eventually.

Provincial officers, independent regional rulers like the Peshwa, and the nawabs and nizams who were the rulers of Mughal successor states also had their own staffs of *akhbār nawīs*, accredited to neighbouring states. Functionally, such a news reporter was also part chronicler and part spy. In form, these reports fell into two major types: the formulaic—reporting on the repetitive, ceremonial occasions of court life; and the editorial—providing comment and analysis of events (Fisher 1993: 49–50; Sarkar 1967: 135–40). Two brief examples:

> Zindan Khan Deccani, a commander of 4000, was reported as being 'used to sacrific[ing] his life in the service of the emperor' and deserving a higher rank. The Emperor sarcastically commented on the rhetorical writing, for how could the mansabdar be still alive if he repeatedly sacrificed his life?
>
> Ibrahim Khan, appointed Governor of Gujarat (1705), used to go to the Jama mosque in a *palki* (palanquin), thereby violating royal prerogative.... To the enquiry of the news-writers, the Khan replied that they might write what they wanted. The Emperor asked the Prime Minister to caution him not to do anything which gave a handle to the news-writers to complain.[5]

After the British gained political ascendancy, their district collectorates and the British Residents at native courts also became the objects of news reports, the *akhbār nawīs* who produced them being employed by individual princes, landed magnates, or merchants who needed to know what was going on. Sometimes news writers sold their reports by subscription to a group of patrons (Fisher 1993: 48–9; Sarkar 1967: 135–40). Surrounded by these eyes and ears, it is no surprise that the British soon employed their own news writers, assigned to native courts. Bayly observes that the British did not simply 'hack into' the Mughal information system, but employed some of its techniques and personnel, while developing their own networks of intelligence (Bayly 1993: 29, 3–43; Cohn 1996: 3–15). A surgeon posted to Lucknow reported on his additional duties assisting the Resident, which involved summarizing reports from *akhbār nawīs* describing the activities of the nawab. He gives an example:

'His Majesty was this morning carried in his tonjon [sedan chair] to the __Mahal [palace], and there he and So-and-So [ladies] were entertained with fights of two pairs of new rams, which fought with great energy, also of some quails. Shawls worth Rs 100 were presented to the *jemadars* [orderlies] who arranged these fights. His Majesty then listened to a new singer, and amused himself afterwards by kite-flying until 4 p.m. when he went to sleep. Reports have come in from the village of __in the district of __that Ram Singh, zemindar [landlord] refused to pay Rs 500 demanded of him by the *amil* [tax-collector], whereon his house was burned, he was wounded, and his two sons and brothers have absconded. Jewan Khan, daroga [superintendent] of the pigeon-house received a Khilat [robe of honour] of shawls and Rs 2000 for producing a pigeon with one black and one white wing. His Majesty recited to the Khas Mahal [private audience] his new poem on the loves of the bulbuls [nightingales],' and so on (Sanial 1934: 112).

Since the quoted source is a hybrid, the example is hardly straightforward. The critical tone relating to *nawābī* excesses comes as much from the British doctor juxtaposing telling excerpts as it does from his *akhbār nawīs* sources.

In any case, the manuscript *akhbār* continued to be produced well after printed newspapers emerged in the nineteenth century and were alternative sources of news, intelligence, and rumour. Published newspapers, in turn, had many similarities in content to the manuscript news reports, whether formulaic coverage of court and government actions, or editorial comment and controversy. The following report from Delhi on the Mughal court that appeared in the *Jām-i Jahān Numā*, a Persian weekly of Calcutta, on 1 October 1825 shows that royals were even then the objects of journalistic curiosity:

Hazrat Jahan Panah (His Majesty) would arrive at the durgah [shrine] of Qutub Sahib after attending the Festival of Flowers (Phool Walon Ki Sair). There His Majesty would listen to music and watch the spectacle of ladies bathing in the canal. The slave-girls would indulge in all kinds of pranks: they would hold each other in groups and thus together jump into the water. Some one would smile and squeeze water out of her hair while another would do the same to her *choli* [blouse]. Someone would try to tear off the *kurti* [shirt] of a play-mate who would thereat blush with shame. One would shout, 'Sister do not enter the current; water flows powerfully there,' and so on. Only those who have seen the playful pranks of such fairy-like creatures know what the spectacle looks like; words cannot describe it. One would hardly believe it to be true (Khan 1991: 32).

Short of frolicking royalty on the Riviera, what could be more titillating? In contrast to the akhbār accounts summarized above, this appears to be an eyewitness account free of editorial comment until the last two sentences, where irony creeps in. The source of this report was apparently a handwritten akhbār, but the *Jām-i Jahān Numā* in other matters quoted from English newspapers and government gazettes, so its editorial point of view is difficult to sort out. This paper had earlier reported critically on the slave girl trade in the Mughal capital.[6] Such scrutiny of native rulers was clearly useful to the British, but when turned towards the East India Company's government in India, made its servants apprehensive. Bayly has made us aware of the complex nature of imperial information, but also of its lacunae, those networks of knowledge that still eluded British control (Bayly 1993: 35–41).

Print in India: The Emergence of Print Journalism

The printing press first came to south India in the sixteenth century under Portuguese auspices, brought by Jesuit missionaries who developed fonts for printing Tamil, as they were anxious to proselytize via the translated word (Kesavan 1985: 13–39). In north India in the late eighteenth century, Protestant missionaries at Serampore—just outside Calcutta—first developed fonts for printing Bengali and Hindi for similar reasons (Kesavan 1985: 189–207). The printing of Arabic, Persian, and Urdu was somewhat more difficult because these languages utilize a script in which letters change shape according to where they occur in a word. Christian missionaries in the Middle East worked out a movable type for the printing of Arabic (*naskh*) script, and this type was also used at Serampore, and at Fort William College in Calcutta. The printing of the more sinuous *nasta'līq* script used in Persian and Urdu, however, demanded a different solution. Resistance to print on the part of Islamic clerics and scribes has been attributed to the Christian origins of the technology, or alternatively, to the tenaciousness—even the sacredness—of the oral tradition in the transmission of knowledge.[7] Without entering into that loaded debate, one could simply point to practicality. As long as literacy was limited to specialists (whether clerics, scribes, merchants, or spies—including Hindus literate in Persian), and these specialists had at their command a script not only intricate but also reducible to shorthand,[8] writing was actually faster for purposes of transmitting information than any mechanical reproduction system yet devised. The solution to printing *nasta'līq* was found in the lithograph, invented in 1796 and soon imported into India.

Calligraphy on stone yielded the required look, and—no small consideration—kept scribes employed. Adoption of lithography, even by the ulama, was almost instantaneous (Metcalf 1982: 199–203).

The British East India Company, in the revision of its charter in 1813, gave a boost to the spread of printing by first permitting missionary activity in British-held territories in India, and secondly recognizing the need for British government patronage of native education (Sharp 1965: 22). The spread of education via the printed word was thereby associated, in many Indian minds, with Christian proselytization. Indians nevertheless took to education in British-run schools in increasing numbers throughout the nineteenth century, and here the practicality argument enters again. For one thing, a knowledge of English became increasingly necessary for worldly success, but in addition, it became apparent to many in the aspiring professional classes that a knowledge of English, the study of calculus, *The Wealth of Nations*, and even *Macbeth*, did not a Christian make.[9] Ram Mohan Roy, a leading advocate of English education for Indians and an important Hindu social and religious reformer in Bengal, denied that he had succumbed to Christian doctrine, and even wrote a treatise questioning the trinity, a notion that gave pause to monists and monotheists alike (Hay 1988: 16, 24–5).

Ram Mohan Roy was also one of the earliest Indian journalists. There had been English newspapers in Calcutta since the late eighteenth century, but by 1820, Ram Mohan had started weeklies in Bengali (*Sambād Kaumudī*), English (*The Brahmunical Magazine*), and in 1822, Persian (*Mir'āt ul-Akhbār*). There was another Persian weekly in Calcutta in the 1820s, the *Jām-i Jahān Numā*—mentioned above—which published an Urdu supplement that has been cited as the first Urdu newspaper.[10] As a reformer, Ram Mohan attracted conservative opponents who brought out their own weekly newspapers. Indeed, the press in Calcutta in this period began to assume the cacophonous quality for which the Indian press has been known ever since. In 1830, there were thirty-three English newspapers in the city reaching 2205 subscribers, sixteen Bengali newspapers, and one in Persian. The circulation of the leading English language daily, the *Bengal Hurkaru*,[11] was around 800 copies. The Calcutta scene was significantly ahead of developments elsewhere in India (Natarajan 1962: 57–9; Khan 1991: 25–42). In Bombay, for example, in this same period there were only two English newspapers, plus papers in Marathi, Gujarati, and Persian; in Madras, three English newspapers, two weeklies in Tamil, one in Telugu, one in Persian, and a bilingual one in Persian and English (Natarajan 1962: 58–9, 61, 69; Khan 1991: 42–64). These were the coastal Presidency cities, well ahead of 'up-country' towns.

Many of these papers commented openly on matters of public policy and did not hesitate to criticize the East India Company's government for either timidity or high-handedness. For example, Ram Mohan Roy's publications attacked the custom of sati and called for government action to suppress it, while his opponents defended the custom on religious grounds and opposed government interference.[12] The *Jām-i Jahān Numā*, meanwhile, published correspondence attacking injustices allegedly perpetrated by the nawabs of Awadh:

[In the issue] of 24th July 1822...the editor, after expressly declaring that he had been unable to judge the truth of what was stated, brought forth a whole series of abusive and disparaging statements against the Oudh [Awadh] government, including a charge against the king of ordering the shops of the shawl-weavers in a certain quarter of the town to be razed to the ground without any cause, and their goods and implements of trade valued at Rs 10,000 to be tossed into the river. A prior number had accused His Majesty of the inconceivable folly of taking out of his wardrobe an immense quantity of valuable articles and setting them on fire merely to enjoy the pleasure of seeing them burn (Sanial 1934: 106).

The government of the nawab protested these dispatches, and the British Resident in Lucknow reported that these accusations had caused the nawab great anxiety, since they implied that the only remedy for his alleged mismanagement was the ultimate takeover of his state. This was a serious diplomatic problem for the government, but it was also a major challenge to its authority, for the natural assumption was that a powerful government would not allow the publication of something it did not approve. How, asked the Resident, could it permit such 'lucubrations of a press operating under its immediate eye at the very seat of its splendour and power' (Sanial 1934: 107)?

The British Indian government responded in 1823 by promulgating an ordinance that restricted the freedom of the press by requiring a licence to publish, much to the dismay of Ram Mohan Roy, normally pro-British, as well as his more recalcitrant compatriots. Roy drew up a memorial to the Calcutta Supreme Court in which he contended that, by its action against the press, the government had silenced some of its most loyal supporters, an argument used generations later by Indian nationalists. Ram Mohan went on to note that:

Another evil of equal importance in the eyes of a just Ruler is that it [the ordinance] will preclude the Natives from making the Government readily acquainted with the errors and injustice that may be committed by its executive officers in the various parts of this extensive country.... Every good Ruler, who is convinced of the imperfection of human nature...must be conscious of the great liability to error in managing the affairs of a vast empire; and therefore he will be anxious to afford every individual the readiest means of bringing to his notice whatever may require his interference. (Hay 1988: 29–30)

He then compared British policy to that of the Mughals:

Notwithstanding the despotic power of the Mogul Princes who formerly ruled over this country, and that their conduct was often cruel and arbitrary, yet the wise and virtuous among them always employed two intelligencers at the residences of their Nawabs or Lord Lieutenants, Akhbar-novees [*-nawīs*], or news-writers, published an account of what happened...which shows that even the Mogul Princes...were convinced that in a country so rich and replete with temptations, a restraint of some kind was absolutely necessary, to prevent the abuses that are so liable to flow from the possession of power.[13]

This is a masterful bit of criticism, since the British were fond of contrasting the justice of their rule with the despotism of the Mughals and other native rulers.

At this juncture, however, the British were more concerned about the seditious capability of the press than its potential as 'intelligencer'. If *akhbārs* served as a check on the despotic powers of imperial subordinates, they nevertheless did not have mass distribution. All the same, we can see that Ram Mohan's criticism of the British press regulations stems not only from a sense of violated civil liberty, but also from his knowledge of Mughal patronage of *akhbār* reporting.

This protest against press regulation brought an eventual response from the British Indian government. In the 1830s, Thomas Babington Macaulay, then law member of the government in Calcutta, commissioned a survey of indigenous manuscript 'newspapers':

The gazettes (*akhbārs*), which are commonly read by the Natives are in manuscript. To prepare these gazettes, it is the business of a numerous class of people who are constantly prowling for intelligence in the neighbourhood of every *cutchery* (court) and every *durbar* (courts of native princes). Twenty or thirty newswriters are constantly in attendance at the Palace of Delhi and at the [British] Residency. Each of these newswriters has among the richer natives several customers whom he daily supplies with all the scandal of the Court and the city. The number of manuscript gazettes daily dispatched from the single town of Delhi cannot of course be precisely known, but it is calculated by persons having good opportunities of information at a hundred and twenty. Under these circumstances it is perfectly clear that the influence of the manuscript gazettes on the native population must be very much more extensive than that of the printed papers in the native languages whose circulation in India by *dawk* [*ḍāk*] (post) does not now—1836—exceed three hundred.

> The manuscript gazettes...are filled with trivial details, with idle reports and often with extravagant falsehood suited to the capacity of ignorant and credulous readers. They are often scurrilous far beyond any papers that appear in print either in English or any native languages. They often contain abuse of the Government and its servants and sarcasms on our national character and manners.[14]

The government reworked the press law in 1835, reasoning that printed newspapers were probably less trouble than the hundreds of unregulated manuscript *akhbār* that still circulated. Under the new press regulations, an Indian press no longer needed a licence but could simply register, and had freedom to print what it would but was still held liable if it printed seditious matter.[15] It is worth noting that in Britain in this period, the press was still strapped by the stamp duty and by high taxation on paper, not repealed until the late 1850s (Koss 1981: 1). This Indian ordinance, consequently, could be considered a significant breakthrough for the freedom of the press.

What is one to make of all this? The impact of print is clearly the greatest in Calcutta, the British Indian capital, and in the other coastal Presidency cities, arguing in favour of British agency, in the standard foreign-impact-and-Indian-response paradigm. On the other hand, we have noted the continuity of the Mughal institution of *akhbār* reporting and its ambiguous legacy as both a source of government intelligence and as a curb on administrative high-handedness. Indian literati readily adopted the printing press, and newspapers and other periodicals emerged in many languages by the 1820s and 1830s, while the manuscript *akhbār* continued to circulate. The government first tried to regulate the press and then liberalized those controls in the face of its patent inability to limit the private circulation of information. Better to tolerate public dissemination of even critical news than to drive sedition underground. A sensible British solution, you might say, but Indian enterprise is obviously a player here too. Ram Mohan Roy, as a member of the Calcutta intelligentsia, may have been ahead of the curve, but his published criticism of the British for some of the administrative arbitrariness that the British were fond of pinning on native rulers was evidence of a nascent political consciousness differentiated from British interests.

Print in Delhi: From *Akhbār* to the News

What of Delhi, an 'up-country station' far removed from the cosmopolitan atmosphere of Calcutta and the other coastal Presidency cities? Delhi, by the early nineteenth century, was a shadow of its former self. Shahjahanabad, the great red-sandstone-walled city built by the Mughal emperor Shah Jahan in the mid-seventeenth century near the ruins of former cities of Delhi, had been sacked successively by the Persians, Afghans, and Marathas during the eighteenth century and finally fell to the British in 1803. It was still the seat of the Mughal emperor, now powerless and a pensioner of the British, while retaining some symbolic shreds of his former glory. The British Resident at the court of Delhi was the real head of the civil administration in the Mughal city, but successive Residents in the early nineteenth century were careful to maintain a facade of deferential behaviour towards the emperor (Blake 1991; Spear 1969).

The intellectual life of Delhi in this period was vibrant, not only because of Pax Britannica. In the late eighteenth century, Delhi had become a centre for the revival of Islamic learning. A number of madrasas flourished, and one of the leading lineages of ulama in the city had taken on the task of translating the Quran into Persian and Urdu, a significant step towards a broader dissemination of religious knowledge. Religious debate not only perpetuated the oral tradition, but lithographic presses printed leaflets and lengthier polemics addressed to sectarian rivals and, with the arrival of Christian missionaries, to those critics as well (Metcalf 1982: 16–52). Delhi was also home to a flourishing poetic culture in Persian and Urdu, centring around the last emperor, Bahadur Shah II 'Zafar', his court poet, Ibrahim 'Zauq', and Zauq's rival, Mirza Asadullah Khan 'Ghalib', and a host of others.

As might be expected, the Mughal capital city had a Persian newspaper, the *Sirāj ul-Akhbār* (founded in 1841), which was the mouthpiece of Bahadur Shah's court. Published weekly from the Red Fort, it was edited by Sayyid Abul Qasim Khan, the court chronicler. It followed the traditional pattern of the formulaic *akhbār*, now in printed form, and circulated among royal retainers and to a few British government officials. John Lawrence noted in 1848 that only thirty-four copies of it were printed, and that 'it has little in it beyond news of the palace and the King in particular, when he sleeps, eats, drinks, goes out, comes in and the like'. Lawrence found this material unenlightening, but the paper did contain interesting literary news, including examples of the latest compositions by Zauq and Zafar himself.[16]

The first two Urdu newspapers in Delhi, the *Delhi Urdū Akhbār* and the *Sayyid ul-Akhbār*, appeared in the late 1830s, significantly following the liberalized press ordinance of 1835. The *Delhi Urdū Akhbār* appeared first, in early 1837, the *Sayyid ul-Akhbār* somewhat later, perhaps as late as 1841; both were weeklies.[17] The *Sayyid ul-Akhbār* was founded by Sayyid Muhammad Khan, whose chief claim to fame was that he was the elder brother of Sayyid Ahmad Khan, a subjudge in the British service who went on to become the major religious and social reformer among Indian Muslims in the late nineteenth century and founder of Aligarh College, later Aligarh Muslim University (Lelyveld 1978). They were the grandsons of a former wazir at the Mughal court and were consequently well connected in the administrative and literary elites of the city. Sayyid Ahmad Khan wrote for this paper[18] and published some of his early works, including *Āthār us-Ṣanādīd* (an archeological study of Delhi), from its press. Sayyid Muhammad Khan died prematurely in 1845, and the press and the paper—its circulation having dropped from fifty to twenty-seven in 1848—both closed down in 1849 (Khan 1991: 111–6).

The *Delhi Urdū Akhbār* was a different story. Even though its circulation in the mid-1840s was a mere seventy-nine, this was good for the time. The paper survived until 1857, with a hiatus or two, with a circulation that fluctuated from a high of eighty to a low of forty-four.[19] The paper and its lithographic press were associated with the family of Maulvi Muhammad Akbar, a Shi'a *mujtahid* who conducted a madrasa in his home, and who was known for his learning and controversial ability.[20] Muhammad Akbar's son, Maulvi Muhammad Baqir (c. 1810–57) was educated by his father to be similarly skilled in controversy, and was acquainted with literary figures at the court, including the poet Zauq. He served as a government tahsildar for several years before taking up journalism. Muhammad Baqir was the sometime manager and long-time editor of the *Delhi Urdū Akhbār*, and its printer and publisher was Pandit Motilal, a Kashmiri who had attended Delhi College. The press was located in Muhammad Baqir's house near Kashmiri Gate and was a successful enterprise, printing books (translations, *dīvāns* of various poets), and religious textbooks (hadith, *tafsīr*), as well as periodicals.[21] Muhammad Baqir's son, Muḥammad Ḥusain 'Āzād' (1830–1910), attended Delhi College, worked with his father at the *Delhi Urdū Akhbār* in the 1850s and later became an illustrious Urdu litterateur, author of, among other things, *Āb-i Ḥayāt*, a classic (if idiosyncratic) history of Urdu poetry.[22]

The *Delhi Urdū Akhbār* contained a variety of news and comment on events at the Mughal court and in native states (Bhopal, Hyderabad, Gwalior, Awadh, Rampur, Punjab), as well as abroad: Persia, Turkey, Afghanistan, Britain, and Europe. There were reports on the wars with Burma and the Sikhs, a story about female infanticide in Rajputana. The journal routinely discussed the emperor's health, his donations to charity and visits to shrines, and the daily ceremonial of the court. For example, the following report appeared shortly after the accession of Bahadur Shah II in late 1837:

> On Juma't-ul-Widā' the emperor rode in state to the Jāmi'-Masjid.... The emperor's procession was still a sight to see. As soon as the prayers were finished, His Majesty gave a khil'at [robe of honour] of six pieces and three jewels to the imam. The nobles

and members of His Majesty's staff all received khil'ats or presents in accord with their rank. The princes and the ladies of the court also were not forgotten. Fairly large sums were given away to the poor in alms. The royal mukhtār [superintendent of the palace] himself supervised the distribution.... In the afternoon His Majesty held a darbār. He put on his robes and jewels. The nobles gave nadhrs [gifts of money] to His Majesty, the heir apparent and Tāj Maḥal Begam. The resident and other European officers came to pay their respects. The resident gave a nadhr of 121 gold muhurs to His Majesty and one of 5 ashrafīs to the heir apparent and received a khil'at and some jewels.[23]

A more critical view of the Mughal court is revealed in the following summary of reports from mid-1837:

The old emperor [Akbar Shah II, r. 1806–37] had not been thrifty. He had been reduced to selling his wife's jewellery [*sic*] and even offices of state. He sold, for instance, a necklace which was really worth Rs 40,000 for Rs 30,000. This happened in June, and in a few months' time the palace was once again in an uproar, for salaries had not been disbursed for some time. Rājah Sohan Lāl, the mukhtār, claimed that he had already spent a couple of lakhs [100,000s] from his own pocket. All the princes clamoured for money, and the emperor every now and then lost his temper. For instance, when Mirzā Tīmūr Shāh pressed him hard for money to pay his servants, the emperor remarked, 'Pay them by selling your clothes!'[24]

In addition to the death of one emperor and the accession of another, 1837 was a year of famine. The *Delhi Urdū Akhbār* reported extensively on the suffering of the poor of the city and surroundings:

From Surat, Ajmer, Kota, and Ludhiana in the west to Calcutta in the east, disturbing news poured in of misery, starvation, and death. As early as July 1837 the effects of a drought had been felt. Akbar Shah II ordered public prayers for rain and arranged to feed a hundred poor every day. The prayers seem to have been partially answered, for there was rain in Qutb Sahib, which gladdened the heart of the old monarch. But it was not enough to avert disaster; cases of theft in the city and robberies on the road increased in number.... The situation grew worse and worse every day. Both the English and the vernacular newspapers were full of the news of dacoities; villages were looted and sometimes set on fire.... The post was looted on some occasions and trade came to a standstill.... On October 5th, the people of Delhi also grew desperate and looted shops in [various bazaars]. The situation got out of control. The boats bringing corn and merchandize were looted on the ghats. Indian soldiers were summoned to restore order.... Mothers could not see their children starving and there were cases of women taking their babies in their arms and jumping into wells to commit suicide...[25]

The editor tried to authenticate all stories that were sent in, and he instituted a letter column to bring grievances of the public to the attention of the authorities. Given the conditions of scarcity, rising criticism of the government was understandable. The following letter protested against the British policy of monopolizing the postal service, raising rates, and imposing other taxes:

How will the poor be able to pay for the British post? If the government, moved by avarice, wanted to establish a monopoly of posts, it should have kept its prices lower than they are now. This would not have weighed heavily on the people and everyone would have given his letters to it gladly.... The special commissioners, who have been appointed to resume the mu'āfī [tax free] lands, are a terror. On the least excuse and the slightest pretext they confiscate land which was granted in perpetuity.... Another more wonderful news is that the members of the bureau want to take 2 per cent on the agricultural produce of the land on the excuse that they want to repair bad roads. How strange it is that they do not heal broken hearts, but they think of repairing roads! The government is not content with this; they have increased the chowkīdārī cess...[26]

The *Delhi Urdū Akhbār* criticized both the Mughals and the British, but recognized where the real power lay, and was consequently more critical of the British and somewhat indulgent of the hapless inhabitant of the Red Fort, blaming the emperor's subordinates for incompetence or corruption:

Maulvi Muhammad Taqi who had last month been appointed *mukhtar* at the royal court by offering a *nazrana* [gift/gratuity] has now resigned his job having fully experienced the actual state of affairs—lack of financial resources, huge expenditure and the amount of debt (exceeding forty thousand rupees). His complaint is that the people working at the court are greedy and do not allow any honest Mukhtar to stay at his post.... Strange stories are being told about the conditions in the Royal Fort. No help or redress is available to the poor people against the high-handedness of the court officials. Salaries have not been paid for the past five months.[27]

The paper also reported routine government matters, such as decisions of the district magistrate's court, births and deaths, and government circulars and notices. More colourful descriptions highlighted the tour of the Governor General, Lord Auckland.[28]

Cultural news also appeared in the pages of the *Delhi Urdū Akhbār*: reports of *mushā'iras*, poetic assemblies held at the homes of Delhi notables such as the Sadr us-Sudur, Mufti Sadruddin Khan 'Azurda', with samples of the poetry recited on a given evening. The poetry of Ghalib, Momin, Zauq—the cream of the literary elite of the city—appeared, not to mention the ghazals of Zafar, the emperor, in almost every issue.[29] As at the court, so in the *Delhi Urdū Akhbār*, Zauq was favoured over Ghalib. The paper reported when Mirza Naushah (Ghalib) was accused of running a gambling den:

It has been heard that a large number of notorious gamblers have been arrested from the house of Mirza Naushah (Mirza Ghalib) in Gali Qasim Jan—Hashim Ali Khan, for example, who had once been committed to sessions. Mirza Naushah's house had become, it is alleged, a den of gamblers but no police officer had so far the courage to interfere and put an end to the nefarious activities going on there. A new police officer, a Sayyid by caste and a remarkably courageous man, has recently been appointed as the Kotwal in the area.[30]

Delhi College also received attention in the *Delhi Urdū Akhbār*. Muhammad Baqir's interest in Delhi College preceded his son's attendance there. His press had published the college's textbooks and translations before the college established its own press, and he had attacked Maulvi Jafar Ali, who taught Shi'a theology there, as unfit for the job. The paper reported on the annual prize days at the college, including the one when Sadruddin Khan Azurda's medal was awarded to Maulvi Nazir Ahmad (1833–1912), another student who went on to a brilliant career as a government official, scholar, reformer, and author.[31]

The *Delhi Urdū Akhbār*, in other words, contained the kind of information found in traditional *akhbārs*: coverage of the palace and reports sent in from neighbouring states by correspondents. *Akhbār nawīs*, as we have seen, were ubiquitous at native courts as well as on the verandas of British courts and collectorates. But the paper also served as a gazette of British government notices, as well as an outlet for the airing of public opinion through letters. The editor did not hesitate to criticize the British and the Mughals for actions he deemed unjust. The publication of poetry meant that the paper doubled as a literary journal and a subtle outlet for social, religious, and political commentary that could be expressed poetically without the British fully comprehending it. Even a cursory reading of the *Delhi Urdū Akhbār*'s contents is enough to convince us that something significant had occurred with this publication: the older *akhbār* forms, both formulaic and editorial, are in evidence here, but so is a newer political, even polemical, press with the enlistment of public opinion and attempts to sway government policies. This had happened earlier in Bengal, but now political discourse in simple but elegant Urdu was emanating from the Mughal heartland. Maulvi Muhammad Baqir's allegiance to the Mughal court and its culture ultimately outweighed his clear-eyed assessment of its incompetence. In 1857, the *Delhi Urdū Akhbār* backed the revolt, and when Delhi was retaken by the British, Muhammad Baqir was among those executed.[32]

Another aspect of the literary and intellectual life of the city of Delhi in the 1820s through the 1850s was the creation of Delhi College. In the 1820s, the local administration took an interest in one of the main madrasas of the city and, adding to it an institution for instruction in English and Western sciences, founded Delhi College. This was a unique institution where the oriental literatures of the madrasa regimen and a Western-style curriculum were both taught through the medium of Urdu. The committee in charge of the college was composed of local notables and literati as well as British administrators. The college had its own press from the mid-1840s, the Maṭba 'ul-'Ulūm, that printed textbooks (both translations and originals), a weekly newspaper, *Qirān us-Sa'ādain*, and two literary and scientific journals, *Fawā'id un-Nāẓirīn*, a fortnightly, and the monthly *Muḥibb-i Hind* (Ḥaq 1962; Minault 1999: 119–34). *Qirān us-Sa'ādain* is an Arabic astronomical term denoting the conjunction of the two benefic planets, Jupiter and Venus. Founded in 1845 by the principal of Delhi College, Dr Aloys Sprenger, *Qirān us-Sa'ādain* referred metaphorically to the interaction of two cultures, Eastern and Western, in the intellectual life of the college.[33]

Muḥibb-i Hind was begun in 1847 and lasted for about five years, edited by Master Ramchandra, a professor of mathematics and science at Delhi College and one of its intellectual leaders.[34] He wrote an original treatise on algebra that received favourable notice in Europe and ultimately won him an award from the government.[35] In his writing and editing of *Muḥibb-i Hind*, Ramchandra gave evidence of a voracious and eclectic mind that also reflected some of the ideas that were being discussed at Delhi College and among the intelligentsia of Delhi in the 1840s and '50s. Titles of articles written by Ramchandra that appeared in the journal exemplify the range of topics that interested him and his readers: 'The Divisibility of Matter—A Strange Description from the Researches of European Scientists and Scholars', 'A Description of a Diving Bell by which means Things Sunken in the Sea may be Retrieved', articles on astronomy, on the work of Sir Isaac Newton, and a discussion of human reason. Ramchandra also included articles about ancient Greece ('On Demosthenes'), about other Asian cultures ('On Confucius'), and serialized translations of Lane's *Customs of the Modern Egyptians*, and a biography of Shah Abbas of Persia. Other serializations included a translation of Elphinstone's *Kingdom of Caubul*, and an original publication of the college press, *Tārīkh-i Yūsufī*, the travels of Yusuf Khan Kambalposh to England.[36] Ramchandra even took on the scholarship of pandits in 'A Discussion of the Mistakes that Indian Scholars have made in Various Studies of the Shastras'. He also discussed new technologies of agriculture and irrigation and summarized works of history and popular science. One of the regular features in this periodical, devoted largely to the dissemination of new knowledge about East and West, was a selection of Urdu poetry from local *mushā'iras*.[37]

Muḥibb-i Hind endured for several years, with a circulation of fifty or sixty that fell off sharply after Ramchandra's conversion to Christianity in 1852, which also caused a scandal at the college and withdrawal of many students (M. Ṣiddīqī 1962: 107–12; M. Ṣiddīqī 1957: 320–48). Its early success, however, demonstrates that there was a market within the literate elite of the city for its synthesis of information about oriental and occidental cultures, wrapped in a vernacular package. This cursory survey of its contents might lead us to conclude that Western science and technology had triumphed in a definitive way, but that is not the whole story. Towards the conclusion of his massive study, *Empire and Information*, C.A. Bayly notes:

> The company's dominion was also an 'empire of opinion' in which Indians were coerced by the reputation for scientific and cultural superiority of their conquerors.... North Indians were late starters in printing and lithography, yet the existence of sophisticated patterns of political debate and the adaptability of older communities of knowledge ensured that the book, the pamphlet, the newspaper, and the British post office had been pressed into use by critics of colonial rule and by those who challenged the West's cultural domination nearly sixty years before the formal date of birth of Indian nationalism. In fact, a study of the information order leads us to query the whole current chronology of the development of that nationalism (Bayly 1996: 365–6).

Returning to some of the questions posed at the outset: what did the increased availability of printed newspapers and periodicals reveal about the market for information in north India in the early nineteenth century? What was the impact of the content of such periodicals on political and cultural consciousness? Did the readers of the periodical press participate in a colonial hybrid culture, or was the emerging arena of vernacular discourse an example of the creative naturalization of Western influences while maintaining links to traditional forms of expression? Judging from the fragmentary evidence presented here, it appears that Indians adopted the Western technology of print on their own terms. Far from being dominated or overwhelmed by Western ways of doing and thinking, literate Indians maintained continuities with their own ways of transmitting information and engaged in selective responses to Western influence. In making Western institutions—like the periodical press—their own, Indians showed their enthusiasm for Western technology while maintaining a critical stance toward British policies. In their adoption of political journalism, Indians infused editorial writing with some of the quality of confidential akhbārs, intermingled with the poetry of the mushā'ira that contained its own subversive subtext. The British may have regarded this vernacular discourse with a certain disdain, but they did so suspecting that they were missing something. They were.

Notes

[1] The repositories consulted are the National Archives of India, New Delhi [NAI], the India Office Library, London [IOL], and the Sajun Lal Collection of newspapers at Osmania University Library in Hyderabad, India.

[2] I am indebted to Bayly 1996, and to *Modern Asian Studies* [MAS] 27: 1 (February 1993), containing the articles by Bayly, Fisher, and Robinson cited below.

[3] Kautilya's *Arthashastra*, cited in Embree 1988: 242–3.

[4] The Mughal system of news reporting is described in detail in Fisher 1993 and Sarkar 1967. Fisher (p. 46) defines the terms as follows: '*Akhbār* stems from the Arabic root kh-b-r, "to know"...*Khabar*...came to denote variously: "news, information, advices, intelligence, notification, announcement; report, rumor, fame; story, account". *Akhbār* (the Arabic "broken plural" form of *khabar*...) came to mean "histories, tales, annals, gazettes, news, relations, advices, chronicles, traditions; a newspaper".... The other part of this title, *nawīs* (or... *nigār*), means "writer". While...today *akhbār* commonly means a printed or lithographed newspaper (thus *akhbār nawīs* means an editor or reporter...), the concept of *akhbār* has historically encompassed a broader semantic range.'

[5] Sarkar 1967: 134, citing Jadunath Sarkar's *Anecdotes of Aurangzeb*. For an example of a newsletter from the court of the nawab of Awadh from 1839, see Fisher 1987: 261–2.

[6] Khan 1991: 30, 32–3, citing the *Jām-i Jahān-Numā* of 23 March 1825.

[7] Robinson 1993: 234–7; for a detailed discussion of this phenomenon in Egypt, *see* Mitchell 1988, Ch. 5.

[8] For the complexities and the shorthand (*shekasta*) of this script, *see* Hanaway and Spooner 1995.

[9] For a discussion of the curriculum at one college, *see* Minault 2000.

[10] Natarajan 1962: 57–60; Sanial 1934: 105–14; Chandan 1992; Aslam Siddiqi 1947: 160–6.

[11] Note the name: it is the Bengali equivalent of *harkāra*, the messenger or spy of the Mughal information network.

[12] See Roy's 'In Defense of Hindu Women,' in Hay 1988: 25–9.

[13] 'Appeal to the King in Council against Press Regulations', cited in Fisher 1993: 81; cf. Sanial, January 1928, 122–40; July 1928, 453–63, quote on p. 453.

[14] Minute by T.B. Macaulay, 2 September 1836, cited in Fisher 1993: 77; and Sanial, July 1928, 454.

[15] Natarajan 1962: 63; texts of press ordinances of 1823 and 1835 in ibid., pp. 325–36.

[16] Khan 1991: 117–9; for an Urdu translation of excerpts from the *Sirāj ul-Akhbār* of 1844–8, *see* Niẓāmī 1964.

[17] There is a difference of opinion about the date of the first issue of the *Delhi Urdū Akhbār*, ranging from 1836 to 1838. According to the calculations of Khan (1991: 64), it was 23 February 1837. As for the *Sayyid ul-Akhbār*, Khan (1991: 112) states that it appeared in 1841, while Natarajan (1962: 69) places it in 1837. M. Ṣiddīqī cites evidence that it appeared in 1837, perhaps before the *Delhi Urdū Akhbār* (1962: 103–4).

[18] If any copies of this paper survive, I have not seen them.

[19] Founded as the *Delhi Akhbār*, by May 1840 it had changed its name (Khan 1991: 66, 74; M. Ṣiddīqī 1962: 100–2; Fārūqī 1972: 93).

[20] M. Akbar founded another Urdu weekly, the *Maẓhar ul-Ḥaq*, published between 1844 and 1850, a religious journal devoted to Shi'a causes and controversies (Khan 1991: 110–11; M. Ṣiddīqī 1962: 105–6).

[21] Sources for this history of the *Delhi Urdū Akhbār* [DUA] include Khan 1991: 65–110; M. Ṣiddīqī 1957: 266–70; Sajun Lal 1950: 16–44; Fārūqī 1972; Files of DUA in Sajun Lal Collection, Hyderabad, and in NAI.

[22] Muḥammad Ḥusain Āzād's *Āb-i Ḥayāt* has recently been translated into English (2001); *see* also Sadiq 1965.

[23] Qureshi 1943: 289–90, summarizing DUA of 29 December 1837 and 5 January 1838; cf. Sajun Lal 1950; for more on late Mughal court ritual, *see* Minault 2003.

[24] Qureshi 1943: 284, summarizing DUA of 16 June, 29 September, and 21 August 1837; n.b.: the issues of DUA cited by Qureshi were not available to me, hence I cite his summaries realizing that they are not the equivalent of translations from the original sources.

[25] Qureshi 1943: 290–1, summarizing DUA reports from June to December 1837.

[26] Qureshi 1943: 293, quoting a letter in DUA of 9 June 1837.

[27] Khan 1991: 75, quoting DUA of 1 March 1840 and 12 May 1841.

[28] Qureshi 1943: 288, summarizing DUA of 23 February 1838; for other coverage of Lord Auckland's tour, *see* his sister's travel account, Eden 1978.

[29] Sajun Lal 1950: 21–3, 27, citing DUA for 8 August and 21 February 1852; Sajun Lal 1942: 131–2; for Azurda, *see* Iṣlāḥī 1977.

[30] Khan 1991: 84–5, citing DUA of 15 August 1841; cf. M. Ṣiddīqī 1957: 273.

[31] Khan 1991: 66–7; for Nazir Ahmad, *see* I. Ṣiddīqī 1971; Beg 1944,1: 13–87.

[32] DUA for 1857, files in the Mutiny Papers, NAI.

[33] Unfortunately, very few copies of this journal survive. I have seen only three issues in the Sajun Lal Collection.

[34] On Ramchandra, *see* Qidwā'ī 1961; and Ja'far 1960.

[35] Ramchandra 1859; cf. Habib and Raina 1989.

[36] See Michael H. Fisher, 'Britain in the Urdu Tongue: Accounts by Early Nineteenth-Century Visitors', in this volume.

[37] Qidwā'ī 1961: 178–94; Habib and Raina 1993: 348–68; *Muḥibb-i Hind*, nos. 14–37 (some missing nos.), (Sept. 1848–Aug./Sept. 1850), IOL.

Bibliography

Anderson, Benedict, *Imagined Communities: Reflections on the Origin and Spread of Nationalism*, London: Verso, 1983.

Āzād, Muḥammad Ḥusain, *Āb-e Ḥayāt: Shaping the Canon of Urdu Poetry*, trans. and ed. by Frances Pritchett in association with Shamsur Rahman Faruqi, Delhi: Oxford University Press, 2001.

Bayly, C.A., 'Knowing the Country: Empire and Information in India', *Modern Asian Studies* [MAS], 27 (1), 1993, 3–43.

______, *Empire and Information: Intelligence Gathering and Social Communication in India, 1780–1870*, Cambridge: Cambridge University Press, 1996.

Beg, Farḥatullāh, 'Ḍākṭar Nazīr Aḥmad kī Kahānī, Kuchh Merī aur Kuchh Unkī Zubānī', in *Maẓāmīn-i Farḥat*, vol. 1, Hyderabad, Deccan: Abdul Haq Akademi, 1944.

Blake, Stephen P., *Shahjahanabad: The Sovereign City in Mughal India, 1639–1739*, Cambridge: Cambridge University Press, 1991.

Chandan, Gurbachan, *Jām-i Jahān Numā: Urdū Ṣaḥāfat kī Ibtidā*, New Delhi: Maktaba-i Jami'a, 1992.

Cohn, B.S., *Colonialism and Its Forms of Knowledge*, Princeton: Princeton University Press, 1996.

Eden, Emily, *Up the Country: Letters Written to Her Sister from the Upper Provinces of India*, London: Curzon Press, reprint, 1978.

Eisenstein, Elizabeth, *The Printing Press as an Agent of Change: Communications and Cultural Transformations in Early Modern Europe*, Cambridge: Cambridge University Press, 1979.

Embree, A.T. (ed.), *Sources of Indian Tradition*, vol. I, New York: Columbia University Press, 2nd edn., 1988.

Fārūqī, Khwāja Aḥmad (ed.), *Dehli Urdū Akhbār (1840)*, Delhi: Urdu Department, Delhi University, 1972.

Fisher, Michael, *A Clash of Cultures: Awadh, the British and the Mughals*, Delhi: Manohar, 1987.

______, 'The Office of *Akhbār Nawīs*: The Transition from Mughal to British Forms', MAS, 27(1), 1993, 45–82.

Habib, S. Irfan, and Dhruv Raina, 'Cultural Foundations of a Nineteenth Century Mathematical Project', *Economic and Political Weekly* [EPW], 24 (37), 16 September 1989, 2082–6.

______, 'The Discourse on Scientific Rationality: A Study of Master Ramchandra', in T. Niranjana, P. Sudhir, and V. Dhareshwar (eds.), *Interrogating Modernity: Culture and Colonialism in India*, Calcutta: Seagull, 1993, 348–68.

Hanaway, William, and Brian Spooner, *Reading Nastaliq: Persian and Urdu Hands from 1500 to the Present*, Costa Mesa, CA: Mazda Publishers, 1995.

Ḥaq, ʻAbdul, *Marḥūm Dehlī Kālej*, Karachi: Anjuman-i Taraqqī-i Urdu, 1962.

Hay, Stephen (ed.), *Sources of Indian Tradition*, vol. 2, New York: Columbia University Press, 2nd edn., 1988.

Iṣlāḥī, ʻAbdur Raḥmān Parvāz, *Muftī Ṣadruddīn Āzurda*, New Delhi: Maktaba-i Jamiʻa, 1977.

Jaʻfar, Sayyida, *Māsṭer Ramchandra aur Urdū Naṣr ke Irtiqā' meṅ unkā Ḥissa*, Hyderabad, Deccan: Abu'l Kalam Azad Oriental Research Institute, 1960.

Kai-Kā'ūs ibn Iskandar (Prince of Gurgān), *The Qābūs Nāma* [AD 1082], trans. by Reuben Levy as *A Mirror for Princes*, New York: E.P. Dutton, 1951.

Kesavan, B.S., *History of Printing and Publishing in India*, vol. 1: *South Indian Origins of Printing and its Efflorescence in Bengal*, New Delhi: National Book Trust, 1985.

Khan, Nadir Ali, *A History of Urdu Journalism*, Delhi: Idarah-i Adabiyat-i Delli, 1991.

Koss, Stephen, *The Rise and Fall of the Political Press in Britain*, vol. 1: *The Nineteenth Century*, Chapel Hill: University of North Carolina Press, 1981.

Lelyveld, David, *Aligarh's First Generation: Muslim Solidarity in British India*, Princeton: Princeton University Press, 1978.

Metcalf, Barbara, *Islamic Revival in British India, Deoband, 1860–1900*, Princeton: Princeton University Press, 1982.

Minault, Gail, 'Delhi College and Urdu', *Annual of Urdu Studies*, 14 (1999), 119–34.

______, '*Qirān us-Sa'ādain*: The Dialogue Between Eastern and Western Learning at Delhi College', in Jamal Malik (ed.), *Perspectives of Mutual Encounters in South Asian History, 1760–1860*, Leiden: Brill, 2000, 260–77.

______, 'The Emperor's Old Clothes: Robing and Sovereignty in Late Mughal and Early British India', in Stewart Gordon (ed.), *Robes of Honour: Khil'at in Pre-Colonial and Colonial India*, Delhi: Oxford University Press, 2003, 125–39.

Mitchell, Timothy, *Colonising Egypt*, Cambridge: Cambridge University Press, 1988.

Natarajan, S., *A History of the Press in India*, Bombay: Asia Publishing House, 1962.

Niẓāmī, Khwāja Ḥasan, *Bahādur Shāh kā Roznāmcha*, 4th ed., New Delhi: Khwaja Awlad Kitab Ghar, 1964.

Qidwā'ī, Ṣadīqur Raḥmān, *Māsṭar Rāmchandar*, Delhi: Urdu Department, Delhi University, 1961.

Qureshi, Ishtiaq Husain, 'A Year in Pre-Mutiny Delhi (1837)', *Islamic Culture* [IC], 17 (3), July 1943, 282–97.

Ramchandra, *A Treatise on Problems of Maxima and Minima Solved by Algebra*, London: Wm. H. Allen & Co., 1859.

Robinson, Francis, 'Technology and Religious Change: Islam and the Impact of Print', MAS, 27 (1), 1993, 229–51.

______, 'Islam and the Impact of Print in South Asia', in Nigel Crook (ed.), *The Transmission of Knowledge in South Asia*, Delhi: Oxford University Press, 1996, 62–97.

Sadiq, Muhammad, *Muhammad Husain Azad: His Life and Works*, Lahore: West-Pak Publishing Co., 1965.

Sajun Lal, K., 'A few newspapers of the pre-Mutiny period', *Indian Historical Records Commission*, 19 (1942), 128–32.

———, 'The Delhi Urdū Akhbār and Its Importance', *IC*, 24 (1), January 1950, 16–44.

Sanial, S.C., 'The Newspapers of the Later Mughal Period', *IC*, 2 (1), January 1928, 122–40; 2 (3), July 1928, 453–63.

———, 'The First Persian Newspapers of India: A Peep into their Contents', *IC*, 8 (1), January 1934, 105–14.

Sarkar, Jagdish Narayan, 'News-Writers of Mughal India', in *The Indian Press*, S.P. Sen (ed.), Calcutta: Institute of Historical Studies, 1967, 110–45.

Sharp, H. (ed.), *Selections from Educational Records*, Pt. 1, 1781–1839, New Delhi: National Archives of India, reprint, 1965.

Siddiqi, Aslam, 'The First Urdu Newspaper', *IC*, 21 (2), April 1947, 160–6.

Ṣiddīqī, Iftikhār Aḥmad, *Maulvī Nazīr Aḥmad Dehlavī: Aḥwāl-o-Āṣār*, Lahore: Majlis-i Taraqqi-i Adab, 1971.

Ṣiddīqī, M. 'Atīq, *Hindustānī Akhbār-navīsī (Kampanī ke 'Ahd Meṅ)*, Aligarh: Anjuman-i Taraqqi-i Urdu (Hind), 1957.

———, *Ṣūbah-i Shimālī-o-Maghrabī ke Akhbārāt-o-Maṭbū'āt*, Aligarh: Anjuman-i Taraqqi-i Urdu (Hind), 1962.

Spear, Percival, *Twilight of the Mughuls*, New Delhi: Oriental Reprints, 1969 [1951].

Britain in the Urdu Tongue: Accounts by Early Nineteenth-Century Visitors[1]

Michael H. Fisher

From the early nineteenth century onward, travellers to Britain wrote in Urdu about that country, which was conquering and ruling India. This essay analyses the two earliest Urdu books about journeys to Britain, written autobiographically by Yūsuf Khān and Karīm Khān, located in the contexts of the ongoing Indian presence in Britain and of British imperialism in India.[2] Both authors were upper-middle-class males of families originally from Afghanistan. The former went as a tourist, the latter as a diplomat. Both observed British institutions first-hand, interacting with Britons of all social classes, and studying Britain's society, politics, history, and culture. In particular, they critically assessed British religious and gender beliefs and practices. However, they adopted different attitudes towards the growing and diverse Indian population in Britain (see Visram 1984 and 2002, Viswanathan 1998, Fisher 1997a and 2003). Through their conversations and actions, they also personally represented India and Indians directly to Britons at a time of expanding British imperialism and 'Orientalism'. By using their own writings (neither available in full English translation even today), supported by other primary sources, we can recover their deeds and perspectives, long overshadowed by Anglocentric accounts of colonialism.[3] Their books 'provide historical evidence of how imperial power was staged at home and how it was contested by colonial "natives" at the heart of the empire itself' (Burton 1997: 1).

Yūsuf Khān 'Kambalposh' travelled to Europe (1836–8) out of *dekhne kā shauq* ('a desire to observe'). He wrote what he called his *Tārīkh-i Yūsufī* ('History of Yūsuf'), promising an accurate autobiographical account of his experiences and encounters with all levels of British society, ranging from elites to streetwalkers (Yūsuf Khān 1983: 98). An unconventional thinker, he debated people of many religions—including Christian, Jewish, and traditional Islamic—critiquing each of them in terms of his own distinctive perspective. He particularly recorded his interactions with British women, so different from gender relations he was familiar with in India. He took little notice of the other Indians in Britain, however. Throughout, Yūsuf Khān represented himself as the central actor in his adventures in Britain, someone who successfully challenged the established cultural categories.

Karīm Khān journeyed to Europe (1839–41), reaching London relatively soon after Yūsuf Khān had left. While he also toured the Occident, he mainly had a diplomatic mission: representing a relative, Nawab Hasan Ali Khan of Jhajjar, before the East India Company's court of directors. In London, he operated at many levels. He persistently (albeit fruitlessly) sought to manoeuvre through the formal bureaucratic and political barriers that British colonialism constructed to frustrate Indian diplomats at the capital. The veracity of his words and deeds in this endeavour is supported by official records in the East India Company's archive. Simultaneously, Karīm Khān personally lobbied powerful Britons of the East India Company's court of directors and Parliament to advance his master's cause informally. His recorded encounters with British women were less extensive than those of Yūsuf Khān. However, Karīm Khān moved cordially among several circles of Urdu-speaking Indians in London, participating in their various social and cultural occasions, and showing solidarity with the members of his own social class among the diversity of Indians present there. He, too, centred his book on his own actions and observations in the West.

These two men apparently never met and wrote independently for Urdu readers. Some aspects of their respective books are strikingly similar, others contrast significantly. Both presented their work as non-fiction, as accurate accounts of their actions and observations, although neither published his book. Both made their own pointed judgements about British customs and values, remaining sceptical of British assertions of moral superiority but wondering at their technical accomplishments and gender relations. Further, both noted with concern Britain's ever-enhanced imperial panoply and, in the case of Karīm Khān, injustices. Yet each chose to socialize in London very differently: one primarily with Britons, the other with Indians there as well. They selected somewhat different writing and literary styles. Yūsuf Khān, who spoke English fairly fluently, nevertheless followed the established *safar-nāma* genre, writing a prose running commentary illustrated with occasional Persian or Urdu verses. Karīm Khān, who knew virtually no English, nevertheless adopted more of a European-style detailed travel journal. He kept a brief record of the people he met or the events of that day (which he identified by Christian and Hijri dates, Urdu day of the week, and place). He further inserted longer commentaries and explanations, with occasional Urdu and Persian verses where he felt appropriate, and added extended accounts of Britain's history and other institutions at the end of his book. Virtually all earlier Indians who chose to write about their journeys to Britain selected either Persian or English, but both these men from Afghan families chose the vernacular Urdu. This reflects both the larger ongoing shift within India from Persian to Urdu literary culture during the thirties and the forties of the nineteenth century and also, to some extent, these men's particular location within Indian Muslim society.

Placed within the environment of the larger Indian presence in Britain, these two Urdu accounts suggest the complexity and internal tensions and contradictions of the imperial process. These accounts also reveal how these authors and other Indian visitors could, to a modest degree, influence British notions of India through conversations and social intercourse. Karīm Khān in particular worked for years to reverse British colonial policies. These two books further demonstrate the ways Urdu speakers created their own body of knowledge about the colonial metropole, in the face of spreading British colonialism in—and Orientalism about—India.

Transnational and Colonial Contexts

The British empire provided a new arena within which novel modes of transoceanic transportation developed. These enabled Urdu speakers to move more easily throughout the globe. The British empire was not, however, the first source of transnational routes for Muslim peoples. Islamic traditions of exploration, and of trading and pilgrimage, meant that there had for centuries been long-established patterns of widespread movement, with rich and extensive works of literature about those journeys. Several distinguished authors have studied Muslim travel literature.[4] Few scholars, however, have as yet written about one fascinating aspect of such literature: accounts by early Urdu speakers from colonized India about their experiences in colonizing Britain.

Indians had been going to Britain about as long as Britons had been sailing directly to the subcontinent, from the early seventeenth century onward. From the mid-eighteenth century, however, a flood of British soldiers, colonial officials, and merchants entered India, while the counter-movement to Britain of Indians also increased significantly. In the early nineteenth century, up to

1,200 Indian seamen and servants went to Britain annually (although the number varied considerably). Dozens of Indian diplomats, scholars, noblemen and women, students, and the wives and children of Britons also visited or settled there. British authorities constructed images of Britain for Indian audiences to support colonialism. But Indian visitors also brought back their own images of Britain, although these spread unevenly in India and were overwhelmed by British colonial representations of the West. By the late nineteenth century, many more Indians would make this journey, but their expectations would be more deeply shaped by British colonialism than earlier visitors (see Raychaudhuri 1988, Viswanathan 1989, Mukhopadhyay 2002).

Clearly, the effects of Indians in Britain and Britons in India during the early nineteenth century were very unequal. On the one hand, British imperialism conquered and ruled India: the East India Company began a series of annexations from 1757 until 1857 that ended in the British Raj (Fisher 1997b and 1998). In all, a million square miles of India came, largely through military force, under the direct rule of the British. The remaining half a million square miles came under British indirect rule, through the many 'princes' of India. Both Yūsuf Khān and Karīm Khān served Indian princes; nevertheless they both explicitly expressed their recognition of the British monarch's sovereignty.

On the other hand, Indians largely travelled to Britain on British-owned and operated ships, often, like Karīm Khān, as petitioners before British authorities. A relatively small number compared to the British population, they nonetheless had some voice in British public discourse about India and its peoples. Indian visitors negotiated roles in British society which changed over time as attitudes towards issues like race and gender shifted both in India and in Britain, in direct consequence of British imperialism (see Bolt 1971, Rich 1990, Sinha 1995). Their experiences of Britain had profound effects on them, which they conveyed in oral or written form to Indians at home. In many ways, British authorities had to respond to this Indian production of knowledge about Britain.

The growing force of British imperialism profoundly shaped British attitudes towards Asian cultures and peoples. Said and Pratt, by highlighting the ways in which Europeans 'appropriated the Orient' and sought to prevent Indians from representing themselves, did much to demonstrate the power of Western constructions of India (Said 1978, Pratt 1992). They and their followers asserted that even the general society of the home nation was directed to support the colonial process, often against the better interests of its general populace, by the picture of the colonized which these European 'Orientalist' works exclusively painted. Cannadine argued for a very different British image of the colonized, one which primarily reflected indigenous British notions of class hierarchy rather than race (Cannadine 2001). Much of the information and many of the values about India eventually reached Britain through European scholars and officials.[5] While British writing about the colonized no doubt dominated the discourse in Britain, Indian voices continually challenged its hegemony. Furthermore, these British constructions of 'India' and 'Indians' in the abstract did not always translate directly into British practices towards the Indian individuals living among them.[6]

Further, Anglocentric analyses do not sufficiently stress the agency of Indians, tending rather to make them appear mainly as victims and objects of scrutiny. Tanika Sarkar critiqued this:

> Most recent works on cultural developments in the colonial period tend to assume the operations of a single, monolithic colonial discourse with fully hegemonistic capabilities. All that Indians could possibly do was to either form a secondary, derivative discourse that simply extended the message of the master-text, or refuse and resist its positions and language.... This position...necessarily robs colonized Indians of effective agency and evacuates an especially complicated historical problem of all complexities... (Sarkar 1993: 61).

Some scholarship has indeed recognized greater Indian (and African) agency through participation in the public sphere, especially the ways they regarded their power to narrate and represent their own experiences in their own terms as powerful modes of resistance to European cultural domination (Abu-Lughod 1963, as-Saffar 1991, Hasan 1993, Said 1993, Bhabha 1994).

In addition, Indian impressions of Britain also changed over time with colonialism. Over the late nineteenth century, many other Indians made this voyage to Britain. Partha Chatterjee contrasts the late eighteenth-century Indian visitor, who went with no 'prior mental map imprinted on his mind telling him how England ought to be seen', with the later nineteenth-century visitor who did (Chatterjee 1998: 1330–6). Our two Urdu authors came chronologically in-between, with some prior expectations but also open to new impressions as well, with admiration for aspects of British culture but resistance to British claims of moral superiority.

Therefore, we must locate these first two Urdu accounts within the changing contexts both of Indians in Britain and also of British colonialism in India. The earlier and the later colonial periods proved very different for visitors from India in Britain. During the visits of Yūsuf Khān and Karīm Khān, British attitudes had not yet hardened against Indians in their midst as they would following the bloody events of 1857, the rise of pseudo-scientific social Darwinism with its construction of race as biological and immutable, and the penetration of imperialism into virtually all aspects of British and Indian societies. This left these Indian authors more scope to define their own roles and express their own voices in the British public sphere. They could also convey their assessments of Britain to Indian readers less indoctrinated by the cultural domination of the British Raj.

Yūsuf Khān, an Early Tourist and Urdu Author about Britain

Throughout his life, Yūsuf Khān (c.1803–61) chose to challenge established cultural categories in search of wider knowledge and experiences. He studied English language and British culture, which increasingly dominated in India; yet he also chose to live most of his life in Indian princely states which retained their distinctive cultural and political identities. Born into a Sunni Afghan family that had settled in Hyderabad (Deccan), Yūsuf Khān began searching from the age of twelve for a truly fulfilling religious path.[7] Finally, he chose what he called the *mazhab-i sulaimānī* (the 'religion' or 'creed' of 'Solomon'): 'the best of all religions/creeds' (Yūsuf Khān, 1983: 133, 158). Others have glossed this as a combination of deism and hedonism, with Yūsuf Khān as its originator and main exponent.[8] Yūsuf Khān's pen-names, Kambalposh and its variant, Kammalposh (literally 'blanket-wearer' meaning 'mendicant'), seem to reflect his counter-cultural self-image.

Yūsuf Khān delighted in challenging established religious authorities of all communities. He recounted how one person of the *qaum* of *mullā* ('caste' or 'sect' of mullahs, 'Muslim jurists') chided him, saying 'you are a Muslim, yet you drink liquor'. To which he replied: 'Ḥaẓrat Paighambar [the Lord Prophet Muhammad] did not forbid the juice of the grape' (Yūsuf Khān 1983: 107). Later, in London, he visited a Jewish synagogue at Tattershall, noting with approval that the women sat in an upper balcony, separate from men. Indeed, he compared religious and social practices with a leader of that community. More frequently while in London, Yūsuf Khān debated religious doctrine and practice with authorities of the established Church of England, concerning such issues as idol worship, diet, and morality. He criticized Britons for hypocrisy: 'those who do not act perfectly should not criticize others'. During one such debate, Father Mortimer 'said, "Christianity had been in India for one hundred years, but the Hindustani people have not understood the right path." I replied that those people are on the right path for them.... He responded, "what right path, they worship idols."' Yūsuf Khān retorted that Hindus kept idols before them, but so too did Christians keep images before them. He concluded his account of this debate by recording his own triumph: 'In truth, they do not know God.... Hearing this, they were silenced' (Yūsuf Khān 1983: 128, 131–2). We can presume that these Muslim, Jewish, and Christian leaders recalled these encounters with Yūsuf Khān somewhat differently.

In his mid-twenties, around 1828, Yūsuf Khān left Hyderabad, the city of his youth. He then explored much of north India, including British-ruled areas and princely states, before settling in Lucknow, the capital of the nominally independent state of Awadh. Yet, British officials ruled Awadh indirectly. There, Yūsuf Khān attracted the patronage of a British military officer, who obtained for him an appointment as a *jam'dār* (lieutenant) and then *ṣūbadār* (captain) of the special Sulaimānī Regiment.[9] Yūsuf Khān thus lived outside of British authority, but he recognized its power.

Living in Lucknow during the 1830s, Yūsuf Khān, like some other men of his class, determined to gain mastery of British culture. Yūsuf Khān, however, went further than many of his contemporaries: 'This slave passed his life with ease and gratitude to God. Suddenly I desired to learn about English knowledge. With great effort, I mastered it. Then, I mostly read history books and was delighted to see accounts of cities and the nature and customs of nations' (Yūsuf Khān 1983: 98). This was the period when Anglicist cultural assertions were starting to dominate in many leading educational institutions and British colonial administration.[10]

Yūsuf Khān thus prepared himself for visiting Britain, developing a set of expectations about what he would find there, although he would not be bound by them after he arrived. He must also have saved sufficient money to support his travels. In 1836 (at about the age of thirty-three) he took a two-year leave of absence to explore British society directly. First, he moved to Calcutta for 5–6 months. From there, he purchased passage to England, sailing (30 March 1837) via South Africa.

On board, Yūsuf Khān further enhanced his English language skills, but he also wrote his travel journal in Urdu. In it, he recorded his actions and his impressions of the new lands that he encountered, relating them to his own cultural categories. During the time he spent in South Africa, for example, he noted the 'Cape Coloured' including their 'beautiful women, neither too dark nor too fair, whose fathers are English and mothers are *bāharwālī* (outsiders)' (Yūsuf Khān 1983: 106). He admired Muslims living at the Cape because their women were 'modest and pure', but he disdained their religious strictures.

On reaching England (21 August 1837), he began his European adventure. First, he evaded royal customs authorities by hiring a small boat which, for £5, landed him and an English fellow passenger at a small seaside village where he spent his first night in England. They then caught a mail coach to London, which brought him into his first physical contact with an Englishwoman.

Yūsuf Khān found her disappointingly a 'very ugly woman...fatter than a mountain' (Yūsuf Khān 1983: 109–10). On reaching London, however, he formed a much more favourable impression of British women of all classes. Walking along the river on his third day in London, he observed 'strolling along the river, English Sahibs with their wives making a show. What beautiful (*ḥusn*) and elegant (*jamāl*) women they were, like fairies (*parī*)' (Yūsuf Khān 1983: 112). He found his ability to gaze upon even respectable British women in Britain surprising, in contrast to India, where elite Indian women were secluded and British women also generally remained distant from Indian men.

Since he intended to spend some time in London, he rented rooms for £10 per month, sharing the house with a British lodger. He recounted how he amused the landlord and servants by bathing in the kitchen instead of the bathroom. They laughed at him because he did not know the difference: 'hearing this I became ashamed and could make no answer' (Yūsuf Khān 1983: 114). Yet, Yūsuf Khān had the self-confidence to record (rather than suppress) this incident, which highlighted his own initial naiveté about British cultural classification of rooms.

While in London, he explored its many conventional and unconventional attractions. He described the most striking tourist sights of London including: Saint Paul's, the British Museum, Westminster Abbey, the Guild Hall, Madame Tussaud's Wax Museum, the Royal Surrey Theatre, a dance hall, the pleasure gardens at Vauxhall, and the Panorama of London in the Coliseum. He also made outings to Greenwich, Woolwich, and the Royal Botanical Gardens at Kew. In all these, he stood physically alongside, yet culturally apart from, British audiences.

Yūsuf Khān's background and orientation provided him with a perspective distinct from the Britons who surrounded him. They were consuming their own culture, he was an outsider comparing theirs to his own. He also sought out cross-cultural encounters. In the British Library, Yūsuf Khān admired particularly its vast collections of books in Arabic, Persian, Hebrew, and Greek. At the Tower of London, he was especially impressed by weapons and mementos taken in the battle that killed Tipu Sultan. At Astley's Amphitheatre, he paid to see an enactment by costumed British actors of an Iranian Safavid prince defeating Turkmans, with a parade of orientally dressed soldiers. This reminded him of his own army of Awadh, which he would later rejoin. He also took a side trip to Paris. In each instance, his background made his 'gaze' different from Europeans in the audience. The various symbols they all observed carried quite different connotations for him and those around him.

While Yūsuf Khān critiqued British cultural and religious customs, he nevertheless accepted Britain's political authority over India. When he joined the admiring throng applauding the teenaged Queen Victoria:

Seeing her face, in my heart arose this prayer: ya Allah, may her horse come near me and she glance at me. God heard. When her horse came before me, it paused and the resplendent visage of the queen looked so serene like the model of divine power. I saluted her. Seeing me, she graciously bestowed a smile on me. On regarding her, I swelled up with unconfined joy and in my heart a prayer arose that, oh God, may this Sultanate never decline and always prosper and continue to expand and acquire perfection (Yūsuf Khān 1983: 139).

Thus, Yūsuf Khān was exceptionally proud of his opportunity to express his devotion personally to the queen.

Among the choices that Indians visiting Britain had to make (and still have to make) were what sartorial and dietary practices to observe. Yūsuf Khān apparently continued to wear his usual clothes. These distinguished him from the Britons around him but did not hamper his movement among them. This contrasted with most early Indian visitors who repeatedly recorded how they found themselves surrounded by polite, curious, and occasionally confining crowds of British gawkers whenever they went out. Since much informal socializing and politicking in British society took place commensally, Indians who eschewed British food, like Karīm Khān, often found themselves disadvantaged. Yūsuf Khān, however, did not observe any eating or drinking constraints, except avoidance of pork. This enabled him to dine out frequently at the homes of a range of British hosts, as his narrative frequently records.

As with so many Indian male visitors, Yūsuf Khān found his interactions with respectable, as well as unknown, British women utterly new and particularly fascinating. For example, he was startled when, in the darkness of the Diorama, he inadvertently put his hand on the shoulder of a woman unknown to him (Yūsuf Khān 1983: 133). Although he was ashamed of himself, he noted none of the Britons around him retaliated. On one outing with a young British man, they entered a coffee house, and struck up a conversation with 'two beautiful-looking women'. One attracted him and he offered to share a coffee with her, which she politely declined, saying 'another time'. He bantered back, 'What confidence is there that we will meet again?' (Yūsuf Khān 1983: 136).

Yūsuf Khān contrasted his easy social intercourse with British people in Britain with that of his experience in India. As an example, Colesworthy Grant (1813–80), a British artist (who had sketched Yūsuf Khān as an ethnographic study of a Pathan), entrusted him with a letter he had written for Grant's sisters-in-law in London. Yūsuf Khān wrote:

I had kept it with me like an amulet.... They received me with great politeness.... This *faqīr* has travelled to many cities but had not met such humane people anywhere else. The English who have come to Hindustan have a changed nature quite different from these.... It is sad that people of Hindustan do not come to this glorious city so that they can see and know with their own eyes the virtues of these people...(Yūsuf Khān 1983: 124).

They thus informally socialized in England in ways not permitted in India.

In addition to these more conventional activities, Yūsuf Khān also explored the seamier side of London. He took a tour of a charitable shelter for prostitutes and orphans. He compared this humane care with the condition of such people

Colesworthy Grant's Sketch of Yūsuf Khān, c. 1834 (Grant 1850?)

in India: 'If any woman there falls into fornication, she remains in that condition all her life; if any boy becomes an orphan, no one will give him bread or clothing. The English have much better arrangements' (Yūsuf Khān 1983: 134–5).

On one excursion into London's nightlife, Yūsuf Khān went with British friends to a crowded cabaret. He described his encounter with a female performer:

The master of the house raised a curtain; at once a woman (*randī*, later meaning 'prostitute'), the daughter of a fairy, came out. The sight of her cooled (*ṭhanḍak*) my eyes. She had a wondrous face that would bring shame to the moon. Having come out, she came and sat by a table and poured water onto her hand and she began to play twelve glasses. From this sound, my heart grew faint. My entire body became an anxious ear in order to hear her; my every organ turned into an eager eye in order to see her. Even the animals in the jungle would have become submissive and obedient to her. I wondered if this was a woman or bewitching fairy (Yūsuf Khān 1983: 123–4).

Yūsuf Khān struggled to put into his own cultural framework this woman's fascinating if (to him) inexplicable behaviour of playing on a crystallophone (musical glasses popular at that time).

Late one night, Yūsuf Khān passed through a narrow alleyway, where he saw a ruffian forcefully grabbing and gagging a woman (*ranḍī*) with a cloth. Seeing no policemen around, Yūsuf Khān himself entered the struggle in order to rescue her. He eventually wrestled the man to the ground and bound him. Finally, allowing the thug to flee, the victorious Yūsuf Khān escorted the woman to her house. She and her mother were very grateful, giving Yūsuf Khān a drink of liquor, although he declined to give them his name or become intimate with them (Yūsuf Khān 1983: 142–3). In his account, Yūsuf Khān thus represented himself acting forcefully, and successfully, in British public space. His demonstrated power to protect this British woman against a British man, reversed the usual gender images in European colonialism, where European men had power and Indian men appeared either effeminate or (especially after 1857) sexually dangerous to European womanhood.

Overall, Yūsuf Khān lauded Britain to his Urdu-speaking audience: 'In truth, *farangistān* ["the land of the Franks," "Europe"] is *parīstān* ["the land of the fairies"]. Every person is wondrously beautiful and graceful. All who come here will forget their native place' (Yūsuf Khān 1983: 155). Nevertheless, London also proved very costly. Yūsuf Khān expended his savings and his two-year leave of absence from the Awadh army. Thus, he left London (8 January 1838), seen off by his many British, predominantly middle-class friends.

He left from Falmouth, journeying via Lisbon, Gibraltar, Malta, Alexandria, Syria, and Ceylon. Thence he travelled via Aurangabad, Nagpur, Benares, Calcutta, and Patna, back to Lucknow.

After his trip, as someone 'England-returned', Yūsuf Khān spoke with authority about Britain to other Indians. He recorded discussing with them the relative merits of Britain and India, such as their respective architectural and sartorial styles, as well as their moral systems and practices. While some suggested that he had lost his status as a 'Hindustani' because he had shared food with the British, he retorted that in Europe, people keep their religion to themselves, and do not eat apart by religion (Yūsuf Khān 1983: 232). Yūsuf Khān particularly contrasted the endless industrious activity of the British, who never allowed even an hour of the day to go to waste, with the more inefficient ways of Indians. He particularly lauded the productive lives of British women:

> Their women do not waste time, they remain engaged in arts and sciences, in contrast to those of Hindustan where [Hindustani] men only waste their time in worthless matters; they, having imprisoned their women in the house, keep them ignorant of the world. Women never see anything of the world except the walls of their home or the sky from their courtyard. Every man constantly thinks this purdah-bound life appropriate for the chastity of his wife. In truth, they restrain them from knowledge and science.
>
> I think that observing purdah is supposed to be for chastity but really a virtuous woman can keep her honour even when seated among one thousand men while an immodest woman, even hidden behind 100,000 curtains, will not refrain from her evil ways...(Yūsuf Khān 1983: 247).

Yūsuf Khān's attitude contrasted with many early Indian visitors who defended purdah as liberating and criticized participation by British women in the public sphere as a burden forced upon them (Fisher 2000).

As Yūsuf Khān moved geographically, he also shifted the people with whom he associated. Unlike many other Indians in London at this time, he apparently eschewed his countrymen, and socialized almost exclusively with Britons there. On his return, until the ship reached Ceylon (Sri Lanka), he continued to mention his interactions with European companions almost exclusively. Even after his return to India, he travelled and visited with Britons, yet he increasingly also began to identify himself with Indians. For example, on reaching Aurangabad, he met a man from Hyderabad who said, 'I recognize you as a fellow of my native place' (Yūsuf Khān 1983: 21).

After his return to Lucknow, Yūsuf Khān wrote up his travel narrative.[11] During the rest of his life, Yūsuf Khān retained his rank as *ṣūbadār*, despite the annexation of Avadh in 1856, and the bloody fighting of 1857. He reportedly died in Lucknow in 1861.[12] His work seems to have remained at first in manuscript, and therefore had somewhat limited readership. Urdu audiences gained greater access in 1847 when Paṇḍit Dharma Nārāyana edited, retitled, and published it in Delhi as *Safar-i Yūsuf* ('Journey of Yūsuf'). Other publishers renamed it *'Ajā'ibāt-i Farang* ('Wonders of Europe') in editions of 1873, 1898, and 1983. It has never been published in English, and has remained largely unnoticed in British Orientalist discussions of Indian authors or histories of colonialism.

In his book, as in his life, Yūsuf Khān broke conventions. Although a soldier, he chose to study English and travel alone as a tourist to Britain. He was the first person to write a book in Urdu about Britain; most other Indian writers who visited Britain up to that point chose Persian (if they came from the traditional administrative elite) or English (if they were Anglicized officials of the British administration). Yūsuf Khān recognized both the opportunities and also the dangers of British colonial rule. Indeed, he openly discussed the potential oppression inherent in British colonialism, should the British administration impose the wrong type of policies (Yūsuf Khān 1983: 227). Yet he also owed much of his employment to British patronage. Unlike many notable Indians who made this dangerous and expensive journey, Yūsuf Khān evidently had no political goal; rather, he went just to see and experience Britain for himself. Contrasting in many ways, but also reiterating some of Yūsuf Khān's attitudes and observations about Britain, stands the nearly contemporary Urdu travel journal of Karīm Khān.

Karīm Khān, Diplomat and Diarist

The visit to Britain by Karīm Khān (born 1811) reveals both the multiple sites of political conflict between British colonial authorities and Indian royalty, and also the growth of Indian communities in Britain. Over the period prior to 1857, more than thirty separate diplomatic and political missions travelled to London, seeking redress of grievances inflicted by British administrators in India. Karīm Khān headed one of these delegations; trying to advance its goals proved a constant source of frustration to him throughout his stay in Britain. He also socialized and exchanged advice and experiences with many of the Indian men of his class in London including other diplomats, noblemen, officials, and students. Thus, while Karīm Khān explored and commented on many of the same London attractions as Yūsuf Khān, his time in Britain had other dimensions as well. From this diary, and from the extensive official correspondence that Karīm Khān exchanged with British officials in London and India, we can reconstruct his life and attitudes in Britain.

Karīm Khān's Sunni Pathan ancestors had emigrated from Afghanistan and settled in Bahraich.[13] Because the family fought alongside the British against the Marathas in 1804, the British gave them a large estate at Jhajjar (near Delhi). After Nawab Hasan Ali Khan lost a succession dispute to his nephew in 1835 he sent one of his relatives, Karīm Khān, to London on his behalf. Karīm Khān was entrusted with the mission of convincing the East India Company's court of directors to overturn the ruling of British officials in Delhi so that Hasan Ali Khan would receive a share of the family property, in addition to his current annual pension of Rs 36,000.

While Yūsuf Khān travelled unaccompanied by either servants or other Indian companions, Karīm Khān, as a courtier-diplomat, travelled with an entourage: a secretary, Mahabbat Khan; a cook, Pir Bakhsh; and a teenaged servant, Genda.[14] The first part of Karīm Khān's diary recounted his journey down the Ganges River to Calcutta, through lands and peoples hitherto little known to him. From Calcutta he sailed (13 March 1840) for Britain. On board (and later in London), Karīm Khān worked hard to improve his rudimentary English, and learned as well to socialize with the British fellow passengers. Nevertheless, he clearly remained most comfortable around other Urdu speakers.

On reaching London, Karīm Khān prepared his campaign to obtain his master's ends but also began to explore the attractions of London. When his apartments in Cornhill (in the City of London) proved too noisy, he rented a house, 14 Caroline Place, much farther north. Here, he and his entourage could live comfortably in control of their own space and food, and could entertain both influential Britons as well as Indian guests on their own terms. Unlike Yūsuf Khān, Karīm Khān observed Islamic dietary strictures: eating only *ḥalāl* meat prepared by his Muslim servant and refusing alcohol. Thus, while Karīm Khān occasionally served a Hindustani-style meal to his British and Indian supporters and friends, he did not accept food cooked in British kitchens (Karīm Khān 1982: 151–2). Like Yūsuf Khān, however, Karīm Khān apparently continued to dress in his customary way.

Karīm Khān's book draws our attention to the growing and diverse Indian population in Britain. Much to Karīm Khān's surprise and complete delight (*kamāl khushī*), on reaching London he discovered a substantial number of other 'Hindustanis' already there (Karīm Khān 1982: 117 and *passim*). While most of these people overlapped in London with Yūsuf Khān, he never mentioned meeting them; in contrast, Karīm Khān recorded spending extensive time in their company. Some of these other Indians were diplomats, on similar missions to that of Karīm Khān. They shared strategies and accounts of successful and—more often—unsuccessful tactics and confrontations with British authorities. These included two delegations from the deposed maharaja of Satara seeking his restoration, totalling about twenty people in all, many of whom spoke Urdu. These Satara missions arrived in 1838 and 1839 respectively; one of these ambassadors remained in London until 1853.

London also attracted Indian nobles, who both lobbied British authorities and enjoyed living there as gentlemen of leisure. One such man, whom Karīm Khān frequently noted in his diary as a companion for social occasions, was Jama'al-Din Muhammad (c. 1792–1842), a son of the late Tipu Sultan.[15] Yet another striking Urdu, Persian, and English-speaking figure on the London social scene, who appeared on half a dozen occasions in Karīm Khān's diary, was David Octerlony Dyce Sombre (1808–51), a man of mixed Indian and European ancestry, heir to Begam Sombre of Sardhana and her £500,000 fortune. He settled in England in 1838. In 1840, he married the daughter of Viscount St. Vincent; Karīm Khān was present in London at that time, but was not invited to their wedding. In 1841, before Karīm Khān had left London, Dyce Sombre had himself elected to the British Parliament from Sudbury. After Karīm Khān had departed from London, Dyce Sombre was expelled from Parliament, was declared legally insane, and died in 1851.

Still another social set in London, whom Karīm Khān noted as his frequent companions, were Parsi officials and students from Bombay. Most had come to Britain in order to enhance their professional shipbuilding expertise, in particular regarding the new technology of steam power. These included Jehangeer Nowrojee Wadia (1821–66), Hirjeebhoy Merwanjee Wadia (1817–83), and Manikjee Kasijee (born c. 1808). Showing solidarity with these fellow Indians in the British capital, Karīm Khān participated in several Parsi religious festivals with them.

While in London, Karīm Khān also met people with wider Indian associations. Captain Richmond Shakespear introduced to Karīm Khān a cavalryman from Rajputana, Fazl Khan (born c. 1816). Fazl Khan had escorted Shakespear to Khiva and then journeyed through Russia to Britain with him (Shakespear 1842: 692–720). Indeed, Shakespear entrusted Fazl Khan to Karīm Khān's hospitality and guidance in London. In addition, Karīm Khān met with Iranians in London, including Prince Mir Buzurg and a professor of Persian at the East India Company's Haileybury College, Mirza Muhammed Ibrahim (c.1800–57).

While Karīm Khān thus spent much of his time meeting with these many other Indians in London, he did not mix with all the Indians there by any means. Present in London at this time, but not mentioned in his account, were a number of Indians who had established themselves in the British middle or lower-middle classes, often in the service sector, and married British women. Sake (Shaikh) Dean Mahomet (1759–1851) of Patna, had come first to Ireland in 1783, and then moved to Britain around 1807, where he opened an Indian restaurant, and then made himself the 'Royal Shampooing Surgeon', operating bath houses in London and Brighton until his death in 1851 (Fisher 1997a). Mohammed Ibrahim Palowkar (c. 1811–55) of Bombay had come to London in 1833 with his father to recover some family lands. While his father left London in frustration, Mohammed Ibrahim married a British woman and stayed on as a tobacconist. Not mentioned by Karīm Khān were a number of Indian wives and mistresses of Europeans, often living in Britain with their children.

Further, he only occasionally mentioned a few among the literally thousands of Indian sailors and servants, both men and women, who visited or settled in Britain at the time. Yet, we can presume that Karīm Khān's servants met with these Indian men and women of their class, since these people had established lively communities especially in London's East End, known as the 'Oriental Quarter'. Thus, Karīm Khān's detailed diary elucidates some of the growing population of Urdu speakers in early nineteenth century London and their internal class divisions.

Karīm Khān had a specific political mission to accomplish for his nawab. After his arrival in London, months before making his first formal approach to the Company, Karīm Khān obtained the advice of influential and politically experienced Britons including Captain Robert Melville Grindlay (1786–1877, founder of the East Indian Agency, later Grindlay's Bank), Sir Charles Forbes (1774–1849, a merchant banker), and Mountstuart Elphinstone (1779–1859, former governor of Bombay), all widely reputed in Indian circles for being sympathetic. These men provided advice in understanding the complex, indeed often bewildering, wording and nature of the many official documents with which Karīm Khān had to deal. Various Britons also helped him compose and translate from Urdu into English his numerous applications to the Company, and translate back the Company's responses. As he stated about several of the letters and documents he received from the Company's directors, 'we read them, but we could not understand them very well' (Karīm Khān 1982: 141). This was due, at least in part, to the Kafkaesque bureaucratic maze into which he had entered.

Despite all his efforts, Karīm Khān's mission stood doomed to failure from its inception, due to the structure of British colonial rule. Indian diplomats like Karīm Khān had been making direct appeals in London since 1766, seeking support from the Company's directors in London against the actions of its officials in India. In order to present a united front against such Indian efforts, the directors had developed a standard policy: all correspondence from Indian rulers must be submitted officially through the Company's authorities in India, who would then channel the important cases on to London. Thus, many of the Indian delegations which made their way to London in order to appeal against injustices done to them in India by British officials found their formal approaches to the Company's court of directors or the board of control routinely rejected. Only a few diplomats managed some success due to their persistence, resources, and the political or legal strength of their cases; but these few gave hope to the rest.

These usual frustrations, however, played themselves out in Karīm Khān's case. After months of consultation, in September 1840, he submitted his documents to the court of directors, who quickly responded, refusing to accept his diplomatic credentials and asserting that local authorities in India would handle the matter.[16] Nevertheless, Karīm Khān persisted. Over the years, Karīm Khān sent and received multiple missives to and from India, and he wrote at least fifteen separate petitions, protests, and explanations to the court of directors, each one of which they considered and then rejected. Meanwhile, the current Jhajjar nawab cut off Karīm Khān's funds and allegedly threatened his family and his employer, Hasan Ali Khan. Eventually, after two years of negotiations with Karīm Khān, the directors voted not to overrule their officials in Delhi.

Strikingly, while all this official correspondence moved back and forth between Karīm Khān and the court of directors, and between Britain and India, there were even more extensive unofficial dialogues and discussions taking place. Karīm Khān's diary is filled with his cordial consultations, gracious socializing, and entertaining excursions with politically powerful Britons, including numerous members of the court of directors, Parliament, and the parliamentary board of control. Many of these Britons clearly gave him informal advice, based on their inside knowledge of his case in particular, and the workings of the British power structure in general. Thus, the official documentation of his repeated and fruitless petitions and appeals to the Company presents a very different narrative from his personal record of his interactions with Britons.

Far too often, the colonial archive remains the sole source for Indian history. The personal papers of Indians like Karīm Khān form an often contrasting body of information about the extensive and direct participation of Indians in the public sphere in imperial Britain. Only by drawing upon such multiple sources by all participants can some of the complexity and multi-sided nature of the imperial process be understood.

When Karīm Khān's funds were exhausted, he finally accepted the need to give up and return home. In order to do so, he had to petition the directors yet again to advance him £300 to pay his debts and purchase a passage for himself and his somewhat rebellious and depleted suite. Even after the directors granted him this money, and his departure was all arranged, two more letters of appeal arrived from Hasan Ali Khan, which Karīm Khān dutifully submitted, and which the directors routinely rejected.

Overall, Karīm Khān gained no apparent political advantage other than drawing the directors' attention to the otherwise unchecked and often arbitrary actions of its officials in India. The negative consequences of his persistent appeals, however, were inadvertently to inflict further hardship on his master's and his own families at the hands of the current Jhajjar nawab and British officials in India. Indeed, in summing up his experience, and that of the other diplomatic missions which he encountered while in London, Karīm Khān wrote bitterly against undertaking such frustrating efforts:

> Let it be known that it will amount to sheer meaningless trouble for the powerless to come to England to plead their case and seek justice. If any pain-filled heart thinks: 'I will go there, submitting myself to such distant travel abroad, then perhaps they will show me mercy,' this is an absolutely wrong idea. These people with whom you must deal here have neither fear of God nor mercy in their hearts. Your very indigence and need will prevent your gaining access to their favour. But any powerful person is welcome to make this attempt, only provided that he brings 10,000,000 rupees cash and forty attendants who are proper companions, reliable supporters, civil, and trustworthy people. Then do not even mention your case for a year, but during this period prepare the preconditions of your case using the money you brought.... Then if you have the Grace of God, you may get a verdict within a year...(Karīm Khān 1982: 283–4).

He warned that even the noble-born (*ashrāf*) Indian men would be immorally seduced by the liberties of living in Britain. He hoped no other Indians would have to endure all that he had, with so little political gain.

Yet, both Yūsuf Khān and Karīm Khān very much desired that their countrymen should learn broadly from their respective first-hand experiences of Britain. Karīm Khān in particular expounded on the little-known (in India) relationship among the British monarch, Parliament, and the East India Company. Karīm Khān also explained to his Urdu readers much of what he had learned about British political and legal history, from pre-Roman times to the present, seeking insights about how to enhance Indian participation in British public polity formation (Karīm Khān 1982: 260–77).

Many Britons were convinced of their own political, economic, technological, and moral accomplishments, desiring that Indians should learn to appreciate them as well. Thus, for example, one of the Company's directors urged Karīm Khān to explain the British economic system in his book, which he did, including the nature of capitalism with its attendant system of stocks and dividends (Karīm Khān 1982: 276ff). Further, British authorities felt that a greater knowledge of British colonial administration might prevent future Indian political missions from venturing to Britain, missions that all parties found so frustrating.

Much of the time that his expensive diplomatic delegation was foundering, Karīm Khān diverted himself by viewing many of the same tourist attractions and British cultural monuments as had Yūsuf Khān. Both admired the British Museum, Astley's Ampitheatre, Vauxhall Gardens, and Woolwich; both made special efforts to meet Jewish communities in London. Further, they both commented in similar ways about British women selling their wares in the streets and in shops, whom Karīm Khān described as 'young and extremely comely women without equal in the arts of buying and selling' (Karīm Khān 1982: 117).

Karīm Khān described himself as less freely mixing with British women than did Yūsuf Khān. Karīm Khān knew far less English, was more orthodox in his practice of Islam, was of higher social class, was accompanied by Indian attendants, and was more protective of his social reputation. Thus, he politely declined even light-hearted offers of British women by his British hosts. On one occasion, Elphinstone (himself unmarried) jokingly urged Karīm Khān to take a British bride to 'remove the sorrow of singleness'. Karīm Khān replied that his peculiar position with respect to British society put him outside of the customary bounds for marriage alliances: '...first of all, those gentlemen in this country who are highborn and noble, their women do not think me worthy; and among the *ajlāf* (commoners), I do not admire their women; because I am *ashrāf* (elite) within my own country, and not ignoble. Hearing this that gentleman laughed and did not pursue this question further (Karīm Khān 1982: 181).' Yet Karīm Khān knew about, and discussed Indians who had British wives, including a professor of Persian and Hindustani at the Company's Addiscombe Military Seminary, Mir Hussain Ali of Lucknow, who had married an Englishwoman while in England and then brought her home with him (Karīm Khān 1982: 277–8, Ali 1832). In his conversations about gender roles, unlike Yūsuf Khān, Karīm Khān defended the practice of purdah.

Karīm Khān came back to Jhajjar via Paris, where he presented a manuscript copy of his book to the French Orientalist scholar, Garcin de Tassy. British commentators quickly noticed his work, publishing an assessment of his arguments, comparing them with the writings of other Indians and Iranians in Britain (*Blackwood's Magazine* 1843: 762–3). This journal judged as clever but unpersuasive his views on gender and Islam. Yet, Karīm Khān's own book remained in manuscript and was only published in Pakistan in 1982.

After Karīm Khān's return to Jhajjar, he continued to write. After the Governor General visited the Qutb Minar in Delhi, he requested Karīm Khān to relate its history. Karīm Khān did so, but in the context of his history of the world, entitled *Mir'āt-i Fatḥnāma.*[17] Although several other British officials solicited copies from Karīm Khān, this book remains in manuscript. In Jhajjar, Hasan Ali Khan continued to receive a pension but, despite continued appeals, failed to obtain a share of the family estate. The last Jhajjar nawab fought the British in 1857; they executed him and annexed the state. Thus, Karīm Khān's diplomatic mission had little long-term political effect, although his long personal discussions with Britons informed them about India, and his extensive experience and writing there informed him and his Urdu audiences about Britain.

Conclusion

Urdu speakers ventured to imperial Britain even at the height of British colonial expansion across India. Once there, they made a place for themselves through a range of interactions with men and women of the local population. They also directly addressed British and Indian audiences, advancing their own positions and representing India to the British and Britain to Indians. Their writing and oral accounts thus belied European assertions of exclusive control over colonial knowledge. These Urdu authors also enable us to understand the process of colonialism in far deeper and more nuanced ways.

Despite the knowledge of Britain carried back by these Indian visitors, it remained unevenly distributed and used in India. Karīm Khān knew of earlier works by Indians who travelled to Britain. For instance, he commented knowledgeably about the assertions of Mirzā E'tiṣām al-Dīn in his Persian book *Shigarfnāma-i Wilāyat* ('Wonder Book of Europe') which described his trip to Britain in 1766–8 (Karīm Khān 1982: 282). Yet Yūsuf Khān, Karīm Khān, and many of the other Indian visitors of their day went relatively unprepared for what they would encounter. Yūsuf Khān's own book remained in only limited circulation until 1847, Karīm Khān's until the late twentieth century. In contrast, British colonial constructions of Britain and of India spread widely throughout the world, even today dominating discourse about colonialism and relations between Britain and India.

Among the repeated themes found in these two Urdu accounts, and earlier ones by Indians in Britain in Persian and English, were those of gender and religion. Most Indian male visitors found their meetings with British women striking. The strong class hierarchy in Britain meant that British women of a lower class than themselves appeared particularly unprotected. Further, British patriarchal authority empowered Indian men even over British women of their own class: an Indian man controlled his British wife's property and she conventionally adopted his name (e.g. Mrs Jane Mahomed). For the fewer Indian women visitors or settlers in Britain, these same patriarchal structures largely subordinated them to British or Indian husbands or employers.

Inherent in British imperial military and political assertions over the Indian colonized was a presumption of British cultural supremacy, including the superiority of Anglican Christianity.[18] This, however, does not appear to have been convincing to either Yūsuf K͟hān or Karīm K͟hān. Each admired British cultural, social, and technological achievements, but neither expressed a desire to give up his own religious values and accept those of his British interlocutors. Neither chose to write in English, but rather directed their remarks to Urdu audiences.

As long as these and other Indian visitors remained in Britain, they evidently had access to public discourse there. They proved able to represent India and Indians directly to the British through their many conversations and debates with Britons. Yet the force of imperialism was such that, following their departure, their words were either forgotten or recast by European writers. It therefore remains for us to attempt to recover the force of their voices, and allow them to inform us about the complexity of both the imperial process and of the diverse roles of these early Indians in imperializing Britain.

Notes

[1] This chapter grows out of my larger project examining the range of Indians who ventured to Britain from about 1600 until 1858. I thank the participants of the conference on 'Urdu Scholarship in Transnational Perspective', Kathryn Hansen, David Lelyveld, Paula Richman, Muzaffar Alam, and Aslam Parwez for their constructive suggestions in developing this paper. I also acknowledge the generous financial support of the American Council of Learned Societies, Oberlin College, and the American Institute of Indian Studies.

[2] Yūsuf K͟hān's book, *Tārīk͟h-i Yūsufī* ('History of Yūsuf') was first published in

1847; the title page of this first edition has in English, *Travels in Europe by Yoosoof Khan Kummulposh*, with the remainder of the book in Urdu, entitled *Safar-i Yūsuf*, ('Yūsuf's Journey'), edited by Paṇḍit Dharma Nārāyana. In 1873, Joseph Johannes brought out a second edition, re-titled *'Ajā'ibāt-i Farang* ('Wonders of Europe'). The Mission Printing Press and Nawal Kishor, Lucknow, republished this in 1898. Makka Books, Lahore, republished it in 1983 with an introduction by Taḥsīn Farāqī. Karīm Khān's autograph manuscript, *Siyāḥat Nāma*, apparently given by him to Garcin de Tassy, is now in the British Library, OR 2163. It was published in facsimile in 1982, edited by 'Ibādat Barelvī.

[3] There have been partial translations of Karīm Khān's book into European languages. Garcin de Tassy translated into French the first part of this diary, up to the time of his leaving India. *Revue de l'Orient et de l'Algérie et des colonies*, 1865: 105–41, 641–63. There is also a paraphrase of parts of Karīm Khān's book in *Blackwood's Magazine*, 54 (336–8), 1843.

[4] The *safar nāma* and the *riḥla* were prominent forms of Muslim travel narrative. *See* Ibn Khaldun (1969), Eickelman and Piscatori (1990). For a later and quite different sort of travel account by a Muslim in Europe, *see* as-Saffar (1991). *See also* Pérès (1940), Abu-Lughod (1963), Lewis (1982), Leed (1991).

[5] For discussion of the ways English culture read India, *see* al Azm (1981), Lowe (1991), Said (1993), Mackenzie (1999), Washbrook (1999). For analysis of dramatic representations of the Orient, *see* Holder (1991), Niranjana (1994).

[6] Matar demonstrates for earlier centuries the difference between the personal reception of Muslim visitors to Britain and the negative images of Muslims in British literature, especially drama (Matar 1999).

[7] H.S. Reid argues unconvincingly that Yūsuf Khān was not Indian but rather a Catholic Italian named Delmerich, of the Medici family. Cited in Introduction to Yūsuf Khān (1983: 52–3). *See also* for a brief mention of Yūsuf Khān, Llewellyn-Jones (1990).

[8] Taḥsīn Farāqī, Introduction to Yūsuf Khān (1983: 72–4).

[9] This regiment was named after King Nasir al-Din Haydar, 'Shah Sulaiman Jah'. Perhaps this is where Yūsuf Khān developed his 'Sulaimānī' religion.

[10] See Zastoupil and Moir (1999). For the further developments of these issues for north Indian Muslims, *see* Lelyveld (1978).

[11] His return to Calcutta was reported in *Jnanannesan*, 25 July 1838, cited in 'Asiatic Intelligence', *Asiatic Journal*, December 1838, 268a.

[12] Garcin de Tassy cited in Yūsuf Khān (1983: 50–1).

[13] According to Garcin de Tassy who knew him, Karīm Khān was the son of Nawab Qā'im Khān and spent two years attached to the Governor General (Yūsuf Khān 1982: 10).

[14] Great Britain Public Record Office, 1841 Census, 14 Caroline Place.

[15] This man, who was universally known in Europe as 'The Prince of Mysore', had been let out of palace confinement in India in order to come to England in 1835, ostensibly for his health. Once in London, he lobbied extensively and somewhat

successfully for an enhanced pension for himself and his younger brothers. He remained a man about town until his death in 1842, while on a pleasure trip to Paris.

[16] For the extensive records of his mission for the period 30 September 1840 to 2 November 1842, *see* East India Company, Minutes of the Court of Directors; Minutes of Military and Political Committee; Home Correspondence, Military Papers, British Library.

[17] Foreign Political Consultations: 17 April 1847, no. 41–6; 30 October 1847, no. 42–3, National Archives of India, New Delhi.

[18] For a study of British use of English literature as a component of imperialism, *see* Viswanathan (1989).

Bibliography

A. *Printed sources*

Abu-Lughod, Ibrahim, *Arab Rediscovery of Europe*, Princeton: Princeton University Press, 1963.

al Azm, S. J., 'Orientalism and Orientalism in Reverse', *Khamsin*, 8, 1981, 5–26.

Ali, Mrs Meer Hassan, *Observations on the Mussulmauns of India*, 2 vols, London: Parbury, Allen, 1832.

as-Saffar, Muhammad (trans. from the Arabic by Susan Gilson Miller), *Disorienting Encounters*, Berkeley: University of California Press, 1991.

Asiatic Journal, 'Asiatic Intelligence', December 1838, 268a.

Bhabha, Homi, *The Location of Culture*, New York: Routledge, 1994.

Bolt, Christine, *Victorian Attitudes to Race*, London: Routledge and Kegan Paul, 1971.

Burton, Antoinette, *At the Heart of the Empire*, Berkeley: University of California Press, 1997.

Cannadine, David, *Ornamentalism*, New York: Oxford University Press, 2001.

Chatterjee, Partha, 'Five Hundred Years of Fear and Love', *Economic and Political Weekly*, 33(22), 30 May–5 June 1998, 1330–6.

Eickelman, Dale F., and James Piscatori, *Muslim Travelers*, Berkeley: University of California Press, 1990.

Fisher, Michael H., *First Indian Author in English: Dean Mahomet in India, Ireland, and England*, Delhi: Oxford University Press, 1997a.

_______, *Politics of British Annexations of India*, Delhi: Oxford University Press, 1997b.

_______, *Indirect Rule in India*, Delhi: Oxford University Press, 1998.

_______, 'Representing "His" Women: Mirza Abu Talib Khan's 1801 "Vindication of the Liberties of Asiatic Women"', *Indian Economic and Social History Review*, 37 (2) 2000, 215–37.

_______, *Counterflows to Colonialism*, Delhi: Permanent Black, 2003.

Grant, Colesworthy, *Sketches of Oriental Heads*, Calcutta: Thacker, 1850?

Hasan, Mushirul, 'Resistance and Acquiescence in North India: Muslim Responses to the West', in Mushirul Hasan and Narayani Gupta (eds.), *India's Colonial Encounter*, Delhi: Manohar, 1993, 39–63.

Holder, Heidi J., 'Melodrama, Realism and Empire on the British Stage,' in J. S. Bratton *et al.* (eds.), *Acts of Supremacy*, Manchester: Manchester University Press, 1991, 29–32.

Ibn Khaldun (trans. from the Arabic by Franz Rosenthal), *Muqaddimah*, N. J. Dawood (ed.), Princeton: Princeton University Press, 1969.

Karīm K͟hān, *Siyāḥat Nāma*, British Library, OR 2163; published in facsimile, 'Ibādat Barelvī (ed.), Lahore: Majlis-i Isha'at-i Makhtutat, 1982; (partially trans. from Urdu into French by Garcin de Tassy), *Revue de l'Orient et de L'Algérie et des colonies*, Paris: Société Orientale, 4 (1), 1865, 105–41, 641–63; partial paraphrase in English, in *Blackwood's Magazine*, 54 (336–8), 1843.

Leed, Eric J., *Mind of the Traveler*, New York: Basic Books, 1991.

Lelyveld, David, *Aligarh's First Generation*, Princeton: Princeton University Press, 1978.

Lewis, Bernard, *Muslim Discovery*, New York: W. W. Norton, 1982.

Llewellyn-Jones, Rosie, 'Indian Travellers in Nineteenth Century England', *Indo-British Review*, 18(1), 1990, 137–41.

Lowe, Lisa, *Critical Terrains: French and British Orientalisms*, Ithaca: Cornell University Press, 1991.

Mackenzie, John M., 'Empire and Metropolitan Cultures', in *Oxford History of the British Empire (The Nineteenth Century/3)*, Andrew Porter (ed.), Oxford: Oxford University Press, 1999.

Matar, Nabil, *Turks, Moors, and Englishmen in the Age of Discovery*, New York: Columbia University Press, 1999.

Mittra, Peary Chand, *Life of Colesworthy Grant*, Calcutta: Bose, 1881.

Mukhopadhyay, Bhaskar, 'Writing Home, Writing Travel', *Comparative Studies in Society and History*, 44(2), April 2002, 293–317.

Niranjana, Tejaswini, 'Translation, Colonialism and the Rise of English', in Svati Joshi (ed.), *Rethinking English*, New Delhi: Oxford University Press, 1994.

Pérès, Henri, 'Voyageurs Musulmans', *Mémoires de l'Institut Français d'Archéologie Orientale du Caire*, 68, 1940.

Pratt, Mary Louise, *Imperial Eyes*, London: Routledge, 1992.

Raychaudhuri, Tapan, *Europe Reconsidered*, Oxford: Oxford University Press, 1988.

Rich, Paul B., *Race and Empire in British Politics*, Cambridge: Cambridge University Press, 1990.

Said, Edward W., *Orientalism*, New York: Vintage, 1978.

———, *Culture and Imperialism*, New York: Knopf, 1993.

Sarkar, Tanika, 'A Book of Her Own, A Life of Her Own: Autobiography of a Nineteenth-Century Woman', *History Workshop Journal*, 36, Autumn 1993, 35–65.

Shakespear, Captain Sir Richmond, 'A Personal Narrative of a Journey from Heraut to Ourenbourg, on the Caspian, in 1840', *Blackwood's Magazine*, 51(320), June 1842, 692–720.

Sinha, Mrinalini, *Colonial Masculinity*, Manchester: Manchester University Press, 1995.

Visram, Rozina, *Ayahs, Lascars, and Princes*, London: Pluto, 1984.

______, *Asians in Britain*, London: Pluto, 2002.

Viswanathan, Gauri, *Masks of Conquest*, New York: Columbia University Press, 1989.

______, *Outside the Fold*, Princeton: Princeton University Press, 1998.

Washbrook, D.A., 'Orients and Occidents: Colonial Discourse Theory and the Historiography of the British Empire', in Robin W. Winks (ed.), *Oxford History of the British Empire (Historiography/5)*, Oxford: Oxford University Press, 1999.

Yūsuf Khān, *Tārīkh-i Yūsufī* published as *Safar-i Yūsuf*, Paṇḍit Dharma Nārāyana (ed.), Delhi: al-'Ulum Madrasa, 1847; republished as '*Ajā'ibāt-i Farang*, Joseph Johannes (ed.), Lucknow: Joseph Johannes, 1873; '*Ajā'ibāt-i Farang*, Lucknow: Mission Printing Press and Nawal Kishore, 1898; and '*Ajā'ibāt-i Farang*, Lahore: Makka Books, 1983.

Zastoupil, Lynn and Martin Moir (eds.), *The Great Indian Education Debate*, Richmond: Curzon, 1999.

B. Unpublished manuscript records

East India Company, Minutes of the Court of Directors; Minutes of Military and Political Committee; Home Correspondence, Military Papers. Oriental and India Office Records, British Library, London.

East India Company, Foreign Political Consultations, National Archives of India, New Delhi.

Great Britain, Public Record Office, 1841 Census.

Iqbal's Imagined Geographies: The East, the West, the Nation, and Islam

Barbara D. Metcalf

apnī dunyā āp paidā kar agar zindoṅ meṅ hai
sirr-i ādam hai ẓamīr-i kun fukāṅ hai zindagī.
If you are among the living, fashion your own world.
Life is Adam's secret, the essence of 'Be, and it was'!

('Khiẓr-i Rāh', 1922, DM: 63)

For the Indian poet and philosopher, Muhammad Iqbal, (1879–1938), widely regarded as the pre-eminent Urdu poet of the first half of the twentieth century, to be truly alive was to be an active, creative shaper of one's own world.[1] For him, words alone had reality, and the creative person was one who successfully named reality. He delighted in the role of Adam, a prophet in the Islamic tradition, who, as he saw it, participated in God's creative power by the naming of the animals. For Iqbal, the poet, like prophets and enlightened saints, could penetrate false worlds to see the essence of truth, to excavate the reality beyond appearances, and to defy the oppressive structures that held individual lives in both Europe and the colonial world in thrall. Iqbal grappled in the interwar period with the problems that engaged European and colonial intellectuals alike. But in contrast to Europeans who typically took Islam as a system of despotism and control, Iqbal found in Islamic symbols precisely the tools to challenge the capitalism, nationalism, and imperialism of his day, and to celebrate a vision of a world of people made free to realize their true selves.

Fazlur Rahman, himself an eminent Islamic modernist, considered Iqbal 'the most serious and daring intellectual modernist the Muslim world has produced' (Rahman 1979: 234).[2] Part of that mid-century modernity was Iqbal's belief in the transformative power of human will and action, directed, in much of his work, to questioning the emerging solidarities of his troubled times. Iqbal, like his contemporary Rabindranath Tagore (1861–1941), was one of those who, in the decades of late colonial rule, articulated what can be called a critical 'alternative modernity' or 'counter-modernity' to that dominant in their societies.

It is, therefore, ironic that Iqbal is primarily remembered in post-colonial Pakistan as the champion of the territorial nationalism, the regnant ideology of the day, that he relentlessly questioned. Dead before any political party made Pakistan its goal and almost a decade before the country was founded, he is, nonetheless, 'the poet of Pakistan'. In India, Iqbal's writings have been largely ignored. But even there, there has been one striking exception: his early song to India, still sung by school children, that celebrates India as the most beautiful place on earth, the garden whose nightingales are its children.[3] The purpose of this essay is to try to reclaim Iqbal from that oddly 'partitioned heritage',[4] partitioned between the two rival nations and partitioned from so much that he in fact represented.

Some scholars have argued for strands in Indian thought, expressive of indigenous 'voice' or 'agency', that assert a place for colonial thinkers *outside* discourses derivative of the West. Alternatively, others have described colonial thinkers as trapped into Western categories they have mirrored, most notably in the discourse Edward Said identified as 'Orientalism' (Said 1978).[5] My emphasis instead is to see Iqbal participating in a *shared* intellectual world whose participants might be in Cambridge or Calcutta, Boston or Munich, Isfahan or Lahore. Iqbal embraced this world and, in part because of his particular cultural heritage and location, enriched it and enlarged it in turn. Ultimately, any attempt, in writing about a thinker like Iqbal, to create an 'archaeology' that identifies thought as 'European' or 'Indian' or 'Eastern' or 'Islamic' falters if such labels suggest organic production.

Iqbal's celebration of human potential, though at home with European philosophers like Bergson and Nietzsche, found expression in re-imagining symbols from the Islamic tradition like that of the ideal individual (his *mard-i momin*) and the passion (*'ishq*) of the spiritual seeker. Central to his intellectual stance was the sophisticated conviction, noted above, that what is articulated is what is real and that in creative action rests the emergence of the realized self (or k͟hudī), the symbol at the centre of his philosophic and poetic thought. This power given to words links individual human creativity with divine creativity, above all in the power of artistic creation that transcends time

(Metcalf 1977). Cantwell Smith has argued that Iqbal's theology is immanentist and that it represents a radical rethinking of the central Islamic doctrine of *tauḥīd*, putting the Divine into the world in partnership with humans to create a new and better world (Smith 1946: 105–6). As Iqbal has the angels complain of him to God: '[the poet] has taught man (*ádam*) divine behavior (*ádáb-i khudāwandī*)'.[6] Iqbal despaired of traditions of what he saw as Islamic passivity and conformity, and, like Islamic modernists generally, claimed his views of human potential and responsibility to be based on his own engagement with the teachings of the Quran. His was a 'this-worldly' emphasis on reform of individual behaviour and social life, true of many Muslim thinkers in the colonial period (Robinson 2000: 105–21), but in his case grounded in what could be called Islamic 'vitalism'.[7]

A second dimension of his participation in shared intellectual currents of the first half of the twentieth century was his poetic romanticism and his Islamic romanticism in particular. After early schooling in Sialkot, Iqbal moved to Lahore, an old Mughal city but now a provincial capital and educational centre. There he joined the Government College, the premier educational institution of the Punjab. Iqbal found a mentor in Sir Thomas Arnold (1864–1933), who had taught at the modernist Muhammedan Anglo-Oriental College at Aligarh (and was remembered for his fondness for lecturing in Islamic dress). Arnold was the first of a handful of English Orientalists, including Iqbal's later translators, A. J. Arberry and Reynold Nicholson, who found in Iqbal, as Iqbal did in them, reinforcement of their Islamic romanticism. After an undergraduate degree at Trinity College, Cambridge, as well as training in law at Lincoln's Inn, he went to Germany to study philosophy where he completed a doctorate in philosophy in Munich. It was there, in Europe, not the Punjab, that he studied Persian metaphysics, and became an unbounded admirer of German romanticism and of Goethe in particular. Goethe's *West Östlicher Divan* (1819), inspired by the poet's reading a translation of the Persian Sufi poet Hafiz (c. 1320–1389), in Iqbal's words, provided 'spiritual sustenance from the [Islamic] East to the West'[8] but in fact sustained Iqbal in turn.

Iqbal's romanticism, while expressed in classic poetic forms and drawing on age-old poetic conventions, would not merely take up traditional themes but address, at times with great specificity, the hard realities of his day as he encountered them in his own Punjab, in the empire, and in the larger world. In so doing, he extended the oppositional strand in European romanticism, enlarging cosmopolitan literary traditions with a new set of concerns and a new Islamic vocabulary even as he transformed the Indo-Persian poetic tradition with new language and new issues.

These philosophical and romantic strands were evident in all that Iqbal subsequently did and said. Although appointed to a position at Government College upon his return to Lahore in 1908, Iqbal soon left teaching for a career as a barrister and, above all, a life as what one might call 'a public poet', engaging with the great moral, social, and political questions of his day in poetry that would be taken up in the emerging urban institutions of civil society—journals, voluntary associations, vernacular newspapers, political rallies, and party gatherings. In 1926, Iqbal was elected to the newly constituted Punjab Legislative Council from a separate Muslim electoral district in Lahore, and he participated in two Round Table Conferences in London, called in 1931 and 1932 to discuss future constitutional reforms.

The issue of Iqbal's 'geography' illuminates the life and thought briefly described to this point and, specifically, points to some aspects of 'fashioning [one's] own world', the charge set out in Iqbal's verse quoted above. Indeed, a fundamental preoccupation of writers, historians, and political actors in this period was in fact the positivist geographic exercise of defining countries and boundaries, locating nation states, and ordering them in terms of power and chronology in relation to each other (Winichakul 1994). The very identification of continents, far from neutral, was a product of European world dominance, reducing China and India to 'subcontinents' while Europe itself was a 'continent' (Lewis and Wigen 1997). Another dimension of this 'world making' was the powerful 'Orientalist' creation of the binary of East and West and the presumed characteristics of nations and individuals dependent on location in one or the other of these presumed arenas. Iqbal, as an artist who reflected on the power of the imagination, was among those who showed remarkable awareness of the extent to which nations and boundaries, material and imagined, although meant to be taken as natural and inherent, were in fact constructed.

Iqbal saw himself as a person who took nothing ready-made, including not only the categories of geography, but also historical periodization, and, central to his thought, 'Islam'. This last, in Iqbal's usage, came to define nothing less than an a-territorial, social and moral space that challenged the priority of the nation state. Similarly, he critically appropriated and used concepts of what could be called colonial sociology and geography in order to lay claim to them. Among these key geopolitical concepts, as one might label them, are 'East' and 'West', with their resonance of cultural and moral characteristics; 'nation', with its territorial boundaries and loyalties; and 'Islam' itself.

The terms 'East' and 'West' as used in colonial or Oriental discourse comment on each other. There is an irony built into the terms 'East' and 'West' from the beginning. 'The East' presents spiritual heights and wisdom in distinct contrast to 'the West's' material, and, quite often, imagined social, political, and moral advance. But even to articulate such concepts is inextricably to make them interdependent as each other's opposite. In the alchemy that transmutes time into space, moreover, 'the East' can become, instead of merely a place of difference, Europe's own past (Said 1978). The usage is essential to pervasive themes in modern thought that posit a break with all that has gone before. Iqbal knowingly claimed 'the East', only to redefine it and at times reject it. In some contexts, he used the term 'East' interchangeably with 'Islam' or even 'Asia' as symbols of a moral order, or potential moral order, as a contrast to the institutions, including the 'nation', taken to be imposed by 'the West'.

Of these terms, Iqbal's use of 'the East' was especially revealing. Self-identification with the East, as Iqbal claimed in such verses as *Payām-i Mashriq* (A Message from the East), gave him a certain kind of right to be heard. Indeed, Iqbal insisted that he *really was* the 'East', for example by calling himself 'the Indian infidel' (*kāfir-i hindī*) who challenged by the depth of his burning passion the Orientalist notion of inauthenticity imputed to non-Arab Muslims ('The Mosque of Cordoba', 1931, DM: 100–1). By identifying himself as part of the East; publishing his writings in the 'Wisdom of the East' series; and accepting a British knighthood in 1922 following the translation of his works, *The Secrets of the Self* and *The Mysteries of Selflessness*, whose very titles resonated with the mystery of Eastern wisdom, Iqbal helped construct one pervasive way of 'mapping' and ordering the world and the peoples within, even while, in significant ways, he sought to undermine it.

Iqbal was not a simple mimic, complicit in ideological structures forged in the context of European colonial ascendancy. Iqbal knew perfectly well the risks of the 'canonical' view that identified 'East' and 'West' as civilizational entities, essentially distinct from each other, but he adopted that essentialism 'strategically' (to use Gayatri Spivak's concept developed in another context [Spivak 1988]). That done, Iqbal was able to expand and subvert these terms until they were nuanced and enlarged at his hand. Indeed, part of Iqbal's own modernity was—to use the term W.E.B. Du Bois coined for the African-American—his 'double consciousness' that allowed him to imagine how he was seen, yet to resist being wholly shaped by that external view (Du Bois 1997: 38). Intellectuals of our day, like the late Iranian political philosopher and activist 'Alī Sharī'atī (1933–77), have seen Iqbal as a precursor in this significant dimension of a 'post-colonial' intellectual style.[9]

Why did the issues of political and moral 'geography', often linked to historical stages, matter to him so much? Iqbal's burning passion, I would argue, was to be free, free not only of physical restraints, but free of any boxes of identity or location that could constrain him. Iqbal sought to lay claim to a seamless world where an individual could be at home in the world anywhere. I thus take from his work a different emphasis from the very widespread one that simplifies his thought into a progression from Indian nationalism (until his trip to Europe and return in 1908) towards an embrace of an 'Islamic world', culminating, after 1930, in the demand for Pakistan. Rather, I see in his emerging identification with Islamic symbols a search, above all, for a language for relentless opposition to capitalist and imperialist exploitation and to *all* imagined boundaries that create divisions. In this, his was a voice that articulated, with its own inflection, a utopian critique of dominant themes in modernity that resonated with contemporaneous dissident critiques in Europe and beyond (cf. Cole 1998).

Iqbal, the poet, constructed new worlds with his words. He did so as one who claimed insight, seeing through the false world of surfaces to the reality within. The metaphor that resonates throughout Iqbal's poetry is that of 'sight' and of 'vision'—of eyes that fail to see reality behind deceptive facades; of the poet who, above all, imagines himself singing of human unity while others, misled by appearances, sow discord. By true vision, Iqbal offered visions of new solidarities, cultural pride, and a programme to seize the future by turning back. It is striking that Tagore used the same metaphor of the need to 'pierce the veil' of the apparent reality of India to find the truth within (Chakrabarty 2000: 150).

I turn now to examples of Iqbal's writings to explore three themes exposed by the poet's vision: the fallacy of the moral superiority of the West; the shared intellectual space in which great thinkers of diverse geographies and all historical ages participate; and, finally, the corrupting system of capitalism, with its corollaries of nationalism and racism, under which all the peoples of the world suffer and for which the spirit of Islam offers a moral alternative.

The *Jāvednāma*, Lord Kitchener, and Pharaoh: The Delusion of the Moral Progress of the West

The years following World War I in India saw mounting anti-government protest at a time of repression and disappointments. In these years, primarily between 1922 and 1932, Iqbal produced the bulk of his Persian poetry. Even to write in Persian challenged colonial expectations that 'modern' Indian intellectuals would eschew what were to be seen as classical, dead languages in India in favour of the vernaculars and English. In using Persian, however, Iqbal made a claim on an identity that transcended the territorially specific colonial category of 'Indian Muslim'. He also rejected the Arab and 'Orientalist' vision of the superiority of the Arab to identify himself with *'ajam*, the pejorative label given by Arabs to non-Arabs denoting the 'barbarity' of those who spoke Persian. In this, he drew from Islamic tradition ways of categorizing groups and territories that were independent of European categories (Majeed 1995: 304–5).

Iqbal's well-known presidential address to the All-India Muslim League in 1930, typically remembered only for its call for a grouping of Muslim provinces in the northwest, also spoke, intriguingly, of the prospect for autonomous Muslim rule as 'an opportunity [for Islam] to rid itself of the stamp that Arabian imperialism was forced to give it' (Iqbal 1948: 14). This issue had continued relevance in terms of how Muslim nations of Iqbal's day related to each other (Majeed 1995: 308). It also had relevance in terms of social status within India since Arab descent served as a pretext for claims to high birth, now enshrined in colonial censuses, in contrast to those (like Iqbal) known to be of local convert stock. Being *'ajamī*, moreover, linked Iqbal to the Persian Sufi poet Rumi, whom he claimed as his master.

Iqbal's *Jāvednāma*, a long epic ascent poem, published in 1932, was the culmination of his Persian writings. It was inspired by the *Commedia* of Rumi's near contemporary, Dante Alighieri (1265–1321), as well as by a long tradition of Arabic and Persian writing, linking an inner spiritual journey to travel through the spheres modelled on the Prophet Muhammad's own *mi'rāj* ascension, that had, in turn, inspired Dante. Nothing in Persianate culture meant more to Iqbal than the writings of Rumi, whose impassioned *maṡnavī*, celebrating the quest for the lost beloved, at once the longing for a human beloved and the soul's passion for the Divine, was widely cherished in the subcontinent. In Rumi, Iqbal found the model for his own interpretation of human creativity and movement, the celebration of passion above intellect, and the unity of cultural bonds over those of residence or birth. It is Rumi who is given the role of spiritual guide in Iqbal's poem, leading the protagonist on a journey from the moon, through Mercury, Venus, Mars, Jupiter, and Saturn to Paradise. This ascent, however, is an occasion to confront contemporaneous challenges of colonial thought and action *on Earth*.

The distance Indian Muslim discourse had travelled from the late nineteenth-century loyalty and deference of Iqbal's modernist forebear, Sir Sayyid Ahmad Khan (1817–98), is evident in this epic, published in the very year of the collapse of the Round Table Conference in London, which

Iqbal had attended. Sayyid Ahmad, in the aftermath of the uprising of 1857 and the targeting of Muslims for blame, was committed to a stance of Muslim 'loyalty' in a polity he understood to be fundamentally like the pre-colonial patronage states he well knew. Even in his own lifetime, with the stirrings of a vision of self-rule and official actions that undermined Muslim interests, on the one hand, and the racism faced by his talented son at the personal level, on the other, Sayyid Ahmad himself knew his policy was flawed. The events of subsequent decades, not least British policies in Ottoman lands as well as acts that clearly showed the repressive and exploitative dimension of imperial politics for all Indians, further undermined Sayyid Ahmad's stance. Iqbal would share Sayyid Ahmad's cry for Muslim renewal from spiritual and political slumber, but he would engage different dimensions of Islam, and, in radically different circumstances, conceive different strategies to achieve the awakening he also embraced. Iqbal, far more immersed in European thought and life, sought both intellectual and political freedom from the dominant European culture that Sayyid Ahmad, with his relatively scant knowledge of Europe and his searing memory of Mutiny horrors, admired.

Iqbal's ferocious anti-colonialism laces the *Jāvednāma* throughout, and it is precisely in his struggle with the events and personages of real history that Iqbal limns a site for seeking eternal truths and spiritual renewal. With great originality, Iqbal infuses worldly political content into traditional poetic forms, as his solution to the problem also faced by his great contemporary, Tagore, who initially compartmentalized his lyrical voice in poetry and his critical, realist, political voice in prose (Chakrabarty 2000: 151–5).[10] Unlike the classic ascent poems in Arabic, Iqbal's celestial journey traverses what turns out to be familiar terrain, namely, earth-like mountains and valleys, rivers and cities, populated by historical saints, thinkers, traitors, poets, spirits, and gods of historic imagination, and political rulers of earth (Prigarina 1997). Encounters with Indian sages, for example, appear in the first and last book. Ghalib (1797–1869), the nineteenth-century Delhi poet, joins classic Sufi lovers on Jupiter. Two heroes who defy Western imperialism, Jamal al-Din Afghani (1838/9–97) and Sa'id Halim Pasha (1864–1921), are central early on in the second book and, in balance, two traitors, Ja'far of Bengal (r. 1757–60) and Sadiq of Tipu's (1750–99) Deccan, who betrayed 'country and people' (*mulk-o-millat*) to the British, dominate the penultimate (Schimmel 1963: 306). There they meet the exquisitely beauteous Spirit of India, doomed to fetters, her heart broken by lamentation. Iqbal chose engagement with such issues of socio-political life—rather than what he sees as the problematic discipline and charisma of the Sufi path—as the key to the individual quest for self-realization.

It is by successive insight into the depth of the inscrutable real world (*az zamīr-i 'alam-i be chand-o-chūn*) that Zinda-rud (The Living Stream), the poem's protagonist and Iqbal's poetic persona, is granted the manifestation of the divine glory (*tajalli-i jalāl*) and learns the truth: to abandon the East and resist the spell of the West. Iqbal's very vocabulary imputes meaning to 'East' and 'West' since he opts for words that are not parallel and mutually defining, as the simple *mashriq* and *maghrib* would be. The 'East' is rather *khāwar*, 'dawn' with its resonance of renewal; the 'West' is *afrang*, the abode of the foreign 'Franks'. He learns another lesson as well, above all to be alone (*be hamā*) and yet engaged with society (*bā hamā*). And he accepts the mission to return to earth, carrying with him the illumination he has gained (Iqbal 1966: 140–1; Iqbal 1962: 179–80). Although not made explicit, the lessons resonate with the detachment of the Sufi and the Prophet's return from his own ascent.

One episode of the epic will serve to illustrate the insight that the poet has acquired: his daring, anachronistic coupling of the British hero, Horatio Herbert Kitchener (1850–1916) and the archetypal despot, Pharaoh. For Iqbal, Pharaoh was the ultimate symbol of cruel and unredeemed tyranny he had always been in Muslim tradition, which had never been dazzled, as had Europe, by the romance of Pharaonic legends and jewels. Pharaoh—in the late twentieth century equated by Islamists with Egypt's Sadat and the Shah of Iran—is here equated with Kitchener of Khartoum, to the British, the very defender of civilization against 'the mad Mahdi' of Sudan, Muhammad 'Ali (d. 1885). Kitchener went on from the Sudan to devise the brutal tactics that secured Boer submission in the Boer War, and—as reward—to be appointed, as viscount, commander-in-chief of British forces in India. His career culminated as consul general in Egypt and Secretary of State for war in World War I.

Imagine Venus. Zinda-rud and Maulana Rumi burn through the clouds and mists to the planet, then through a surging sea of pitch to a valley, to find the gods of the ancient world. Rumi speaks:

> I know them all, one by one—
> Ba'al, Mardukh, Ya'uq, Nasr, Fasr
> Ramkhan, Lat, Manat, Asr, Ghasr (1966: 73; 1962: 81).

Mardukh addresses the travellers first, providing the ingenious explanation of the gods' new-found prosperity: the modern excavations, museums, and scholarship of the West, which—far from mere service to historical and archaeological knowledge—turn out to be coupled with the flight 'from church and sanctuary' in a new idolatry that leads men to 'gaze backwards to the past age' (1966: 74; 1962: 82). Hearing that explanation, Ba'al breaks into song, with each stanza concluding in a joyous refrain, 'Ancient gods, our time has come!' The imperialists, far from heralds of real progress, turn out to be nothing more than revivers of paganism.

Rumi then silences the gods with *his* song in the poetic form of the ghazal whose subject is the inner quest that abandons the pagan world. The two travellers approach the translucent, utterly still—and hence, in Iqbal's imaginary, dead—ocean to find that most unlikely pair, Lord Kitchener of Khartoum and the Pharaoh of Moses's Egypt.

For Iqbal, no strategy in his poetry is more central than to show the hidden truth behind a misleading exterior, and no less is this true here. The two men, whom British history would never link, turn out to be *virtually the same*—for both are fundamentally power-drunk and arrogant:

> that one from the East, the other from the West,
> both at war and blows with the men of God (1966: 77; 1962: 85).

Both, literally, received blows to the neck, one from the staff of Moses, one from the Mahdi's sword. Both, uncannily, died by the same means, each 'dying of thirst in the embrace of the sea', equally God's judgement whether by the Red Sea's waters or in the sinking of the H.M.S. *Hampshire*. These are not mere coincidences.

Pharaoh calls on rulers to take a lesson from his fate, and returns to Mardukh's theme, now to condemn and not to praise European scholarship, and to expose the arrogance and avarice of those who rob the tombs:

> A human shape dwells in a museum
> with a legend upon its silent lips
> telling the story of imperialism
> and giving visions to the blind.
> What is the grand design of imperialism?
> To seek security by contriving division (1966: 78; 1962: 87).

Iqbal knows perfectly well the presumed motive of 'science and wisdom' to justify European archaeology, museums, and histories—he puts that explanation into Kitchener's mouth (1966: 78; 1962: 87). But, Foucauldian *avant la lettre*, he also knows the indissoluble link of knowledge and power, not least in the 'contriv[ed] divisions' and categories that self-proclaimed objective European knowledge created and used to serve their imperial rule.

Pharaoh, the symbol of evil, emerges as older and wiser than Kitchener. He sees the link of his tyranny and today's imperialism, and he would undo his past errors if he could:

If I could only see God's interlocutor [*Kalīm Allāh*, i.e. Moses] again
I would beg from him a heart aware (1966: 78; 1962: 86).

He challenges Kitchener to justify *his* violating the Mahdi's tomb, if the justification of tomb robbery is indeed to advance knowledge. Before Kitchener has an opportunity to reply, at the very word of the Mahdi's name, with lightning 'the Sudanese Dervesh' himself appears, bearing with him the rose scent of Paradise:

He cried, 'Kitchener, if you have eyes to see,
behold the avenging of a dervish's dust!
Heaven granted no grave for your dust,
gave no resting place but the salty ocean.'[11]
Then the words broke in his throat;
from his lips a heart-rending sigh was loosed
'Spirit (*rūḥ*) of the Arabs,' he cried, 'awaken;
like your forebears, be the creator of new ages!
Fu'ad, Faisal, Ibn Sa'ud,
how long will you twist like smoke [up]on yourselves?' (1966: 79; 1962: 88)

With that, Zinda-rud and Rumi recall their journey to the Beloved with the heart-stopping refrains of Sufi poetry:

'Cameleer, our friends are in Yathrib, we in Nejd....'
My camel is drunk with the grass, I for the Beloved (*dost*);
the camel is in your hands, I in the hands of the Beloved (1966: 80; 1962: 89).

And they resume their quest.

At one level, Iqbal's theme is the universal one of the attraction of the Divine, the pull of constant search and unsatisfied love, the need to see the true light and not the glitter of externals (Vahid 1959: 158–9). But Iqbal does not engage this theme through meditation in the hermit's cave. He does it by a 'this-worldly' devastating critique of British imperialism. Iqbal demonstrates a kind of stubborn self-confidence that throws to the wind the chronologies and the unquestioned justifications, not only of imperial rule but also of the intellectual enterprise of which he himself is a product. In these verses, Iqbal implicitly challenges the notions of time and history that posit the 'progress' and 'advance' of the modern West: its rulers are no better than the ancient tyrants. And he challenges 'whiggish' geographic teleologies that see East and West as eternally distinct: mirror-image tyrants take root in West and East. Zinda-rud has been led to clarity of vision; the misguided West, its sight distorted, gazes backwards and is left, in Pharaoh's words, with only 'visions of the blind' (1966: 78).

'The Prophet of Islam...Belongs to the Modern World': Dialogues Across Time and Space

The rejection of East and West as separate categories, as well as the assumption of 'modernity' as a decisive rupture in human morality and achievement, are themes that reappeared in Iqbal's seven lectures published as *The Reconstruction of Religious Thought in Islam* (1928). These lectures illustrate Iqbal's utter commitment to the notion of the free individual, and the conviction that it was in the realization of that individual's selfhood, driven by passion for divine love or truth, that life found its fulfilment. This conviction is relevant to such notions as 'East' and 'West' because it would be unthinkable to Iqbal that an individual would mechanically reproduce in microcosm some larger cultural world: the simplistic dualism that would trace genealogies of Western thought and Eastern thought, hermetically sealed from each other.

Again, as in the *Jāvednāma*, Iqbal insisted that only an ethnocentric pride would represent 'modernity' as a fundamental rupture in human consciousness. No individual should be trapped by the presumed chronology that limited rationality, for example, to the contemporary period, let alone by the mire of unchanging stasis imputed to the East. The free individual claims the whole world and engages on equal terms with intellectuals of any place and of any time.

Thus, *The Reconstruction* proceeds on the cavalierly 'un-modern' approach to time and place, already encountered in the *Jāvednāma*, where individuals from all times and places interact because they are assumed to share a common intellectual framework. In doing this, Iqbal implicitly communicates his conviction that Muslim thinkers have engaged with great philosophical issues, with precisely the same erudition and sophistication as have the thinkers of modern Europe:

> [Kant's] *Critique of Pure Reason* [1781] revealed the limitations of human reason and reduced the whole work of the rationalists to a heap of ruins.... Ghazali's [d. 1111] philosophical skepticism...virtually did the same kind of work in the world of Islam in breaking the back of that proud but shallow rationalism which moved in the same direction as pre-Kantian rationalism in Germany (Iqbal 1978: 5).
>
> Ghazali further amplified [Nazzam's principle of doubt] in his *Revivification of the Sciences of Religion*, and prepared the way for 'Descartes' Method' [1637].... Abu Bakr Razi [d. 923] was perhaps the first to criticize Aristotle's [d. 322 BCE] first figure, and in our times his objection, conceived in a thoroughly inductive spirit, has been reformulated by John Stuart Mill [1806–73].... It is a mistake to suppose the experimental method is a European discovery (Iqbal 1978: 128–9).

Iqbal identified what he saw as the great intellectual issues of his time and placed the great Muslim thinkers of the past in equal dialogue as full contributors with them.

Iqbal—in considerable company—imagined a genealogy of rationalism that produced modern science, but he was clear in his mind that the participants in that trajectory were not only 'the West', if that meant only Europeans and Christians. Indeed in one of his striking passages he turned to the Prophet of Islam who, he maintained, 'in so far as the spirit of his revelation is concerned ...belongs to the modern world.... The birth of Islam...is the birth of inductive intellect' (Iqbal 1978: 126). Central to his version of seventh-century modernity was the scope given to the individual without 'priesthood and hereditary kingship, the constant appeal to reason and experience in the Qur'an, and the emphasis that it [laid] on Nature and History as sources of human knowledge' (Iqbal 1978: 126). The West, as Iqbal encountered it in Darwin and Bergson, Nietzsche and Schopenhauer, was, in his formulation, quite simply 'us' (Shaikh 1992: 62).

Iqbal explicitly challenged the assumption of Spengler's *The Decline of the West* (1914)—with us down to Samuel Huntington of our day (1996)—that each culture was a specific organism, having no point of contact with cultures that historically preceded or followed it. Iqbal was specifically interested in the contribution of Muslim thinkers to Renaissance thinkers, often presented as a kind of conduit service in which Arabic translations preserved heretofore lost writings in Greek. Iqbal, in contrast, presented an intellectual heritage forged by the very revolt of Muslim thinkers against the classics.

Iqbal was, however, not only concerned with linear historical influence but with shared cultural worlds at any given time. Iqbal knew that recent scholarship had demonstrated Dante's familiarity with Islamic ascent texts, based on the Prophet's own *mi'rāj* ascension through the heavens. Indeed, Dante's whole enterprise of the quest for beauty or truth, with the vision of the absent beloved as muse and the tension of scholasticism and mysticism, resonates broadly with intellectual currents shared over a wide geographic space in the thirteenth and fourteenth centuries. Indeed, this description could well serve, for example, for nothing other than the work of Jalal al-din Rumi himself. The *Jāvednāma*, centuries later, took *The Divine Comedy* as its poetic model and engaged with worldwide issues of the mid-twentieth century. To describe *The Divine Comedy* and the *Jāvednāma* as, respectively, poems of the West and the East is less revealing than an appreciation of the culturally fluid and permeable worlds in which each was created.

Iqbal's own poetry also suggests this permeability. Iqbal called himself the

Muhammad Iqbal photographed in a characteristic pose as the romantic poet, lost in thought.

'Poet of the East'. But his poetry, like the poetry of many other Indian writers of the 1920s and 1930s, could not have existed without the European romanticism they knew and loved. Like the English romantics, Iqbal created a world of identities between the thoughts, moods and yearning of the poet and of nature (Mujeeb 1967: 484); he celebrated the individual; he was a poet of revolt. The photograph of Iqbal that is endlessly reproduced bespeaks the romantic poet—the beardless face, downcast eyes lost in thought, the face in profile, the rumpled dress.[12]

One sees this romanticism in Iqbal's many Urdu poems set by rivers, at once, in their movement, symbols of life as well as symbols of the passage of time. Rivers are a stimulus to nostalgia, whether the Ganga, the Neckar, the Ravi, the Guadalquivir of Cordoba, the south Indian Kaveri, or the Tigris.[13] The Persian Sufi tradition of poetry, of course, often posited an identity between the soul and natural symbols—the nightingale, the rose, the tulip, the moth—and these continue, enriched, in Iqbal's verse. But Iqbal linked natural symbols to his own inner absorption in visions of hope for worldly change:

Sāḥil-i daryā pe maiṅ ek rāt thā maḥv-i naẕar
Gusha-i dil meṅ chhupā'e ek jahān-iẕṭarab...
Mauj muẕṭar thī kahīṅ gaharā'iyoṅ meṅ mast-i khwāb!
One night on the bank of the river I was lost in my vision.
In the recesses of my heart I concealed a world of anxiety....
Somewhere, in the depths, the wave was restless, drunk in dreams.

('Khiẓr-i Rāh', DM 58–9)

Iqbal participated in and enlarged a shared intellectual and literary world that the poet claimed as his own.

The Insight of Khizr: Capitalism, Nationalism, and 'Community' as Narcotics

Nowhere were Iqbal's social concerns more evident than in his 'Khizr of the Road' (1922), an extended poem centred on the mysterious prophet of the

Islamic tradition, Khizr. Khizr is taken as the unnamed prophet in a Quranic passage (Quran 18: 65–82), described as 'one of Our servants, whom We gave Mercy from Ourself and whom We taught knowledge from Our Presence'. In the passage, Moses is permitted to follow Khizr on a journey provided that he does not question his actions. Khizr, as they proceeded, damaged the ship of poor ferrymen who had transported them, killed a seemingly innocent boy, and built up a fallen wall in a town that had repulsed them. But Khizr had seen through appearances to the reality of each situation: he protected the ferrymen's boat from confiscation by a tyrannical king; he saved the parents from an evil child; and he protected the hiding place of the inheritance of two orphans, which otherwise would have been stolen by the town's inhabitants. Khizr is Iqbal's model, ever in motion, ever defying expectations, ever in quest of justice.

In Iqbal's poem, Khizr reveals that not only the colonial world but the entire world suffers under the tyranny of capitalism since materialism, greed, and the inhumane exploitation of capitalism, distort human relations not only in Asia but in Europe as well. 'When,' asks Iqbal, putting the defiant question into the mouth of Lenin, addressing God, in one of his final and most celebrated poems, 'will the ship of capitalism sink?' ('Lenin', 1935, DM: 110–11). Banks surpass churches; women are without children; and democracy, in Europe as in India, is only magic to mask the realities of power. Iqbal and Lenin transcend any presumed geographic divide.

Khizr identifies constitutional reforms as only cosmetic, a ploy of 'the West' in holding on to its rule:

> *hai wahī sāz-i kohn maghrib kā jamhūrī niẓām*
> *jis ke pardoṅ meṅ nahīṅ ghair az nawā'e qaiṣarī*
> The democratic system of the West is the same old instrument
> In whose frets are nothing but the songs of imperial Caesars.
>
> ('Khiẓr-i Rāh', 1922, DM: 66–7)

Constitutional assemblies, reforms, rights—the focus of imperial wrangling in India in the twenties—Khizr labels mere 'soporifics'. The categories of the imperial state—race, nations, church, princes, culture, colour—are the 'narcotics' of imperialism that drug subject peoples into fighting over illusory power.

The truth of Khizr is a devastating critique of the West—of materialism, of the exploitation of the poor, of the categories like race and community. Khizr reveals kingship to rest in consciousness—it is nothing but mere 'magic-making'. Iqbal used the old Sufi images of intoxicated love that lead to the Divine, but now the firefly circles not the shrine (performing *ṯawāif*), but the false light of Europe; drinks not the wine of love, but the wine of the Farangi salesmen. Khizr's secret is detachment from the bonds of place that allows him to see these truths—a detachment that the poet and intellectual must share. Europe's economic and political dominion was based on advances in science and in rationalism, as Iqbal's lectures, described above, make clear. But Europe in no sense was to be taken as a spiritual mentor, as Iqbal warned his young compatriots in one of his last poems, 'Afrańgzada', ('besotted by the place inhabited by Franks'). Europe allures but is nothing but surface glitter: 'a gold-ornamented scabbard without a sword' which seduces one's sight ('Afrangzade', DM: 132–3). A common theme in notions of East and West is a kind of equivalence: first the East was great, and now the West. In fact, for Iqbal, there is no equivalence. The East, in its day, brought Europe civilization and moral nurture, *tarbiyyat* ('Masjid-i Qurtaba', DM 104–5), as Europe does *not* do in return today.

Today, far from offering nurture, Europe thwarts moral development, as some Europeans also argued. Thus A. J. Arberry, Iqbal's great translator, wrote, 'Europe...is the greatest hindrance in the way of man's ethical advancement', a comment appropriately published in 'The Wisdom of the East Series' (Iqbal 1953: xiii). Hope lay in reclaiming—to use, for example, the title of a book of Iqbal's beloved teacher, Sir Thomas Arnold—*The Legacy of Islam* (1931). Iqbal, like Marx, attributed a value to the capitalist exploitation of an inert Asia only in so far as its dislocations produced the unanticipated stimulation of its society and cultures, just as pearls, Iqbal wrote, are created 'by the buffeting of the seas'. Going beyond Marx in an arresting phrase in 'The Rise of Islam' (1923), Iqbal wrote, *musalmān ko musalmān kar diyā ṯūfān-i maghrib ne*, 'The storm of the West has made the Musalmaan into a Musalmaan' ('Tulū'-i Islām', DM: 74–5).

Iqbal in his life and work responded to his direct experience of a vibrant, dynamic, but, in his view, godless Europe. He knew both a Europe whose poetry and philosophy he loved, as well as a Europe whose particularly brutal form of twentieth-century imperialism in the Punjab he experienced first hand. College years in Cambridge were coupled with the experience of the Rowlatt-engendered terror of post-World War I Punjab; what seemed a charade of constitutional reform in the 1920s and 1930s; and endemic racism. In the end, Iqbal's focus was on a global fraternity of Muslims, but the way he imagined a Muslim 'nation' in India and the nature of his 'pan-Islamic' vision were as much about his anti-colonialism and anti-capitalism as about Islam.

The 'Islam' that Iqbal celebrated, moreover, was one of 'spirit', defined above all by openness and freedom for the individual who would realize himself within a community guided by moral values. His interest in Islamic traditions focused not on the core texts of the Quran and Hadith, in contrast for example to Sayyid Ahmad Khan, but on the minor intellectual traditions of philosophy. He had no interest, as later Islamist parties would, in 'Islamic law' or an 'Islamic system', as again his 1930 presidential address made clear:

> Nor should the Hindus fear that the creation of autonomous Muslim states will mean the introduction of a kind of religious rule in such states.... It is a state conceived as a contractual organism long before Rousseau ever thought of such a thing.... The character of a Muslim state can be judged from what the *Times of India* pointed out some time ago in a leader on the Indian Banking Enquiry Committee. 'In ancient India,' the paper points out, 'the state framed laws regulating the rates of interest, but in Muslim times, although Islam clearly forbids the realization of interest on money loaned, Indian Muslim states imposed no restriction on such notes' (Iqbal 1948: 14–15).

In Islam, Iqbal hoped for moral guidelines that would overcome exploitation and divisive ethnicity as well as the nationalism that was the currency of the day. In a frequently quoted verse, Iqbal celebrated the Prophet's *hijra*: *hai tark-i vaṯn, sunnat-i maḥbūb-i ilāhī*—'to depart the homeland is the example of God's Beloved' ('Vaṯaniyyat,' Iqbal 1989: 187).

For Iqbal, support for Muslim political autonomy would seem less a good in itself than simply a strategy to foster in one place a less divided and less exploitative society on the basis of the moral system he found in Islam. Nationalism would seem in the end a *pis aller* against Iqbal's larger vision, which chafed at the arbitrary units—nations, tribes, ethnicities—which imperialism created. Iqbal witnessed nationalism in two forms: the arbitrary carving up of the Ottoman empire after the war and the manipulations of interest groups within colonized India. In an allusion to the Quran, Iqbal spoke of national identities primarily as matters of convenience, 'for facility of reference only and not for restricting the social horizon of [their] members' (Iqbal 1978: 159). The nation he imagined would be—as Pakistan, ironically, never would be—free of communalism, on the one hand, and class interests, like those in his day of the dominant Punjab party, the Unionists of landlords and landed *pīrs*, on the other. At the tomb of the reformer Shaikh Ahmad Sirhindi (1564–1624), who refused to bow before the Mughal and whose spirit, Iqbal says, gave forth 'the ardour of free men', Iqbal prayed for vision, not mere 'seeing', but vision based on true poverty of spirit, *faqr*:

Ānkheṅ merī bīnā haiṅ, wa lekin nahīṅ bedār!
My eyes can see, but they have not been opened! ('Panjāb ke Pīrzādoṅ se', DM: 124–5).

His prayer was denied. Instead, he was told that there was no access to such poverty of spirit since the holy men themselves had traded the cap of poverty for the turbans of government service! (See also Gilmartin 1988).

Just as the Muslim leadership of the Punjab offered no hope to Iqbal, neither did existing Muslim rulers in general. 'Pan-Islam' was in no sense part of an existing, or even hoped for political community for Iqbal, but, again, offered a kind of spiritual antidote to the political and social domination he opposed. When he dreamed of 'Hijaz', he was not dreaming of a physical place or an existing polity: remember that the Sudanese dervish included Ibn Sa'ud (1880–1953) among those ensnared in error. Iqbal did not support the Khilafat movement.

Iqbal's turning away from Indian nationalism or a common Indian nationality was rooted in his conflation of materialism and racism with nationalism. As for some competing vision of an alternative pan-Islamic community, Iqbal made clear that it had 'no geographic basis' (Shaikh 1992: 62–5). In a famous verse, he spoke of Mecca giving Geneva the advice to forego a League of Nations (*aqwām*) for a League of Humankind (*insān*). Mecca, Mazheruddin Siddiqi suggests, is a symbol for a world that transcends race and nation, East and West (Siddiqi 1965: 27). For Iqbal, a renewed Islam would serve the interests of all peoples. This was one of Khizr's secrets:

rabṭ o ẓabṭ-i millat-i baiẓā hai mashriq kī nijāt
aishiyā wāle haiṅ us nukte se ab tak be khabar
The cohesion of the Radiant Community is the salvation of the East
The people of Asia are so far ignorant of this point ('Khiẓr-i Rāh', 1922, DM: 72–3).

'Islam', as Iqbal used it, was a unifying symbol and a source of pride for Muslims, but it was also a moral alternative intended to transcend division and hierarchy.

Imagined Geographies, Shared Modernity, and Historical Irony

Iqbal believed that the creative self, through the power of vision that sees into the nature of things, could literally—through the power of words—construct a new reality. He made the East, like 'Asia' and 'Islam', a space of moral wisdom and potential, not a geographic designator at all. Iqbal's 'East' was, specifically, not a 'legacy', as Orientalists would constrain it, but, in his imagination, fortuitously the place of the sunrise, as he put it in his famous poem, 'The Rise of Islam'. As for 'the West', in his judgement it represented neither progress nor moral superiority. Its arrogance blinded it to the roadblocks it created to human freedom and creativity—qualities others thought defined it.

But Iqbal also rejected the very divisions of East and West, for he sang of a world of permeable boundaries, and he took for granted shared intellectual and creative exchange throughout time. Indeed, 'the East' was not a geographic designator at all. As Suroosh Irfani writes, 'the East' for Iqbal implied 'an *inner* geography where the Adamic "trust" of divine viceregency lies obscured' (Irfani 1997: 1, emphasis mine). In his introduction to *Payām-i Mashriq*, his 'Message from the East', Iqbal wrote of his mission as an effort 'for raising the mental horizons of individuals and nations above geographical boundaries' in order to 'revive *human* nature (*insānī sirat kī tajdīd*)' (Irfani 1997: 4, italics added). In a letter to his translator, R. A. Nicholson, Iqbal made clear that his vision was meant to transcend race and nations, and to include not only Muslims but non-Muslims as well:

> I find that the nationalistic creed based on race or geography is gaining ground in the Muslim countries.... Therefore, as a Muslim and a lover of mankind, I would remind them that they are in duty bound to work for the progress of the entire humanity...(Siddiqi 1965: 31).

Iqbal, in the end, dreamed of the free individual gathered in a moral society, undivided by East or West, India or Pakistan, Arab or 'Ajam, or even Muslim or non-Muslim. In an Urdu ghazal of repartee with God on the injustices of 'this passing world'—where the Europeans thrive and the possessors of the Quran distort it—the poet, courting, Sufi-like, the displeasure of his own people as well as of strangers, declared himself outside them all:

> *darvesh-i khudāmast na sharqī hai na gharbī*
> *ghar merā na dillī, na ṣafāhān, na samarqand!*
> The dervish, drunk with God, belongs neither to East nor West
> My home is not Delhi, not Isfahan, not Samarqand! (Ghazal 16, DM: 90–1).

These are extraordinary verses for someone celebrated as a nationalist.

Iqbal's verse was incomparable, but his hopes to engender a new society through his words, Adam-like, were not to be. He denounced the divisions among subcontinental Muslims created, as he saw it, by the imperial powers who sought to divide by region and sect and, in his own Punjab, by the economic interests of the urban and the rural, big landlords and others. But in denouncing one set of divisions, he inevitably embraced another, that between Muslims and all others. His calls for cohesion in the face of what he saw as imperial stratagems provided Muslims with symbols of a 'charismatic community', to use David Gilmartin's term, above all in the decisive area of the Punjab. His verse thus served the territorially defined community of 'Indian Muslims' that he had long resisted by such strategies as fostering linkages to *'ajam*, to a larger Muslim world, and humankind generally.[14] Iqbal came to see a consolidated Muslim population as a space for his idealistic Muslim values to flourish. As Javed Majeed has pointed out, Iqbal thus emphasized the very British sociology he deplored (Majeed 1995: 323–4). By celebrating community (*millat*, as he used it) as the context for the emergence of the realized self, he reinforced the ethnicized nationalism that colonial sociology had defined.

Even as Iqbal turned to Islamic symbols to seek solutions to the problems of his day, his voice was uniquely his. Iqbal's emphasis on an Islamic spirit and Islamic ethics differed from the emerging vision of a totalizing Islamic system formulated by the pre-eminent 'Islamist' thinker of the twentieth century, Maulana Syed Abul A'la Maududi (1903–79), Iqbal's younger contemporary. It also differed from the diverse voices of the Islamic scholars, the ulama, and the holy men of his day, whom for the most part Iqbal simply dismissed. He specifically rejected the pragmatic embrace of Indian nationalism on the part of many of the religious scholars who supported the Indian National Congress and imagined a kind of 'jurisprudential apartheid' for Muslims within a free and democratic India (Hardy 1970: 34). But he was like these other Islamic thinkers, and like virtually every other political figure of the day of whatever religious background,[15] for whom, in the end, the religious 'communities' were regarded as the primary constituents of society. With heroic philosophy and poetic virtuosity, Iqbal had conjured from the depths the mysterious Khizr, the great Sufi Rumi, the Prophet himself in dialogue with great exponents of modernity, all to guide, instruct, and put colonialism—its institutions, its divisions, and its moral superiority—in their place.[16] But the competition of 'religious communities' in British India proved the power of the pervasive discourse, the 'narcotic', that even Iqbal, in the end, could not resist.

Notes

[1] I thank Kathryn Hansen and David Lelyveld as organizers of this volume and the conference that preceded it for an opportunity to celebrate the work of C. M. Naim. An essay on Iqbal's 'imagination' would seem a fit offering because of Naim's own commitment to humane and universal values.

[2] It is with some diffidence that I write about Iqbal, study of whom has defined the careers of many scholars. I was inspired to think again about Iqbal a few years back by an invitation from the Institute for Policy Research (IKD), Kuala Lumpur, to participate in a conference, 'Muhammad Iqbal and the Asian Renaissance' (3–5 June 1997), intended to be one of five such events, the others studying Jose Rizal, Rabindranath Tagore, Sun Yat Sen, and Jamal al-Din Afghani as beacons for today's nations of Asia. I am grateful to Abdul Rahman Adnan, director; the then deputy prime minister of Malaysia, Anwar Ibrahim; and other hosts on that occasion. I am also thankful, as always, to Muhammad Khalid Masud for helpful suggestions. I also acknowledge with thanks the constructive comments of several colleagues gathered at North Carolina State University (where I presented a draft of the Kuala Lumpur paper), in particular, David Gilmartin, Sandria Freitag, Mushirul Hasan, Muhammad Kalam, Mohamad Tavakoli-Targhi, and Umar Qureshi. Thanks also to Rachel Sturman for her careful reading of a later draft. I also express gratitude and admiration for the edition of Iqbal's Urdu poetry, noted in the bibliography, prepared by David Matthews, which was indispensable for this project ('DM' in the embedded notes).

[3] 'Taranna-i Hindi' (1904, DM: 16–17.) As Farina Mir notes, however, that song was eclipsed in the 1990s with Hindu nationalist preference for 'Bande Mataram' (oral communication).

[4] The phrase is that of Shankha Ghosh, Kolkata, who has translated Iqbal into Bengali in order to resist such partitioning. Comments of Pabitra Sarkar, Kuala Lumpur, 5 June 1997.

[5] In this regard, it is irresistible to quote one of Iqbal's favourite lines from Rumi:

> *Shud pareshān khwāb-i man az kaṣrat-i ta'bīrhā.*
> My dreams are distraught from too many interpretations.
>
> From his 'Speech on the motion for adjournment regarding communal riots delivered in the Punjab Legislative Council on the 18th July, 1927' (Iqbal 1948: 67).

[6] Quoted in Vahid 1959: 30 from *Bāl-i Jibrīl.*

[7] In addition to Iqbal's attraction to Bergson and, albeit with many reservations, Nietzsche, he also was drawn to now dated scientific discoveries of his day. According to Fazlur Rahman, he took subatomic theories, for example, as proof of human free will, free of cause and effect (Rahman 1982: 153–4).

[8] Iqbal's *Payām-i Mashriq* (1923) was an explicit offering to Goethe in return and carried on its cover the Quranic verse 'To God belongs East and West' (Vahid 1959: 77–8).

[9] See 'Alī Sharī'atī 1982. With thanks to Mohamad Tavakoli-Targhi and Clarence Walker.

[10] In the *Jāvednāma*, Iqbal made use of several familiar poetic forms. The poem as a whole is written as an epic *maṣnavī*, using even the same meter that Rumi had used in his own great *Maṣnavī*. Iqbal, with great originality, however, used two other forms in his verse, both represented in the section below: poetic drama with exchanges

in the mouths of dramatis personae as well as interspersed lyric ghazal (Iqbal 1966: 12).

[11] The poet's point is that the Mahdi's grave in Omdurman is an honoured site of pilgrimage while Kitchener's watery grave is forgotten.

[12] *http: //philo.8m.com/Iqbal1.jpg*

[13] See as examples 'Kinār-i Rāvi'(1905, DM: 23), 'Ek Shām,' written in Heidelberg (1907, DM: 25), 'Tarāna-i Millī' by the Ganga (1910, DM: 30).

[14] *See* Majeed (1995) for a stimulating analysis of Iqbal's use of '*ajam*, for example, in the context of discourses of racism.

[15] The tiny numbers embracing leftist Marxism are the only exception to this.

[16] He admired, for example, Iranian utopians and universalists going back to the Baab (Sayyid 'Ali Muhammad Shirazi, 1819–50), who inspired the modern Baha'i movement. Tahira, the Babi poetess and martyr (d.1852), finds her place in the *Jāvednāma* with the martyr Hallaj (858–922) and others who accept death rather than deviate from their vision.

Bibliography

Chakrabarty, Dipesh, *Provincializing Europe: Postcolonial Thought and Historical Difference*, Princeton: Princeton University Press, 2000.

Cole, Juan R. I., *Modernity and the Millennium: The Genesis of the Baha'i Faith in the Nineteenth-Century Middle East*, New York: Columbia University Press, 1998.

Du Bois, W.E.B., *The Souls of Black Folk*, David W. Blight and Robert Gooding-Williams (eds.), Boston: Bedford Books, 1997 [1903].

Gilmartin, David, *Empire and Islam: Punjab and the Making of Pakistan*, Berkeley: University of California Press, 1988.

Hardy, Peter, *Partners in Freedom—and True Muslims: The Political Thought of Some Muslim Scholars in British India 1912–1947*, Scandinavian Institute of Asian Studies Monograph Series No. 5. Lund: Studentlitteratur, 1970.

Huntington, Samuel P., *The Clash of Civilizations and the Remaking of World Order*, New York: Simon & Schuster, 1996.

Iqbal, Muhammad, *Speeches and Statements of Iqbal, compiled by 'Shamloo'*, 2nd ed., Lahore: Al-Manar Academy, 1948.

———, *The Mysteries of Selflessness: A Philosophical Poem*, trans. A. J. Arberry, Wisdom of the East Series, London: J. Murray, 1953.

———, *Kulliyāt-i Iqbāl Fārsī*, Delhi: Kutubkhana Naziriya, 1962.

———, *Javid-Nama*, trans. Arthur J. Arberry, London: George Allen & Unwin Ltd., 1966.

———, *The Reconstruction of Religious Thought in Islam*, Lahore: Sh. Muhammad Ashraf, 1978 [1928].

———, *Kulliyāt-i Iqbāl Urdū*, Lahore: Iqbal Akademi, 1989.

Irfani, Suroosh, 'Iqbal's Critique of the "East"', Paper presented at the 1997 conference,

'Muhammad Iqbal and the Asian Renaissance', Institute for Policy Research, Kuala Lumpur, Lahore: Institute for Strategic Studies, Typescript.

Lewis, Martin W., and Karen E. Wigen, *The Myth of Continents: A Critique of Metageography*, Berkeley: University of California Press, 1997.

Majeed, Javed, 'Pan-Islam and "Deracialisation" in the Thought of Muhammad Iqbal', in Peter Robb (ed.), *The Concept of Race in South Asia*, Delhi: Oxford University Press, 1995, 304–26.

Matthews, D. J. (ed. and trans.), *Iqbal: A Selection of the Urdu Verse*, London: School of Oriental and African Studies, University of London, 1993 (hereafter DM).

Metcalf, Barbara D., 'Reflections on Iqbal's Mosque', *Journal of South Asian and Middle Eastern Studies*, 1: 2, 1977, 68–74.

Mujeeb, Muhammad, *The Indian Muslims*, London: George Allen & Unwin Ltd., 1967.

Muzaffar, Chandra, 'Iqbal and Reform in the Muslim World', Paper presented at the 1997 conference, 'Muhammad Iqbal and the Asian Renaissance', Institute for Policy Research, Kuala Lumpur, Kuala Lumpur: Centre for Civilizational Dialogue, 1997, Typescript.

Prigarina, Natalia, 'Poetic World of Muhammad Iqbal', Paper presented at the 1997 conference, 'Muhammad Iqbal and the Asian Renaissance', Institute for Policy Research, Kuala Lumpur, Moscow: Institute of Oriental Studies, 1997, Typescript.

Rahman, Fazlur, *Islam*, 2nd ed., Chicago: University of Chicago Press, 1979 [1966].

______, *Islam and Modernity: Transformation of an Intellectual Tradition*, Chicago: University of Chicago Press, 1982.

Robinson, Francis, *Islam and Muslim History in South Asia*, New Delhi: Oxford University Press, 2000.

Said, Edward W., *Orientalism*, New York: Pantheon, 1978.

Schimmel, Annemarie, *Gabriel's Wing: A Study into the Religious Ideas of Sir Muhammad Iqbal*, Leiden: E. J. Brill, 1963.

Shaikh, Farzana, 'Azad and Iqbal: The Quest for the Islamic "Good"', in Mushirul Hasan (ed.), *Islam and Indian Nationalism: Reflections on Abul Kalam Azad*, New Delhi: Manohar, 1992, 59–76.

Sharī'atī, 'Alī, *'Allāmah Iqbāl, Muṣliḥ Qarn-i Ākhir*, trans. Kabīr Aḥmad Jā'isī, Srinagar: Iqbal Institute, Kashmir University; New Delhi: Maktaba-i Jami'a, 1982.

Siddiqi, Mazheruddin, *The Image of the West in Iqbal*, 2nd ed., Lahore: Bazm-i-Iqbal, 1965.

Smith, Wilfred Cantwell, *Modern Islam in India*, Lahore: Sh. Muhammad Ashraf, 1946.

Spivak, Gayatri, 'Can the Subaltern Speak?', in Cary Nelson and Lawrence Grossberg (eds.), *Marxism and the Interpretation of Culture*, Urbana: University of Illinois Press, 1988, 271–315.

Vahid, Syed Abdul, *Iqbal: His Art and Thought*, London: John Murray, 1959.

Winichakul, Thongchai, *Siam Mapped: A History of the Geo-Body of a Nation*, Honolulu: University of Hawaii Press, 1994.

PART 2

The Critical Project and Its Revision

The Poet in the Poem or, Veiling the Utterance

Shamsur Rahman Faruqi*

Choudhri Mohammed Naim spent very nearly two decades perfecting his translation of *Z̲ikr-i Mīr*, Mir's autobiography. Written in difficult, somewhat idiosyncratic, and occasionally quite obscure Persian, it has fascinated scholars and students of Mir ever since it was discovered in the late 1920s and printed in 1928 (Mir 1928). Yet, apart from the fact that its author is perhaps the greatest Urdu poet ever, it signally fails to do what autobiographies are supposed to do: it tells us practically nothing about Mir as a person, or even as a poet. What Mir claimed to have done in *Z̲ikr-i Mīr* is as follows (in Naim's excellent translation):

> Now says this humble man, Mir Muhammad Taqi whose *takhallus̤* is Mir, that being unemployed these days and confined to my solitary corner, I wrote down my story [*aḥvāl-i khud*], containing the events of my life [*ḥālāt*], the incidents of my times [*savāniḥ-i rozgār*] and some [other related] anecdotes [*ḥikāyāt*] and tales [*naqlhā*] (Naim 1999: 26).

Naim tells us in his Introduction that in *Z̲ikr-i Mīr*:

> The account of Mir's own life is scattered and quite summary in nature. He does not give us the kind of personal details we expect in an autobiography. He does not tell us what year he was born in, or got married in, or how many children he had and when; he is silent about his peers and his interaction with them in literary gatherings; he doesn't even mention any of his writings (Naim 1999: 11).

*Note: All translations from Urdu and Persian have been made by the author, unless specified otherwise.

So what was the purpose of the exercise, or experiment in autobiography that Mir undertook apparently in all seriousness? Judging from what little we know of Mir, the autobiography seems to present a picture—if at all it can be called a picture—of Mir which is not on all fours with his real personality. To quote Naim once again:

> Contrary to the image created by Muhammad Husain Azad in *Āb-i Ḥayāt*, the most influential of all histories of Urdu poetry, and his own frequent remarks in ZM, Mir was not always a dour recluse. In fact, on the evidence of many of his topical poems, he could be said to have been a man of appetites. He could feel strongly for his friends and lovers and openly find pleasure in their company, just as he could launch scurrilous attacks against those who would enrage him for any reason. The poems he wrote about his patron Asaf-ud-Daulah's hunting expeditions—they are thematically unique in Urdu poetry—display a keen appreciation of natural beauty. He also appears to have been quite fond of animals—at various times, he kept cats, dogs and goats as pets, and wrote delightful poems about them (Naim 1999: 4–5).[1]

Thus *Ẕikr-i Mīr* seems to conceal much more than it reveals, and what it does reveal about its author is either inconsequential or not quite in conformity with the image of Mir that has reached us through sources other than this so-called autobiography. One might almost say that Mir composed *Ẕikr-i Mīr* to dissemble, rather than reveal. It is true that no autobiographer reveals everything, but one can expect a responsible autobiographer to reveal something, and to ensure that whatever he does reveal is not false. A good example is the autobiography of Bertrand Russell. It merely hints at or suppresses almost all the unsavoury aspects of the author's life and character; it edits the truth to present the author in the best possible light (Russell 1967–9). Yet what it does present is substantial and true information about its author.[2]

Mir's autobiography reads in part like a hagiography of his father's and grandfather's spiritual merits, and in part like notes of contemporary events hurriedly jotted down in a private journal. A lot of the material has no date, and a good bit of it does not observe any chronological sequence. Small wonder, then, that while Urdu critics have assiduously mined Mir's poetry to glean details about his life and circumstances, they have rarely alluded to or made use of *Ẕikr-i Mīr* to support their assertions about Mir's personality and what they regard as the 'true details' of his life. And even in poetry, only that much has been used which supports the critic's pet notions. Whatever doesn't, doesn't make it to the horizon of the critic's attention. For instance, the popular myth is that Mir was an intensely unhappy person, especially in love, So, a successful love affair of mature years as described in the apparently autobiographical *Mu'amilāt-i 'Ishq* (Episodes of Love) has been passed over in silence, and the unhappy love story, *Khvāb-o-Khiyāl-i Mīr* (Mir's Dreams and Imaginings), also apparently autobiographical, has been savoured by our critics 'as much as their lips and teeth could permit' (in Ghalib's phrase, though in another context). Russell and Islam cheerfully satisfy the demands of inclusiveness by flying in the face of the poem's evidence and asserting that the 'woman in the case' in both *Mu'amilāt-i 'Ishq* and *Khvāb-o-Khiyāl-i Mīr* is the same, and that the *Khvāb-o-Khiyāl* is actually a sequel to the *Mu'amilāt* (Russell and Islam 1968: 96–7).

Much of our Mir criticism shows a somewhat amusing, somewhat annoying conjuncture of two myths. The first myth is that poetry, especially ghazal, is necessarily the expression of the poet's personal feelings, and the events and circumstances narrated in it are, if not entirely factual, based certainly on facts. Myth number two is that since Mir's poetry reveals him to be a sad, embittered man, his life and personality also were sad and embittered. Another way of stating this myth is to say that since Mir's life was sad and embittered, so his poetry is full of sadness and bitterness. Let me elaborate this a little.

Poetry is the expression of personality: versions of this view have been held sacred in our criticism ever since we realized that there is a business of criticism and some people are specially equipped to transact it. The late Professor Nūrul Ḥasan Hāshmī, a respected teacher of C.M. Naim's, used to observe quite casually and frequently that 'poetry was a *dākhilī* thing', *dākhilī* here being taken to mean anything from 'heartfelt', 'authentic in some autobiographical sense', to 'the spontaneous overflow of powerful feelings', this last, of course, being a statement made by Wordsworth (1919: 26), and made popular among us by undergraduate teachers of literature.[3]

One inevitable and perhaps initially unanticipated result of this stress on the *dākhilī* nature of poetry was that much of the *maṡnavī*, almost all *qaṣīda*, and all ghazal that was not based on Sufistic themes or 'sacred love' was considered to be out of the pale of *sachchī shā'irī* (true poetry). The term 'true poetry' could be interpreted as (1) texts that truly deserved to be called 'poetry,' and (2) texts that stated 'true' things. When influential literary personages like Rashīd Aḥmad Ṣiddīqī declared that the ghazal was the *ābrū* (honour and good name) of Urdu poetry, they clearly intended this to apply to the 'authentic', 'undefiled' ghazal, the ghazal that expressed the poet's 'true and natural feelings' and was based on 'reality' (Anṣārī 1997: 112).

The principle that poetry is, or should be, the expression of the poet's 'personality' was a natural derivative of the assumption that poetry expressed the poet's 'true feelings'. This principle was also stated in the following form:

poetry is, or should be, based on 'reality', or 'truth', or 'true facts'. It was again only a small percentage of extant Urdu ghazals that could make the grade according to this formulation. The main demand was that in the ghazal one should narrate or depict only those events and states that one had experienced in person. Thus, the ghazal was seen as something like autobiography.

'Andalīb Shādānī, in a series of famous and very influential articles published in the Urdu monthly *Sāqī* from October 1937 to November 1940, declared that all good ghazal was based on the poet's real-life experience (Shādānī 1945). Judging from this standpoint, he found the productions of all contemporary ghazal writers to be 'false', or poetry of 'inferior grade'. Their ghazals were not based, according to Shādānī, on what he believed should be the true events of love, events that had occurred in the poets' real life, and in fact many of the events described in modern ghazals, like the 'death' of the 'poet', could not have happened at all, because the poet obviously had to be alive to compose the poem.[4] According to Shādānī, the essential requirement for the ghazal was 'intensity of feeling and true emotions'. He declared further:

> Only those should be considered truly qualified to compose ghazals or narrate the story of love who, in addition to being possessed of poetic powers, give word to their own emotions, write about what has really transpired in their life, and write only what they have personally felt (Shādānī 1945: 14, 12–13).

Shādānī held the curious theory that while the 'artificial' themes and tropes that abound in Urdu ghazal were purely imitative of Persian and therefore 'unnatural', it was quite all right for the Persian ghazal to have them, because 'in the early times, such ideas and themes came into Persian poetry because of the poets' circumstances, and their environment' (Shādānī 1945: 28). For example, the Iranians were excessively given to drinking, so it is all right for Persian poetry to be full of images and themes related to wine and song. But in Urdu, the addiction to drink has been a rare occurrence among our poets from the earliest to the modern times. It is therefore impermissible for Urdu poets to wax eloquent on themes of drinking and inebriation (Shādānī 1945: 39–40).

Firāq Gorakhpurī had urged that the modern Urdu ghazal should not be blamed for being full of the themes of sadness and pain, for the air of sadness, lament, and anguish of the heart that one encountered in English poems like *The Shropshire Lad*, *The Waste Land*, and Hardy's *Wessex Poems*, was much more intense than anything found in Urdu. Shādānī took the trouble to translate some passages from these works (he chooses 'Death by Water' from *The Waste Land*) to 'prove' that:

> Whatever has been said in these poems is entirely *natural* [English word used in the original]. Some of this poetry is a dirge on love's martyrs, some of it a lament on the untimely death of friends, some of it is an involuntary sigh on the death by drowning of someone whose heart's desire remained unfulfilled...(Shādānī 1945: 61–5)[5]

In any other literary environment, such statements would arouse derisive laughter, but in Urdu they became the guiding light for later critics like Nūrul Ḥasan Hāshmī and Abūl Laiṡ Ṣiddīqī who found the poetry of the so-called 'Lucknow School' wanting in *dāk͟hiliyat*, devoid of the narration of real circumstances, much given to *k͟hārijiyat* (that is, depiction of external things like the beloved's dress, her toilette, her speech and mode of conduct in a somewhat explicit, faintly erotic manner) and therefore inferior. This also established the principle that poetry that concerns itself with the beloved's physical attributes, even if only in a mildly erotic way, and perhaps based on the poet's own experience and observation, is inauthentic, 'effeminate' and not of the first order.[6]

By the time our understanding of 'good' and 'bad' poetry (or at least ghazal poetry) became firmly established within the discourse of 'truth' and 'personality', we discovered yet another nugget of 'truth' about the nature of poetry. Critics who were led to believe that 'individuality' of voice and therefore 'originality' of style was a positive value, found Buffon's maxim 'le style c'ést l'homme même' very congenial to the theory that poetry was the expression of the poet's personality. The English translation of this dictum, 'Style is the man', was understood to mean that personality colours, or even creates a writer's style. This was conveniently added on to pseudo-psychological critical speculations like: Byron would not have been Byron but for his club foot. John Middleton Murry's nebulous semi-metaphysical notions about style also came in handy, and his name was often invoked in discussions of this subject. Though his observation, that style was 'organic—not the clothes a man wears, but the flesh and bone of his body' (Preminger and Brogan 1993: 1225), was not actually quoted very often, it informed our critics' assumptions about how the writer's personality revealed itself through his style.

Given the paucity of facts or even clues about the manner of life and feeling of early Urdu poets, there was no better way to determine the contours of a poet's personality than extrapolating inferential facts from his poems, or from whatever 'sources' presented themselves. The conclusions were then patched on to the poet's status as a literary person. For example, it could be argued that if Mir was seen in *Ẕikr-i Mīr* as telling a lot of lies, we could infer that such a person could not be a good poet, for he would have lied about his affairs of the heart as well, and since poetry, in order to be good, must be based on truth, Mir's love poetry cannot be regarded as good poetry. While we didn't go quite that far in regard to Mir, Ghalib's detractors often found in the 'questionable' aspects of his character a suitable stick to beat him with: a person given to drinking, gambling, sycophancy, jealousy, etc., could not be a good poet.

The Urdu modernists avoided the pitfalls of 'personality', but insisted that poetry was *iẕhār-i ẕāt* (expression of the inner being). This formulation was used as a counterpoint to what was later described as 'committed' literature, but was actually the literature of the party line. The modernists said that the poet should write whatever he really feels or thinks. He should not be fettered by outside pressures or persuasions. A true poet describes the truth as he sees it. He narrates truths, conveys to his reader his personal vision; he deals in truths that he discovers for himself. In other words, the poet does not purvey communal or communitarian truths; he gives to the world only what his inner being says is the truth.

There is no doubt that this principle works very well for the 'new' poetry, that is, the poetry written and promoted by the modernists and their immediate inspirations: Miraji, Rashed, Akhtarul Iman. And it continues to work for the Urdu poetry being written even today. But as a tool for understanding 'classical' or pre-modern Urdu poetry, it is useless. It must go to the great credit of the Urdu modernists that they did not try to read and judge classical Urdu poetry in terms of the 'expression of the poet's inner being'. They, however, did say that there was no unbridgeable difference between the old poetry and the new, for both were, after all, true poetry. Thus, they paved the way for the notion that poetry is not necessarily, and not always, the expression of the 'inner being'.

The principle that remains on the whole even now dominant in our main-line criticism is that poetry, and especially ghazal poetry, in some way mirrors the poet's life and personality. This implies two things: (1) we can derive some truths about a poet's life from his poems, and (2) we can legitimately derive some conclusions about his poetry from the facts of a poet's life and personality.

Different Urdu critics used these principles within limits set apparently unconsciously by themselves. If some critics stressed the personality of a poet as a foundation on which to erect opinions about his poetry, others used the poetry in order to make generalizations about his personality. For instance, Muḥammad Ḥusain Āzād depicted Nasikh as a somewhat aristocratic and arrogant person of good culinary appetites who was also fond of 'worldly' or 'unpoetic' pastimes like physical exercise and wrestling. Against this portrait of Nasikh, Āzād posited, perhaps unconsciously, the figure of Atash as a person of no desires, unworldly to the point of being naive, self-respecting though not self-regarding, devoid of hypocrisy, and austere like a Sufi. Our critics were not slow in concluding that given these personal traits, Nasikh produced a poetry that was the epitome of Lucknow-ness: a poetry replete with *khārijiyat* and empty of *dākhiliyat*, while Atash's poetry was something else—steeped in the 'Delhi' style, a model of *dākhiliyat*, and devoid of the preoccupation with the beloved's body and raiment, so characteristic of Lucknow-ness.[7] That both were actually poets of the same type, and in fact sometimes the poetry of one is practically indistinguishable from the other's, was a fact that does not seem to have occurred to any of our critics.

The contradictions and errors bred by the approach—poetry reflects biography, or biography is mirrored in the poetry—can further be seen in our treatment of Naẕīr Akbarābādī and Amīr Mīnā'ī. Seeing in Naẕīr's poetry an apparent abundance of religious and social multivalence, a proclivity for free, or at least liberal thought, and a lack of stress on religious ritualism, we made no delay in concluding that Naẕīr displayed these properties of character in his everyday, 'non-poetic' life too. Basing ourselves on the poems, we declared Naẕīr to be an *'avāmī shā'ir* (poet of the people).[8] We ignored Naẕīr's ghazals because the ghazals could support no such conclusion. As for Naẕīr's putative liberal and multivalent religiosity, no one seems to have noticed that Naẕīr, who lavishly praises Hindu and Sikh religious figures, does not have a word for the *shaykhain* (the first two caliphs of Islam).

The exemplary personal piety of Amīr Mīnā'ī rubs uncomfortable shoulders with his numerous erotic *she'rs*, some of which he liked so much that he put them in a selection of his poetry which he himself compiled.[9] If poetry is an expression of personality, should it not be inferred that Amīr Mīnā'ī was a man of worldly delights, and a free-living lover of erotic pleasures? Major details of the life of Amīr Mīnā'ī are well known, and speculation of the kind that was freely yielded to in Naẕīr's case was not possible here. So our critics maintained a discreet silence. With all the self-assurance of one who need not see very far, Rashīd Aḥmad Ṣiddīqī pronounced it impossible for a 'bad' person to be a 'good' poet.

For obvious reasons, Mir has had more than his share of theory-flaunting, poetry-twisting critics. For example, 'Andalīb Shādānī was quite persuaded that since Mir has a number of *she'rs* with homoerotic, or homosexual, or plain boy-love themes, he was an *amrad parast*, a term that means all the above modes of homosexual eroticism.[10] Contrariwise, some of Mir's famous *she'rs* which sounded conventionally 'sad', or had themes of unsuccessful or unrequited love, led the critic to decide that Mir did nothing in his life but weep and sigh sad sighs. His clearly humorous or light-hearted *she'rs* were dismissed as 'lowly', or 'vulgar', or somehow darkened by the murk and gloom of personal loss and tragedy. In the Preface to Maulvī 'Abdul Ḥaq's extremely popular *Intikhāb-i Kalām-i Mīr, Ma' Muqaddama, jis meṅ Mīr ke Ḥālāt aur Kalām kī Khuṣūṣiyāt par Baḥṣ kī ga'ī Hai* (Mir's Selected Poetry, with a Preface, which Discusses Mir's Circumstances and the Characteristics of his Poetry), Ḥaq had this to say about Mir and his humorous *she'rs*:

Light-heartedness and gaiety were not allotted in Mir Sahib's portion; he was the very embodiment of despair and [emotional] deprivation. This is the state of his poetry too. Or rather, his poetry is a true image of his disposition and life-story, and probably this is the reason why it is not devoid of genuineness and reality...

Man's temperament has two aspects: pleasure and delight, or then affliction and grief. Mir Sahib's she'rs, whether based on love or on wisdom, all reflect grief and affliction, failure and despair. This was the cast of his temperament. He might have been in any circumstance, may have been overpowered by any state, whenever he uttered something from the heart, it would be saturated in despair and failure. The taste of jesting, or fun, is just not there in his poetry.... His works do have some humorous she'rs, but they are either of such vulgarity that they smack of bad taste, or then they have that very unfulfilled longing and despair which stuck with him through his living days (Ḥaq 1945: 16, 31).

Majnūn Gorakhpurī detected some sort of 'revolutionary', or at least a moral and didactic agenda in Mir's poetry, but still he designated Mir 'the poet of sorrow', and said something curious to support his contention:

Mir is the poet of sorrow. Mir's age was the age of sorrow. And Mir, had he not been the poet of sorrow, would have committed treason against his age, and would not have been such a great poet for us either. Posterity has regarded only those poets as great who were the true children of their age, and fully representative of it (Gorakhpurī 1996: 196).[11]

All this would be risible, if the matter was not deadly serious, for criticism such as this has governed our appreciation of Mir for the last seventy or seventy-five years. Going back to Maulvī 'Abdul Ḥaq's judgement on Mir's humour, let me recall here that Maulvī 'Abdul Ḥaq has quoted just one *she'r* of Mir's (Ḥaq 1945: 32) to 'prove' that even the comic verses of Mir are charged with sorrow and despair:

Mir too was mad, but while passing by,
In a jesting way
He would rattle the chains
Of us, the shackled ones.[12]

So what does Majnūn Gorakhpurī do to account for Mir's humorous *she'rs*? He says, 'Let it be remembered that Mir's humour was not of the shallow and cheap kind. His humour had very deep layers of gravity and meaningfulness.' This remark is intended by Majnūn Gorakhpurī as a comment on the very *she'r* about the 'jesting Mir' that Maulvī 'Abdul Ḥaq quoted to 'prove' that Mir's humour was overlaid with tones of sorrow and despair.

It is interesting and symptomatic that these two senior critics, who are often praised for establishing the place of Mir in the modern canon, are entirely unable to come to grips with Mir's humour and his pleasantries. Both quote the same *she'r* to prove two different points. According to 'Abdul Ḥaq, Mir's lighter verses are both vulgar and plebeian, or are actually darkened by the shadow of his sorrows and frustrations. Majnūn Gorakhpurī, on the contrary, judges Mir's humour as having 'serious' purposes underneath.

It must be concluded, however reluctantly, that neither of these critics seems actually to have read Mir carefully. Or then they have deliberately distorted the personal and literary picture of Mir to suit their own favourite theories. Both are quite convinced that Mir is a poet of sorrow and pain. Majnūn Gorakhpurī attributes this to Mir's age. For it was his age, and his personal circumstances, which had turned Mir's life, and therefore his poetry, into a 'perpetual hanging on the gallows'. His poetry, especially his ghazals, prove that 'Mir's voice expresses the whole pain and anguish of his times in an extremely sophisticated and dignified manner' (Gorakhpurī 1996: 191). Against this is Maulvī 'Abdul Ḥaq's formulation to the effect that Mir's temperament itself was extremely susceptible to the experience of pain. According to Majnūn Gorakhpurī, Mir's poetry reflects his life; according to 'Abdul Ḥaq, Mir's life reflects his poetry. That is, 'Abdul Ḥaq diagnoses Mir's temperament to have made his life unhappy, and since his life was unhappy, his poetry was unhappy too. Majnūn Gorakhpurī goes the other way round: Mir's age was an age of sorrow, so Mir's life was sorrowful, hence his poetry was sorrowful too. Thus, according to 'Abdul Ḥaq, Mir was essentially an uncouth type who lapsed into indecorous drollery the moment he slipped out of his tenebrous moods. According to Majnūn Gorakhpurī, Mir's was a life of unrelieved gloom and even his humour veiled serious meanings and grave purposes.

The poetry of humour or banter does not translate well, if at all. Yet it seems worthwhile here to invoke Mir's own evidence and present some of his light-hearted *she'rs* to show what actually he was doing when he wrote in that mode:

I now depart the idol-house, oh Mir,
We'll meet here again, God willing (Mīr 1968: 138).

Friendship with boys now darkens my destiny;
My father used to warn me
Often, against this very day (Mīr 1968: 145).

If I was so minded
I'd fill my arms with you
And lift you up in a trice:
Weighty you may be, but you are
Just a flower before me (Mīr 1968: 237).

Pious Sheikh, your asinine nature
Is known the world over;
You do your hops and skips everywhere,
In refined assemblies, or arid places (Mīr 1968: 584).

I visited Mecca, Medina, Karbala,
I sauntered around and came back
Just the way I was (Mīr 1968: 620).

On the Day Of Judgement
By way of punishment for having written poems,
They flung against my head
My own book of poems (Mīr 1968: 623).

It should be obvious even from these random selections that in range, mood, and verbal subtlety, these *she'rs* present a degree of variety and sophistication which the reductionist mindset of our critics was unequipped to handle. The three senior critics whose work I have briefly discussed above, I hope without oversimplifying their positions, considered their assumptions about Mir's poetry more reliable than the poetry itself. The assumption that they shared was that poetry is the expression of personality. The only difference was that for Shādānī and 'Abdul Ḥaq, personality meant disposition and temperament, and for Majnūn Gorakhpurī it was the sum total of the poet's personal history and the social and political circumstances prevalent in his time.

I need not emphasize here that questions like 'personal expression' or 'poetry as self-revelation' never arose in classical Urdu poetics, or in Sanskrit poetics, nor yet in Perso-Arab poetics. Nor were issues like 'authenticity' or 'true expression of real emotions' ever raised in any of the literary traditions that Urdu is heir to. None of the contemporary or near contemporary accounts of Mir, for instance, say a word about his so-called hardships, disappointments, and sorrows, or that his poetry is an expression of his bitter personality and the sadness of his life trickles through everywhere in his poetry. The censures of critics like Shādānī and the extenuations offered by critics like Firāq Gorakhpurī were both conceived in terms of what they thought was the literary idiom of the Western world.

The important thing from the point of view of the sociology and politics of Urdu literary criticism is not the truth or validity of the literary theory offered by Shādānī and others. The important thing is that in its essentials, the theory was believed by our critics to be Western in origin, and also (or perhaps therefore) universally true. The fact of the matter, as every student of Western literary thought knows, is that poetry as expression of personality is not a universally recognized notion in the West. On the contrary, up until the advent of Romanticism in England, it had long been recognized in the West that literary texts, especially poems, breed other literary texts, and that no literary artefact can be understood outside the rules and conventions of the genre in which it was written. When a new genre came into existence, every effort was made to present it as not essentially different from the pre-existing literary artefacts of a similar nature.

A good example of this can be seen in the romances (we would now call them 'novels') of Madeleine de Scudery, and the prefaces that her brother Georges wrote for them as their putative author. In the Preface to *Ibrahim* (1641), Georges wrote:

> The works of the spirit are too significant to be left to chance; and I would be rather accused of having failed consciously, than of having succeeded without knowing what I was about.... Every art has certain rules which by infallible means lead to the ends proposed;...I have concluded that in drawing up a plan for this work I must consult the Greeks..., and to try by imitating them to arrive at the same end.... It would be as stupid as arrogant not to wish to imitate them (de Scudery 1964: 580–1).

This was not just a casual appeal to the ancients to justify what would have been at that time a novelty. We see Fielding adopting the same strategy in his Preface to *Joseph Andrews* (1742). He wishes his text to be read as a 'comic romance', and finds justification for it in the practice of the ancients. Having declared that 'poetry may be tragic or comic', and that it 'may be likewise either in verse or prose', he designates his 'comic romance' as a 'comic epic poem in prose':

Now, a comic romance is a comic epic poem in prose; differing from comedy, as the serious epic from tragedy: its action being more extended and comprehensive; containing a much larger circle of incidents, and introducing a great variety of characters (Fielding 1954: 17–18).

Similarly, in regard to making extensive and even blatant use of the texts of one's literary forebears, it is interesting to see Fielding say in *Tom Jones* (1749):

The ancients may be considered as a rich common, where every poor person who hath the smallest tenement in Parnassus hath a free right to fatten his muse. Or, to place it in clearer light, we moderns are to the ancients what the poor are to the rich....

In like manner are the ancients, such as Homer, Virgil, Horace, Cicero, and the rest, to be esteemed among us writers as so many wealthy squires, from whom we, the poor of Parnassus, claim an immemorial custom of taking whatever we can come at (Fielding 1966: 501).

Fielding's tone is facetious, but in essence his point is well supported by past theory and practice. I cite Madeleine de Scudery and Fielding to illustrate the point that in the literature of pre-industrial Europe, even new genres were sought to be understood in terms of old genres, and that literary artefacts were not seen there as creations in the void. A very vague and generalized maxim to the effect that poetry expresses the personality of the poet may be extracted from the writings of some of the English Romantics. But it would be a brave critic indeed who would believe that a 'lyric' poem like Shelley's 'A Lament' (1821) expressed not only his real feelings, but also that those feelings were permanent, and that the second (concluding) stanza was true and accurate for Shelley's later life too:

Out of the day and night
A joy has taken flight;
    Fresh spring, and summer, and winter hoar
Move my faint heart with grief, but with delight
        No more—Oh, never more (Shelley 1954: 576).[13]

Had 'Abdul Haq and other Urdu critics had their way, Shelley, on the strength of 'A Lament' would have been held out as a poet of unmitigated sadness and frustration at least after 1821. Critics (see Firāq Gorakhpurī and 'Andalīb Shādānī above) who could believe 'Death by Water' to be a personal poem of loss could believe anything.

A genuine question arises here. After all, the poet does put something in his poem, even if it is mere words. So does his utterance, or his words, give us no clue about his personality?

In order to attempt any coherent answer to this question, we shall first have to decide what we mean by 'personality'. Caroline Spurgeon, in her *Shakespeare's Imagery and What it Tells Us* (1935) had, by offering not unfanciful interpretations of Shakespeare's image clusters, even tried to determine Shakespeare's likes and dislikes, his habits, his personal experiences, and similar (minor?) details of his personality. But if 'personality' is the sum total of a person's genetic inheritance, education, and domestic and cultural environment, it is a moot point if poetry does express it all, and if it does, whether it can be descried by the reader in distant times and climes.

Then there is another question. Even if we do succeed in determining some or even all features of the pre-modern Urdu poet's personality, what insights would that information give us that could be relevant to an understanding or appreciation of his poetry? Or let us go the other way round: let us study the *she'rs* in which the poet seems to be speaking of himself. What information would we get about his character and personality from such *she'rs*, and how reliable would that information be, never mind its usefulness as a tool for critical assessment of the poetry?

Even a less than close reading of a pre-modern Urdu ghazal poet would make one thing instantly clear: he is not a reliable informant about himself, if at all the word 'informant' would apply here. Muṣḥafī (1750–1824) and Mir are notable among our poets for their sensuous and erotic imagery. Both also say things that can be taken as information about their sexual interests. Here are some *she'rs* from Muṣḥafī:

> Master Mushafi, you didn't miss out on a single lad;
> Obviously you are quite a maestro
> At your calling (Muṣḥafī 1968: 515).
>
> Well, Mushafi, I am not
> Much of a lover of boys—
> But I do have intercourse, more or less
> With womankind (Muṣḥafī 1968: 225).
>
> Even if she ever came to hand
> I shouldn't be guilty of the wicked deed;
> Please oh pure and perfect Lord,
> Grant me this prayer (Muṣḥafī 1971: 65).
>
> I grant that beardless brats
> Do give pleasure in a way, yet one finds
> The pleasure of love in females alone (Muṣḥafī 1974: 56).

It is obvious that these *she'rs* are useless as material for a personality profile of Muṣḥafī. In fact, it is easy to see, were one familiar with the principle of *maẓmūn āfirīnī* (theme creation, that is, finding new themes for poems), that more than anything else, these *she'rs* are exercises in theme creation. Mir sometimes affords even more telling examples. Here is one:

How could a plain human being
Keep company with such a one?
Impudent, thieving, restless, shallow, rakish, profligate (Mīr 1968: 726).

This *she'r* occurs in Mir's fifth *dīvān*, completed perhaps not earlier than 1798 and not later than 1803. Even if the earlier date is taken as more probable, Mir was seventy-five years of age at that time. And if this *she'r* is based on Mir's real circumstances, we should be bound to conclude that Mir was possessed of a personality that inclined towards what he himself describes as the very dregs of society. And if poetry expresses personality, one may wonder if a poet with such a personality could really have composed those noble *she'rs* that are the glory of our literature.

Here again, the principle of *maẓmūn āfirīnī* provides a more reliable key for opening up such texts to us. First and foremost, the pre-modern Urdu poet was engaged upon the business of finding new themes, or giving new slants to old themes. Mir said:

Your soul free from torment for the mazmun,
Your heart devoid of pain,
What avails?
Even if your visage is paper pale,
What avails? (Mīr 1968: 649).

Here the poet's office has been equated with that of the lover or the Sufi whose heart is tender and full of pain: one should have a heart full of pain, or a soul afflicted with torment, searching for new *maẓmūns*, or torment for *maẓmūns* not coming at all, or those that came but disappeared before they could be captured in words. One's true station in life is to have a concern in the ḥeart for *maẓmūns*, or pain in the heart caused by love. One must have either one or the other, or one's life is profitless. Creation of themes, and not self-revelation, is the proper business of the poet.

The following *she'r* occurs in Mir's first *dīvān*, completed before 1752:

I used Rekhta as a veil
Over my true utterance;
And now it has been fated
To stay as my art (Mīr 1968: 132).

This could be just another *maẓmūn*. But experience has taught me to regard poetics-related utterances of pre-modern Urdu poets as genuine statements in literary theory. This is particularly true of the poets who wrote roughly during the century and a half from around 1700 to around 1850 when Urdu's 'new' poetics was being developed and refined. I have given an inadequate translation; the keywords here are *sukhan*, *parda*, and *fan*, translated by me as 'utterance', 'veil', and 'art' respectively, although other meanings of these words are pertinent here: 'conversation', 'speech', 'poetry', 'words', 'discourse' for *sukhan*; 'screen', 'curtain', 'pretext', 'covering' for *parda*; and 'artifice', 'craft', 'accomplishment', 'cunning' for *fan*.

The word *rekhta* too has more sides than one: the language called *Rekhta*, the poetry written in that language, the ghazal written in the language called *Rekhta*, or *Hindī*. The basic theory is clear: the accomplishment of poetry conceals, throws a veil over the real utterance, or speech, or poetry, which remains unheard and unrevealed. Poetry veils the true utterance, and dissembling is the true art of the poet. Should this then be taken to mean a confession that one can never express one's true thoughts? Again, my experience of pre-modern Urdu poetry tells me not to do so. The problem of the failure of language is a modern phenomenon; the pre-modern poet was supremely confident in his power to find words for any theme. Mir possessed all *sukhan*, all words; what he did not have (according to this *she'r*) was the desire, or the will, to unveil his words.

So what words could those words be? They could be anything, a declaration of love before the beloved, a mystical, gnomic vision, a proclamation of war upon a world that valued form over meaning, the ritual over the spiritual, illusion over reality. The fact that he does not tell us what his real utterance was, or could be, is entirely appropriate: the utterance remains veiled.

So are we fated forever to remain ignorant of the poet's true purpose? My answer is, yes. And it is not such an intolerable state of affairs so long as we can manage to divine all, or at least some, of the poem's true purposes. Trying to discern the poet's true purpose will almost certainly lead us to nothing more than a handful of trivialities. In Mir's third *dīvān* there is a stunning *she'r*:

The world is the chessboard, Heaven the Player,
You and I the pieces. Like a true tyro
Heaven's only interest is in taking the pieces (Mīr 1968: 604).

The cold passion of the tone, the laconic satire, and the telling observation about novice chess players create a dramatic space where distant reverberations sound from a *rubā'ī* attributed to Khayyam, and from *King Lear* (though the latter should owe entirely to the reader/listener for their existence), and where a somewhat conventional theme is transformed into a cosmic dance of death. Added to this is the underlying irony: the sky is conventionally described in Urdu poetry as incredibly old. (That is why it appears 'bent', or it is 'bent' because it is so old.) So there is a new dimension of irony in describing a traditionally ancient being as an abecedarian chess player. What made the *she'r* even more memorable to me was another image drawn from the realm of chess, in the following *she'r* from the fourth *dīvān* of Mir:

> How I wish you had
> At least a chessboard and pieces around—
> Mir is an artful chess-playing companion,
> Not a burden upon the heart (Mīr 1968: 680).

Putting aside the felicity with which Mir made use of two double-rhyming phrases *(bār hai k̲h̲āṯir, yār-i shāṯir)* in a single line, the easy flow of the *she'r*, the tongue in cheek humility of the tone, and the polysemy of *yār-i shāṯir*,[14] I was immediately struck with the chess imagery, and coupled with the previously quoted *she'r* from the third *dīvān*, it led me to conclude that Mir must have been interested in chess. This happy inference was shattered when some time later I came across the following sentence in Chapter II of Sa'dī's *Gulistān* (1258):

> In the people's service I should be an artful chess-playing companion (*yār-i shāṯir*), not a burden upon the heart (*bār-i k̲h̲āṯir*) (Sa'dī 1909: 68).

I ruefully concluded that the only knowledge about the personality of Mir that I could extract from the two *she'rs* was that Mir may or may not have been interested in chess, but he knew *Gulistān* better than I did.

Notes

[1] For an English translation of Āzād's account of Mīr's life, personality, and poetry, see Āzād 2001: 185–203. Regarding Mir's appreciation of nature, it might be worthwhile to mention here that Mir never saw a body of water larger than a small though wide and tumultuous river in north Avadh, variously called the Sarju or the Ghaghra. Yet he has written some most hauntingly resonant and richly textured poetry about the ocean or turbulent river waters.

[2] Russell does not even hint at the circumstances of his divorce with Dora, his second wife, and the endless bickerings and bitterness, and his own obduracy over the

divorce settlement. Or consider, for example, Russell's laconic remark about his divorce with his third wife Patricia ('Peter') Spence. Russell says, 'When, in 1949, my wife decided that she wanted no more of me, our marriage came to an end' (Russell 1967–9: 3.16). For fuller information one has had to wait for Monk 2000.

[3] Earlier in his Preface to the second edition of *The Lyrical Ballads* (1800), Wordsworth said, 'The poet thinks and feels in the spirit of human passions' (1919: 21). Doubtless, in his long essay Wordsworth had hedged his bets in several subtle ways, but the glitter of his grand propositions so dazzled our theory makers that they did not stop to read the fine print.

[4] It is curious that practically none of our early twentieth-century critics could see their way to making the elementary distinction between the 'poet/author', and the 'protagonist' or 'speaker' or 'narrator' in a *she'r*. The initiator of the literalism that effected this conflation was the great Alṭāf Ḥusain Ḥālī in his famous *Muqaddama-i She'r-o-Shā'irī* (1893). Such conflation is entirely repugnant to the principle of *maẓmūn āfirīnī*. Failure to distinguish the protagonist from the poet/author also resulted in the failure to differentiate between metaphorical (or 'false') statements and non-metaphorical (or 'true') statements. Shiblī Nūmānī, despite his disapproval of what he thought was 'excessive metaphoricity' in the Indian Persian poetry of the Mughal period, astutely noted that in this poetry metaphor was treated as true in the literal sense, and was then made the basis of more metaphor making. *See* Shiblī Nūmānī, *She'rul 'Ajam*: 'They treated the literal [=idiomatic, accepted] meaning of the word as real, and made it the foundation of their *maẓmūn*' (Nūmānī 1954–8: 3.20). *Also see* his discussion of the extension of the beloved-as-murderer metaphor in Persian poetry (Nūmānī 1954–8: 4.76). Shādānī does not mention Shiblī at all, but quotes Ḥālī in extenso, or paraphrases him freely.

[5] On the term 'natural', see Pritchett 1994: 155–68.

[6] *See* Hāshmī (1971) and Ṣiddīqī (1967 [1965]). Both works have remained popular. These works bring to their logical conclusion the ideas about 'natural' and 'authentic' poetry introduced by Ḥālī (1893), then 'Abdus Salām Nadvī (1926), and 'Andalīb Shādānī. For a good discussion of what these people meant by 'Delhi-ness' and 'Lucknow-ness' in the context of Urdu poetry, *see* Petievich 1992: 13–25.

[7] For character sketches of Nasikh and Atash by Muḥammad Ḥusain Āzād, *see* Āzād 2001: 279–84 (Nasikh), and 311–12, 17 (Atash).

[8] *See*, for instance, the papers of Majnūn Gorakhpurī, Ehteshām Ḥusain, and Sīmāb Akbarābādī in the monthly *Nigār* (January 1940). These papers have been reproduced in Uṣmānī 1979.

[9] Here are two of my favourites, from the first fifteen pages:

I'll now bring back your picture
Before you, and
I'll clasp it to my breast,
I'll kiss it (Mīnā'ī 1873: 10).

Arm under the head, last night
She went to sleep with me.
It was so comfy, my arm
Went to sleep (Mīnā'ī 1873: 15).

[10] 'Mīr Ṣāḥib Kā Ek Khāṣ Rang', Shādānī 1963. Originally published in the monthly *Sāqī* (Delhi: October 1940). Shādānī's and Russell's conclusions on Mir's love poetry have been well and searchingly examined in Pritchett 1979: 60--77.

[11] Majnūn Gorakhpurī's essay was first published in the 1940s.

[12] Mīr 1968: 616. The *she'r* occurs in the fourth *dīvān*, composed before 1794, though after 1785.

[13] There are also other, somewhat different versions of the poem. I give the one that is considered most acceptable.

[14] This phrase has at least the following meanings: a friend or companion who is (1) an expert chess player, (2) extremely clever and artful, (3) swift in speed (as a messenger or runner, or one who walks with the master's mount), (4) deceitful, (5) roguish and unreliable, (6) wanton. The Arabic root *shin, toe, ra*, also means 'to go away from, to withdraw from'.

Bibliography

Anṣārī, Aslūb Aḥmad, *Aṯrāf-i Rashīd Aḥmad Ṣiddīqī*, Aligarh: Universal Book House, 1997.

Āzād, Muḥammad Ḥusain (ed. and trans. by Frances Pritchett and Shamsur Rahman Faruqi), *Āb-e Ḥayāt: Shaping the Canon of Urdu Poetry*, New Delhi: Oxford University Press, 2001.

de Scudery, Georges, 'The Preface to *Ibrahim* (Selections)', in Allan H. Gilbert (ed.), *Literary Criticism: Plato to Dryden*, Detroit: Wayne State University Press, 1964 [1940].

Fielding, Henry, *The History of the Adventures of Joseph Andrews and his Friend Mr Abraham Adams*, New York: Penguin, 1954 [1742].

———, *The History of Tom Jones, A Foundling*, New York: Washington Square Press, 1966 [1749].

Gorakhpurī, Majnūn, 'Mīr aur Ham', in M. Ḥabīb Khān (ed.), *Afkār-i Mīr: Ma'tarmīm va Izāfah*, Delhi: Abdul Haq Academy, 1996 [1967].

Ḥālī, Alṭāf Ḥusain, *Muqaddama-i She'r-o-Shā'irī*, Delhi: Maktaba Jami'a Limited, 1981 [1893].

Ḥaq, Maulvī 'Abdul, *Intikhāb-i Kalām-i Mīr, Ma' Muqaddama, jis meṅ Mīr ke Ḥālāt aur Kalām kī Khuṣūṣiyāt par Baḥṣ kī ga'ī Hai*, Delhi: Anjuman Taraqqi-i Urdu (Hind), 1945 [1929].

Hāshmī, Nūrul Ḥasan, *Dillī kā Dabistān-i Shā'irī*, Lucknow: Uttar Pradesh Urdu Academy, 1971.

Mīnā'ī, Amīr, *Gauhar-i Intik͟hāb*, Rampur: Ra'isul Matabi', 1873.

Mīr, Mīr Muḥammad Taqī (ed. and trans. by Ẕill-i 'Abbāsī 'Abbāsī), *Kulliyāt*, vol. 1, Delhi: Ilmi Majlis, 1968.

______ (ed. by Maulvī 'Abdul Ḥaq), *Ẕikr-i Mīr*, Aurangabad: Anjuman Urdu Press, 1928.

Monk, Ray, *Bertrand Russell: The Ghost of Madness, 1921–1970*, New York: Free Press, 2000.

Muṣḥafī, Shaik͟h G͟hulām Hamadānī (ed. by Nūrul Ḥasan Naqvī), *Kulliyāt-i Muṣḥafī, Dīvān I*, Lahore: Majlis Taraqqi-i Adab, 1968.

______, *Kulliyāt-i Muṣḥafī, Dīvān III*, Lahore: Majlis Taraqqi-i Adab, 1971.

______, *Kulliyāt-i Muṣḥafī, Dīvān IV*, Lahore: Majlis Taraqqi-i Adab, 1974.

Nadvī, 'Abdus Salām, *She'rul Hind*, 2 vols, Azamgarh: Matba'-i Ma'arif, 1926.

Naim, C.M. (ed. and trans.), *Zikr-i Mir: The Autobiography of the Eighteenth Century Mughal Poet: Mir Muhammad Taqi 'Mir' (1723–1810)*, New Delhi: Oxford University Press, 1999.

Nūmānī, Shiblī, *She'rul 'Ajam*, vols 1–5, Azamgarh: Ma'arif Press, 1954–8.

Petievich, Carla, *Assembly of Rivals: Delhi, Lucknow and the Urdu Ghazal*, Delhi: Manohar, 1992.

Preminger, Alex and T.V.F. Brogan (eds.), *The New Princeton Encyclopedia of Poetry and Poetics*, Princeton: Princeton University Press, 1993.

Pritchett, Frances, 'Convention in Classical Urdu Ghazal: The Case of Mir', *The Journal of South Asian and Middle Eastern Studies*, 3 (1), Fall 1979, 60–77.

______, *Nets of Awareness: Urdu Poetry and Its Critics*, Berkeley: University of California Press, 1994.

Russell, Bertrand, *The Autobiography of Bertrand Russell*, vols 1–3, London: Allen and Unwin, 1967–9.

Russell, Ralph and Khurshidul Islam, *Three Mughal Poets: Mir, Sauda, Mir Hasan*, Cambridge: Harvard University Press, 1968.

Sa'dī Shīrāzī, *Gulistān*, Kanpur: Matba'-i Majidi, 1909 [1258].

Shādānī, 'Andalīb, *Daur-i Ḥāẓir aur Urdū G͟hazalgo'ī*, Delhi: Parvez Book Depot, 1945.

______, *Taḥqīq kī Raushnī Meṅ*, Lahore: Ghulam Ali & Sons, 1963.

Shelley, Percy Bysshe (ed. by Edmund Blunden), *Selected Poems*, London and Glasgow: Collins, 1954.

Ṣiddīqī, Abūl Laiṡ, *Lakhna'u kā Dabistān-i Shā'irī*, Lahore: Urdu Markaz, 1967 [1965].

Spurgeon, Caroline, *Shakespeare's Imagery and What it Tells Us*, New York: Macmillan, 1935.

Uṡmānī, Shamsul Ḥaq (ed.), *Naẓīr Nāma*, Delhi: Subuhi Publications, 1979.

Wordsworth, William, 'Preface to the Lyrical Ballads, Second Edition, 1800', in Edmund D. Jones (ed.), *English Critical Essays of the Nineteenth Century*, London: Oxford University Press, 1919 [1916].

Poet of the Bazaars:
Naẕīr Akbarābādī, 1735–1830[1]

Aditya Behl

Born in Delhi around 1735 and resident in Agra from 1749 until his death in 1830, the Urdu poet Naẕīr Akbarābādī was contemptuously dismissed by the critic and connoisseur Nawāb Muṣṭafā Khān 'Shefta' (1806–69) as a writer of much poetry popular among the vulgar people in the bazaars of northern India (*ash'ār bisyār dārad ke ba-zabān-i sūqīyyīn jārī ast*). Shefta concluded from this observation that it was not necessary to count Naẕīr's poems among the works of established poets. Shefta's judgement had the effect of excluding Naẕīr's works both from the genteel classicism of the older order in Urdu poetry as well as from the reformed canons of the modernist Muḥammad Ḥusain 'Āzād' (1830–1910) and the high-minded Islamic revivalism of the Urdu poet Alṭāf Ḥusain 'Ḥālī' (1837–1914). Both these eminent transmitters of the canon of Urdu poetry left Naẕīr out of their history of literature. Yet Āzād and Ḥālī's exclusion of Naẕīr from the Urdu canon could not prevent his poetry from being consistently popular throughout the eighteenth and nineteenth centuries. The British lexicographer S.W. Fallon, compiler of the *Hindustani-English Dictionary*, noted in his preface: 'Naẕīr is the only poet whose verses have made their way to the people. His verses are recited and sung in every street and lane, especially in his native town of Agra.... In the broadest sense of the word, he was greatly independent, original, philosophic, catholic. The versatility of his genius is seen in the many-coloured variety of subjects which he handled. The poetry which he has evolved from common things...is ignorantly regarded by native scholars as the surest proof that he was no poet. "He has written," they say, "on such common subjects as flour and *dāl* (pulses), flies and musquitoes [*sic*]."...His poems are a picture gallery in which may be seen speaking pictures of the sports and pastimes, pleasures and enjoyments, pain and misery, and the mind and feelings of the natives of India' (Fallon 1879: viii–x). Naẕīr's works have enjoyed something of a revival among modern Urdu critics. Muhammad Sadiq's *History of Urdu Literature* devotes a chapter to Naẕīr and applauds his 'exuberant vitality, his passion for life at the sensuous level, and his involvement in the variegated panorama of life' (Sadiq 1984: 155).

It is against this critical background that one must articulate ways of understanding and enjoying Naẕīr's poetry. Enthusiastic critics have praised Naẕīr for presenting us with a moving 'picture gallery' (Fallon) of the eighteenth century, and for his exuberant descriptions of the 'variegated panorama of life' (Sadiq), but without tackling the considerably more difficult questions of aesthetic mediation and value. The major enthusiasts and apologists for Naẕīr work back from his poetry to present an image of his life. The deeper assumption hidden here is that poetry 'reflects' life directly and unproblematically, without any attention to the mediations of genre, aesthetic purpose, historical place, and audience. Are we to view Naẕīr's poetry as a simple 'reflection' of his turbulent times? Is he a realistic poet? 'Abdul Ghafūr 'Shahbāz', the canonical Urdu biographer of Naẕīr, fills in wide gaps in his life by referring to the poems and assuming that the experience, say, of Naẕīr's childhood must have been like one of his happy descriptions of childhood (Shahbāz 1981: 18–22). That this is a perilous procedure should be all too apparent, since there are also unhappy moments in his poems. Are we to assume that they reflect unhappiness in Naẕīr's life?

A connected problem is the sensuality of Naẕīr's verse, some of which has even been bowdlerized from the Nawal Kishor printing of 1870 in editions such as the *Āsī Kulliyāt* (1951) and the Salīm Ja'far anthology of the same year. Shamsur Rahman Faruqi claims that Naẕīr's view of sexuality carried with it the 'feeling that he's smacking his lips' over sex, as if he were sexually frustrated. He continues:

> Naẕīr Akbarābādī has treated all aspects of sexual pleasure but he mentions young boys too often, and his repetitious talk of teasing them, enticing them, and coaxing them to cooperate makes me think that he was psychologically impotent and could not conceive of sexuality like mature, experienced, and 'well-adjusted' people like Mīr.[2]

That Naẕīr should be faulted for his homoeroticism at a time when such themes were common in Urdu poetry seems particularly unjust. Mir himself includes in his poetic corpus many homoerotic verses (Naim 1979: 122–3, 141; Rahman 1990: 9, 12–18) and, like half of eighteenth-century Delhi, was probably infatuated with the devastatingly handsome 'Abdul Ḥai 'Tābāṅ', so tragically young to die of overdrinking (Ḥaqq 1935: 1).

Rather than judging them as faulty or impotent, Naẕīr's poems about sexual experience need to be viewed as expressive of an engagement with pleasure, a sensual sensibility. They represent a poetry of sensation, of feeling recreated, rather than one focused purely on creating new shades of subtle meaning (*ma'nī āfrīnī*) out of the limited range of topoi (*maẓmūn*, pl. *maẓāmīn*) of the classical ghazal world. Canonical critics may sniff at Naẕīr's verses, but admit to a certain guilty pleasure in reading Naẕīr. When Shahbāz, Naẕīr's Urdu biographer, went to Shiblī Nu'mānī for help with his research, Shiblī promised to help but commented snidely: 'When I found out that you were writing about his life (*ḥālāt*), I understood the matters to which you were paying special attention.'[3] Naẕīr represents a range of sensations and fixes them in poetic form for readers and audiences to savour, to consume. How are these sensations in poetic form aesthetically and socially mediated?

In order to answer this question, we must step back to the larger eighteenth-century north Indian context of Naẕīr's poetry. The declining political fortunes of the Mughal emperors and the invasions of Nadir Shah (1739) and other freebooters and adventurers provide merely the external markers of a century of tumult and transition, frequently painted in crepuscular tones by colonial historians (Irvine 1989, Spear 1991). After the pioneering work of Richard Barnett, Christopher Bayly, Sudipta Sen, and others, the eighteenth century is now understood as a period of regional dynamism, enhanced trans-regional networks of trade, and the foundation of viable successor states to the Mughal imperium.[4] Concomitant with the rise of regional states like Avadh, Hyderabad, and Bengal ran the rise of predatory powers like the Jats and Marathas. Criss-crossing this landscape of battling local powers ran networks of overland and riverine trade along historic routes like the Grand Trunk Road and the rivers Ganga and Jamuna. Enthusiastic participants in this scene of exchange and movement were ascetics and religious virtuosi or mercenaries from a plurality of lineages, with fixed or seasonal bases at mosques, Sufi shrines, fairs, or Hindu places of pilgrimage. Local religious, musical, literary, and artistic cultures flourished in these dynamic and changing public spaces.

At key points along these networks of trade, religious authority, and communication were situated market towns, from small village markets (*ḥāt*) and market towns (*qaṣba*) dominated by Muslim gentry to larger imperial centres like Delhi, Lahore, and Agra. Sen characterizes it as a 'society of marketplaces as much as one driven by land and its cultivation' (Sen 1998: 1). He describes a landscape dominated by 'passages of authority', a useful notion to indicate rights—imperial, aristocratic, religious, customary—over the revenue of marketplaces, roads, and rivers. Passage along these networks and exchange at nodal points was controlled and taxed by a variety of zamindars, toll collectors, religious authorities, and holders of customary or inherited rights over the productivity of markets. Markets were malleable and contingent: the increasing disruption of political stability caused some service elites to abandon older imperial centres like Delhi and Agra to travel to more prosperous lands to seek employment and patronage. There were also roving bands of robbers and traders such as the Banjaras, immortalized in perhaps Naẓīr's most famous poem, *Banjāra-Nāma.*

Naẓīr offers us a self-conscious poetic engagement with this society of marketplaces, the world of the bazaars of north India in the eighteenth and early nineteenth centuries. Pleasure itself, like trade, is culturally conditioned; in Bayly's phrase, it is a 'moment in culture' (Bayly 1992: 61). Naẓīr composed a wide variety of poems, but in his *naẓms* or connected poems he offers us a range of pleasures as vital and dynamic and colourful as the north Indian bazaar. In his marketplace of words, Naẓīr describes what it is like to enter the urban landscape, to consume the pleasures on sale. Naẓīr delineates the feeling of entering into the city of Agra, enjoying its pleasures, consuming its commodities, celebrating its festivals, and living in the public spaces of the bazaars, nodes in the networks of revenue, trade, consumption and desire.

These arenas for pleasure contain a cast of ideal typical characters like the courtesan, the pimp, and the merchant. Words are the currency of Naẓīr's ideational bazaar, and the act of authorship involves entry into the sensual imaginal world of the marketplace. His poems summon up a hierarchy and calendar of pleasures, an ideational structure that is built on the bazaar's festive joys and daily rhythms, describing the feelings of participating in these festivals and exchanges.Thus, he was not a 'realistic' poet in any straightforward way. While his poems engage with the realia of north Indian life in the eighteenth and early nineteenth centuries, he does not conform to any conventions of realism. Instead, his poetry is an intense engagement with realia, a reaching out for the sensations and feelings that attend particular experiences.

The world of Naẓīr's verse is also an ideal world, although one that is different in scope and emphasis from the poetic worlds created by ghazal poets like Ghalib and Mir. His poems push the range of Urdu poetry further than any more aristocratic canonical poet, going well beyond the hypertrophied aestheticism of the accepted topoi of roses and nightingales, the paradise-like garden and its flowers, and the longing for wine and the beautiful cup-bearer.

Naẕīr's descriptive poems are executed with considerable technical skill and employ a rich cultural and literary vocabulary. In addition, he has left a canonical *dīvān* or collection of ghazals and longer stanzaic poems responding to older poets such as Sirāj Aurangābādī and Ḥāfiẕ. A preliminary typology may be helpful here. In sorting through the poems, one notices several different types, by no means exhaustive of Naẕīr's total output of verse: (1) poems that *respond to older classics* in Persian and Urdu by crafting macaronic or *javāb-go* (responsive) verses in the same metre and rhyme; (2) poems about the feel and texture of *everyday life*: descriptions of items of daily use, of what it is like to slip in the mud in the monsoons, to go swimming in the Jamuna, to enjoy the ordinary pleasures of north Indian life; (3) poems that delineate the *culture of the bazaars*: life among the courtesans, profligates, banias, lowlifes, fakirs, and bhang addicts; erotic verses (poems on masturbation and the female orgasm, often bowdlerized), bawdy jokes, as well as satires of mercantile deception ('Pickled Rats'); and (4) poems of *social critique*, in which Naẕīr exposes the hypocrisy of people in power and the hollowness of social position. For Naẕīr, the world is full of sham and deception; the only attitude one can have towards it is philosophical detachment.

Placing Naẕīr: Pen Portraits

The eighteenth-century Agra of Naẕīr's life was the former Mughal capital, an agricultural and commercial centre where local artisans could sell their products. Naẕīr spent most of his life as a teacher in this city. He has left us a self-portrait in verse, in which he describes himself as a poor provincial schoolteacher. Despite the claim of Sayyid ancestry, he is not shy about his Indian extraction:

> *sust ravish, pasta qadd, sāṅvla, hindī niẕhād*
> *tan bhī kuchh aisā hī thā qadd ke muvāfiq 'ayān*
> Slow-paced, short in height, dark, and of Indian extraction
> His body was just as plain as his stature.
> *māthe pe ik khāl thā chhoṭā sā, masse ke ṭaur*
> *thā vo paṛā ān kar abru'oṅ ke darmiyān*
> He had a little mole on his forehead, somewhat like a wart
> It had come to rest there, just between his eyebrows.
> *vaẕa' subuk us kī thī, tis pe na rakhtā thā resh*
> *mūnchheṅ thīṅ, aur kānoṅ par paṭṭe bhī the panba sāṅ*
> His temperament was naturally cheerful; moreover, he did not have a beard
> He had moustaches, and his sideburns were white as cotton too.
>
> (Naẕīr 1989: 15–16).

A contemporary description confirms that Naẓīr had 'a temperament both measured and frisky' (*ṭabī'yat mauzūṅ aur chulbulī rakhte the*).[5]

Naẓīr was one of a class of service people catering to the pleasures and tastes of the nobility and the *ashrāf*, petty zamindars and rajas, as well as those of wealthy Jain, Agraval, or Khatri merchants who prospered off the inland trade of Hindustan. In his self-portrait, he represents himself as 'fearful at heart and cowardly', but doing what he knew best: teaching. He was keenly aware of the limits of his knowledge:

> None of the books for his lessons were clear to him
> If he knew the meanings, he'd say them, otherwise just carry on teaching.
> He couldn't comprehend any knowledge in Arabic
> But in Persian, yes, he did perhaps understand some 'this' and 'that'.
>
> (Naẓīr 1989: 15)

Despite these shortcomings and expressions of false modesty, however, he declares himself passionately devoted to composing and reciting couplets and ghazals. He concludes by thanking Allah for providing for him:

> Through His grace, Allah gave him throughout his life
> With dignity and respect, clothing and water and bread (Naẓīr 1989: 16).

The poem places him within the class of the people of the bazaar, a small schoolteacher who provided for himself adequately by teaching the boys of the *shurafā* of Agra. Thus, he would be the equivalent of the munshis or the maulvis that visit elite north Indian homes to tutor the children, respected for erudition but not exactly social equals. Naẓīr offers us the literary identity of the professional or service classes of late Mughal India, the one Urdu poet who used his command over language and verse to represent their world. Naẓīr comes from the world of the bazaar around the Taj, at a little distance from the imperial fort of Akbarabad, teaching boys and composing verses in everyday language that appealed to ordinary people.

As far as physical appearance and mode of dress go, Shahbāz, the Urdu biographer, describes him as follows: 'His complexion was wheatish, his height middling, and he had a high and broad forehead, shining eyes, a high nose, salt-and-pepper beard, and big moustaches. He dressed in the style that had been current in the Delhi of Muhammad Shah Rangila's time, that is, a turban with an opening in front, an *angarkhā* of thick cloth with the aperture towards the right, a new coat, below that a kurta, a pair of pyjamas a yard wide, shoes with pointed toes, a splendid cane in his hand, and rings of turquoise and cornelian on his fingers' (cited in Āsī 1951: 3). One could not ask for a better picture of the urbane late-Mughal bon vivant, all dressed up and ready to sample the excitements of an evening out. Naẓīr's works prove that Urdu was not simply the language of the military camp or the royal court, but enjoyed a much more heterogenous set of origins, with a range of class sensibilities and locations. Urdu's enduring status in modern South Asia is partly due to its intimate and historic ties with the networks and nodal points of exchange: the bazaars, *ganj*s, and *hāṭ*s of Hindustan.

Naẓīr and the Canon

Explanations of the beginnings of Urdu in north India in the early eighteenth century exemplify what can best be called an absent literary origin. Critics have tended to push the origins of Urdu back to some putative point in the distant past (Amir Khusrau, the invading army of the Punjab as agent of linguistic change, early works such as Afẓal's *Bikaṭ Kahānī*, the *Maṣnavī Kidam Rā'o Padam Rā'o*, etc.). However, as Shamsur Rahman Faruqi notes in a recent monograph, the earliest extant Urdu literary productions are from the Deccan and Gujarat, overwhelmingly penned by Sufis. A 'true beginning' for Urdu in the north was only possible in the eighteenth century (Faruqi 2001: 111). The process of establishing Urdu involved developing poetic talents and new listening and reading publics:

> In Delhi, during the middle decades of the century and under the nurturing attention of the poet-linguist-scholar Sirajuddin Ali Khan Arzu and the Sufi-poet Mirza Mazhar Jan-i Janan, there appeared two remarkable generations of Urdu poets, including such masters as Hatam, Abru, Yaqin, Dard, Qa'im, Sauda, and Mir (Naim 1999: 2).

Naẓīr, who was a contemporary of these poets, has not been given his place within this scene of new canon formation in Urdu. Instead, he remains a half-liminal figure at odds with retrospective critical orthodoxies such as those of Āzād and Ḥālī.

Yet Naẓīr tried his hand at high literary forms such as the ghazal, and his compositions demonstrate that he had a good understanding of Persian and Urdu canons of poetry. He frequently responded in macaronic verse to Persian ghazals by masters such as Ḥāfiẓ and Sa'dī, as well as those of other Urdu poets like Sirāj Aurangābādī. In this form of response, called *javāb-go'ī* in Persian and Urdu, the poet composes a reply to the earlier *ustād* by crafting verses in the same metre and rhyme. It is precisely this pleasure, an interlinguistic sense of call and response, that Naẓīr invokes when he is responding to the works of canonical masters. The term he uses is *taẓmīn*, the taking of another poet's verses into one's own verse, both preserving it and presenting a response to it. *Taẕmīn* is related to the verbal root *ẕaman*, the provision of surety or safe keeping. As an attitude to the canon, it seems to refer both to preservation and pleasure, as in his macaronic response to a famous ghazal of Ḥāfiẓ:

rahūṅ kāhe ko dil-jasta phirūṅ kāhe ko āvāra
agar ān turk-i shīrāzī ba-dast ārad dil-i mārā
Why should I remain broken-hearted, why wander aimless,
If that Turk of Shiraz takes my heart in his hand?
k͟hudā gar mujh gadā ko salṭanat bak͟hshe to maiṅ yāro
ba-k͟hāl-i hindū-ash bak͟hsham samarqand-o-buk͟hārā rā
If God were to grant this beggar an empire, then, O friends,
I would give, for that Hindu mole, all of Samarqand and Bukhara!
'Naẕīr' is luṭf se taẕmīn kar tū miṣra'-i 'Ḥāfiẓ'
ke bar naẓm-i to afshānad falak 'aqd-i ṡurayyā rā
Nazir, take Hafiz's verse into your own with such pleasure
That the sky scatters over your poetry the knot of the Pleiades!

(Naẕīr 1951a: 7)

Here Naẕīr interspaces the concluding line of each couplet of Ḥāfiẓ's Persian original (Ḥāfiẓ 1988: 98) with a line in Urdu. More importantly, he links his response with a notion of literary pleasure, *luṭf*, making it clear that what he seeks from his audience is an appreciation of how skilfully he revivifies in Urdu the familiar Persian classic.

Naẕīr defines his position by deriving his own poetic practice from earlier paradigms of literary eloquence, but then extends them into new semantic fields in Urdu. For instance, his *muk͟hammas* (poem with five-line stanzas) on a ghazal of Sa'dī begins by tying literary enjoyment to the pleasures of the rose garden:

kal ham jo ga'e bāg͟h meṅ ṭuk luṭf uṭhāne
aur dil ko lage sair gulistāṅ kī dikhāne
itne meṅ kahūṅ kyā tujhe ai yār yagāne
ba-rubūd dilam dar chamane sarv-i ravāne
ẕarrīn-kamare, sīm-bare, mū'e-miyāne
Yesterday, when I went to the garden to enjoy myself,
And to show my heart the pleasure of the rose garden,
When suddenly, what shall I say, O friend, that peerless one—
That moving cypress in the garden stole my heart—
Golden waist and silver body, and waist as slender as a hair!

(Naẕīr 1951a: 190)

Here the poet's aesthetic appreciation of the garden is skilfully invoked in the very first line and connected with the pleasure of a stroll in the rose garden, enhanced by an encounter with a peerless beloved. In the English translation, each Persian couplet by Sa'dī is italicized, marking off the original to which Naẕīr responds in each verse. Naẕīr frequently fixes such pleasures in textual form for the enjoyment of his readers, who could enjoy both the experience described and the poetics of its representation.

This double pleasure can best be linked to the twin ideas of derivation and extension. Naẕīr derives models, imagery, and ideas from older classics, but then extends them into fuller poetic elaborations for the delectation of his audience. He follows up on his chance encounter in the garden by filling in the shades and nuances of the beauty of the beloved:

gul-fām gul-andām dil-ārām nikū'e
dil-dār dil-āzār jafā-kār do-rū'e
āhū sifate kabk tage anbarīn mū'e
bedād-gare kaj-kulahe 'arbada-jū'e
shakar shikane tīr-qade sakht-kamāne

Rose-cheeked, rose-bodied, heart's solace, so lovely,
Captivating the heart and heart-tormenting, cruel two-faced one,
A gazelle, a partridge running gracefully, with ambergris-scented hair—
Unjust one with cap askew, always looking for a fight,
With sugared speech, arrow-straight in stature, and stubborn as a bow!

(Naẕīr 1951a: 190)

Here Naẕīr carefully chooses his words for rhythm, assonance, and semantic interplay. Thus, the beloved is described both as *dil-dār* (heart-captivating) and *dil-āzār* (heart-tormenting), and the string of adjectives that follow expand on the different aspects of the beloved's grace and cruelty. Naẕīr responds to the authority of the Persian by creating an Urdu context and set of explanations for its couplets.

Naẕīr respects the bounds of form and sees himself as following in a canonical series. He expresses his admiration for the older masters and extends their poetry into Urdu, creating his own literary paternity and genealogy. He ends with a nod to Sa'dī:

How can I praise the beauty of my love's charms enough?
The loveliness of both worlds just ends with that tease!
Then, like 'Naẕīr', attach your heart to that seductive idol—
'Sa'dī', without that lock and cheek and ruby lip, there were
Sighs and lamentations, fever and fret and smoke! (Naẕīr 1951a: 191).

The hierarchy of the Persian original and the Urdu response is thus transformed into a poem in which Sa'dī's ghazal forms the refrain of Naz̤īr's composition. In a literary tradition that operates with a limited set of topoi (*maẓāmīn*), what counts as innovation is the skill with which the poet extends a derivative set of ideas. While Naz̤īr amply demonstrates his ability to respond creatively to the canon, he also extends the range of topoi outwards by embracing the realia of life as subjects for poetry. As such, he pushes canonical bounds further than any Urdu poet of his century, and it is to these worldly engagements that we must turn in order to understand his distinctive contribution to Urdu literature.

The Texture of Everyday Life

It is a commonplace that Naz̤īr's verses are expressive of the feel of everyday life, its texture, its material culture and objects, its structures of emotion, exchange, and ideation. Yet, he does not describe this material culture directly or straightforwardly. Naz̤īr expresses an emotional relationship with it, making the material world the subject of the poem but seeing it through a poetic filter. Thus, in his poem on the fan ('Pankhā') he elucidates how the glittering object is part of wider networks of exchange, desire, and craftsmanship. The fan is the jealous poet's rival, closer to the beloved than Naz̤īr can ever hope to get:

kyā mausam-i garmī meṅ numūdār hai pankhā
k͟hūboṅ ke pasīnoṅ kā k͟harīdār hai pankhā
gul-rū kā har ik jā pe ṭalabgār hai pankhā
ab pās mere yār ke har bār hai pankhā
    garmī se muḥabbat kī baṛā yār hai pankhā

How it appears in the season of summer, the fan
A buyer of the perspiration of beautiful ones is the fan
At every place, a seeker of the rose-faced one is the fan
Now at every turn, close to my beloved is the fan
    A great fan, from the heat of love, is the fan (Naz̤īr 1951a: 570).

The fan is not here merely an article of comfort in the hot weather; it has entered the marketplace of beauty as 'a buyer of the perspiration of beautiful ones' (*k͟hūboṅ ke pasīnoṅ kā k͟harīdār hai pankhā*), a 'great fan' (*baṛā yār*) of the seductive beloved.

The poet goes on to describe the sensations emanating from the beloved's use of the fan in their own close association, whether after a bout of love-making or to cool his own ardour:

dil bāgh huā jātā hai phūloṅ kī bhabak se
aur rūḥ basī jātī hai khushbū kī mahak se
kuchh khaṣ se kuchh us pānī kī būndoṅ kī ṭapak se
nīnd ātī hai ānkhoṅ meṅ chalī jin kī jhapak se
kyā yār ke jhalne kā maze-dār hai pankhā
From the blazing up of the flowers the heart is happy, a garden
And the spirit is pervaded with the scent of perfume
From the scent of vetiver, from the dripping of the water
Sleep comes to the eyes from its being waved around,
How pleasant it is when my love waves the fan! (Naẕīr 1951a: 571).

Here the rhythmic and sensuous end-rhyme in each line (*bhabak*, *mahak*, *ṭapak*, *jhapak*) lulls us into the sensation of closing one's eyes gently in the gentle breeze of the fan. Naẕīr evokes erotic sensations, the slow progress of a love affair in the Indian heat through the exchange between lover and beloved, with the fan imagined sometimes as a rival, sometimes as a necessary companion.

Naẕīr is minutely observant of the splendour of the fan as a craft object, and indeed his poetry collectively offers us a cultural vocabulary for artisanship in many spheres. Many embellishments are possible with the fan, a piece of cloth variously shaped and attached to a wooden rod:

Softly and cleanly, with delicacy and flashing splendour
With the tacking on of gold braid and with the shine of spangles
The brocade's threads of gold fall from its flapping
From the glitter of satin and gold braid and lace edge,
How it sparkles in the hand of that infidel, the fan! (Naẕīr 1951a: 571).

The gold brocade and lace edging (*kinārī*), the spangles and sequins, are used with a play on the word *lagāvaṭ* or attachment, which can mean both emotional and material attachment. Above all, the proximity to the beloved makes the fan the ultimate object of desire:

In the summer, from the evening until the day's dawning
The fan is the constant companion of the fairy-born
For the lover, why shouldn't it be an object of desire? (Naẕīr 1951a: 572).

Naẕīr uses an everyday object to delineate an economics of desire in which value resides in the beloved's arms. From a customer in the market of beauty, the fan becomes the ultimate commodity because of its closeness to the beloved. It is precisely through a material object that he *can* describe desire, rather than through abstract notions or high metaphysical conceits.

This is apparent even in his poems on the consumption of quite ordinary commodities, as for instance his poem on the watermelon ('Tarbūz'). He begins by describing the appearance of a watermelon and the physiological and emotional effects of eating it:

kyoṅ na ho sabz zumurrud ke barābar tarbūz
kartā hai khushk kaleje ke ta'īṅ tar tarbūz
dil kī garmī ko nikāle hai ye akṣar tarbūz
jis ṭaraf dekhiye behtar se hai behtar tarbūz
ab to bāzār meṅ bikte haiṅ sarāsar tarbūz
Why should it not be green as an emerald, the watermelon?
It makes the dry liver wet, does the watermelon
Often, it casts out the heart's burning, the watermelon
Wherever you look, one's better than the last, the watermelon
Now all through the bazaar it's on sale, the watermelon (Naẓīr 1951a: 577).

From its physical appearance, green as an emerald, Naẓīr slides easily into the emotional satisfaction afforded by biting into a watermelon in the hot season. If one's liver, the seat of the emotions, is 'dry' (*khushk*), the freshness and coolness of a watermelon will irrigate it. It is *the* commodity that rules the marketplace when it is in season, on sale at every fruit and vegetable stall.

But the poet-lover cannot enjoy this commodified emotional satisfaction in peace. Naẓīr places the watermelon within the exchange between him and a saucy boy, who torments him by first demanding a watermelon, then rejecting it peremptorily:

mujh se kal yār ne mangvāyā jo de kar paisā
us meṅ ṭānkī jo lagā'ī to vo kachchā niklā
dekh tyaurī ko chaṛhā ho ke ghaẓab ṭaish meṅ ā
kuchh na ban āyā to phir ghūr ke ye kahne lagā
kyoṅ be lāyā hai uṭhā kar ye merā sar tarbūz
Yesterday, my friend gave me money and asked for a watermelon
When we cut a square piece out of it, it turned out raw
When he saw this, he got annoyed and flew into a rage
And when he couldn't think of anything, he glared at me and said,
'Hey you, what sort of stupid watermelon did you get?' (Naẓīr 1951a: 577).

Although the poet protests, the boy gets angrier and angrier. The exchange culminates with the boy picking up the watermelon and flinging it at the poet's chest (*khīnch mārā mere sīne pe uṭhā kar tarbūz*).

From here the exchange descends to low burlesque, for when the boy lovingly asks him for another melon, Naẓīr supplies it but has to face the consequences:

pyār se jab hai vo tarbūz kabhī mangvātā
chhilkā us kā mujhe ṭopī kī t̤arḥ de hai pinhā
aur ye kahtā hai ke phenkā to chakhā'ūnga mazā
kyā kahūṅ yāro maiṅ us shokh ke ḍar kā mārā
do do din rakkhe hu'e phirtā hūṅ sar par tarbūz
Sometimes, when he lovingly sends for a watermelon,
He puts the rind on my head as a cap
And says: 'If you throw it away, I'll teach you a lesson!'
What can I say, friends, from fear of that tease
I wander around with the watermelon on my head for two full days!
(Naẕīr 1951a: 578).

The joke is on the hapless poet-lover, who is completely under the spell of the coquettish boy. And while the boy enjoys the melon, Naẕīr is finally condemned to the agony of unrequited love: 'He stays cool, while my liver is burning up!' The entire poem ends with the poet watching the watermelon taking the boy in a luscious embrace:

phānk bījoṅ kī bharī le hai vo jab muṅh se lagā
tab lipaṭ jātā hai kyā pyār se hans kar tarbūz
When he takes a slice full of seeds to his mouth,
How it embraces him lovingly, the laughing watermelon! (Naẕīr 1951a: 578).

The boy's bite into a succulent slice of watermelon is rendered through the idiomatic phrase *muṅh lagānā*, which, besides its literal meaning of applying something to the mouth, signifies becoming overfamiliar with someone, especially a social inferior. The seeds suggest that the fruit itself is laughing, here imagined as the union of the object of desire with a concrete subject. The watermelon's physical appearance and juiciness help Naẕīr to name a pleasure (the loving embrace) and to render it simultaneously out of reach.

It is precisely this shuffle between the satisfaction of desire and its unattainability that marks Naẕīr's use of these items of daily use like fans and ordinary pleasures such as the eating of watermelons in the hot season. These are inscribed into the arch exchanges between objects of desire and eager lovers, as tangible markers of the erotic encounter. While these poems are evocative of a rich vocabulary of culture and life in the eighteenth century, we cannot approach them as straightforwardly 'realistic' works. The texture of everyday life that emerges from them is mediated through material exchange, through the game of desire deferred and delayed, through the sensations and emotions of the progress of love.

Culture of the Bazaars

Material exchange is fundamental to Naẓīr's poetry, which renders emotion concrete and places it within the public spaces and objects of the bazaar rather than in a subtly introspective poetic world. He invests ordinary articles such as watermelons and fans with larger symbolic meanings, invoking a wider world of exchange and interaction. This is both an historical world, the society of marketplaces within which Naẓīr lived and breathed, as well as an ideal world with conventions of representation and stock characters such as whores, pimps, banias, fakirs, bhang addicts, and other profligates. It is a world into which the reader must enter with Naẓīr, savouring its pleasures, consuming its commodities, and enjoying its sensations. In a recent essay on the marketplace as a governing trope for religious thought in eighteenth-century Bengal, Hugh Urban goes beyond the simple materialist argument that makes poetry a simple mask for economic interests: '[the] ambivalent status of the marketplace—as both a center of power and as a potential site of contestation and critique—also holds true on the religious plane. Not only was the marketplace a key metaphor for political dominance, but it was also used in many cases as a metaphor for religious dominance and spiritual authority' (Urban 2001: 1089).

It is not surprising that religious sects should take economic models of the marketplace and use them to respond to the massive changes attendant on the East India Company's conquest of Bengal. As Sudipta Sen points out, this was a conquest of marketplaces, for the marketplace was the 'knot in the fabric of social mediation' where economic forces, political power, and religious authority came together (Sen 1996: 19 and passim). In order to enter Naẓīr's marketplace of words, however, we have to take one step back from the transition to colonial rule and focus on Agra's history as a key Mughal city. Naẓīr's Agra was an imperial and commercial centre that dominated both an agricultural hinterland and a larger empire, a nodal point for many overland and riverine trade routes.

Besides the market, Agra also had its own Red Fort (Akbarabad) and the famous shrine of the Taj Mahal and its surrounding neighbourhood, Taj Ganj (the home of Naẓīr). Along with the rest of Mughal India, Agra passed through many turbulent upsets through Naẓīr's lifetime. The wealthy city was a natural target for invaders and freebooters, and contributed to the levies demanded by Nadir Shah in the wake of the sack of Delhi in 1739. Through the tumultuous eighteenth century, the Mughals, Jats, and Marathas controlled the city at various times. After Lord Lake's victory over the Mughal emperor at the battle of Patparganj in 1803, the British laid siege to the city and took it. In 1805, Agra was placed under a British collector and after 1835 served as capital to the north-western provinces until the Rebellion of 1857 (Latif 1896: 57–65).

Naẕīr's response to Agra's history is not directly descriptive, but takes the form of a 'Lament for the City' (*shahr-āshob*). The Urdu *shahr-āshob* is itself an adaptation from the Persian form of the genre, which was basically a poem about the pretty boys of the different trade guilds of a city. In Naẕīr's hands it is an elegy for the many and various subjugations suffered by the city, but these are only implied as the cause for the lament. His *shahr-āshob* is much more an encapsulating description of the social groups that make up the urban fabric. The famous poem begins:

hai ab to kuchh sukhan kā mere ikhtiyār band
rahtī hai ṭabaʿ soch meṅ lail-o-nahār band
daryā sukhan kī fikr kā hai maujdār band
ho kis ṭarḥ na muṅh meṅ zabāṅ bār bār band
jab agre kī khalq kā hai rozgār band
Now poetry is somehow beyond my control, closed.
My temperament remains closed, by day or night, in thought.
The ocean of poetry, the waves of thought, do not move.
Why shouldn't the tongue in my mouth remain locked, time after time?
For Agra's people, all their business is closed (Naẕīr 1951a: 465).

Despite these protestations of modesty and silence, Naẕīr produces a poem with forty-five five-line stanzas (*mukhammas*) that describe all the groups of people who inhabit the market of Agra and their condition through the tumultuous upsets suffered by the city:

māre haiṅ hāth hāth pe sab yāṅ ke dastkār
aur jitne pesha-dār haiṅ rote haiṅ zār zār
kūṭe hai tan luhār to pīṭe hai sar sunār
kuchh ek do ke kām kā ronā nahīṅ hai yār
chhatīs peshe vāloṅ kā hai kārobār band
All the craftsmen sit here, hitting one hand with the other,
And all the professional people cry piteously.
The ironsmith pounds his body, the goldsmith beats his head.
It's not just one or two whose work has suffered, friend!
All the thirty-six serving groups find their business closed

(Naẕīr 1951a: 466).

Ironsmiths, goldsmiths, artisans, paper-makers, petty traders, grocers, peddlers, cobblers, prostitutes, barbers, dancing boys—these are the people who make up the thirty-six professional groups and who populate the pages of Naẕīr's *Kulliyāt*.

It is helpful here to remember Shefta's aristocratic sneer at the vulgar audiences of Naẕīr's poetry. Shefta places Naẕīr within a class of social inferiors—the *sūqīyyīn* or *bāzāriyān* ('market people')—and politely but firmly excludes his verses from the exalted canons of established poetry. Sudipta Sen helpfully summarizes elite Mughal attitudes towards the lower orders:

Most professions attending to the elite were held in disdain and looked upon as fit only for the mean and the vile...personal servants, watering men, elephant-keepers, venders, perfumers, sweets sellers, and breadmakers were considered scoundrels (*pājī*)...even among ten-rupee officeholders (*mansabdārs*), an elephant-keeper with a monthly allowance of five hundred rupees was seen absolutely as a social unequal. The company of people engaged in mean professions or the market (*bāzāriyān*) was to be carefully avoided. No aristocrat, Mughal, Shaikh, Sayyad, or Afghan, would marry into their ranks, have them join their table, or entertain them at their social gatherings (Sen 1998: 29).

These people were the focus of Naẕīr's ideational world. His poems celebrate life among them, bringing their pleasures and preoccupations into the charmed circle of Urdu poetry. Except when they are named historical or religious personages, his bazaar characters tend to be stock types engaging in typical behaviour: the merchant or bania, the whore (*ranḍī*), the bhang addict, and so on. To the mocking aristocrats, Naẕīr presents a view from the bazaar, a social critique levelled at the hypocrisy and deception of those in power.

As an example of how Naẕīr treats a stock character, let us examine the figure of the courtesan or prostitute. In his *shahr-āshob*, he mentions that economic hardship has affected even the oldest profession in the world:

be-rozgāriyoṅ ne diye aise hosh kho
roṭī na peṭ meṅ ho to shahvat kahāṅ se ho
dekhe na ko'ī nāch na ranḍī kī sūṅghe bo
yāṅ tak to muflisī hai ke kasbī kā rāt ko
do do mahīnoṅ tak nahīṅ khultā izār-band

Unemployment has robbed men of their senses.
If they don't have bread in their stomachs, how can they satisfy their lusts?
No one watches dancing any more, nor smells the scent of a prostitute.
Poverty has increased to such an extent that at night the whore
Does not open her drawstring for two full months! (Naẕīr 1951a: 467).

The closely fastened drawstring of the prostitute ties economics and sexual desire into a knot that can only be opened by a paying customer. Of course, the pleasure does not come cheap, as the list of coquetries, ploys, and deceptions aimed at extracting money from customers is extremely long (and constantly growing).

At the heart of the matter is the woman herself as commodity, perhaps most concretely summed up in another verse from Naẕīr's elegy on Agra:

vo bākira bhī mānge hai dil meṅ yahī du'ā
yārab tū mere motī ko jaldī se ab chhidā
kuchh achhā khā'ūṅ pahnūṅ jo ho zīst kā mazā
That virgin too now prays in her heart as follows:
'O God, quickly get my pearl pierced now,
So that I may eat and dress well, enjoy the pleasures of life!'

(Naẕīr 1951a: 467).

The verse cannot be about a decently brought up *sharīf* girl, who would not be represented as wishing for the 'piercing of her pearl'. The ceremony that the girl of the bazaars longs for is the *nath utrā'ī*, 'taking off the nose-ring', an idiomatic phrase for deflowering a virgin. In the context of a courtesan's establishment, this is a special *rite de passage* for which a rich customer would pay handsomely. The result would be, of course, that the virgin would become a courtesan in her own right, entertaining men and entrapping them in her wiles, earning a good living from her beauty and talents and enjoying herself.

Yet these verses also land us into a conceptual difficulty, viz., how to classify these women of the bazaar? In the context of ancient Greece, James Davidson has spoken eloquently of the tyranny of a division between the Wives and the Rest, which deprives women of agency and flattens out the distinctions between different kinds of sex workers (Davidson 1997: 73–7). In Urdu, the distinction is drawn perhaps most sharply in *Umrā'o Jān Adā*, Rusvā's famous novel about the life of a Lucknow courtesan. At one point in the narrative, the author exclaims: 'the fact of the matter is that there are three types of women: the first, virtuous (*nek bakht*), the second, sinful (*kharāb*), and the third, women of the market-place (*bāzārī*). Of the second type, there are two kinds: those who sin in secret and those who plunge into sin openly and publicly' (Rusvā 1991: 224). The first two may be classified as *sharīf*, respectable, though their actions determine whether they are judged as virtuous or not. It is the third type, the *bāzārī* woman, that is our concern here.

The alert reader will have noticed that Naẕīr has used at least two terms already for the woman of the marketplace: *raṇḍī*, the prostitute, and *kasbī*, the whore who does it for a fixed sum of money, her *kharchī* or wage. To these a third, more polite term may be added: *ṭawā'if*, the term used for the grand courtesans whose salons were a gathering place for wealthy patrons. Veena Talwar Oldenburg nicely sums up their place and power before the transition to colonial rule:

Women, who had once consorted with kings and courtiers, enjoyed a fabulously opulent living, manipulated men and means for their own social and political ends, been the custodians of culture and the setters of fashion trends, were left in an extremely dubious and vulnerable position under the British.... At all Hindu and Muslim courts in the many kingdoms that made up the subcontinent before the British began to conquer them and displace their rulers, the courtesans were an influential female elite (Oldenburg 1990: 260, 262).

That these women inhabited a sliding scale between the cheapest two-bit whores and the most powerful madams of the *demi-monde* should come as no surprise. At the low end of the spectrum, they sold sex. At the upper end, their company, their music and dancing, and their emotional sympathy were the commodities that were for sale.

The working girl could manipulate the ambiguities along this sliding scale expertly to carve out a place for herself. Oldenburg delineates the ways in which courtesans overturn gender hierarchies that keep *sharīf* women oppressed and establish their own social and economic position as independent women (Oldenburg 1990). The commodifying language of the marketplace is made explicit in the label *bāzārī*, applied to all non-*sharīf* women. But courtesans themselves would resist this classification. As the madam in *Manḍī* ('The Market'), Shyam Benegal's modern film about Hyderabadi courtesans, exclaims to the earnest moral reformers who wish to legislate her out of existence, 'We are artists!' (*ham kalākār haiṅ*!) She of course is able to exploit artfully the foibles of local politicians and their sons to establish an independent *koṭhā* or house for herself and her girls.

Naẕīr's poems about courtesans are set in this space, the *koṭhā*, the domain of beauty and pleasure and coquetry. This is explicitly a house in the marketplace, where men gather to enjoy an evening's entertainment and perhaps more. The *koṭhā* can be a violent place:

girāyā shor kiyā gāliyāṅ dīṅ dhūm machī
'ajab ṭarḥ kī hu'ī vārdāt koṭhe par
[They] knocked [me] over, created a tumult, shouted abuse, and a commotion ensued.
A strange kind of incident happened at the *koṭhā*. (Naẕīr 1992: 544).

The longing of the rejected lover is conveyed through sexual innuendo:

likheṅ ham 'aish kī takhtī ko kis ṭarḥ ai jān
qalam zamīn ke ūpar, davāt koṭhe par
kamand zulf kī laṭkā ke dil ko le līje
ye jins yūṅ nahīn āne kī hāth koṭhe par
How can I inscribe the tablet of pleasure, my love?
The pen is on the ground, the inkpot on the *koṭhā*.
Let the lasso of your lock of hair hang down and take my heart
This is a commodity that won't come to you just like that, at the *koṭhā*.
(Naẕīr 1992: 544).

Instead of the courtesan's body, Naẕīr makes his heart a commodity here. Significantly, the heart is a commodity with no price on it, unlike his female interlocutor. He invests the courtesan with the power over his heart, reversing the usual relations of exchange and hiding the real transaction that underwrites the evening's pleasure. It comes to a successful conclusion:

lipaṭ ke so'e jo us gulbadan ke sāth 'naẕīr'
tamām ho ga'īṇ ḥall mushkilāt koṭhe par
When I slept clinging to that rose-bodied one, Naẕīr
All my difficulties were resolved at the *koṭhā* (Naẕīr 1992: 544).

The sexual act resolves all difficulties: the rivalries, the pecuniary embarrassments, the mutual exploitation inherent in the exchange between courtesan and customer.

The key unnamed factor in this exchange is money, which underwrites all relations and renders them into impersonal transactions. It is no accident that one of the characters in *Umrā'o Jān Adā*, in a fight with a prostitute, calls her *māl-zādī*, 'daughter of the coin' (Rusva 1991: 218). The commodification of a prostitute's time, her talent, her body—this is possible only with money. Naẕīr composed numerous poems on the subject of money, and in them he spells out the relations between sexual pleasure and monetary exchange:

kauṛī hī ḍāltī hai ṭawā'if ke ta'īṅ latāṛ
kauṛī hī us kī letī hai angiyā-o-kurtī phāṛ
kauṛī hī launḍe-bāẕī kī kartī hai chheṛ-chhāṛ
laṛkā bhī dam meṅ ātā hai sun kauṛiyoṅ kī jhāṛ
kauṛī ke sab jahān meṅ naqsh-o-nagīn haiṅ
kauṛī na ho to kauṛī ke phir tīn tīn haiṅ
It's the penny (cowrie) that crushes the courtesan,
The penny is the one who tears her blouse and shirt.

The penny is the one who teases and flirts with boys.
The boy comes running when he hears the jingling of the pennies.
The entire world is under the sway of the penny.
If you don't have a penny, then you're just three for a penny!

(Naẕīr 1951a: 644–5).

Here Naẕīr lays bare the economic core of the marketplace, the penny or cowrie, which allows the possessor of money to enjoy every pleasure that is offered for sale. He invests the money with the true agency, the power to tear off the prostitute's clothes, the power to flirt with boys, the power to rule the world.

Yet this is not simply a libidinous economy, but one tied with larger historical changes such as the increasing monetization of both agrarian and trading systems. As Bayly notes:

... the slow imposition of a cash revenue demand and the long-term growth of trade in the Ganges valley had made money an essential feature of agrarian politics...the requirements of post-Mughal regimes for cash and legitimacy had strengthened the influence of corporations of merchants, gentry and service people...these classes were more than a 'new elite'. They were bearers of a locally rooted culture which was emerging beneath the centralised pattern of Mughal India (Bayly 1992: 34).

Naẕīr helps us to understand the *mentalité* of the agents who were undergoing this shift, the 'merchants, gentry and service people' whose life and preoccupations he renders so well. His poetry delineates the social mediation that took place through the institutions of the bazaar, through its periodic fairs and temporary marts, through the sharp practices of the new elites of Agravals and Khatris who dominated the marketplaces of northern India in the eighteenth century.

Naẕīr is acutely sensitive to the power of money, but he does not merely 'reflect' it in his poetry. There is, to borrow a phrase from E. P. Thompson, a 'moral economy' of the marketplace. For instance, his satire on mercantile deception, 'Pickled Rats' *(Chūhoṅ kā Āchār)* sets the poet up as a seller of rat pickle:

phir garm hu'ā ān ke bāzār chuhoṅ kā
ham ne bhī kiyā khwāncha taiyār chuhoṅ kā
sar pā'oṅ kuchal kūṭ ke do chār chuhoṅ kā
jaldī se kachūmar sā kiyā mār chuhoṅ kā
kyā zor maze-dār hai āchār chuhoṅ kā

Once again, the market for rat pickle has warmed up!
I too prepared a small tray of rat pickle.

I crushed the heads and feet of a few rats,
And killed them and quickly prepared a fresh rat pickle.
  How wonderfully tasty it is, a pickle made of rats!

(Naẓīr 1951a: 696–7).

Naẓīr apparently found a dead rat in a jar of pickle he had ordered from the grocer, and this poem is a response to the situation (Naẓīr 1992: 547). The bulk of the poem lists the ingredients that would go into his rat pickle, sparing no disgusting article: worms, snakes, scorpions, rotting red chillies, flies, spiders, muskrats, midges, owls' wings and the pubic hair of vultures (*gidh kī jhānṭeṅ*). Throughout, he parodies the pretensions of the grocer, quoting outrageous prices for his pickle:

āge jo banāyā to bikā tīs rupe ser
aur gahakī ga'e le pachīs rupe ser
jāṛe meṅ ye biktā hai battīs rupe ser
aur holiyoṅ meṅ biktā hai chālīs rupe ser
  kyā zor maze-dār hai āchār chuhoṅ kā
When I made it formerly, it sold for thirty rupees a seer,
And customers bought it at twenty-five rupees a seer.
In the winter, it sells for thirty-two rupees a seer
And at Holi, the price is forty rupees a seer!
  How wonderfully tasty it is, a pickle made of rats!

(Naẓīr 1951a: 698–9).

A seer is a weight of approximately two pounds. Naẓīr uses these unheard of prices to show up the tricks and cozening language of merchants, who often adulterate their goods and sell shoddy merchandise to unsuspecting buyers.

Naẓīr's marketplace of words, with its norms and conventions, its stock characters and crooked merchants, is thus a reified fictive world. He represents the economic basis of life through articulating vividly the experiences of customers and passers-by. His addressees, the readers of his poetry, must suspend their disbelief and enter this urban space with him. Naẓīr appeals to experience, fixing sensations in textual form for readers to recognize as part of their own knowledge of the social world of the bazaar. This reification goes along with a sense of morality, of what is right and what is not, anchoring a poetic attitude of social contestation and critique. He tells us what it feels like to live life outside the palaces of the rich and famous, poking fun at their shallow displays and the pretence that attends social position. In this poetic world of sensations critically understood and represented, each experience is evaluated and set down as part of the celebrations and exchanges of bazaar life. This spectrum of experiences includes his poems on sex, so often bowdlerized by editors or misunderstood by modern critics, to which we now turn.

Pleasures, Private and Public

Does writing in pleasure guarantee—guarantee me, the writer—my reader's pleasure? Not at all. I must seek out this reader (must 'cruise' him) *without knowing where he is*. A site of bliss is then created. It is not the reader's 'person' that is necessary to me, it is this site: the possibility of a dialectics of desire, of an *unpredictability* of bliss: the bets are not placed, there can still be a game.

(Barthes 1989: 4)

Naẕīr's poems on sex invite the complicity of the reader in the pleasures of his text by involving him/her in a game in which no bets can be placed—the erotic encounter. Naẕīr's poems are located at the nexus of a private and a public world, making visible, in Barthes's phrase, the 'dialectics of desire' between the subject and the object of pleasure. Sex is both a human and a social experience, demanding the truth of our being, defining us in relation to ourselves and to others through the ultimate physiological release. Naẕīr is sensitive to the nuances and feelings that attend the erotic encounter, making it possible for us to approach sensually the private and public pleasures of the eighteenth century. His poems on sexual experience address a range of subjects: masturbation, the female orgasm, the saturnalian festival of Holi, and so on. Naẕīr places pleasure within a broad and inclusive humanism that defies modern labels, forcing us to come face to face with an expansive and unpredictable sexuality that can encompass all sorts of experiences and feelings.

Let us begin with his poem on masturbation, perhaps the ultimate sexual solipsism. A solitary pleasure, masturbation is necessarily also carried out in response to an imagined other, an object of desire from our fantasies. Naẕīr describes, in his opening stanzas, the physical experience:

hai hāth kī garmī meṅ jo az bas ke bharā ras
kahte haiṅ isī vāsṭe is kām to hathras
sau ʿaish ke lete haiṅ maze hāth ko kas kas
lazzat jo hai is kām kī kyā kyā maiṅ kahūṅ bas
laḍḍu meṅ na peṛoṅ meṅ na oloṅ meṅ mazā hai
jo mard-i mujarrad ke muṭhauloṅ meṅ mazā hai

The warmth of the hand is so full of juice!
That's why they call this act 'juice-in-the-hand.'

Tightening the hand, one can enjoy a hundred pleasures.
What can I tell you about the delight of this act?
There is not the pleasure in laddus, sweets and sugarballs,
That the fist of a masturbating man affords to us.

(Naẕīr 1951a: 695)

Here Naẕīr uses the loaded word *ras*, the juice or semen or sap that runs through humans and plants, which can also denote the essence of aesthetic awareness. The warmth of the hand joins the aesthetic with the physical experience, bringing them together in the term *hathras*, 'juice-in-the-hand'.

If one does not wish to savour this 'juice' all by oneself, one could go to a prostitute (*ranḍī*) and ask her to help the process along:

chūṛī ko bajā dil kā maẕā apne nibāhā
kyā 'aish muṭhaulon̈ ke bhī hote hain̈ a-hā-hā
Making her bangles ring, one fulfils the delight of one's heart.
Ah, what pleasures there are in the fist of the hand!

(Naẕīr 1951a: 696)

This encounter with an object of desire is totally self-directed—all the prostitute can provide is the rhythmic movement of her hand to provide the pleasures of the fist to the poet. Naẕīr ends by recognizing the vital role of masturbation for the sexually celibate:

gar hotī na 'ālam men̈ muṭhaulon̈ ke liye rāh
to 'ābid-o-ẕāhid kā na hotā kabhī nirbāh
ranḍī kī na darkār na launḍe kī rahī chāh
If there were no way open for fists in this world,
The devotee and the ascetic would never be able to manage.
The prostitute would be no use, there'd be no desire for boys!

(Naẕīr 1951a: 696)

In a sly dig at recluses and hermits, Naẕīr claims that not even devotees and ascetics can get along without masturbation. The range of pleasures that is available to the customer in the marketplace of desire cannot match the delights of masturbation, which allows the sexual subject to satisfy himself according to his own whim.

If masturbation allows a man to please himself, what about pleasing the other, one's partner in any sexual encounter? Naẕīr addresses this concern in his poem on the female orgasm, in which he imagines himself in the position of the woman who is being mounted by an active man. The woman issues a pressing invitation:

rāẓī hūṅ maiṅ is dam mujhe āsan meṅ kuchal ḍāl
jis chīẓ ke malne kī khushī hai so vo mal ḍāl
bekal hūṅ merī jān merī jān meṅ kal ḍāl
peṛū bhī ragaṛ aur merī chhātī bhī masal ḍāl
hotī hūṅ khalāṣ ab to yahī jān ga'ī maiṅ
ik aur bhī dhakkā tere qurbān ga'ī maiṅ
I'm willing at this very moment, crush me tight in a posture!
Rub away at the thing that yields happiness when rubbed.
I am restless, my love, breathe new life into my life.
Rub hard at my mound, press and squeeze my breasts!
I'm about to come, know this, I'm just about gone!
One more push, I sacrifice myself on you!

(Naẓīr 1951a: 692)

Here the excitement of the woman *in coitu* translates itself into these passionate entreaties. This is not pornography, but a vividly realized set of dialogues about the progress and sensations of a sexual experience. It is the unpredictable bliss of orgasm the woman demands, enthusiastically wishing to be penetrated and enjoyed. She teeters on the edge, begging for just one more push to send her into ecstasy.

As the encounter moves to a climax, Naẓīr makes clear the identity of the poet's sexual partner. In the ultimate male fantasy, the prostitute does not demand a wage for her labour:

ab tujh se maiṅ ik kauṛī bhī kharchī nahīṅ lūṅgī
hāṅ khol tujhe apnī maiṅ champā-kalī dūṅgī
Now I won't ask you for even a penny as my fee.
Yes, I'll unfasten my *champā*-bud necklace and give it to you!

(Naẓīr 1951a: 693).

Here the prostitute reverses the usual relation of exchange, giving Naẓīr her golden necklace as a reward for the pleasure he has given her. The poem ends with the woman declaring herself Naẓīr's slave girl forever:

Listen, Naẓīr, my lover, now all I say to you is this:
'As long as I live, I shall remain your slave girl (*launḍī*)!'

(Naẓīr 1951a: 693)

Naẓīr thus paints himself as the ultimate sensualist, to whom even the professional courtesans pay deference. The experience of sexual ecstasy is tied to relations of exchange and dominance, which Naẓīr can redefine through the erotic encounter.

Thus far, we have looked at pleasures enjoyed behind closed doors, but

Naẕīr's depiction of sexuality is not limited to these delights. He describes the pleasures of the public spaces of the bazaar, where crowds gather for festivals such as Holi. He carries the reader/listener along with the intoxication that lies behind the springtime play with colours:

gulzār khile hoṅ pariyoṅ ke aur majlis kī taiyārī ho
kapṛoṅ par rang ke chhīnṭoṅ se khush-rang 'ajab gulkārī ho
muṅh lāl gulābī āṅkheṅ hoṅ aur hāthoṅ meṅ pichkārī ho
us rang bharī pichkārī ko angiyā par tak kar mārī ho
sīnoṅ meṅ rang ḍhalakte hoṅ tab dekh bahāreṅ holī kī
When rose beds blossom with fairies, and everything is ready for a party,
When squirts of colour on the clothes create marvellous patterns of flowers,
When faces are red and eyes pink, and water guns come out in people's hands
When that colour-filled water gun is aimed and shot at the blouse,
And colours flow among the breasts, look at the festive season of Holi!

(Naẕīr 1951a: 438).

Naẕīr plunges the reader deeper into his world of pleasure and joy as the horseplay of Holi gets more boisterous. He is frank about the ensuing revelry, describing the public celebration, music, dance, banter, and people who take part in these festive exchanges:

us rang rangīlī majlis meṅ vo ranḍī nāchne vālī ho
muṅh jis kā chānd kā ṭukṛā ho aur āṅkh bhī mai kī pyālī ho
bad-mast baṛī matvālī ho har ān bajātī tālī ho
mai-noshī ho behoshī ho bhaṛve ke muṅh meṅ gālī ho
bhaṛve bhī bhaṛvā bakte hoṅ tab dekh bahāreṅ holī kī
aur ek ṯaraf dil lene ko maḥbūb bhavaiyoṅ ke laṛke
har ān ghaṛī gat bharte hoṅ kuchh ghaṭ ghaṭ ke kuchh baṛh baṛh ke
In that colourful party, when the dancer is a courtesan,
Her face is a piece of the moon, and her eye a goblet of wine,
That drunken one, very intoxicating, claps her hands in rhythm every second.
There's wine-drinking and unconsciousness, and the pimp speaks only abuse.
When even the pimps call him a pimp, look at the festive season of Holi!
And on one side, to steal one's heart, are the darling dancing boys
At every moment, they dance away, sometimes retreating, sometimes advancing.

(Naẕīr 1951a: 438).

Here some of the dramatis personae of Naẕīr's ideal world take their place on the stage of the bazaar, the courtesans, musicians, and dancing boys who are part of the drunken festivities. Not a single one has a name; it is their participation and its emotional nuances, its appeal to our feelings, that is the key. All the *matériel* for a party is present: music, wine, beautiful people, and licence to play Holi. What more could any self-respecting bazaar poet want?

The guilty pleasures of consorting with such lowlifes and bazaar people are expertly delineated by Naẕīr (in verses hastily bowdlerized by all the modern editors, who leave out the terms for body parts). Here the women who are being molested complain about the groping hands of the *bāẕāriyān*:

ko'ī nīche dab kar kahtī ho chillā kar hā'e kuchal ḍālā
chhātī par mār ke hāthoṅ ko peṛū bhī ṣāf masal ḍālā
ko'ī peṭ pakaṛ kar bhāgī ho yūṅ kahtī hai hai mal ḍālā
ko'ī dhūm machā kar kahtī ho kam-bakht ne sīna dal ḍālā
jab ye ghul shor khaṛakte hoṅ tab dekh bahāreṅ holī kī

One is pressed down and screams, 'You're crushing me!
You're fondling my breasts, and pressing on my crotch!'
Another holds her belly as she runs, crying 'You've rubbed me up!'
Yet another creates a tumult, 'That wretch, he's ground up against my breasts!'
When such a commotion crackles forth, look at the festive season of Holi!

(Naẕīr 1951a: 439).

These furtive gropings under the mask of a saturnalian festival are designed to titillate the audience, to make them complicit in pleasure. In all the poems discussed in this section, it is not just the explicitness of the names for body parts that is so offensive to the modern editors, but rather the sensations that Naẕīr so deftly invokes.

Naẕīr's representation of sexual experience runs the gamut from masturbation to orgasm to public molestation, demanding an imaginative leap into a world of intimacies both private and public. The reader cannot help being seduced by the familiarity and ease of the depictions, a far cry from the idealized cup-bearers, roses and nightingales of other Urdu poets. Naẕīr is a poet of concrete experience, whose poetry allows us to excavate an archaeology of pleasure for the eighteenth century, an insider's look into what it felt like to be alive and passionately engaged in the things of this world. He depicts the realia of life enthusiastically, rendering them accessible for the reader who is willing to meet him halfway. What is needed is a sensual sensibility, an openness to experience that echoes the attitude of this strikingly original literary figure. We now come to the question of the social attitude and valence of his poems, to delineate the rough humanism that marks Naẕīr's verse.

A Rough Humanism

This discussion of Naẕīr's poems has so far left unexplored the question of the social sensibility of his poems, except to note their anti-aristocratic bias. Naẕīr frequently meditates on the stability, authority, and power that were so much in question through the turbulent eighteenth century. He does not hesitate to deflate the high and mighty who put on airs but are subject to the world's transience and the inexorability of death. He ruthlessly exposes the hypocrisies of rank and position, pointing to death as the great leveller. In his famous *Banjārā-Nāma*, or 'Song of the Gipsy', he invokes the figure of an itinerant trader and pillager who will pack up our lives when he moves on:

ṭuk ḥirs-o-havā ko chhoṛ miyāṅ mat des bides phire mārā
qazzāq ajal kā lūṭe hai din rāt bajā kar naqqārā
kyā badhiyā bhainsā bail shutur kyā gauneṅ pallā sar-bhārā
kyā gehuṅ chāval moṭh maṭar kyā āg dhuāṅ kyā angārā
sab ṭhāṭh paṛā rah jāvegā jab lād chalegā banjārā
Leave aside greed and lust, my friend, don't roam desperately from land to land!
The Cossack of death loots and plunders, beating his drum by day and night.
What are cattle and bullocks, bulls and camels, sacks and panniers and headloads?
What are wheat and rice and lentils and peas, what are fire and smoke and sparks?
All your splendour and goods will be useless, when the Banjara loads them up to go! (Naẕīr 1951a: 541).

Here Naẕīr gives us the graphic image of a robber or plunderer loading up to go, a member of one of the bands of thugs, Jats, Pindaris, Banjaras, and other itinerant groups that travelled through the north Indian countryside. Naẕīr outlines worldly life through material goods: agricultural produce and the animals and accoutrements for its transport to market. He evokes a caravan camp, all the material goods being transported, but also the ever-present danger of highway robbers and thugs.

Throughout, Naẕīr pokes fun at the aristocratic and wealthy obsessions of his day, sketching a satiric portrait of an elite culture on the verge of collapse:

kuchh kām na āvegā tere ye laʿl-o-zumurrud sīm-o-zar
jab pūnjī bāṭ meṅ bikhregī phir ān banegī jān upār
naqqāre naubat bān nishān daulat ḥashmat faujeṅ lashkar
kyā masnad takiyā mulk makāṅ kyā chaukī kursī taḵẖt chhatar
sab ṭhāṭh paṛā rah jāvegā jab lād chalegā banjārā
None of this will be any use, these rubies and emeralds, silver and gold.
When your capital is scattered on the road, your very life will be in danger.
Drums, kettledrums, distinctions, flags, wealth and power, armies and battalions,
What are thrones and cushions, land and house? What are chair, seat, throne, and parasol?
All your splendour and goods will be useless, when the Banjara loads them up to go! (Naẕīr 1951a: 542).

Here Naẕīr evokes the late Mughal aristocratic world by mocking the trappings of status, power, and wealth that men sought so desperately. Death the leveller would leave none of these intact.

As for the mercantile classes, Naẕīr tells them through the poem that death, the greatest merchant of them all, would foil all their plans for profit. Robbers would steal all their goods-in-transit, all their capital would be lost in the face of death. He ends by reinforcing the message:

jab marg phirā kar chābuk ko ye bail badan kā hāṅkegā
ko'ī nāj sameṭegā terā ko'ī gaun siye aur ṭāṅkegā
ho ḍher akelā jangal meṅ tū khāk laḥad kī phāṅkegā
us jangal meṅ phir āh 'naẕīr' ik bhungā ān na jhāṅkegā
sab ṭhāṭh paṛā rah jāvegā jab lād chalegā banjārā

When death swings his whip and leads off this bullock of a body,
who will reap your grain, who will stitch and hem your sacking?
Utterly alone in the forest, you'll taste the dirt of the grave!
Then in that forest, ah, Naẕīr! Not even a gnat will glance at you!
All your splendour and goods will be useless, when the Banjara loads them up to go! (Naẕīr 1951a: 543)

In the second line, the phrase *ko'ī gaun siye aur ṭāṅkegā* is used expertly by Naẕīr to suggest the stitching of a shroud for a human body, and the very next line presents us with the perspective from inside the grave. In the different verses of the *Banjārā-Nāma*, Naẕīr uses the objects that make up the material culture of wealth and power to give us the cultural vocabulary of everyday life in eighteenth-century north India. In the end, we are all human beings who have to die, he says, so why the pretence today? The poem's framework is well within the traditional limits of the *tanbīh-ul-ghāfilīn*, the 'Warning to the Negligent'; what is remarkable is Naẕīr's capacity to evoke the diverse world of eighteenth-century north India.

Although the fact of death points to the transience of worldly life, Naẕīr is still able to celebrate the common being that unites humankind. A respect for humanity resonates through the pages of his collected verses, inflecting his attitude towards his historical and social world. In his *Ādmī-Nāma* (Song of Humanity), he articulates well the basis of human sympathy:

yāṅ ādmī pe jān ko vāre hai ādmī
aur ādmī hi tegh se māre hai ādmī
pagṛī bhī ādmī kī utāre hai ādmī
chillā ke ādmī ko pukāre hai ādmī
aur sun ke dauṛtā hai so hai vo bhī ādmī

Here, human beings give up their lives for other humans,
And those who kill others with the sword are also human.
It's only humans who strip the turban from others to degrade them.
It's humans who cry out to other humans for help,
And those who run to aid them are also human (Naẕīr 1951a: 683).

Naẕīr looks with open eyes at the human condition and the evils that humans visit upon each other, but is able to express a vision that transcends these limitations. Humans may hurt and kill others, but they are also there for one another in times of crisis and need. Just so, the world is evanescent, but it is our only source of joy and delight.

Naẕīr's poems present us with a broad and expansive vision of humanity, a rough humanism that goes beyond distinctions to the sensation of being in this world. Although Naẕīr composed his poems in the context of the eighteenth century boom in Urdu literary production, he did not merely reproduce the rarefied aestheticism of Persian lyric poetry. He chose to turn the techniques and topoi of Urdu poetic composition to new experiences, allowing readers and listeners to enter his ideational and social world through a sensibility open to sensual experience. As we have seen, Naẕīr situates himself as a follower of the received canon while composing verse that stretched canonical boundaries well beyond other classical Urdu poets. The texture and pleasures of everyday life, the bazaar culture of his day, popular devotion, sexual desire and flirtation, deflating sham and hypocrisy, cultivating detachment towards the (transient) world—these are some of Naẕīr's central concerns. He is able to approach them through a sustained attention to the conditions and relationships that attend material exchange, the heart of the marketplace.

Recent revisionist scholarship on the eighteenth century has sought to attack the myths of cultural decay attached to the political narrative of Mughal decline and the takeover by the East India Company. While we can now accept that the late eighteenth century was not, to borrow a phrase from the historian Percival Spear, the era of the 'twilight of the Mughals', the work of specifying the vitality and dynamism of the age through its cultural remains is yet to be done. Naẕīr is a poet who responds to the concerns of the ordinary people of his day, a poet of sensation, of reaction to real life, of social critique, of popular devotionalism. Bayly notes in his pioneering book that 'the study of changing popular mentalities' looks dauntingly difficult in the Indian context (Bayly 1992: vii). Naẕīr offers us a literary way into the bazaar, to the types of people who frequented that world, their life, its outlines and hierarchies, rhythms and celebrations, its experiences, sensations, material culture; it is an invitation we cannot afford not to accept.

Notes

[1] I wish to thank Jeffrey Donaghue for his exemplary generosity in making available his entire cache of research materials on Naẕīr to me. But for his kindness, these rare editions would have perished. He has enabled the next generation of work on Naẕīr. I also wish to express my gratitude to Yavar Abbas, Eugene Irschick, Michael Maas, and Jameela Siddiqi for their stimulating and probing conversations on the subject of Naẕīr; they helped me to clarify my argument enormously.

[2] 'Naẕīr Akbarābādī ne jinsī lazzatoṅ ke tamām pahlu'oṅ ko bartā hai lekin unke yahāṅ naujavān laṛkoṅ kā ẕikr zyādā hai aur unse chheṛ chhāṛ, unko varghalāne, unko phuslā kar rāh par lāne kī bātoṅ kī takrār se mujhe andāza hotā hai ki vo nafsiyyātī ṭaur par nā-mard the aur bāligh, tajurba-kār yā "well-adjusted" logoṅ kī ṭarah (maṣlan mīr ki ṭarah) jins kā taṣavvur nahīṅ kar sakte the' (S. R. Faruqi, 'Naẕīr Akbarābādī kī Kā'ināt', in 'Uṣmānī 1979: 415).

[3] Shiblī to Shahbāz: 'Jab ma'lum huā ki āp uske ḥālāt likh rahe haiṅ, maiṅ samajh gayā ki ap kī naẕar kin bātoṅ par hai.' Shahbāz 1981: 383.

[4] *See* Barnett 1980, Bayly 1992, Sen 1998.

[5] Hakim Asghar Husain Farrukhabadi, in Shahbāz 1981: 378.

Bibliography

Primary Sources

'Ḥāfiẓ' Shīrāzī, *Ḥāfiẓ Qazvīnī-Ghanī*, Muḥammad Qazvīnī (ed.), Tehran: UNESCO, 1988.

'Naẕīr' Akbarābādī, Valī Muḥammad, *Kulliyāt-i Naẕīr*, Agra: Matba'-i Ilahi, 1862.

———, *Muntakhab-i Naẕīr*, Kanpur: Matba'-i Nizami, 1869.

———, *Kulliyāt-i Naẕīr*, Lucknow: Munshi Nawal Kishor Press, 1870.

———, *Kulliyāt-i Naẕīr*, Kanpur: Matba'-i Ahmadi, 1890.

———, *Kulliyāt-i Naẕīr Akbarābādī*, Qutbuddīn Aḥmad (ed.), Lucknow: Matba'-i Nami, 1897.

———, *Kulliyāt-i Naẕīr*, 'Abdul Ghafūr 'Shahbāz' (ed.), Lucknow: Munshi Nawal Kishor Press, 1900.

———, *Kulliyāt-i Naẕīr*, Kanpur: Munshi Nawal Kishor Press, 1902–3.

———, *Dīvān-i Naẕīr*, Mirzā Farḥatullāh Beg (ed.), Delhi: Anjuman-i Taraqqi-i Urdu (Hind), 1942.

———, *Kulliyāt-i Naẕīr Akbarābādī*, Maulānā 'Abdul Bārī Āsī (ed.), Lucknow: Raja Tej Kumar Press (Waris-i Nawal Kishor Press), 1951a.

———, *Gulzār-i Naẕīr*, Salīm Ja'far (ed.), Allahabad: Hindustani Academy, 1951b.

———, *Intikhāb-i Naẕīr Akbarābādī*, Delhi: Maktaba Jami'a, 1989.

———, *Naẕīr Granthāvalī*, Naẕīr Muḥammad (ed.), Lucknow: Uttar Pradesh Hindī Sansthān, 1992.

'Rusvā', Mirzā Muḥammad Hādī, *Umrāo Jān Adā*, Delhi: Maktaba Jami'a, 1991.

Secondary Sources

Āsī, Maulānā 'Abdul Bārī, 'Naẕīr kī Qalamī Tasvīr', in *Kulliyāt-i Naẕīr Akbarābādī*, Lucknow: Raja Tej Kumar Press (Waris-i Nawal Kishor Press), 1951.

Barnett, Richard B., *North India Between Empires: Awadh, the Mughals, and the British, 1720–1801*, Berkeley: University of California Press, 1980.

Barthes, Roland, *The Pleasure of the Text*, Richard Miller (trans.), New York: Noonday Press, 1989.

Bayly, C. S., *Rulers, Townsmen, and Bazaars: North Indian Society in the Age of British Expansion, 1770–1870*, Delhi: Oxford University Press, 1992.

Davidson, James N., *Courtesans and Fishcakes: The Consuming Passions of Classical Athens*, New York: HarperCollins Publishers, 1997.

Fallon, S. W., *A New Hindustani-English Dictionary, with Illustrations from Hindustani Literature and Folklore*, Benares: Medical Hall Press, 1879.

Faruqi, Shamsur Rahman, *Early Urdu Literary Culture and History*, Delhi: Oxford University Press, 2001.

Ḥaqq, 'Abdul, 'Muqaddima', in Mīr 'Abdul Ḥai 'Tābāṅ' (ed.), *Dīvān-i Tābāṅ*, Aurangabad: Anjuman-i Taraqqi-i Urdu, 1935.

Irvine, William, *Later Mughals*, New Delhi: Taj Publications, 1989.

Latif, Syad Muhammad, *Agra Historical and Descriptive, With an Account of Akbar and His Court, and of the Modern City of Agra*, Calcutta: Calcutta Central Press Company Limited, 1896.

Naim, C. M., 'The Theme of Homosexual (Pederastic) Love in Pre-modern Urdu Poetry', in Muhammad Umar Memon (ed.), *Studies in the Urdu Gazal and Prose Fiction*, Madison: South Asian Studies, University of Wisconsin-Madison, 1979.

______ (trans. and ed.), *Zikr-i Mir: The Autobiography of the Eighteenth Century Mughal Poet: Mir Muhammad Taqi 'Mir' (1723–1810)*, Delhi: Oxford University Press, 1999.

Oldenburg, Veena Talwar, 'Lifestyle as Resistance: The Case of the Courtesans of Lucknow, India', *Feminist Studies*, 16 (2), 1990, 259–87.

Rahman, Tariq, 'Boy-Love in the Urdu Ghazal', *Annual of Urdu Studies*, 7 (1990), 1–20.

Sadiq, Muhammad, *A History of Urdu Literature*, Delhi: Oxford University Press, 1984.

Sen, Sudipta, 'Passages of Authority: Rulers, Traders, and Marketplaces in Bengal and Benares, 1700–1750', *The Calcutta Historical Journal*, 17: 1 (1996), 1–39.

______, *Empire of Free Trade: The East India Company and the Making of the Colonial Marketplace*, Philadelphia: University of Pennsylvania Press, 1998.

Shahbāz, 'Abdul Ghafūr, *Zindagānī-i Benaẕīr*, Delhi: Taraqqi-i Urdu Board, 1981 [1903].

Spear, Percival, *Twilight of the Mughuls: Studies in Late Mughul Delhi*, New Delhi: Munshiram Manoharlal, 1991 [1951].

Urban, Hugh B., 'The Marketplace and the Temple: Economic Metaphors and Religious Meanings in the Folk Songs of Colonial Bengal', *Journal of Asian Studies*, 60: 1 (2001), 1085–1114.

'Uṣmānī, Shams al-Ḥaqq (ed.), *Naẕīr-nāmā*, Delhi: Subuhi Publications, 1979.

Feminine Authorship and Urdu Poetic Tradition: *Bahāristān-i Nāz* vs *Tazkira-i Rekhtī*

CARLA PETIEVICH

Sab kahāṅ kuchh lāla-o-gul meṅ numā'iyāṅ ho gayīṅ
Khāk meṅ kyā ṣūrateṅ hongī ki pinhāṅ ho gayīṅ
Not all, but some, have manifest themselves as tulips and roses
What faces must there be still lying buried 'neath the dust!

More than seeking to recover voices of women lost to patriarchal historiography, this essay looks at what the Urdu literary tradition can tell us about identifiable feminine voices—about women poets who made it into the historical record, and about male poets who spoke in 'women's' voices. Innumerable women writers have been lost to us and do indeed lie 'buried 'neath the dust', to borrow from the famous verse by Mirza Ghalib (1797–1869). But my project here is to consider the idea of the feminine in Urdu literary history, based on the voices we have.

Though not so named, notions of *écriture féminine* ('writing the feminine') arose for Urdu literati well before 'Western' feminists took it up in the 1970s. Speculative experiments with what women would write about if women could be Urdu poets, and questions about what would mark their art as distinctly feminine go back some two hundred years. Participation of women poets in an otherwise male tradition begins to be recorded in biographical compendia (*tazkiras*) from shortly before the turn of the nineteenth century. *Ṭabqa'āt us-Sho'arā* by Qudratullā Shauq (d. 1809) is probably the earliest *tazkira* to mention the Hyderabadi poet Māh Laqā Bāī 'Chandā', who is also featured in the *Bahāristān-i Nāz* discussed below. Around 1802, a poetic genre called *rekhtī*—narrated by male poets in the feminine voice—was introduced into Lucknow literary circles by the (male) poet Sa'ādat Yār Khān 'Rangīn' (d. 1834). *Rekhtī*, long dismissed in Urdu critical literature, has recently received a spate of scholarly interest (Naim 2001; Petievich 2002, 2001a, 2001b; Vanita and Kidwai 2000).[1] This essay will consider the first known *tazkira* of women poets, *Bahāristān-i Nāz* by Faṣīḥuddīn 'Ranj' (1864), and the earliest known chronicle of Urdu's male-authored 'feminine' voice, Tamkīn Kāẓmī's *Tazkira-i Rekhtī* (1930). My speculations about the Urdu poetic tradition's conscious representation of 'feminine' authorship will be based on these two texts.

The History of Feminine Voices in Indic Literatures

The two-century-old tradition of writing the feminine in Urdu is young by comparison with other imaginative expressions of 'women's writing' or 'women's consciousness' in non-Muslim Indic literatures. In *akam*, a sub-genre of Tamil *Caṅkam* poetry (2nd–4th c.), the feminine lyric voice predominates (Hart 1975, 1979; Ramanujan 1994, 1985; Selby 2000). Poems in women's voices have been central to other Indic traditions too, especially lyrics narrated in the voice of the *virahinī*, a woman separated from her beloved. The most famous examples are probably the songs of Mirabai, but this voice goes back to Sanskrit *kāvya*, to twelfth-century Punjabi *dohās*, and to Jayadeva's *Gīta Govinda*. By contrast, 'classical' ghazals were gendered entirely masculine, leaving little space for feminine voices in Urdu lyric poetry.[2]

This contrast cannot be attributed to any profound cultural or aesthetic difference in lyric poetry's role. Urdu readers might not be familiar with *Caṅkam* poetry, and some not even with Mirabai, but love in separation is as central to the Urdu lyric as it is to Tamil *akam* or bhakti poetry. In all these traditions, a poem's aesthetic core is approached through evoking images of nature to convey and reflect the poem's emotional essence. The significant difference is this: while the feminine voice is normative in other Indian literatures, Urdu marks it as deviant. Speaking of it in rather condescending terms, Urdu literati often dismiss it as disreputable, as something borrowed from the so-called Hindi tradition, and as, therefore, not quite authentically 'Muslim' or 'Islamic', but rather as something inferior (cf. Faruqi 1981: 30).

Dismissive attitudes towards 'Hindi' tradition have not always characterized Urdu writers' understanding, nor their practice, but are modern, reflecting a change in thinking from earlier times. They probably date from the late nineteenth century. This was when the social status of women became linked to an Indo-Muslim community engaged in the process of self-articulation as

British colonial subjects, in competition with a rival community, 'the Hindu', engaged in a parallel process. The articulation involved both assertive and defensive strategies. Because Urdu language and poetry were so intimately linked to Indo-Muslim identity, Urdu literature was an obvious and ready medium in which to express identity through differentiation from 'the Hindu'.

The social subjugation of Indian women was, of course, a cornerstone of British colonial discourse, and the decrying of low educational levels for women was its most prominent feature. Thus, whether in the context of reform movements such as the Bengal Renaissance (Hindu) or the Aligarh Movement (Muslim) of the late nineteenth century, Indian male elites felt obliged to respond to its accusations. The work of numerous scholars bears ample witness to this (Lelyveld 1978; Metcalf 1992; Minault 1983, 1994, 1998; Chatterjee 1993, Sangari and Vaid 1990).

Ambivalence marked the response of Urdu literati to the onslaught of colonial discourse. Urdu critics faced a twofold dilemma: the British had argued that Indians were unfit to rule themselves because of a decadent effeminacy in the culture, and feminization of poetic expression seemed to bolster this claim. Yet Europeans in India had simultaneously pointed, as evidence of backwardness, to the notable absence of female participation in cultural and political life. Gender segregation, practised among both Muslim and Hindu elites of northern India, put the literati so much on the defensive that they never pointed out (perhaps did not even perceive) the contradictions within colonial discourse. Accusations levelled against Indians could well have been redirected towards the miserable social status of women in Victorian culture.[3] Instead, Urdu's literati developed critical formulations like the Two School theory, which institutionalized questionable distinctions between the literatures of Delhi and Lucknow in hopes of salvaging the civilizational honour of the Mughals at the expense of the otherwise celebrated Indo-Muslim cultures (Petievich 1992; Faruqi 1999; Pritchett 1994).

Another response, that of Progressive Writers in the mid-twentieth century, was to focus on and celebrate the working class and feminine experience.[4] In a famous speech inaugurating the Progressive Writers' Association in Lucknow in 1936, Premchand tied the importance of compassionate, even valorizing, literary treatment of women's suffering to developing Indians' fitness to overthrow colonial rule and establish independence (Russell 1992: 204–28). Critical marginalization of literary genres like *rekhtī*, or anything else deemed vulnerable to accusations of effeminacy and/or decadence, must be understood in the light of this discursive struggle.

But all these attempts to disguise or deflect critical attention away from 'effeminacy' in Muslim expressive culture were misguided. The Urdu literati would have had to go back to the earliest Islamicate literature in India to root out completely experimentations with feminine experience. Feminized expression is found throughout Punjabi literature, as when Bābā Farīd Ganj-i Shakar (d. 1265 CE) sang as a *virahinī* in his *dohās* (Anand 1990). It is found in greater abundance in the *kāfīs* of the sixteenth- and eighteenth-century Sufi poets 'Mādho Lāl' Ḥusain and Bulleh Shāh; or in the *qiṣṣas* of Damodar (sixteenth century) and Wāriṣ Shāh (eighteenth century), narratives recounting the misadventures of the star-crossed lovers, Hir and Ranjha.

Court poetry too, from the Muslim kingdoms of the Deccan plateau, features feminine-narrated poems, as in Urdu's first credited *dīvān*, that of Sultan Muḥammad Qulī Quṭb Shāh of Golconda (r. 1566–1611). Numerous other sixteenth- and seventeenth-century Dakani court poets also wrote ghazals in the feminine voice (Petievich 2000). Moreover, scholars have amply documented this voice in earlier non-elite Sufi writings, wherein women's work songs were adapted for didactic purposes (Jalibi 1977, Eaton 1978, Asani 1995). It would seem then, that until modern times the feminine was either celebrated in Indo-Muslim poetry, or was at least so ubiquitous as to be unremarkable, except in the classical ghazal.

In the twentieth century, actual female authorship comes into its own, and there is abundant feminine experience depicted in novels, short fiction, and poetry. Thus, female participation in representing feminine consciousness and experience finally emerges widely in Urdu nearly two millennia after the emergence of an Indian male-authored feminine poetic voice. Male authors, it seems, were 'effeminating' a long time before effeminacy became critically suspect.[5]

Why has Urdu literary scholarship been so reluctant to claim this heritage? There can be no doubt that the past one-and-a-half century's process of canonization in Urdu poetry has rendered a lyric feminine 'I' hard to come by. Although critical writing does acknowledge it minimally, the feminine voice occupies a marginal place at best in Urdu literary histories and survey literature.[6] But why?

Authorship, Literary Voice, and Literacy

While we may never satisfy ourselves as to the precise cultural politics behind this marginalization, we can speculate on connections among authorship, a feminine literary voice, and female literacy. What were the kinds of textual knowledge produced in Urdu on women's authorship, and what may be extrapolated from such texts about attitudes towards female literacy in the modern era? Metcalf, Minault, Naim, and others have done definitive work in the much larger field of women's education and reform. This essay merely attempts to draw insights gleaned from examination of two texts. Each is a *tazkira*, a compendium of poets featuring their names, biographical remarks and selections of their verse, almost always in ghazal form. *Tazkiras* represent, arguably, the earliest form of critical writing on Urdu poetry, predating such formal literary histories as Maulānā Āzād's *Āb-i Ḥayāt* (1880), or Alṭāf Ḥusain Ḥālī's critical treatise, *Muqaddma-i She'r-o-Shā'irī* (1893). What might these *tazkiras* tell us of wider concerns about women's place in the formation of a modern Indo-Muslim national community (*qaum*) during the last quarter of the nineteenth century and the first few decades of the twentieth? As much attention must be paid to the biographers as to their subjects.

Bahāristān-i Nāz

This text ('The Garden of Blandishment', hereafter *BN*) represents women poets as an authorial category. It was first published in 1864, compiled by Ḥakīm Faṣīḥuddīn Ranj of Meerut (d.1885). Subsequent editions were published during Ranj's lifetime (1869, 1882) and thereafter (Fateḥpūrī 1972: 631). As *BN*'s twentieth-century editors explain, it was the first *tazkira* of its kind in Urdu (Ranj 1965: 52). The first edition, not extant, seems to have been rather short, comprising thirty-eight pages.[7] By the third edition, it had expanded to 114 pages listing 174 poets. While the catalogue of poetic names grew, the *tazkira* yet remained disappointingly short on actual poetic samples, a situation standard to the genre (Fateḥpūrī 1972: 461).

On the other hand, the biographical remarks, composed in characteristic rhyming prose phrases (cf. Āzād's *Āb-i Ḥayāt*), offer a fascinating picture of how *tazkira-nigārs* (compilers) promoted the personae of 'poetesses' and presented them to the Urdu readership. By way of example, Māh Laqā Bāī Chandā, the famous courtesan of Hyderabad, is represented literarily in *BN* by a single *she'r*. Ranj's full entry is as follows:

> Chandā *Randī*: earliest owner of a full collection of poems (*ṣāḥib-i dīvān*), a resident of Hyderabad, Deccan. Her name was also Māh Laqā. On account of her wealth she kept quite a magnificent retinue. Five hundred soldiers ate her salt, among them some foot soldiers, some cavalry. She also patronized poets. Her wrestling was such that renowned wrestlers paid tribute to her strength. Such an archer was she that her arrow never missed its mark; she rode such that even the best horsemen couldn't keep stride with her. She was the dutiful pupil of Sher Muḥammad Khān, *takhalluṣ* 'Bā-Īmān'. This was the time of the Deccan Subedar Aristu Jah, the time of Alamgir II.

Poetesses in her time were seen but not heard, yet the legend of her beauty and accomplishment was on every tongue. The author of the *Ṭabqa'āt us-Sho'arā* wrote that in a 1799 assembly she presented her *dīvān* as tribute to an English dignitary. It is present in the Qaisari Library, but the poetry (*kalām*) is not found there. I happen to have on hand this verse, whose refrain (*radīf*) caused me great amusement:

> *Akhlāq se to apne vāqif jahāṅ hegā*
> *Par āp ko ghalaṭ kuchh ab tak gumāṅ hegā*
> The whole world is aware of my virtues
> Yet somehow *you* still have your doubts! (Ranj 1965: 127–8).

This is a paltry representation by Ranj. Chandā may, in fact, be Urdu's best-known early female poet, and there are extant at least three manuscripts of her *dīvān*.[8] It has been published repeatedly, most recently in 1990 from the Majlis-i Taraqqi-i Adab, Lahore. Though the *dīvān* contains no ghazal with the *hegā radīf*, it runs to sixty-two pages and 125 ghazal selections. In *Women Writing in India*, the sole pre-twentieth century entry on Urdu is Māh Laqā Bāī Chandā (Tharu and Lalita 1991: 120–2). Tharu and Lalita, not Urdu specialists, still offer a full ghazal in English translation and refer to Chandā's extant *oeuvre* as comprising a total of thirty-nine ghazals. It seems difficult to believe that Ranj's one-verse offering was all that was available to the connoisseur of his time.

Ranj does much in his presentation to promote and celebrate the notoriety of Chandā while actually doing little to represent her as a poet, even less to treat her poetry seriously. This is reflected even in the *tazkira*'s title, in its employment of the word *nāz*: while it can mean 'elegance, delicacy, or gracefulness', *nāz* also connotes coquetry and blandishment (Platts 1968: 1114). Thus, the first critical collection devoted to Urdu women poets is packaged in the garb of dalliance—and this in a cultural tradition which takes poetry as serious business. Even more than this, we must consider that Ranj's prefatory remarks evince greater concern for the preservation of the names (or the legends) of poets than for their poetry. Ranj observes that Chandā's *dīvān* is held in the Qaisari Library, but not her *kalām* (*oeuvre*). In other words, *the book without its contents* has been kept safe for posterity! Far more interesting to Ranj's readers ought to be her skills in archery, horse(wo)manship, wrestling and patronage,[9] each of which carries a dual connotation in the context of her advertised profession. *Randī* did not always carry the connotation of a prostitute, apparently having served merely to indicate a woman in earlier times. But Chandā, a renowned courtesan—as were many pre-modern female poets—is the only 'poetess' in *BN* introduced by that term.[10]

Contrary to the expectation Ranj sets up, in the following ghazal Chandā inhabits the standard persona of the seeking *'āshiq* (lover/narrator), oscillating between melancholic lament and attempts at righteous assertion towards the withholding beloved. The poet manipulates standard tropes to create exaggerated visual images while carrying claims of his/her own denigration and dissolution to the level of braggadocio:[11]

Dil ho gayā gham se dāgh-dār khūb
Phūlā hai kyā hī josh se ye lāla-zār khūb
Grief has branded my heart but good:
Could its heat have caused this tulip-bed
to burst forth into bloom?
Kab tak rahūṅ ḥijāb meṅ maḥrūm vaṣl se
Jī meṅ hai kīje pyār se būs-o-kinār khūb
How long shall this veil sequester me from union?
My heart demands passion's kisses and embraces!
Sāqī lagā ke barf meṅ mai kī ṣurāhī lā
Ānkhoṅ meṅ chhā rahā hai nashe kā khumār khūb
Cup-bearer, pack a wine-pitcher in ice and bring it here!
Intoxication is clouding my vision.
Āyā na ek din bhī tū va'de pe rāt ko
Achhā kiyā sulūk taghāfil she'ār khūb
Not a single day did you prove faithful
to your promises concerning night:
Such are your loving ways, Neglectful One!
Aisī havā bandhī rahe chandā kī yā 'alī!
Bā-ṣad bahār dekhe jahāṅ kī bahār khūb
May Chandā's renown remain as is, O 'Ali!
And may it flourish to witness
A century of springtimes! (Chandā 1990: 99).

This is reminiscent of poetry by the great *ustāds* of Lucknow or Delhi during the middle of the nineteenth century, the narrator's gender being entirely ambiguous, save in the second verse where the narrator refers to being trapped in a veil. But Ranj's exoticization of Chandā draws attention away from the verses, redirecting it to the poet's gender and, thus, her social status.

Another poet who stands out in this *tazkira* is Munnī Bāī 'Ḥijāb', and she too dates from the early nineteenth century.[12] Of her *oeuvre* Ranj offers us one full ghazal (seven *she'rs*), selections from two other ghazals (four and two *she'rs* respectively), and four miscellaneous verses. She is given just over two full pages, at least two-thirds of which contain verse. Ḥijāb is another of the very few women poets in Urdu for whom we can find an extant *dīvān*.[13] Ranj refers to it in passing as 'smallish' and suggests that its purpose was to serve as a memento of her lovers (Ranj 1965: 135). He does go on to say that she equals or betters the renowned 'poetesses' of his own day in giving account of a life of pleasure (*paimānā-i luṭf zindagī*). As illustration we have this ghazal:

Ḥāl-i ḥijāb qābil-i sharḥ-o-bayāñ nahīñ
Ānsū na ṭapke sun ke ye vo dāstāñ nahīñ
The plight of Hijab is not the stuff
Of annotation and explication:
This is not that dry sort of tale that, once heard,
Leaves the eyes unflowing.
Dil meñ jigar meñ sīne meñ pahlū meñ ānkh meñ
Ae 'ishq terī sho'la-fashānī kahāñ nahīñ
Heart, liver, breast, flank, eyes:
O Love, what part of me has your flame-throwing *not* scorched!
Karte ho qatl bu'l-havasoñ ko ghazab hai ye
Samjhe ho tum magar ko'ī 'āshiq yahāñ nahīñ
It's amazing how you slay those desiring you
Then aver there to be no good prospects around![14]
Pūchho na ḥāl-i zār mirā tum se kyā kahūñ
Gum-karda rāh-i bāgh hūñ yād āshiyāñ nahīñ
Don't ask after my sorry plight—
what could I tell you?
I've lost the way back to the garden,
forgotten my nest.
Ham bhī kharīd lete tire zulm ke liye
Bāzār-i dahr meñ ko'ī dil kī dukāñ nahīñ
I, too, would stock up against your cruelty,
But in this worldly market
There's no shop purveying hearts.
Dete haiñ chheṛ chheṛ ke kyūñ mujh ko gāliyāñ
Samjhe hu'e haiñ vo mire munh meñ zabāñ nahīñ
Why does s/he [do they] tease me and torment me so?
S/he [they] must think I've no tongue in my mouth to respond![15]
Vo āvar mere ghar meñ chale ā'eñ khud-ba-khud
Sar par mire ḥijāb magar āsmāñ nahīñ
S/he might come to my house of her [his] own accord—
My head is veiled, Ḥijāb, but there is no sky![16]

It is anybody's guess why Ranj sees in this ghazal a chronicle of a life of pleasure, as his prefatory remarks indicate. Mixing melancholic lament with bravado, employing standard forms of wordplay, this poem stands out in no way from a hundred other ghazals of its time.[17] Importantly, Ḥijāb conforms to convention, as did Chandā, by narrating in the first person masculine voice. Except for the mention of *ḥijāb* (head-covering) in the final verse (*maqṭa*ʻ), internal indications of female authorship are absent. It is clear from the ghazals presented above that both Ḥijāb and Chandā are actually good poets. Why then Ranj's emphasis on their life circumstances, which are normally considered irrelevant to *rekhta-go'ī*?

Despite his worthy endeavour to bring these female poets to light, Ranj appears afraid of what their participation might say about Urdu culture. Introducing Ḥijāb's *dīvān* as 'smallish', one 'that served as a memento of her lovers', represents an expression of male anxiety about female authorship. Perhaps Ḥijāb rivalled—even surpassed—other (male) poets in *ghazal-go'ī* just as Chandā challenged them on horseback and in the wrestling ring. Moreover, these poets, as women of erudition, education, and wealth, may have exceeded some noblemen in their acts of patronage and cultural production. Recall that Chandā's household was cited as five-hundred-strong. We know very well the arguments about protecting women's chastity and, thereby, the honour of their community through seclusion. But do we see here, perhaps, men of the Urdu elite also sidelining professional competitors of the opposite sex?

The *ḥijāb* is one of the central signs of female seclusion. Its adoption as a *takhalluṣ* theoretically serves to protect the reputation of the woman poet who uses it. It ostensibly reassures the socially conservative, who might castigate her for the immodesty of engaging in poetry's public discourse, that their censure is unnecessary. Yet seclusion acts as a double-edged sword: it presents a demure shield to the outside world, but it also creates mystery and anxiety about what veiled women do together when men are absent. For a poet to adopt this *takhalluṣ* as a *rekhtī-go* is to reinforce the very premise on which the genre rests, viz., the shenanigans women might be getting up to in the *zanāna*. The *takhalluṣ* offers voyeuristic titillation to its audience while simultaneously trivializing feminine poetic expression.

In his entire *tazkira*, Ranj credits a single poet with composing *rekhtī*. Writes he, 'Rashk Maḥal Begam by name, all-powerful in *rekhtī* is her fame' (*Rashk Maḥal Begam nām, rekhtī meṅ dast-gāh tamām*) (Ranj 1965: 113). Ranj says of Begam, 'though a resident of Punjab, [she] fully adopted the language of the fort [court]'; and that she 'is in Calcutta as a contracted member of Wajid Ali Shah's retinue', by which we might understand her to have been married, or perhaps under a separate contract, to the deposed King of Awadh.

Ranj goes on to say that though still 'open-hearted',[18] Begam was, at the time of his writing, physically veiled; and he records three *she'rs* from one of her ghazals and a single *maṯla'* from another:

> *Na bhejūngī sasurāl meṅ tum ko khānum*
> *Nahīṅ mujh ko dūbhar hai khānā tumhārā*
> I won't send you to your in-laws' place, Khanum,
> Your cooking is not so hard for me to bear.
> *Mirī kanghī choṭi kī letī khabar ho*
> *Ye aḥsān hai sar par dogānā tumhārā*
> That the comb watches out for the braid—
> May this be the blessing on your head, my sweet.
> *Hu'ā bāl bīkā jo mirzā hamārā*
> *To phir sang hai aur shānā tumhārā*
> If anyone touches a hair on my head, Mirza,
> A stone will be your comb![19]
>
> And
>
> *Ghar si-gāna kī do-gānā mirī mahmān gayī*
> *Maiṅ ye angāroṅ pe lūṭī ki mirī jān gayī*
> My girlfriend was my houseguest in three different ways
> I rolled around on embers till my last gasp (Ranj 1965: 113).

Exhibiting a feminine narrator—*rekhtī*'s defining characteristic—this excerpt lives up to the genre's reputation as racy, both in tone and content. In this way it contrasts with the typically melancholy tone of *'ishq*'s love-in-separation theme that we saw in the ghazals preceding it. It is also the only instance I have ever encountered of female-authored *rekhtī*, and Ranj may have confused 'her' with another *rekhtī-go* 'Begam'(who is mentioned in the *Tazkira-i Rekhtī*).[20] This brings us to the second *tazkira* under consideration.

Tazkira-i Rekhtī

Tamkīn Kāẕmī's *tazkira* (hereafter *TR*) is a representation of *écriture féminine* rather than of women poets. Not a compendium of women poets, this text compiles a list of thirty-four poets—all men—who wrote in the feminine voice. In his preface, Kāẕmī says he was intrigued with *rekhtī* as a genre from the moment he saw the *dīvān* of the renowned north Indian *rekhtī-go* Jān Ṣāḥib (1818–86), but that, being a Dakani man, he (Kāẕmī) could not understand most of the verses he read. *Rekhtī* represents the quintessential exoticism of feminine expression, and this *tazkira* manifests a typical ambivalence towards the genre: it is simultaneously an attempt to establish a historical record and an invitation to the voyeur to enter intriguing and mysterious realms.

Kāẕmī reports having studied many *re<u>kh</u>tī dīvāns*, but specifically names the four most famous authors of the genre: Jān Ṣāḥib, Rangīn, Inshā, and Nāznīn.[21] Sa'ādat Yār <u>Kh</u>ān Rangīn is, as noted earlier, the genre's purported creator,[22] and Inshā Allāh <u>Kh</u>ān 'Inshā' (1756–1818) was tremendously famous as a poet of *re<u>kh</u>ta* as well; but the most renowned *re<u>kh</u>tī-go* poet by far is Mir Yār 'Ali 'Jān Ṣāḥib'. Indeed, Kāẕmī's introduction says, 'If Jān Ṣāḥib were to be called the Great Poet (*shā'ir-i 'aẕam*) of *re<u>kh</u>tī*, it would not be unfitting' (Kāẕmī 1930: 24). The *TR* offers a near-200-verse selection (*inti<u>kh</u>āb*) of Jān Ṣāḥib, running to ten pages of text in the main body of the *taẕkira* out of a total of eighty-eight. Inshā and Rangīn, whose extant *kalām* is among the most voluminously represented, claim in *TR* only six pages (sixty-four *she'rs*) and seven pages (sixty-four *she'rs*) respectively. Jān Ṣāḥib's opening ghazal is a *ḥamd* (poem of praise, usually for God or the Prophet Muhammad or, in this case, the twelve imams), which self-consciously sings the praise of Jān Ṣāḥib's own writing along the way. This *ḥamd* lacks the raciness normally associated with *re<u>kh</u>tī*. Indeed, this work by Jān Ṣāḥib supports the few claims made for him as a serious poet:

> If there's one Urdu poet who has interpreted the heart it is Jān Ṣāḥib. Although he has interpreted the hearts of women, still there is also no doubt that he gives them not just voice, but consciousness (*ḥāl*) too. From the highest class of women to the lowest, he presents their affairs. The work they do, the things they say, the ideas born in their hearts—Jān Ṣāḥib has presented it all. The love of a father; motherly affection; the affection of brother and sister; the love between a husband and wife, including their quarrels; envy between co-wives; dalliance with acquaintances; fights with mother-in-law and sister-in-law; a bride's veil; sister-in-law jokes; the state of confinement; the condition of children, their education and upbringing; housekeeping details; marriage and wedding customs; matters concerning dancers, singers and musicians; treatment of female slaves; remedies for the sick; laments for the dead; magic and incantations; weakness of faith; clothing; jewelry; items of adornment...in short the basics of this world. And the truth is that this *dīvān* is a picture of the state of society at that time (Naqvī, 59–60).

Re<u>kh</u>tī's standard characteristics can be seen, however, in the following selection from Rangīn, the genre's official creator:[23]

Mujh pe ṭūfāṅ na le chāh kā chal dūr dadā
Jhūṭ se munh kā tere jāyegā aṛ-nūr dadā
Don't flood me with desirous words—keep your distance, Nurse!
These lies will blacken your face, O Nurse!

Ek to shakl ḍarānī hai terī be-chā sī
Tis pe yūṅ phāṛ ke dīde mujhe mat ghūr dadā
For one, your ugly face is frightful—
And Nurse, don't stare at me wide-eyed like that!
Pak gayā hai tere hāthoṅ se kalījā merā
Tujh ko dūṅ chīloṅ ko gar ho mirā maqdūr dadā
Nurse, at your hands I've been cut to the quick—
I'd feed you to the vultures if I could!
Is lagāne se tere aur bujhāne se tere
Tere tālū meṅ ilāhī kare nāsūr dadā
From your spreading and squelching of rumours, Nurse,
May God make your mouth ulcerate! (Kāẕmī 1930: 43).[24]

From another ghazal:

Ṭes perū meṅ uṭhī ūhi merī jān gayī
Mat sitā mujh ko dogānā tere qurbān gayī
This throb below has nearly killed me
Dear One, don't tease so, you've already done me in!
Tere sadqe gayī rangīn g͟hazal ik aur to kah
Jagat ustād hai tū maiṅ tujhe pahchān gayī
Your acclaim is a done deal, Rangīn, so
Recite one poem more:
I recognize you as Ustad of the World! (Kāẕmī 1930: 45).

And from yet another:

Ae dogānā tū mujhe lūṭne ko āyī phir
Phir satak jāvegī ghar par mire suthrāyī phir
Ah, Sweetheart, when you come again to ravage me
my house will once more be in disarray.
Merī aur merī zanāk͟hī ke hai guṛiyoṅ kā byāh
Āj sāchiq hai mere ghar se būrī jātī hai
My sweetheart's and mine is a doll's wedding:
Today's the bridegroom's feast—
How dare she leave my house! (Kāẕmī 1930: 45).

Here we see all the expected tropes of *rek͟htī*: the typical *begamātī zabān* (Minault 1984, 1994), the racy idiomatic expression thought to be particular to secluded women of the elite; interactions with household servants and other domestic concerns; and lesbian allusions. Rangīn employs his pen-name in such a way as to 'enter' this segregated space at the end of each ghazal, thus underlining the voyeuristic nature of *rek͟htī*; and to reinforce his own persona as an errant roué among the Begams. This also serves to remind us that the feminine milieu of *rekhtī* is invoked by males, the 'real experts' on women!

Nāznīn is another *rekhtī-go* of intriguing biography. Kāẓmī introduces him as a resident of Delhi, a pupil of Shaikh Ibrāhīm 'Zauq' (d. 1854),[25] citing as his sources Mirzā Qādir Bakhsh Ṣābir's *tazkira Gulistān-i Sukhan* (1855) and, on the date of Nāznīn's birth (AH 1271/1856–7 CE), Nassākh's *Sukhan-i Sho'arā*. Nassākh claims that Nāznīn 'wrote better *rekhtī* than Jān Ṣāḥib, composing this *rekhtī* epitaph on the occasion of Zauq's death':

Nahīṅ nāznīn ranj kartī kisī kā
Gayā jab se yār aur ḥurmat hai khū'ī
Nāznīn laments for no one
Since both beloved and reputation have passed on
Balā se rahūṅ shād dil ko to apne
Agar maiṅ ne kumbe kī 'izzat ḍabū'ī
May I of joyous heart remain afflicted
If I should e'er besmirch the family name
Khaṣam jab mu'ā launḍiyoṅ ko rulāyā
Ki is parde meṅ nām rakkhe na ko'ī
When my husband died all the maids grieved
No one's good name remains intact here in purdah
Valekin mujhe kāmiloṅ se hai ulfat
Gham-i zauq meṅ rāt bhar maiṅ na soyī
For all that I love the masters
I couldn't sleep all night for sorrow for Zauq
Likhī us kī tārīkh aur ye hu'ā gham
Miyāṅ zauq ko maiṅ bu'ā āp royī
I wrote his date and this sorrow descended
Auntie, I myself weep for Master Zauq (Kāẓmī 1930: 73–4).

TR goes on to list another four pages of Nāznīn's poetry, totalling twenty-one further *she'rs* and an eight-stanza *mukhammas* (poem of five-line stanzas), apparently culled from five different sources. The following set gives a fair idea of why some critics dismiss *rekhtī* as mere doggerel:

Hu'ī 'ushshāq meṅ mashhūr yūsuf-sā javān tākā
Bu'ā ham 'auratoṅ meṅ thā baṛā dīda zulaikhā kā
I gained fame among lovers for my pick
of a handsome, Joseph-like youth:
Auntie, we women claim
Zulaikhā's discerning eye!

Maiṅ apne sar ko dhotī hūṅ bu'ā aur ye tamāshā hai
Mu'ā baiṭhā hai kyā khush khush ki din āyā taqāẓā kā
As I wash my head, Aunt, here's a spectacle—
That miserable dolt sits merrily;
When day comes there'll be hell to pay![26]

****

Sonā kabhī shohar ko muyassar nahīṅ hotā
'Aurat! inhīṅ bātoṅ se terā ghar nahīṅ hotā
It's never easy for a husband to sleep;
Woman! These affairs will bring your house down!

****

Merī namāz khoyī us murdu'e ne ā kar
Uṭhī thī ae dadā maiṅ kambakht abhī nahā kar
Nurse, when that miserable wretch came
He made me lose track of my prayers;
And damned if I hadn't just got up and bathed![27] (Kāẕmī 1930: 74).

Nāznīn has no extant *dīvān* as far as this author can discern, but as a historical character he has been preserved in the novel, *Dillī kī Ākhrī Shama'* (see Qamber 1979) in which he is depicted as providing light entertainment by draping himself in a dupatta and reciting *rekhtī*.[28] Despite this paltry evidence of his life and work, Kāẕmī mentions Nāznīn along with Rangīn, Inshā, and Jān Ṣāḥib as the most famous *rekhtī-gos*. Either his *oeuvre* has been completely suppressed, or his legend is apocryphal.

Of the other thirty poets listed in *TR*, only the Dakani master, Hāshmī Bījāpurī, a seventeenth-century court poet of 'Ali 'Adil Shah II (r.1646–72), is a writer of enduring repute. His attributed *kalām* comprises a *dīvān* of 327 ghazals, many of which are *rekhtīs* (Hāshmī 1961: 14–16); *masnavīs*, including the famous *Yūsuf-Zulaikhā*;[29] *qaṣīdas* and *marṣiyas*, which Kāẕmī tells us Hāshmī composed in great number though they are no longer extant (Kāẕmī 1930: 80–1.) Here are some verses from the best-known *rekhtī* of Hāshmī, which present a qualitative difference in tone from the *rekhtī* we have seen so far:

Sajan āveṅ to parde sun nikāl kar bhār baiṭhūngī
Bahānā karke motīyāṅ kā pirotī hār baiṭhūngī
If my sweetheart were to come then I'd
emerge from purdah, sit outside;
I'd sit there on some pretext,
threading pearls into a garland.

Uno yāṅ ā'o kahenge to kahūṅgī kām kartī hūṅ
Athaltī aur mathaltī chup ghaṛī do-chār baiṭhūṅgī
Should he approach me
I'll say to him, 'I'm working.'
I'll dawdle and dally and sit a while
Quietly facing him.
Nazīk meṅ un ke jāne ko khushī sūṅ shād ho dil meṅ
Vale logāṅ meṅ dikhlāne kūṅ ho bezār baiṭhūṅgī
Were I to draw near to him
my heart would swell with joy
But to others I'd show a sorrowful face (Hāshmī 1961: 244).

Here the feminine narrator is decidedly submissive to her grammatically male lover, displaying all the standard tropes of feminine modesty that apparently please men. The marked difference in tone between Hāshmī's *rekhtī* and that of the other poets discussed here gives some idea of how problematic it is to lump Dakani *rekhtī* together with Lakhnavi (Petievich 1990). It seems that this use of the feminine voice is heterosexual and normative to prescribed social relations, manifesting none of the anxiety we perceive in the voices and personae presented to us by such nineteenth- and twentieth-century mediators as Ranj and Kāẓmī. As to how this feminine voice fits into the larger picture of Urdu poetry and Indic poetry, Kāẓmī cites an excerpt from Karīmuddīn's *tazkira Ṯabqa'āt-us Sho'arā-i Hind* (early nineteenth century) which offers the standard explanation:

In Arabia men are the lovers of women and most *she'rs* are narrated by men; in Iran man is the lover of man, in Hindustan woman is man's lover; this is how it seems from reading Hindi verses such as *kahat*, *dohrā* and other genres. Miraculously, in the Glorious Quran love of woman is recounted by men. So Hāshmī also composed the story of *Yūsuf-Zulaikhā* in this manner, that is, with the woman expressing *'ishq* (Kāẓmī 1930: 80).

In the case of a seventeenth-century Dakani poet, this explanation seems plausible, if not entirely illuminating. It seems clear that while the narrator described here is a *virahinī*, the tone is not devotional, as in bhakti; and it lacks the complexity of Sanskrit *kāvya* or Tamil *akam*. It seems to be a reverse fantasy of the mischief so central to the imagination of later, northern *rekhtī-go* poets.

Of the other poets listed in the *TR*, we can say that they are obscure, or have been obscured from the view of Urdu readers. It is interesting to note that Rashk Maḥal, listed in the *Bahāristān-i Nāz* as a *rekhtī-go* poet, goes unnoted by Tamkīn Kāẓmī. The only 'Begam' he lists—and he presents a thirty-four verse *qaṣīda* plus seven full ghazals by this poet—is 'Ābid Mirzā 'Begam', born in 1857 in Lucknow to a father in the service of Wajid Ali Shah. Kāẓmī notes that, as of the date of his *tazkira* (1930), 'Begam' was still alive and dwelling in Hyderabad under the occasional patronage of the Asaf Jahi Nizams. Clearly, s/he would have been too young to attract the notice of Faṣīḥuddīn Ranj, even by the time of the *BN*'s final edition in 1882, though his/her poetry was quite familiar to Kāẓmī, a contemporary Hyderabadi. Curiously, despite 'Irfān 'Abbāsī's 1989 citation of *TR* as a source for his mention of Rashk Maḥal 'Begam' (in the *Tazkira-i Sho'arā-i Rekhtī*), Kāẓmī makes no mention of 'her'.[30]

'Begam' and 'Ḥijāb' prove to have been popular *takhallus*, both for poets of *rekhta* and *rekhtī*. But as we have said, the actual evidence for women writing *rekhtī* is very slim—just the four *she'rs* from one ghazal[31] and another lone *she'r* in a different *zamīn*, all exactly the same in each of the three *tazkiras* that cite 'her' ('Abbāsī 1989: 64–5, Nassākh 1982: 573, Ranj 1965: 113). Moreover, what is clearly going on here is a subversion: the mark of respectability (*ḥijāb*) and the title of respectability (*begam*) are being manipulated, the first juxtaposed against the association of female poets with courtesanship in *BN* and the second against the naughtiness and non-respectability of *rekhtī* in *TR*.

Female Authorship vs Female Literacy

What we can determine about female literacy from these sources is actually limited, implicit, and speculative. But we can infer, to paraphrase the critical introduction of the 1965 edition of *BN*, that the ranks of poetesses were largely comprised of women of ill repute. Although literacy is not strictly necessary to compose poetry in this tradition, it should not surprise us that women with a degree of learning sufficient for composing poetry would be either courtesans or noblewomen. This state of affairs seems also to have pertained in ancient Greece among the hetaera, in Japan among the geisha, and in Renaissance Italy (Stortoni 1997: xviii–xxi). Female literacy the world over has been low as a rule, and women who pursued education were often obliged to forego domestic respectability in exchange for this rare privilege. But to return to the case of Indian women, one editor of *BN*, Khalīlur Raḥmān Dāūdī, writes:

> It is not only in *BN* that we find *ṭavā'ifs* mentioned in connection with poetry, subsequent *tazkiras* are full of them. Following *BN*, in 1878, Durgā Parshād 'Nādir' published a *tazkira* entitled *Chaman-i Andāz*. In it he mentions 144 poetesses. From among these 144 only 57 were respectable women, the rest *ṭavā'ifs*.

Dāūdī goes on to say:

One should not conclude...that only *ṯavā'ifs* composed poetry. This is not the case at all, in fact, women of the great houses of culture and civilization also 'said' poetry, but they did not think it fitting that they should become known for it, given their status and position. So their *dīvāns* and other writing were confined to the four walls of their homes. Even so, the author of *BN* makes such poetesses known to us as much as he can and we are indebted to him for it.[32]

The Purpose of *Tazkira*

We have said that *tazkiras* represent the earliest genre of secondary literature on poetry, and that the past one-and-a-half century's self-conscious tradition of writing literary history in Urdu has, overwhelmingly, taken the *tazkira* form. But these texts must be read against the grain to some extent. As others have also observed, the motivation behind this genre is to make mention (*zikr*), to create genealogies of literary and cultural production, rather than to actually preserve or study the poets' work or the literary tradition itself. As a *tazkira-nigār* Ranj reveals very little in *BN* about his own literary sensibilities or his critical vision. Indeed, it is generally thought that such qualities were absent from the tradition of writing *tazkiras* until the time of Āzād's *Āb-i Ḥayāt* in 1880 (Pritchett and Faruqi 2001). The remarkable authority attached to this pioneering work, its dominance in literary criticism throughout the twentieth century, rests in great part on the critical insights with which Āzād suffused his genealogy. Ranj, who came just before Āzād, was operating under a standard different from that set by *Āb-i Ḥayāt*.

We can speculate that while *BN* was designed to offer a testimonial to the participation of women in the realm of cultural life, and to thereby refute one aspect of colonialist discourse around Indian backwardness, Ranj did not take it upon himself, as Āzād later chose to do, to make literature the subject of scientific study and thereby to refute another aspect of colonial discourse surrounding the superiority of Western culture because of its scientific and technological advances. Ranj exhorts his readers to appreciate the accomplishments of women, but those that seem to attract his attention appear to be brazenness or modesty as much as scholarship or poeticity. In fact, he lists the names of female poets as evidence of Urdu culture's inclusive credentials but, in so doing, gives short shrift to actual poetry composed by women.

BN and *TR* lend insight into the possible differences between poetry women have written in Urdu, and what men have written when aurally impersonating women. *TR* allows us to visit male imaginings about how women might express themselves poetically; while *BN* offers us a picture of female poets as a category, along with a smidgeon of their verse, as presented by a man of letters.

It is worth reiterating that women writing *rekhta* chose to adopt the normative, masculine voice rather than a feminine voice. Thus, the notion of a special *écriture féminine* might be more a male rather than female concern in the early modern Urdu context. Here is an example by the poet 'Sharm' (Bashfulness, Modesty): [33]

Pahle ṡābit kareṅ is vaḥshī kī taqsīreṅ do
Phir mujhe shauq se pahnāyeṅ vo zanjīreṅ do
First let's establish my savage transgressions
Then have the pleasure of shackling me!
Ek būsa liyā kis din hoveṅ taqsīreṅ do
Kyūṅ mire pā'ūṅ meṅ pahnāte ho zanjīreṅ do
I stole a kiss: whatever day it was, lay blame
Why do you dress my feet in shackles?
Kahā qāṣid ne ki lāyā hūṅ maiṅ paighām-i viṣāl
Āj khil'at mujhe pahnā'o ki jāgīreṅ do
The messenger said, 'I've brought you news of a tryst.
Now dress me in robes of honour and grant me land.'
Donoṅ zulfoṅ kā tirī āyā jo vaḥshat meṅ khayāl
Par gayīṅ pā'ūṅ meṅ mere vahīṅ zanjīreṅ do
In the wilderness I remembered both your locks:
Both spread across my legs and shackled them.
Yā to ghar us ke maiṅ jā'ūngā o yāṅ āyegā yār
Vaṣl ke khvāb kī bas haiṅ yahī ta'bīreṅ do
Either I go to 'his' house or my love comes to mine—
Let this be the shape my dreams of union take.
Munh pe munh rakhne kā iqrār hai inkār ke sāth
Ek mazmūṅ kī likheṅ yār ne taḥrīreṅ do
Along with refusal came a 'mouth to mouth' pledge
My love has composed a Writ of Manumission!
Mujh ko hairāṅ terā aur tujhe hairāṅ merā
Ḥaq ne kyā khūb banāyī haiṅ ye taṣvīreṅ do
I'm amazed by you and you're amazed by me
What fine pictures have Truth and Right drawn!
Ae muṣavvar tujhe dūngā maiṅ bahut-sā in'ām
Merī aur us kī bāham khainch de taṣvīreṅ do
O painter, I shall give you great rewards!
Please, just draw a picture of him/her and me together.

Dard-i dil dūr hu'ā sīne kī sozish bhī gayī
Sharbat vaṣl meṅ tere haiṅ ye tāsīreṅ do
My heart's pain lies at a distance,
my chest affliction gone as well:
May the potion of our union always render such effects!
Yā bahāne se bulāyeṅ use yā khaṭ likheṅ
Sharm kyā khūb ye sujheṅ hameṅ tadbīreṅ do
Either find some excuse to summon her/him
or pen an invitation—
Sharm, how fine these visions are—make plans! (Ranj 1965: 156).

While the fifth and eighth *she'rs* bear witness that the poet has adopted a masculine persona, it is not at all clear to this reader how the poet could be identified—from the poem's expression itself—by gender. We see clearly that women who composed lyric poetry chose to speak in a masculine voice. Surely, they did so because they understood the deep conventions of the poetic system in which they were participating, valued the system, and wished to participate fully in it. To adopt the voice of *rekhtī* would not have effected full participation.

Female Literacy

Among the most visible efforts at social and cultural reform in late nineteenth-century northern India were those concerned with women's education. Yet reformists did not all share the same vision, and it seems clear that even those calling for the most radical reform remained somewhat ambivalent about its potential outcomes. The great Sayyid Ahmad Khan, for instance, argued that women should be taught to read, but not to write (Minault 1998), and he was not alone. Naim relates the moving story of one woman's struggle to overcome her enforced illiteracy at the hands of male elders. Bibi Ashraf's father and uncle had attended Delhi College and pursued the modern profession of law. But her grandfather warned against how women might begin speaking to men, once educated (Naim 1987: 103). By contrast, the more progressive Alṭāf Ḥusain Ḥālī, very nearly a contemporary of Bibi Ashraf's father and Ranj, made a point of advocating for women's education and decried the condition of women such as she (Minault 1983, Naim 1987).

Those who compiled *tazkiras* of women poets would seem to have viewed things more like Ḥālī. Far less famous than he, but contemporary, were Ranj—a putative fellow *shāgird* of Mirza Ghalib—and Durgā Parshād 'Nādir', who was apparently inspired by Ranj to bring out *Gulshan-i Nāz* (1876) and

Chaman-i Andāz (1878), two other *tazkiras* of 'poetesses'.[34] Ranj, like Ḥālī, decried women's lack of education and declared ignorant those husbands who failed to make use of existing arrangements for female scholars at government facilities (Fateḥpūrī 1972: 462). The several *tazkiras* of Indo-Muslim poetesses compiled by Ranj and Nādir between 1864 and 1882, in tacit conjunction with reformist writers like Ḥālī and Deputy Nazīr Aḥmad, consciously attempted to reverse the status quo and to introduce women of letters to mainstream literati so that they might occupy a place in the historical register. But the actual place Ranj wanted women to occupy is open to question, and the preceding discussion suggests that, to any inferred altruistic impulses he harboured, perhaps meaner motives may be added as well.

Ranj, in the rather salacious pleasure with which he introduces poetesses, including his own liaisons with them, also seems intent upon reducing their literary stature. Whatever the quality of their poetry—and we have seen that it could be high—Ranj ultimately framed his *tazkira* around these poets' roles as quasi-public women, leaving his reader with a sense of ambivalence: 'poetesses' should enter the historical register, but perhaps not on the same line as male poets.

Tamkīn Kāzmī's *Tazkira-i Rekhtī* reflects anxieties and fantasies somewhat differently. While *BN* seems to use the notion of female poets as courtesans to compromise their literary credentials, simultaneously inviting the (assumed male?) reader into the realm of voyeuristic pleasure, *TR*'s *rekhtī* texts reinforce the notion that secluded women band together to exclude men from their own realm of pleasure, referring to husbands in deprecating terms and behaving lewdly with other men, even with one another. This, of course, contradicts the organizing principle behind seclusion as a social practice, preservation of chastity, and posits *rekhtī* as the problem rather than purdah.

One is tempted to think that the shenanigans depicted in *rekhtī* are exactly the results Sir Sayyid and his ilk wished to nip in the bud by inducting women into a community of readership but not of authorship. For authorship is agency, and there were already a number of—perhaps too many—competing agents in the social space under negotiation in post-1857 British India.

Not that *rekhtī* really tells us what secluded women did behind the curtain. It is, after all, a male invention, a delegitimized adaptation of a pre-existing voice in a literary tradition that once enjoyed legitimacy. Among the myriad ironies of sorting out these texts is that the courtesans of *tazkiras* such as *BN* are, in some ways, more real than the allegedly respectable and veiled, *parda-nashīn* 'women' depicted for us in *rekhtī*. The idiomatic expressions for which *rekhtī* is known underline the fact that seclusion has kept women different from men. While their particular idiom is 'preserved' for us through *rekhtī*, so is a sense of the exotic. The language used by *BN*'s women when they compose is indistinguishable from that of male poets, so the 'poetesses' themselves are reified as exotic. This is not, then, a chronicle of India's respectable Muslim women emulating their European counterparts, *mems* whom Ranj claimed 'participate[d] fully in every profession', 'were world-renowned in their own fields', and had attained 'excellence in matters of language and education' (Ranj 1965: 85–6).

Aside from what and whether women ought to write, there is the question of what texts were taught them when they did learn to read: (1) the primary text was the Quran, without emphasis necessarily placed on young girls' comprehension of what they were reading (Naim 1987: 102); (2) Maulvī Ashraf ʿAlī Thānawī's *Bihishtī Zewar* usually accompanied the Quran in any bride's dowry, in order that she might become a properly socialized wife and mother, thereby contributing to the reform and resurrection of Muslim civilization in India (Metcalf 1992); (3) some elite women were taught to read from Persian classics like Saʿdī's *Bostān* and *Gulistān* so as to inculcate an appreciation of fine discourse (*khush sukhan*)—apparently women were to learn the art of fine discourse but to practise it only in private. In 'How Bibi Ashraf Learned to Read and Write', Professor Naim refers to the 'books on matters of faith and religious observervances' that were the staple of reading matter in the *zanāna*. He also cites authoritative texts that exhort Muslim men to 'teach the girls neither reading nor writing' (Naṣīruddīn Tūsī in *Akhlāq-i Nāṣirī*). Thānawī himself recommended reading and writing for domestic purposes, but only if the girls involved were not thought to be 'brazen by nature' (Naim 1987: 105, 113). Knowledge is power, as is literacy; the issue of female literacy was being negotiated in a competitive, gendered realm, with social and political power at stake. Sir Sayyid and other proponents of Muslim power in British India, therefore, made plain that Muslim men must be ensured 'first dibs' over women in the race towards education (Minault 1983: 40, Naim 1987: passim).

His sincere concern for the 'Muhammadans' of India notwithstanding, I am by no means the first to take exception to claims of Sir Sayyid's feminism (Minault 1983, 1998; Naim 1987). Nor is it particularly original to remark here that lack of women's education and social uplift came to be a negotiating chip between competing South Asian and European male elites more than it reflected any of the competitors' commitment to universal human rights. The status of women became, primarily, a debating point between foreign and indigenous male elites, the debate being over whether or not Indian culture was really as inferior to European culture as was claimed by the colonialists. Concern for women was secondary at best. The situation reminds us of similar problematics within Marxist discourses in the early and mid-twentieth century, wherein gender equality was consistently deferred in favour of class (and, in America, of racial) equality.

On the other hand, to read and ponder these rather obscure(d) Urdu *tazkiras* is fascinating and edifying work; to keep the light of historical record shining on them is the imperative of committed cultural historians. And to remember the socio-political climate prevailing in the late nineteenth and early-twentieth centuries helps make sense of the pushes and pulls of reformist agendas concerning literacy and education in Muslim British India. We would do well to remember that the *Tazkira-i Rekhtī* produced a kind of knowledge deemed by the custodians of Urdu culture (and by extension, Indo-Muslim culture overall) to reflect poorly on the community with which it was associated, as yet another negotiation dawned—that of the movement for Pakistan.[35] Without bearing these factors in mind, how to make sense of the near-complete suppression of both *rekhtī* poetry and the chronicle of its authors? By contrast, efforts to publish and preserve the work of twentieth-century female poets have been far more successful, and one hopes that the corner has been turned irrevocably on this particular form of censorship.

But *tazkiras* will remain selective representations of the Urdu tradition, perhaps inevitably sustaining the legends of poets rather than their poetry. *BN*'s fanciful introductions and *rekhtī*'s phony women's voices deflect attention away from the real literature authored by women with real biographies. They bring forth a few roses and tulips but leave a plethora of possibilities still lying hidden in the dust of patriarchal history. Indeed we can lament, as did Mirza Ghalib:

> *Sab kahāṅ kuchh lāla-o-gul meṅ numā'iyāṅ ho gayīṅ*
> *Khāk meṅ kyā ṣūrateṅ hongī ki pinhāṅ ho gayīṅ!*

Acknowledgements

I would like to thank Shabana Mahmud of the British Library's India and Oriental Office collection for her generosity and collegiality over the years, and for having first introduced me to the poetry of Chandā and Ḥijāb. My sincere thanks also to Professor Naim for his gracious mentorship; to Saleem Kidwai for having encouraged me to pursue the study of *rekhtī*; to Prof. Sadiqur Rahman Kidwai for his generosity of time and spirit in reading more *rekhtī* with me than he probably would have preferred; and to Ramya Sreenivasan for pounding the Delhi pavements with me through the long, hot summer of 1999 in search of any Delhi library that might be holding a copy of Tamkīn Kāẕmī's *Taẕkira-i Rekhtī.*

Notes

[1] Other recent work touching on the feminine voice in Urdu literature includes Faruqi 1999, and Naim and Petievich 1997.

[2] The 'I' is expressed in the grammatical masculine, as are the ghazal's 'you' and 'they'. For fuller discussion of this phenomenon, see Petievich 1990, 2000, 2001 (a) and (b), and 2002. A fair amount of scholarly attention has been paid of late to the issue of gender, but it has yet to enter mainstream discussion in Urdu circles. Clearly, much more discussion is still needed. See Faruqi 1999, Naim 2001.

[3] Indeed, Fisher in this volume demonstrates that Indian perceptions of Victorian women's status was much at odds with contemporary feminist understandings. *See also* the remarks of Ranj (Ranj 1965: 85–6).

[4] *See* the novels and short stories of the Urdu-turned-Hindi writer Premchand, Rashid Jehan, and the *Angāre* group, Rājinder Singh Bedī, Krishan Chander, 'Iṣmat Chughtāī, Khadīja Mastoor, Hājira Masroor, and a host of others from the 1930s and 1940s. The literature on Progressive Writers is legion, but for useful introductions, *see* Sadiq 1984, Russell 1992, Coppola 1975, and Mahmud 1988.

[5] 'Effeminate: to make like a woman'. *Webster's New International Dictionary*, 2nd edition (unabridged), 1942, 819.

[6] Cf. the standard histories of Urdu literature: Bailey 1932, Jālibī 1977, Sadiq 1984 [1964], Saksena 1940, Schimmel 1975, and Zaidī 1993.

[7] I have been unable to ascertain how many poets it listed. The *taẕkira*'s length expanded with each subsequent edition, the second edition (1869) adding another seventy-eight pages. The third (1882) included ninety pages of *taẕkira* with sixteen pages of introductory *ḥamd-o-na't* (Fateḥpūrī 1972: 459). The Majlis-i Taraqqi-i Adab edition of 1965 runs to 240 pages.

[8] Shabana Mahmud of the Oriental and India Office Collections of the British Library reports one manuscript held in the British Library, one in Karachi and a third in Hyderabad (personal correspondence, 20 December 1993). She reports that the selection of ghazals varies in each collection, noting that some thirty ghazals, each five *she'rs* long, though contained in this 1990 edition, are not found in the British Library manuscript of Chandā's *dīvān*. Tharu and Lalita refer to a biographer, Sameena Shaukat, but not to her biography of Chandā (1991: 122). They also mention, without citation, that Māh Laqā's poems were compiled and published after her death as *Gulẕār-e Māhlaqā* (Māh Laqā's Garden of Flowers).

[9] Courtesans came to be conflated, by the nineteenth century, with the ghazal's beautiful, cruel, elusive Beloved. In the ghazal it is highly conventional that a beloved shoot the arrows of her piercing glance into the hearts of her admirers; whereas poetry

would represent the more public side of Māh Laqā's profession, reference to her archery, her 'wrestling', and her 'riding' direct our imagination to its more private practice.

[10] Schimmel tells us that Garcin de Tassy, on p. 8 of his 'Les femmes poètes dans l'Inde' 'makes [Māh Laqā] a queen, but the literary role of courtesans is well-known...' (Schimmel 1983: 57)

[11] This is known as *ma'nī āfirīnī* and characterizes a good deal of highly acclaimed ghazal poetry. See Pritchett 1994 and Petievich 1992 for expanded discussions of classical poetic convention in the ghazal.

[12] In addition to this Munnī Bāī 'Ḥijāb', Ranj (pp. 132–3) lists three other 'Ḥijābs':

(1) 'Asg͟harī Begam Lakhnavī,

(2) a Kashmiri poetess sighted in Bombay by an informant of Ranj, and

(3) Nawab Begam, a member of the Lakhnavi nobility born in AH 1259

For each of these three poets Ranj gives only a single *she'r*.

[13] I am indebted, again, to Shabana Mahmud of the British Library's Oriental and India Office Collections for first bringing Ḥijāb's poetry to my attention in 1993.

[14] Literally this line reads: 'But then, you've realized that there are no real *'āshiqs* here'. The first reading of this verse emphasizes the cruelty of the Beloved who slays his/her admirers, then complains that s/he has none. The second reading imputes to the Beloved the wisdom to know who is worthy to be called an *'āshiq*, and seeing all her/his admirers to be unworthy, slays them. Yet to be slain by the Beloved is a true *'āshiq*'s goal, so after the fact, these victims' worth has actually been proven. The slippage between rebuke and tribute is one characteristic of a successfully expressed *she'r* in classic ghazal tradition.

[15] I apologize to the reader for the cumbersome treatment of pronouns in this translation, but gender is so central to my argument that I cannot follow the highly problematic convention of reading the beloved always as a 'she'.

[16] In other words, 'Though I veil myself, Heaven above would not protect me from the disgrace of an unsolicited caller'.

[17] Except, perhaps, that mention of the poet's name in the *maṯla'* (initial *she'r* of a ghazal) carries the force of introducing a narrative, a conceit rather reminiscent of the *mas̱navī* form.

[18] Widely available?

[19] Both K͟hānum (f) and Mirzā (m) are terms of respectful address but can be proper names.

[20] This Rashk Maḥal 'Begam' is to be distinguished from others with the same *tak͟hallus̤*:

(1) 'Ābid Mirzā 'Begam' Lakhnavī, another *rek͟htī-go* who wrote *rek͟htī* under the *tak͟hallus̤* 'Begam', but *rek͟hta* under a separate *tak͟hallus̤*, 'Be-G͟ham' (Without Sorrow) (Kāẓmī 1930: 13, 'Abbāsī 1989: 65);

(2) an otherwise unnamed daughter and pupil of the great Mir Taqi Mir, not a *rek͟htī-go* (Kāẓmī 1930: 112, Nassāk͟h 1982: 572);

(3) one Tārā Begam (Nassāk͟h 1982: 573).

[21] *Rek͟htī dīvāns* are clearly much harder to come by now than they were in the

late 1920s when Tamkīn Kāẓmī undertook his study of the genre. Over the past half-decade I have been able to locate only a few manuscript versions of the work of Rangīn, Inshā, and Jān Ṣāḥib, one published collection each of Hāshmī Bījāpurī and Inshā, and two editions of a combined volume of Rangīn's and Inshā's *rekhtī* (Badāyūnī 1924, Badāyūnī n.d.). A few out-of-print published editions of the *Dīvān-i Jān Ṣāḥib* can be found here and there as well, but I have never seen a copy of Nāznīn's *rekhtī dīvān*. As far as I know none of these editions is currently in print.

22 This has been contested: some people have argued for Inshā, others for the Dakani poet 'Qais', still others for 'Hāshmī' Bījāpūrī, and, according to Farmān Fateḥpūrī, 'Shauq' attributes the invention of *rekhtī*, via Mīr Muḥammad 'Khāksār', author of *Tazkira-i Hindī*, to Nawāb Amīr Khān Anjam Umdatul (Fateḥpūrī 1972: 149). But we may accept, for the present, that the distinction belongs to Rangīn, based on the evidence before us.

23 *TR* also excerpts the *ḥamd* with which Rangīn's *Dīvān-i Angekhta (rekhtī dīvān)* opens.

24 This translation of '*dadā*' is literal, but its colloquial usage applies to a senior maidservant, who, an anonymous reviewer of this chapter observes, 'can be very gossipy (hence the curse)'.

25 Zauq's two most famous pupils were, of course, Bahadur Shah 'Zafar', the last Mughal emperor, and Mirza Ghalib.

26 The *double entendre* so characteristic of *rekhtī* can be seen in this verse. The narrator is washing her head after sexual intercourse, in preparation for getting on with her routines, yet the 'dolt' hangs around, threatening to give her away by his presence there.

27 Again the *double entendre*: bathing precedes prayers as well as succeeds sexual intercourse. The narrator is afraid that (1) she'll be given away by 'his' return and (2) that she may end up having to bathe again.

28 This incident was either recreated from popular legend by the author, or has become the stuff of it, as later histories, especially Sadiq 1984, evoke *rekhtī* and associate Jān Ṣāḥib with such practice.

29 The story of Joseph and Potiphar's wife (known in Islamic legend as Zulaikhā, though she has no proper name herself in the Bible) is a favourite among Urdu poets, especially those of Sufi bent. Indeed, one of the *she'rs* above attributed to Nāznīn evokes the theme of their love, reiterating Joseph's legendary beauty and Zulaikhā's discriminating eye.

30 'Abbāsī does, however, reproduce Nassākh's entry on Rashk Maḥal in the *Sukhan-i Sho'arā*. Perhaps he intended to cite Tamkīn for the following entry on 'Ābid Mirzā, and some editorial confusion ensued.

31 The ghazal's *radīf* is '*tumhārā*' with a *qāfiya* of '-ā'.

32 Ranj 1965: 54. In her discussion of Abul Qāsim Muhtasham's *tazkira* of Persian poetesses, Schimmel notes that the author's mother herself, Ḥasīna, was accomplished and educated, and an acknowledged disciple of Khwāja Wazīr in poetry, though 'she did not want her verse to become famous' (Schimmel 1983: 54).

[33] About her Ranj writes: '*Sharm* [Nawāb Shamsunnisā Begam, daughter of Ḥakīm Qamaruddīn Ṣāḥib], pupil of Khwāja Wazīr Lakhnavī; born in Banaras, resident of Lucknow. Masterfully modest and chaste (*ṣāḥib-i 'iṣmat-o-ḥayā*), exceedingly intelligent and intellectually acute, manifestly proficient in the rules of prosody and versification (*'urūẓ-o-qawāfī*), [she] achieved as much as one would wish in the art of poetry. Here is a fresh (*tāẓī*) ghazal of hers published in the *Punjābī Akhbār* of Lahore on 25 December 1868, along with some earlier work...' (Ranj 1965: 155–6).

[34] Nādir's final compilation and expanded edition (1884) was entitled the *Taẓkiratun Nisā-yi Nādirī*.

[35] Recall Jinnah's historic 1940 speech at Lahore, calling for the creation of Pakistan, when he asserted that Muslims and Hindus did not just constitute two communities; they constituted two completely distinct civilizations within the subcontinent.

Bibliography

'Abbāsī, 'Irfān, *Taẓkira-i Sho'arā-i Rekhtī*, Lucknow: Nasim Book Depot, 1989.

Anand, Balwant Singh, *Bābā Farīd*, New Delhi: Sahitya Akademi, 1990 [1975].

Asani, Ali. 'Spinning Songs, Yearning Brides and the Bridegroom Prophet: Muslim Literatures in the South Asian Vernaculars', in Ali Asani *et al.* (eds.), *Celebrating Muhammad: Images of the Prophet in Popular Muslim Poetry*, Columbia, S.C.: University of South Carolina Press, 1995.

Badāyūnī, Niẓāmī (ed.), *Dīvān-i Rangīn-o-Inshā*. Badayun: Nizami Press, 1924.

———, *Dīvān-i Rangīn-o-Inshā*, 2nd ed., Badayun: Nizami Press, n.d.

Bailey, T. Grahame, *A History of Urdu Literature*, Calcutta: Association Press, 1932.

Chandā, Māh Laqā, *Dīvān-i Chandā*, Lahore: Majlis-i Tarraqi-i Adab, 1990.

Chatterjee, Partha, *The Nation and its Fragments: Colonial and Postcolonial Histories*, Princeton: Princeton University Press, 1993.

Coppola, Carlo, *Urdu Poetry, 1935–1970: The Progressive Episode*, Unpublished PhD dissertation, University of Chicago, 1975.

Eaton, Richard M., *Sufis of Bijapur, 1300–1700: Social Roles of Sufis in Medieval India*, Princeton: Princeton University Press, 1978.

Faruqi, Shamsur Rahman, 'Conventions of Love, Love of Conventions: Urdu Love Poetry in the Eighteenth Century', *Annual of Urdu Studies*, 14, 1999, 3–32.

———, 'Expression of the Indo-Muslim Mind in Urdu Ghazal', in Shamsur Rahman Faruqi (ed.), *The Secret Mirror: Essays on Urdu Poetry*, Delhi: Academic Literature, 1981.

Fateḥpūrī, Farmān, *Urdū Sho'arā ke Taẓkire aur Taẓkira-Nigārī*, Lahore: Majlis-i Taraqqi-i Adab, 1972.

Hart, George L. III, The *Poems of Ancient Tamil, Their Milieu and Their Sanskrit Counterparts*, Berkeley: University of California Press, 1975.

———, *Poets of the Tamil Anthologies*, Princeton: Princeton University Press, 1979.

Hāshmī Bījāpurī, *Dīvān-i Hāshmī*, Hafeez Qateel (ed.), Hyderabad: Idara-i Adabiyat-i Urdu, 1961.

Jālibī, Jamīl, *Tārīkh-i Adab-i Urdū*, vol. 1, Delhi: Educational Publishing House, 1977.

Kāẓmī, Tamkīn, *Tazkira-i Rekhtī*, Hyderabad: Shamsul Islam Press, 1930.

Lelyveld, David, *Aligarh's First Generation: Muslim Solidarity in British India*, Princeton: Princeton University Press, 1978.

Maḥmūd, Shabāna, *Angāre: Ek Jā'iza*, London: Kitabiyat, 1988.

Metcalf, Barbara Daly, *Perfecting Women: Maulāna Ashraf 'Alī Thānawī's Bihishtī Zewar: A Partial Translation with Commentary*, Berkeley: University of California Press, 1992.

Minault, Gail, 'Hali's *Majālis un-nissā*: Pardah and Woman Power in Nineteenth Century India', in Milton Israel and N. K. Wagle (eds.), *Islamic Society and Culture: Essays in Honour of Professor Aziz Ahmad*, New Delhi: Manohar, 1983, 39–49.

______, '*Begamātī Zubān*: Women's Language and Culture in Nineteenth-Century Delhi', *India International Quarterly*, 9: 2, 1984, 155–70.

______, 'Other Voices, Other Rooms: The View from the Zenana', in Nita Kumar (ed.), *Women as Subjects: South Asian Histories*, New Delhi/Calcutta: Stree, 1994, 108–24.

______, *Secluded Scholars: Women's Education and Muslim Social Reform in Colonial India*, New Delhi: Oxford University Press, 1998.

Naim, C. M., 'How Bibi Ashraf Learned to Read and Write', *Annual of Urdu Studies*, 6, 1987, 99–115.

______, 'Transvestic Words: The *Rekhtī* in Urdu', *Annual of Urdu Studies*, 16, pt. 1, 2001, 3–26.

Naim, C. M. and Carla Petievich, 'Urdu in Lucknow, Lucknow in Urdu', in Violette Graff (ed.), *Lucknow: Memories of a City*, New Delhi: Oxford University Press, 1997, 165–80.

Naqvī, Muḥammad Mubīn, *Tārīkh-i Rekhtī ma' Dīvān-i Jān Ṣāḥib*, Allahabad: Matba 'Anwar Ahmadi, n.d.

Nassākh, 'Abdul Ghafūr, *Sukhan-i Sho'arā*, Lucknow: U.P. Urdu Akademi, 1982 [1874].

Petievich, Carla, 'The Feminine Voice in the Urdu Ghazal', *Indian Horizons*, 39, nos. 1–2, 1990, 25–41.

______, *Assembly of Rivals: Delhi, Lucknow and the Urdu Ghazal*, New Delhi: Manohar, 1992.

______, 'Dakani's Rādhā-Krishna Imagery and Canon Formation in Urdu', in Mariola Offredi (ed.), *The Banyan Tree: Essays on Early Literature in New Indo-Aryan Languages*, vol. 1, New Delhi: Manohar/Venezia: Universita Degli Studi di Venezia Dipartimento di Studi Eurasiatici, 2000, 113–30.

______, 'Gender Politics and the Urdu Ghazal: Exploratory Observations on *Rekhta* vs. *Rekhtī*', *Indian Economic and Social History Review*, 38: 3, 2001a, 223–48.

______, '*Rekhtī*: Impersonating the Feminine in Urdu Poetry', *South Asia*, XXIV, 2001b, 75–90.

______, '*Dogānās* and *Zanākhīs*: The Invention and Subsequent Erasure of Urdu Poetry's "Lesbian" Voice', in Ruth Vanita (ed.), *Queering India: Same-Sex Love and Eroticism in Indian Culture and Society*, New York: Routledge, 2002, 47–60.

Platts, John T., *A Dictionary of Urdu, Classical Hindi and English*, London: Oxford University Press, 1968 [1884].

Pritchett, Frances W., *Nets of Awareness: Urdu Poetry and Its Critics*, Berkeley: University of California Press, 1994.

Pritchett, Frances W. and S. R. Faruqi (trans. and ed.), *Āb-e Ḥayāt: Shaping the Canon of Urdu Poetry*, New Delhi: Oxford University Press, 2001.

Qamber, Akhtar (trans.), *The Last Mushā'irah of Delhi: A Translation of Farhatullah Baig's Dillī kī Akhrī Shama'*, New Delhi: Orient Longman, 1979.

Ramanujan, A.K. (trans.), *The Interior Landscape: Love Poems from a Classical Tamil Anthology*, Delhi: Oxford University Press, 1994 [1967].

———, *Poems of Love and War from the Eight Anthologies of the Ten Long Poems of Classical Tamil*, New York: Columbia University Press, 1985.

Ranj, Ḥakīm Faṣīḥuddīn, *Bahāristān-i Nāz: Tazkira-i Shā'irāt*, Khalīlur Raḥmān Dāūdī (ed.), Lahore: Majlis-i Taraqqi-i Adab, 1965 [1864].

Russell, Ralph, *The Pursuit of Urdu Literature: A Select History*, London: Zed Press, 1992.

Sadiq, M., *A History of Urdu Literature*, 2nd edition, New Delhi: Oxford University Press, 1984 (1964).

Saksena, Ram Babu, *A History of Urdu Literature*, Allahabad: Ram Narain Lal, 1940.

Sangari, Kumkum and Sudesh Vaid (eds.), *Recasting Women: Essays in Indian Colonial History*, New Brunswick, N.J.: Rutgers University Press, 1990.

Schimmel, Annemarie, 'A 19th c. Anthology of Poetesses', in Milton Israel and N. K. Wagle (eds.), *Islamic Society and Culture: Essays in Honour of Professor Aziz Ahmad*, New Delhi: Manohar, 1983, 51–8.

———, *Classical Urdu Literature from the Beginning to Iqbal*, Wiesbaden: Otto Harrassowitz, 1975.

Selby, Martha Ann, *Grow Long, Blessed Night: Love Poems from Classical India*, New York: Oxford University Press, 2000.

Stortoni, Laura Anna (ed.), *Women Poets of the Italian Renaissance: Courtly Ladies and Courtesans*, New York: Ithaca Press, 1997.

Tharu, Susie and K. Lalita (eds.), *Women Writing in India, 600 B.C. to the Present*, vol. 1, New York: The Feminist Press of the City University of New York, 1991.

Vanita, Ruth and Saleem Kidwai (eds.), *Same-Sex Love in India: Readings from Literature and History*, New York: St. Martin's Press, 2000.

Zaidī, 'Alī Jawād, *A History of Urdu Literature*, New Delhi: Sahitya Akademi, 1993.

'The Meaning of the Meaningless Verses': Ghalib and His Commentators

FRANCES W. PRITCHETT

The 'classical' (*klāsikī*) Urdu ghazal is a Persian-derived genre of romantic/mystical lyric poetry that was widely cultivated in north India during the eighteenth and nineteenth centuries. Its hegemony ended only when the aftermath of the Rebellion of 1857 destroyed the aristocratic Indo-Muslim society and patronage networks that had kept the tradition alive: there was less and less leisure for master poets (*ustād*) to correct the poetry of the pupils (*shāgird*) they were training, and the famously conflict-prone *mushā'iras*—at which poets performed for each other and for a small circle of patrons and connoisseurs—could no longer be maintained.

Mirzā Asadullāh K̲h̲ān 'G̲h̲ālib' (1797–1869) is universally considered to be one of the two greatest poets of the classical ghazal tradition. Lovers of Urdu ghazal have struggled over the past century to maintain access to his poetry, which at its best is some of the finest in the world. Ghalib is also known as a notoriously 'difficult' poet, and more than a hundred commentaries (*sharḥ*) have been written to explicate his work (Anṣārullāh 1972, 1998). Ghalib is the only Urdu poet to have acquired such a commentarial tradition. Even today, still more commentators are constantly appearing; I am now, for my sins, in the process of becoming one of them. (My commentary is available at *http: //www.columbia.edu/fp7.*)

Yet the commentators are for the most part astonishingly unhelpful. Their work is radically limited, often in ways that seem actually counter-intuitive. Their explanations do not at all suffice to elucidate for a serious reader what Ghalib is actually doing. How to explain such a failure? How to account for so many voices earnestly saying such a limited, narrow range of things?

Historically speaking, there might seem to be an obvious place to point the finger. The development of the commentarial tradition coincided with the growth of the post-1857 'natural poetry' movement, which emphasized a Wordsworthian notion of poetry as realistic, biographically informed, emotionally 'sincere', sociologically accurate, progressive, devoted to inspiration and national uplift—everything, in short, that the classical ghazal was not. The rise of the 'natural poetry' movement, like the death of the classical ghazal, resulted from the complex changes wrought by the (intellectual and cultural) aftermath of 1857. I have written in detail in *Nets of Awareness* about the 'natural poetry' movement and its hostile approach to classical ghazal, and so will not provide an extensive account here. It might seem that the 'natural poetry' movement would provide an obvious culprit—can it not readily and plausibly be blamed for promoting unsatisfactory commentary on Ghalib? As we shall see, Āzād and Ḥālī, the two canonical founders of the movement, both contributed to the body of commentary on Ghalib's poetry.

But in this case such finger-pointing will not get us very far. After all, the commentators stepped forth as admirers and defenders of Ghalib, rather than hostile detractors; they were volunteers, and they spent hundreds of hours of their lives analysing the whole corpus of his verses. Why would so many of them take so much trouble to provide their readers with (however inadequate) readings of the poetry, if they did not themselves feel that their work had value, and that they were accomplishing something significant?

In this essay I would like to lay out the dimensions of the problem, and then offer my own best guess at a solution.

Let us, therefore, take a brief tour through commentarial history. For demonstration purposes I shall choose the first verse of the first ghazal in Ghalib's *dīvān*. Ghalib himself selected and arranged his verses for publication; he was the first Urdu poet to have had the opportunity to do so. His poetry was popular enough, and printing presses were by then widely enough available, to permit four editions of his *dīvān* to appear in his lifetime (in 1841, 1847, 1861, and 1862). He knew that this verse would be in a specially marked position, and particularly exposed to scrutiny.

I want to show that most commentators, including Ghalib, provide only prose paraphrase; and when they do engage in literary argumentation, it is often a thrust-and-parry about 'meaning'.

'The Meaning of the Meaningless Verses'

The first verse of the first ghazal is, by tradition, the only verse from a classical poet's whole *dīvān* that has a strongly prescribed theme: everybody knows that it is to be a *ḥamd*, or verse in praise of God. And what does Ghalib give us instead ('Arshī 1982: 159)?

> *naqsh faryādī hai kis kī sho<u>kh</u>ī-i taḥrīr kā*
> *kā<u>gh</u>az̤ī hai pairahan har paikar-i taṣvīr kā*
> 1) The image/painting is a plaintiff—about whose mischievousness of writing?
> 2) Of paper is the robe of every figure in the picture.

The translation is mine (as are all others in this essay except where marked); it is of course painfully literal. The verse is one that has proved confusing to many readers, and has provoked extraordinary outbursts by commentators. But certainly no serious critic has ever mistaken it for a genuine *ḥamd*.

We know that the hue and cry about it began during Ghalib's lifetime. The ghazal that contains it goes back to 1816, when the poet was all of nineteen years old. The earliest form of the ghazal had nine verses, of which verses 1–4 and verse 9 were—twenty-five years later—selected for publication (Raẓā 1988: 112). Throughout his lifetime, Ghalib's friends and correspondents asked him for interpretive help with his poetry. Maulvī Muḥammad 'Abd ur-Razzāq 'Shākir' was one such correspondent. Writing to him in 1865, near the end of his life, Ghalib gave a direct and straightforward explanation of several difficult verses:

> First listen to the meaning of the meaningless verses (*pahle ma'nī-i abyāt-i be-ma'nī suniye*). As for *naqsh faryādī*: In Iran there is the custom that the seeker of justice, putting on paper garments, goes before the ruler—as in the case of lighting a torch in the day, or carrying a blood-soaked cloth on a bamboo pole [to protest an injustice]. Thus the poet reflects, of whose mischievousness of writing is the image a plaintiff?—since the aspect of a picture is that its garment is of paper. That is to say, although existence (*hastī*) may be like that of pictures (*taṣāvīr*), merely notional, it is a cause of grief and sorrow and suffering (<u>Kh</u>alīq Anjum 1985, 2: 837–8; Daud Rahbar 1987: 281–3).

Ghalib's explanation is direct and straightforward, that is, except for the first sentence. How are we to judge the implications of a cryptic phrase like 'the meaning of the meaningless verses'? The words themselves are clear. They seem to respond to a query by Shākir, but in what tone of voice? Teasing? Irritated? Rueful?

To find Ghalib's verses difficult—or even at times 'meaningless'—is a common frustration, and to have any explanatory words from him is a rare luxury. By my count, he has only commented on fourteen verses out of the 1,459 in his published Urdu *dīvān*. Yet at least to this limited degree, we must consider Ghalib himself to be the first and in some obvious ways the most significant commentator on his poetry.

Leaving aside for the present two early works of little influence (Vālah Dakanī 1893; Shaukat Meraṭhī 1899), the second important commentator was Alṭāf Ḥusain 'Ḥālī' (1837–1914), and the third was 'Ali Ḥaidar 'Naẓm' Ṭabāṭabā'ī (1852–1933). Ḥālī completed his great work *Yādgār-i Ghālib* (A Memorial of Ghalib) in 1897, and Naẓm published his commentary *Sharḥ-i Dīvān-i Urdū-i Ghālib* (A Commentary on the Urdu *Dīvān* of Ghalib) in 1900. These two early commentators have been quoted constantly ever since, both with and without attribution, by later entrants into the field.

These two primal commentators assumed archetypally opposite attitudes. Ḥālī was the devoted and admiring pupil, the collector of anecdotes and provider of lavish praise. (Never mind the inconvenient fact that his 'natural poetry' ideology had helped to overthrow the popular reign of the classical ghazal; here he is almost doing penance for his iconoclasm.) Ḥālī has nothing to say in the whole course of his memoir about *naqsh faryādī*. He apparently found the verse to be neither a major problem nor a great glory, and thus did not feel that he had to make a point of mentioning it.

In marked contrast to Ḥālī, Naẓm Ṭabāṭabā'ī is something like a fellow-*ustād* with a prickly ego: he judges Ghalib not reverently but critically, even jealously, and definitely as an equal. Throughout his commentary he is acerbic and nit-picking; although he occasionally offers high praise, he is more than ready to point out flaws and problems. And Naẓm makes a point of starting out the way he means to go on. No other opinion of his has been so famous, so controversial, so shocking to the sensibilities of later commentators, as his all-out attack on the verse *naqsh faryādī*. This attack is here translated in full:

> The author's meaning is that in life, we become separated and divided from the True Source, and separation from that Beloved is so grievous that even a figure in a picture complains about it. And after all, the existence of a picture is no existence! But it too longs to become lost in God: it laments its life.
>
> The suggestion of the paper dress of a plaintiff is present in Persian too, and in Urdu in the poetry of Mīr Mamnūn, and I've seen it in the poetry of Momin Khān too. But the author's saying that in Iran there is a custom that the justice-seeker puts on paper robes and goes before the ruler—I have never seen or heard any mention of this anywhere.
>
> As long as in this verse there is no word that would make manifest an ardour for becoming lost in God, and a hatred for worldly existence, we cannot call it meaningful. Nobody deliberately composes things without meaning. What happens is that because of the constraint of metre and rhyme, there was no scope for some necessary words, and the poet considered that the meaning had been expressed. Then, however many

meanings have remained in the poet's mind, they should be called [in Arabic] 'meanings internal to the poet'.

In this verse, the author's intention was that the figure in the painting is a plaintiff about an insubstantial, unworthy existence. And this is the reason for its paper robe. There was no scope for 'insubstantial existence' (*hastī-i be-'itibār*) because it was awkward and his purpose was to compose an opening verse (*maṭla'*). In place of 'existence' he put 'mischievousness of writing', and from this no presumption about the cutting out of 'existence' was created. Finally, even to his face people said, 'This verse is meaningless' (Naẓm 1900: 1–2).

This famous attack raises a number of issues. The one that I want to leave out of our present discussion is the question of whether in ancient Iran justice-seekers really did customarily wear paper robes. Naẓm's rather hair-splitting critique is not clearly developed. (If he has never heard of the custom, does that in itself constitute a poetic flaw? If in truth the custom never existed, does that constitute a poetic flaw? If so, why, when the ghazal is full of such conventions?) With few exceptions, later commentators simply produce more examples of poetic reference to the custom, but this does not advance the discussion, since Naẓm has already recognized that such literary examples exist. In fact, Naẓm seems to be objecting to the claim of historicity that Ghalib makes in his letter, rather than to the paper-robe imagery in the verse itself.

Naẓm's real attack rests on the alleged meaninglessness of the verse. He intends this claim of meaninglessness in a technical sense, and he locates and explains his objections clearly—or at least, relatively clearly—as these things go in the world of Ghalib commentary. The verse is meaningless, he says, because the phrase 'mischievousness of writing' does not specify precisely enough the nature of the complaint made by the paper-robed justice-seekers. The poet should have contrived to put in something like 'insubstantial existence' instead, and then the verse would in fact have the meaning that the poet intended it to have. Naẓm himself, however, seems to find no difficulty in understanding and explicating the intended meaning of this 'meaningless' verse—a fact which must cast significant doubt on his argument.

Naẓm wraps up his attack with a stinging report of audience response, one of very few such observations in the whole commentarial tradition. The verse is so patently incoherent, he says, that people actually confronted the poet and told him so. 'Finally, even to his face people said, "This verse is meaningless."' Which of course makes us wonder: does this fit in with Ghalib's reply to Shākir's query? Did Shākir report such continuing objections, and is that why Ghalib began his reply as he did? Probably we will never be able to be sure, but the possibility is well worth considering.

In the commentarial tradition, a gap of twenty-odd years follows Ḥālī and Naẓm, punctuated only by the fragmentary work of Muḥammad 'Abd ul-Vājid 'Vājid'(1902) and the brief and partial work of 'Ḥasrat' Mohānī (1905), who, on this verse, merely paraphrases Ghalib's own words. Then we find another pair of important commentators, the two 'Bekhud's: Sayyid Muḥammad Aḥmad 'Bekhud' Mohānī (1883–1940), writing around 1923, and Sayyid Vaḥīd ud-Dīn 'Bekhud' Dihlavī (1863–1955), writing around 1924. Both of them, and in fact all the later commentators, generally agree with the paraphrased prose 'meaning' of the verse as outlined first briefly by Ghalib himself, and then at more length by Naẓm. In fact, it is striking how little the commentators disagree among themselves in their explication of this 'meaningless' verse; many of Ghalib's verses generate a considerably wider range of commentarial readings.

Of all the commentators, Bekhud Mohānī is unique in the passion he brings to refuting Naẓm's charges of 'meaninglessness'. He is moved to a furious defence that goes on at much more length than Naẓm's original attack. These excerpts are typical of its lively, readable, polemical tone:

I am entirely astonished at Janāb [Naẓm]'s words. Five objections to one verse, and those objections too such that a sound taste puts its finger to its teeth [in amazement]! The aforementioned gentleman does not find any word in this verse that expresses aversion to insubstantial existence. Although in the first line, not to speak of aversion, a powerful word like 'plaintiff' is present. And the complaint too is such that the plaintiffs, like those seeking vengeance for the murder of an innocent, have donned paper robes. 'Aversion' was a commonplace word; so in such a place why would a pulse-taker of words and meaning like Mirzā have selected it? After a look at what I have submitted, probably (*ghāliban*) it cannot be said that the verse is in the realm of 'meanings internal to the poet'....

As for the claim that people told Mirzā to his face that this opening verse was meaningless, in my opinion it is not necessary to give a reply, because the aforementioned gentleman has not given any source for this information. But it is necessary to say this much: if such a thing happened, it is no cause for astonishment. There are many such 'connoisseurs' today; nor were they few in Mirzā's time either....

I am astonished at Janāb [Naẓm]'s presumption—that he did not even reflect that Mirzā chose this opening verse (*maṭla'*) for the opening verse of his *dīvān*. He ignored the fact that the rank Mirzā held as a poet, he also held as a judge of poetry. The pitilessness with which Mirzā made a selection from his own poetry [for publication]—such examples are not to be seen even in the case of the Persian purists. Then, those venerable elders were destined to have the honour of taking part in the making of the selection. In that day there was heartfelt acceptance of their understanding of poetry, their grasp of subtle points; and even today people do not dispute their decisions. Everyone also knows that Mirzā's *dīvān* was published in his lifetime. Even after the publication of his *dīvān*, Mirzā lived for some time. It's astonishing that he never had the suspicion, 'My opening verse is meaningless!' [Arabic:] 'Take heed, you who are insightful' (Bekhud Mohānī 1970: 1–3).

What a fine and vigorous riposte! According to Bekhud Mohānī, why is Naẓm's accusation groundless? 1) because the word 'plaintiff' and the wearing of paper robes show plenty of aversion to 'insubstantial existence'; 2) because no source has been given for the allegations that contemporaries found the verse meaningless; 3) because even if some contemporaries did make such claims, they were pretentious poetasters seeking to augment their own glory; 4) because Ghalib himself was both an excellent judge of poetry, and an admirably severe critic of his own work; and 5) because his friends who helped him choose verses for publication were revered connoisseurs. Here, one might think, the battle has been fairly joined. How will later commentators advance the debate?

As it turns out, they will advance it minimally if at all. Bekhud Dihlavī, writing at almost the same time as Bekhud Mohānī, illustrates a much more typical commentarial approach. His remarks are given in their entirety:

The meaning is that existence is a cause of pain and suffering because of its instability and mortality. The commentary is that the world—that is, the population of the world—is a plaintiff, about the Eternal Engraver's mischievousness of writing. (The dress of a plaintiff, according to an ancient custom of Iran, used to be of paper, the way in Hindustan those with complaints used to carry a lighted torch in the day, or in Arabia they used to put a murdered person's clothing on a spear and go to seek vengeance.) The meaning of 'mischievousness' is 'not to stay fixed'. And 'not to stay fixed' is already proved because of the picture's having a paper robe. That is, the common custom is that a picture is made on paper, and paper is a thing that gets ruined quickly. By 'every figure in the picture' is meant the totality of animals and plants. And all these things are destined for oblivion. The only difference is that a flower withers in the course of a day; for a human's death, no [fixed] interval has been decreed. Even things made of wood, stone, metal finally become useless and broken. When all the things in the world are in this state, for an image of existence to be a plaintiff about its instability and contingency is a complete proof of the poet's lofty imagination and uncommon inventiveness. In my opinion this verse is meaningful, and the thought is one heretofore untouched. To call this verse meaningless is to do violence to the claims of justice (Bekhud Dihlavī 1934: 9).

Bekhud Dihlavī thus takes the high road: he does not argue with Nazm in detail, but simply provides an eloquent prose paraphrase and explanation of the verse. He then concludes that the verse is so manifestly meaningful that to call it meaningless is 'to do violence to the claims of justice'. Bek͟hud Dihlavī unquestionably represents the commentarial mainstream. The synthesizing commentator Āg͟hā Muḥammad 'Bāqir' (1917?–72), writing in 1939, sums up the situation pretty accurately: 'Except for [Naẓm], all the commentators call this verse meaningful' (Bāqir 1943: 7).

Thus, the main line of the commentarial tradition: prose paraphrase including disputes about 'meaning', interspersed with prose paraphrase not including disputes about 'meaning'. If space permitted, I could provide many more examples, most on the order of Bek͟hud Dihlavī's comments. But let us move on to consider some of the neglected possibilities—tools that were conspicuously available to every commentator, and were conspicuously not used.

Roads Not Taken, Tools Not Used

We can also marshall internal evidence from the commentarial tradition to provide a sort of minority report: to show rare examples of the use of some of the critical tools that the commentators so routinely neglected.

Around 1950, there appears a brief and unusually lucid commentarial analysis of *naqsh faryādī*—that of Labbhū Rām 'Josh' Malsiyānī (1883–1976). Josh provides a more precise and technically focused analysis than any we have seen before, including Ghalib's own:

> Some say that this verse is nonsensical. But this is entirely an injustice. Mirzā Ṣāḥib says in a style of 'sophisticated naiveté' (*tajāhul-i 'ārifāna*), 'Who has, through his artisanship, displayed so much mischievousness in the image of every creature, that each individual is unable to endure that mischievousness, and can be seen to make a complaint?' In the second line is the verbal device (*ṣan'at*) of 'elegantly assigning a cause' (*ḥusn-i ta'līl*). The clothing of a picture is of paper. Mirzā takes that clothing to be the clothing of plaintiffs. 'Mischievousness' refers to the coming into being, and destruction, of substances, and thus to the various types of events that keep erasing one creature after another (Josh 1950: 49).

For the first time, we see a commentator who goes beyond arguments about meaning, and beyond prose paraphrase. Josh's use of technical terms enables him to describe the verse more incisively and compactly than any previous commentator. Let us pause to consider the critical tools that enable him to say a lot in a small space.

'Elegantly assigning a cause' (*ḥusn-i ta'līl*) is a well-established technical term in the classical poetics of the Persian-Urdu ghazal. It is defined by an authoritative modern handbook as follows:

Ta'līl means 'to establish a reason' or 'to express a reason'. *Ḥusn-i ta'līl* is to give a fine and superior example of that action. If a reason is expressed for something such that even if it is not real, it has in it some poetic richness and subtlety, and it has some affinity with reality and nature as well, that is called *ḥusn-i ta'līl* (Fārūqī *et al.* 1981: 49–50).

In the most massive classical handbook of poetics, Najm ul-Ghanī's 1232-page *Baḥr ul-Faṣāḥat* (Ocean of Eloquence), *ḥusn-i ta'līl* is not only defined in similar terms (though with more detail), but is systematically analysed into four subclasses, each of which is then elaborately explained through the analysis of many illustrative verses (Najm ul-Ghanī 1925: 1076–82.).

Josh has, it seems to me, identified exactly the primary 'verbal device' that Ghalib was using in his verse. In classical ghazal, most lines were end-stopped; enjambement, though by no means non-existent, was relatively uncommon. And because each two-line verse had to make its own independent poetic impact, manipulating the relationship(s) of the two lines to each other was one of the poet's most effective strategies. One line could give a cause, and the other its effect; one line could ask a question, and the other could answer it; one line could make a general assertion, and the other provide a specific example; and so on. Handbooks of rhetoric provided many subtle analyses of possible intra-verse (which in practice almost always meant inter-line) relationships (Najm ul-Ghanī 1925: 1015–1117). Reversing the expected logical order (first effect, then cause; first answer, then question; and likewise) was another source of piquancy, especially under conditions of oral performance in a *mushā'ira.* Such reversal forms the framework of *naqsh faryādī*: the first line expresses an interrogative reaction, while the second line—for which, in oral performance, the listeners would have had to wait—provides the crucial piece of observational evidence on which the first is based.

So relevant are the traditional Persian-Urdu analytical categories, in fact, that Josh has casually invoked not one but two of them. For he points as well to Ghalib's use of what I have translated as 'sophisticated naiveté' (*tajāhul-i 'ārifāna*); this is itself considered a verbal device. Its meaning is 'to knowingly become unknowing'. That is, 'despite knowing about something, to express one's unawareness, so that extravagance can be used in explaining it'(Fārūqī *et al.* 1981: 46). And in this case too, *Baḥr ul-Faṣāḥat* not only recognizes the device but carefully analyses its use into two subcategories: those in which the poet proposes two possible explanations for something; and those without such an either-or structure (Najm ul-Ghanī 1925: 1059).

I want to offer one further example, this one from the very recent commentarial tradition: two excerpts from an extended analysis by the distinguished modern critic and all-round literary figure Shams ur-Raḥmān Fārūqī (1935–), whose own selective commentary was published in 1989. Fārūqī makes several additions to our repertoire of technical terms; and in the process, further deepens our understanding of the verse:

In addition to the 'semantic affinities' (*murā'āt un-naẓīr*) ('image', 'writing', 'of paper', 'robe', 'figure', 'picture') Ghalib has also taken good care in this verse to have 'resemblance of sound' (*tajnīs-i ṣautī*) (*faryādī, kis kī, shokhī, kāghazī hai pairahan har paikar*). In the second line there is a special emphasis on *har*, which knocks against the two *r*'s of *paikar-i taṣvīr* and increases the elements of intensity and mystery in the line (Fārūqī 1989: 23).

Here we notice two technical terms, suggesting two kinds of analysis that can be performed on the verse. The meaning of the first term, *murā'āt un-naẓīr*, can be recognized simply from the examples Fārūqī gives: the verse is crammed with interrelated and mutually evocative words from the vocabulary range pertaining to painted/written images. In fact, out of the verse's fifteen words, six are part of this domain. Technically, *murā'āt un-naẓīr* (which is so fundamental a poetic quality that it goes by several other names as well, such as *tanāsub* and *munāsibat*) is defined as occuring when 'in the poem words are gathered together the meanings of which have a relationship to each other, but this relationship is not one of contrariety or opposition' (Fārūqī *et al.* 1981: 56–7). In fact, this semantic affinity goes deeper in Urdu than my translation can even show. Consider just the following multi-faceted examples: *naqsh*, which I have translated as 'image/painting', is defined as: 'a painting, a picture; portrait; drawing; a print; a carving, an engraving; a map, or plan'. And *paikar*, which I have translated as 'figure', means: 'face, countenance, visage; form, appearance, figure; resemblance, portrait, likeness' (Platts 1930: 1145, 300).

The other term that Fārūqī uses, 'resemblance of sound' (*tajnīs-i ṣautī*), refers to a broad range of sound effects and kinds of alliteration. These are indeed conspicuous: in the nine words he mentions, *-ī* occurs four times, *-ai* and *-ar* three times each. And then there are, of course, the special effects created in the second line by the use of *r* sounds, as he points out. To see how closely sound effects are analysed within the classical poetic tradition, consider just one example: the special term 'stitched-together resemblance' (*tajnīs-i marfū'* applies to lines like this one of Dabīr's: *lo tegh-i barq dam kā qadam darmiyāṅ nahīṅ*, in which stitching together *barq dam* replicates the sound of *qadam* (Fārūqī *et al.* 1981: 59–62, esp. 61). And of course *Baḥr ul-Faṣāḥat* analyses a whole range of such *ṣan'at-i tajnīs* into a remarkable number of categories, with examples even more detailed and varied (Najm ul-Ghanī 1925: 894–920).

Commentators do sometimes point out 'semantic affinities' within a verse of Ghalib's, though usually only casually: they may mention a couple of strikingly related words, but without undertaking a careful survey of the whole verse. However, far more commonly, they do nothing at all along these lines. As the reader will have noticed, in the case of this verse, which has extremely conspicuous semantic affinities involving fully 40 per cent of its total words, no commentator so far has even once alluded, even in passing, to the presence of this important structural device.

But the second sentence in Fārūqī's analysis is far more remarkable, indeed even unique, in the tradition of Ghalib commentary. On the face of it, it looks quite normal: 'In the second line there is a special emphasis on *har*, which knocks against the two *r*'s of *paikar-i taṣvīr* and increases the elements of intensity and mystery in the line.' And yet, it is not normal within the commentarial tradition. Not only in the analyses of this verse, but in all the analyses on all the verses that I have read so far, I cannot recall that even one commentator has ever closely analysed the sound effects in even one verse. And this despite the fact that quite a number of Ghalib's verses, which after all were composed for oral recitation, have the most astonishing sound effects. The verse *jān dī dī hu'ī usī kī thī / ḥaq to yūṅ hai ki ḥaq adā na hu'ā* ('Arshī 1982: 193) comes to mind at once, but many others cry out almost as loudly for analysis in terms of sound effects. Invariably, they cry out in vain; the commentators are simply not listening.

Let me conclude this brief tour through the commentarial approaches to *naqsh faryādī* with one more excerpt—the conclusion of Fārūqī's analysis of the verse:

The first line is also constructed as *inshā'iya*, that is, interrogative. Interrogation is Ghalib's special style. It is possible that he learned the art of interrogation and other *inshā'iya* principles from Mir. But the first verse of the *dīvān*, the theme of which ought to have been founded on praise of God, calls the arrangement of the two worlds into question. This mischievousness, or free-spiritedness, or lofty-mindedness, is Ghalib's characteristic manner. Mir too has called the arrangements of the Creator of the universe into question; for example, in his very first *dīvān* he says,

ko'ī ho maḥram-i shokhī tirā to maiṅ pūchhūṅ
ki bazm-i 'aish-i jahāṅ kyā samajh ke barham kī
If anyone would be intimate with your mischievousness, I would ask:
What were you thinking (that it was) when you overthrew the gathering of enjoyment of the world?

Seeing the word 'mischievousness' the suspicion arises that Mir's verse might have stuck in Ghalib's mind. But to use the theme of the mischievousness of the Creator of the universe, and on top of that to turn that mischievousness into a subject for question and place such a verse at the head of the *dīvān*—this mischievousness was possible only from Ghalib (Fārūqī 1989: 23–4).

This resonant and suitable conclusion gives Ghalib and Mir well-warranted praise of a kind that they surely would have appreciated. It invites us to consider the term 'mischievousness' (*sho<u>kh</u>ī*), as many other commentators do as well. In fact, Yūsuf Salīm Chishtī (among others) also makes the point about the special 'mischievousness' of using such a verse as a *ḥamd* (Chishtī 1983: 231–2). But no other commentator has directed our attention towards the poetic value of *inshā'iya* speech, although interrogative discourse is such a prominent feature both of this verse, and of Ghalib's poetry in general.

The concept of *inshā'iya* or non-informative (i.e. interrogative, prescriptive, hypothetical, or exclamatory) discourse, as opposed to *<u>kh</u>abariya* (informative or falsifiable discourse), is far from new within the Arabic-Persian-Urdu poetic tradition (Fārūqī 1993: 23–37, 1997; Pritchett 1994: 106–8). It is considered at length in *Baḥr ul-Faṣāḥat*; and just look at how elaborately it has been appreciated and analysed. Its internal categories, all individually discussed, consist of:

> *bayān-i tamannā*, 'expression of desire', twenty examples, some explained;
> *bayān-i istifhām*, 'interrogative expression', twenty examples, some explained (with subsections devoted to all the important interrogatives);
> *bayān-i amr*, the imperative mood, thirty-four examples, some explained;
> *bayān-i nahī*, prohibitive expression, fourteen examples, some explained;
> *bayān-i nidā*, the vocative mood, thirty-six examples, some explained;
> *bayān-i du'ā*, expression of supplication, five examples, some explained (Najm ul-<u>Gh</u>anī 1925: 595–627).

In short, the classical Urdu ghazal poets did not exactly lack for technical explication of their poetics; *Baḥr ul-Faṣāḥat* alone is 1,232 pages long.

Since these off-the-shelf analytical categories were so readily available, why do the commentators generally ignore them? Ghalib himself, when he explains his own verses in letters, rarely goes beyond the simple prose paraphrase level he employs in explaining *naqsh faryādī*. And why does a major critic, literary figure, and connoisseur like Naẓm generally ignore these well-established analytical categories? And why do virtually all the other commentators do the same? (I have not looked at every commentary, but I have looked at the most important and influential ones.) In the case of this particular verse, Josh has mentioned two such categories, but within Josh's whole commentary such terminology, alas, remains rare. Fārūqī has given us three more categories, but he is quite exceptional within the commentarial tradition, since he is, among other qualifications, a devoted student of classical poetics.

To sum up, two features of the commentarial tradition are worthy of note. First, commentators almost always provide an interpretive prose paraphrase of a verse, either brief or expanded (or sometimes twofold, for two interpretations); once in a while they will also defend or (more rarely) attack the 'meaning' of the verse. And second, commentators generally ignore both the technical terminology of Persian-Urdu poetics, and the formal analysis that this terminology is designed to facilitate; though they occasionally use a technical term or briefly point out a formal feature within the verse, this is haphazard and rare.

It is this second observation that I have found so perplexing. Here we have in the ghazal an extremely stylized genre of poetry, one that takes shape within the tiniest possible verbal space, one that both possesses and requires a tremendous repertoire of technical knowledge. And here we have a poet who writes its most difficult and complex verses. And here we have a number of volunteers, some of whom were, in theory at least, highly competent insiders within the tradition, who offer to help us understand the poetry. Why in the world do they do so partial and limited a job of it? Why do they not use the wide range of tools their own tradition had developed for exactly this purpose?

What Price 'Meaning'?

As we have seen, Ghalib undertook to tell Shākir 'the meaning of the meaningless verses', starting with *naqsh faryādī*. And what he then provided was a brief, coherent prose paraphrase, spelling out in more detail the thought that was latent in the fifteen words of the verse. He also offered some background information about the history and meaning of paper robes as plaintiff's attire (though he did not point out the extra piquancy of positioning this verse as the *ḥamd*). Not only did he not mention such terms as 'elegantly assigning a cause', 'sophisticated naiveté', 'semantic affinities', 'resemblance of sound', or 'interrogative discourse', he also did not suggest in layman's language any of the domains they were designed to investigate. That is, he did not say, 'Take a look at how many of the words in the whole verse come from the domain of painted/written images', or 'How about those interesting sound effects involving *i* and *r*!', or 'Did you notice that you first get the conclusion (and that too in the form of a question), and only afterward learn the reason for it?' Even if Ghalib had considered Shākir a poetic novice, he himself was a masterful letter-writer and could certainly have conveyed this kind of analytical information if he had wished to do so. Apparently, to tell 'the meaning of the verse' was, for his purposes at the time, to provide something much simpler than a full exposition or analysis of the verse.

This letter was written late in his life, and perhaps in a spirit of courtesy and resignation. For after all, by then he was used to being asked variations on this question. He had been asked them at frequent intervals for almost fifty years. We have a smallish amount of anecdotal evidence that documents a much larger amount of controversy on the subject—controversy that apparently continued throughout Ghalib's life.

Muḥammad Ḥusain 'Āzād', author of the great canon-forming literary history *Āb-i Ḥayāt* (Water of Life, 1880), conspicuously dislikes Ghalib, and never misses an opportunity to take potshots at him. Introducing the classical ghazal tradition, Āzād explains that Ghalib's work has grave problems as compared to that of earlier *ustāds*: 'Ghalib, on some occasions, followed excellently in their footsteps—but he was a lover of "meaning creation" (*ma'nī āfirīnī*), and he gave more attention to Persian, so that in Urdu, the number of his largely (*g͟hāliban*) unblemished verses has not turned out to be more than one or two hundred' (Āzād 1982: 77; Pritchett and Fārūqī 2001: 103–4.).

Poor Ghalib, what a piquant situation: because of his love of 'meaning creation', his poetry is attacked as flawed and even meaningless. The situation is so dire, in Āzād's eyes, that only one or two hundred of Ghalib's Urdu verses are really satisfactory. In case we might have missed the point, Āzād spells it out for us later on with even greater care. Because of the central role of *Āb-i Ḥayāt* in shaping poetic attitudes over the past century, the relevant passage is given at length:

> One day the late *ustād* [Z͟auq] and I were discussing Mirzā [G͟hālib] Ṣāḥib's style of 'delicate thought' (*nāzuk k͟hiyāli*), and Persian constructions, and people's various temperaments. I said, 'If some verse manages to come out without convolutions, it's as devastating as Doomsday!' He said, 'Very good!' Then he said, 'Even his better verses, people fail to appreciate. I will recite some of his verses to you.' He recited a number of individual verses. One is still in my memory:
>
> *daryā-i ma'āṣī tunuk-ābī se hu'ā k͟hushk*
> *merā sar-i dāman bhī abhī tar na hu'ā thā*
> The river of sinfulness dried up for lack of water;
> As yet, not even the hem of my garment had become wet.

There is no doubt that through the power of his name ['Asad' means lion], he was a lion of the thickets of themes (*maẓmūn*) and meanings. Two things have a special connection with his style. The first is that 'meaning-creation' and 'delicate thought' were his special pursuit. The second is that because he had more practice in Persian, and a long connection with it, he used to put a number of words into constructions in ways in which they are not spoken. But those verses that turned out clear and lucid are beyond compare.

People of wit did not cease from their satirical barbs. Thus once Mirzā had gone to a *mushā'ira*. Ḥakīm Āg͟hā Jān ''Aish' was a lively-natured and vivacious person [who recited some verses that included the following]:

We understood the speech of Mīr, we understood the language of Mirzā [Saudā],
But his speech—he himself might understand, or God might understand.

For this reason, towards the end of his life he absolutely renounced the path of 'delicate thought'. Thus if you look, the ghazals of the last period are quite clear and lucid (Āzād 1982: 494–6; Pritchett and Faruqi 2001: 405–6).

As Āzād tells it, Z̲auq emphasizes the unappreciatedness of even Ghalib's better verses, while 'Aish mocks him in a specially composed verse sequence. And this is not the only such incident reported by Āzād. He also tells us a long story of how this same 'Aish sets up a foolish, bumbling schoolmaster as a poet, giving him the pen-name 'Hudhud' (Hoopoe) and making him a figure of fun at court *mushā'iras*. Composing his poetry for him, 'Aish puts into his mouth many satiric verses:

At the secret instigation of the Ḥakīm Ṣāḥib, Hudhud pecked at the nightingales of poetry with his beak. Thus he recited some ghazals before the whole *mushā'ira*, of which the words were extremely refined and colorful, but the verses absolutely without meaning. And he would say, 'I've written this ghazal in the style of Ghalib'. I remember one opening verse:

markaz-i maḥvar-i girdūṅ ba-lab-i āb nahīṅ
nāk͟hun-i qurṣ-i qarak͟h shubh-i miẓrāb nahīṅ
The circle of the axis of the heavens is not at the lip of the water.
The fingernail of the arc of the rainbow does not resemble a plectrum.

The late Ghalib was a flowing river. He used to listen, and laugh (Āzād 1982: 469; Pritchett and Faruqi 2001: 381).

Āzād thus pretends, in his clever and sneaky way, to end with a tribute to Ghalib's sense of humour. But the rhetorical point has been amply made: Ghalib wrote poetry in which 'the words were extremely refined and colorful, but the verses absolutely without meaning', and everybody knew this and mocked him for it.

Nor is Āzād our only source for such anecdotes. Ghalib's loyal biographer and *shāgird*, Alṭāf Ḥusain Ḥālī, contributes another such wryly amusing account:

Once Maulvī 'Abd ul-Qādir Rāmpūrī, who was a great jester by temperament, and who had for some time been connected with the Fort of Delhi [the Court], said to Mirzā [Ghalib], 'I don't understand one of your Urdu verses.' And at that moment he composed two lines of verse and recited them before Mirzā:

pahle to roghan-i gul bhaiṅs ke aṅḍe se nikāl
phir davā jitnī bhī hai kul bhaiṅs ke aṅḍe se nikāl
First take the essence of the rose out of the eggs of buffaloes—
And other drugs are there; take those out of the eggs of buffaloes.

Hearing this, Mirzā was quite astonished, and said, 'Far be it from me—this is not my verse!' Maulvī 'Abd ul-Qādir said, keeping up the joke, 'I myself have seen it in your *dīvān*! And if there's a *dīvān* here, I can show it to you right now.' Finally Mirzā realized that in this guise the Maulvī was objecting to his work, and was insisting that there were verses like this in his *dīvān* (Ḥālī 1986: 112; Russell and Islam 1969: 40).

Ḥālī notes that Ghalib was not easily intimidated: to the contrary in fact, for he incorporated into his verses a firm defiance of his critics. Perhaps the most explicit example was this one (Ḥālī 1986: 112; 'Arṣhī 1982: 266):

na satā'ish kī tamannā na ṣile kī parvā
gar nahīṅ haiṅ mire ash'ār meṅ ma'nī na sahī
Neither a longing for praise, nor a care for reward—
If there's no meaning in my verses, then so be it.

Both this and another similar verse cited by Ḥālī (Ḥālī 1986: 112–3; 'Arshī 1982: 259) are quite early (1821), and Ḥālī goes on to argue, just as Āzād does, that in later life Ghalib duly saw the error of his ways and ceased to write such difficult poetry. This is the official 'natural poetry' view, and we do not have the scope in which to discuss it here; but whether we accept this view or not, it is clear that despite all the friendly and not-so-friendly harassment he received, Ghalib never repudiated the 'meaningless' poetry of his youth. He retained dozens of verses like *naqsh faryādī*—and some far more obscure and rebarbative—in his *dīvān* through all four editions (1841, 1847, 1861, 1862), and still seemed quite content with the 'meaningless' verses that he explained to Shākir only four years before he died. In the case of another of these 'meaningless' verses, he wrote to Shākir with apparent pleasure that it contained a 'new idea I have brought forth from my temperament', and he explicated all three verses without the least hint of anything other than pride in them (Khalīq Anjum 1985, 2: 837–8).

Certainly Ghalib had to endure the hostility of those who genuinely preferred a simpler and more colloquial style, and of those who preferred an emphasis on romantic emotion rather than a more cerebral metaphysics. In general, people who liked their ghazal verses to be flowing (*ravāṅ*) and readily, colloquially, intelligible, ended up furious at him: he could write such verses brilliantly when he chose, as his *dīvān* amply demonstrates, yet he so often did not choose! Why did the wretch not write more verses like: 'The river of sinfulness dried up for lack of water, / As yet, not even the hem of my garment had become wet'? Behind the mockery of his contemporaries one can sense the deep irritation of envious colleagues and frustrated connoisseurs who see a major talent being misdirected into folly.

And in some cases, one can quite well sympathize with the critics. No one could possibly understand *naqsh faryādī* without knowing that plaintiffs wear paper robes when they come in search of justice; but at least that literary convention, whether or not it was historically true, had a proper 'warrant' (*sanad*), or historical lineage of prior use by authoritative *ustāds*, within the ghazal world. Consider a far more dire situation: a totally arbitrary warping of language, with no other defence than sheer caprice ('Arshī 1982: 283).

qumrī kaf-i k͟hākastar-o-bulbul qafas-i rang
ai nāla nishān-i jigar-i sok͟hta kyā hai
Turtledove, a fistful of dust, and nightingale, a cage of colour
Oh lament, what is the sign of a burnt liver?

Now this is one that you could think about for an awfully long time without being able to figure it out. It is another very early ghazal, composed (like *naqsh faryādī*) in 1816. (Composed by a nineteen-year-old boy!) But please note that Ḥālī was not even born until 1837, and his conversations with Ghalib took place in the last thirteen or so years of Ghalib's life. Here is his report on this particular verse:

I myself asked Mirzā the meaning of this. He said, 'In place of "oh" (*ai*), read "except" (*juz*); the meaning will come to your understanding by itself. The meaning of the verse is that the turtledove, which is not more than a fistful of dust, and the nightingale, which is not more than a cage of elements—the proof of their being liver-burnt, that is, lovers, is only from their warbling and speaking.' Here, the meaning in which Mirzā has used the word *ai* is obviously his own invention.

One person, having heard this meaning, said, 'If in place of *ai* he had put *juz*, or if he had composed the second line like this, "Oh lament, except for you, what is the sign of love," the meaning would have become clear.' This person's utterance is absolutely correct, but since Mirzā avoided common principles as much as possible, and did not want to move on the broad thoroughfare, rather than wanting every verse to be widely understandable he preferred that inventiveness and unheard-ofness (*nirālāpan*) be found in his style of thought and his style of expression (Ḥālī 1986: 114; Russell and Islam 1969: 39).

Who would not sympathize with this hapless 'person', whose own plaintive lament is perfectly justified? Such a spectacular level of youthful poetic arrogance does seem to be an aberration; it is hard to find other such blatant, in-your-face redefinitions of common words elsewhere in the *dīvān*. In the case of a verse like this one, the charge of making 'meaningless' poetry could be said to be well grounded. Ghalib is guilty at times of his own form of *shokhī-i taḥrīr*, 'mischievousness of writing'. But there is no evidence that in his conversations with Ḥālī—or anywhere else, for that matter—he ever showed any regret for this youthful arrogance and *shokhī*.

Ghalib the poet of 'meaning creation' (*ma'nī āfirīnī*) and 'delicate thought' (*nāzuk khiyālī*) was always a high flyer, as he himself insisted and as Ḥālī points out so aptly (and as Āzād points out so accusingly). He wanted to create his own meanings, and to have them apprehended subtly. He wanted to do brilliantly what others had done well; and he also wanted to do what no one had done before. He wanted to make more meanings, and more complex meanings, and in a more compressed and multivalent way, than anybody else in the whole Persian-Urdu poetic world. To a large extent he succeeded, and he knew it. But his success was contested and controversial, and came at a price. He died in poverty, humiliated at the end, dependent in old age on unresponsive patrons.

Throughout his life he expressed frustration that he did not find hearers or readers who could grasp the full dimensions of what he was doing. He did not suffer fools gladly, but he responded to genuine *shāgirds* and lovers of the ghazal. He no doubt gave Shākir the 'meaning' that he thought was suitable and sufficient to the occasion. And he gave Ḥālī rather more. In the case of another verse, Ḥālī tells us how Ghalib suggested to him not only interpretations, but also an interpretive process:

kaun hotā hai ḥarīf-i mai-i mard-afgan-i 'ishq
hai mukarrar lab-i sāqī meṅ ṣalā mere ba'd
Who can withstand the man-killing wine of passion?
Many times there is a call on the lips of the cup-bearer, after me.

This verse ('Arshī 1982: 199) is another early one (1821). It was certainly not unfathomable, since it had an 'apparent' meaning that was perfectly clear to Ḥālī. But Ghalib did not want him to stop there. Ghalib urged him to think harder, and to dig more deeply into the verse. As Ḥālī reports:

The manifest (*ẓāhirī*) meaning of this verse is that since I have died, the cup-bearer of the man-killing wine of passion—that is, the beloved—many times gives the call—that is, summons people to the wine of passion. The idea is that after me, no buyer of the wine of passion remained; thus he had to give the call again and again. But after further reflection, as Mirzā himself used to say, an extremely subtle meaning arises in it, and that is, that the first line is the words of this same cup-bearer's call; and he is reciting that line repeatedly. At one time he recites it in a tone of invitation.... Then when in response to his call no one comes, he recites it again in a tone of despair: Who can withstand the man-killing wine of passion! That is, no one. In this, tone (*lahaja*) and style (*ṭarz-i adā*) are very effective. The tone of calling someone is one thing, and the way of saying it very softly, in despair, is another. When you repeat the line in question in this way, at once the meanings will enter deeply into your mind (Ḥālī 1986: 130–1).

Mirzā used to say that 'after further reflection' another meaning—in fact, an 'extremely subtle/refined/delightful meaning' (*nihāyat laṭīf ma'nī*)—arises in the verse. And how is that meaning created? Why, first of all, by rearranging the relationship of the two lines, so that instead of reading the second as an explanatory sequel to the first—'1) Who can endure the wine of passion? (not me, I died of it!) 2) (Thus) after my death the cup-bearer often calls out (in vain)'—we read the first as a result of the logically prior second: '2) After my death the cup-bearer goes around calling out many times, 1) Who can endure the wine of passion?' In short, more meanings can be provided by rearranging the logical and semantic relationships of the two lines, just as classical poetic theory would lead us to expect; and with a special piquancy provided by putting the secondary or reactive line first, and the logically prior or informative line second—just as in *naqsh faryādī*.

Moreover, we notice that the first line is in the *inshā'iya* mode, and in Ghalib's greatly favoured *inshā'iya* category, the interrogative (just as in *naqsh faryādī*). Ghalib has been guiding Ḥālī not only to read the verse with two different line relationships, but also to read it with different kinds of *inshā'iya* intonation. And he has tactfully implied to Ḥālī that such subtleties have become evident even to Ghalib himself not initially but only 'after further thought', although it is impossible to believe that a veteran 'meaning creator' like Ghalib would not do these tricks with deliberate intention, subtle planning, and the maximum possible technical expertise. We know that Ḥālī had had a patchy, often interrupted classical education with which he was never satisfied (Pritchett 1994: 13–14), so perhaps he was not too good on his terminology; perhaps Ghalib is patiently playing the *ustād* here, and explaining technical tricks in non-technical language. But explain them he does, so that Ḥālī ends up provided with a cluster of meanings for that verse that he did not have before. Moreover, he can then explain them clearly and intelligibly to us, and does so. We see that it can be done, and that he can do it. Why does he so rarely carry over this excellent critical approach to other verses? (And why does Ghalib never do so at all?)

How Much 'Meaning' Is Enough?

In short, why the parlous state of the commentary on *naqsh faryādī*, and of the commentarial tradition in general? It is clear that the typical, least-common-denominator commentarial entry for any given verse is a prose paraphrase of the 'meaning', rather than anything analytically more sophisticated; but it is much less clear why this is so consistently the case. Why do the commentators give us so frustratingly little access to the huge, sophisticated, invaluable set of analytical tools developed within the Persian-Urdu poetic tradition?

S.R. Fārūqī writes in his commentary about verses that have 'layer upon layer of wordplay (*ri'āyateṅ*) and verbal affinities (*munāsibateṅ*), but the commentators have generally not mentioned them, because...they have followed the opinion of [Naẕm] that wordplay and verbal affinities are nothing worthy of respect' (Faruqi 1989: 61). Faruqi's view, however, does not account for the fact that Ghalib himself explains the 'meaning' of his verses in a similarly stripped-down way.

To me, the most plausible explanation for the commentators' tunnel vision is the fact that the commentarial tradition springs directly out of the lifelong, no-holds-barred conflict between Ghalib and his critics, on the question of meaning. The commentarial tradition assumes that Ghalib is always under suspicion of creating the kind of poetry that Āzād mocks: verses that are full of 'extremely refined and colorful' words, but that remain 'absolutely without meaning'. Ghalib's verses are thus in danger of having zero meanings; the commentators seek to vindicate them by providing at least (and usually at most) one meaning apiece. The commentators' primary goal is to provide not ten meanings rather than one, but one meaning rather than none. A verse with one meaning is quite sufficiently vindicated and equipped, and need not be greedy for more. Once the commentators have winkled out such a meaning, they tend to show the pride and enthusiasm of successful crossword puzzle solvers. Shaukat Meraṭhī, author of one of the earliest commentaries, entitles his work *Ḥal-i Kulliyāt-i Urdū-i Mirzā G̲h̲ālib Dihlavī* (A 'Solution' to the Complete Urdu Verse of Mirzā G̲h̲ālib Dihlavī). Bek̲h̲ud Mohānī uses the same term, 'solution', for his interpretation of each verse; if he finds two meanings for a verse, each one is labelled as a separate 'solution' (*ḥal*), and numbered accordingly. When you have finished a crossword puzzle, it is done; the problem has been solved, and you are well entitled to move on.

How egregious this notion is, readers of Shamsur Raḥmān Fārūqī's work will understand. However it is to be explained, the impoverished state of the commentarial tradition with regard to the very resources that one might think would be most suitable and closest at hand—the technical analytical categories of the classical Persian and Urdu poetic tradition—is a striking and depressing reality. The commentators' 'solution' approach is opposed to Ghalib's own poetic practice and theory, as well as to the best poetic practice and theory of our own time (and, of course, of practically every other time too). How the Empson of *Seven Types of Ambiguity* would have loved to work on Ghalib!

To us, of course, the best defence would be a good offence: to insist that Ghalib offers not one meaning, but *four or five*! Four or five meanings in two little lines! Plus wordplay, sound effects, and every poetic device he could fit in! Reading the commentators makes you feel like putting on paper robes, carrying a lighted torch in the daytime, and going in search of justice.

And yet the deficiencies of the commentarial tradition serve also to highlight a strange triumph: that Ghalib's poetry lives, and is loved, despite more than a century of naturalistic criticism and grossly inadequate interpretation. And the commentaries serve also to evoke the memory of another of Ghalib's great verses about letters on paper and their all too ephemeral fate ('Arshī 1982: 337):

> *yā rab zamānā mujh ko miṭātā hai kis liye*
> *lauḥ-i jahāṅ pe ḥarf-i mukarrar nahīṅ hūṅ maiṅ*
> Oh Master, why does the age erase me?
> On the tablet of the world I am not a repeated letter.

Bibliography

Anṣārullāh, Muḥammad, *Ghālib Bibliyogrāfī*, Aligarh: Aligarh Muslim University, 1972.

———, *Ghālib Bibliyogrāfī (Kitābeṅ)*, New Delhi: Ghalib Institute, 1998.

'Arshī, Imtiyāz 'Alī, *Dīvān-i Ghālib*, 2nd ed., New Delhi: Anjuman Taraqqi-i Urdu, 1982.

Āzād, Muḥammad Ḥusain, *Āb-i Ḥayāt*, Lucknow: Uttar Pradesh Urdu Academy, 1982 (facsimile of 1907 ed., Lahore) [1880].

Bāqir, Āghā Muḥammad, *Bayān-i Ghālib: Sharḥ-i Dīvān-i Ghālib*, Lahore: Shaikh Mubarak Ali & Sons, 1943 [1939].

Bekhud Dihlavī, Sayyid Vaḥīd ud-Dīn, *Mirāt ul-Ghālib*, Calcutta: Usmaniyah Book Depot, 1934 [1924].

Bekhud Mohānī, Sayyid Muḥammad Aḥmad, *Sharḥ-i Dīvān-i Ghālib*, Lucknow: Nizami Press, 1970 [1923].

Chishtī, Yūsuf Salīm, *Sharḥ-i Dīvān-i Ghālib*, New Delhi: Itiqad Publishing House, 1983 [1959].

Daud Rahbar (trans. and ed.), *Urdu Letters of Mirza Asadullah Khan Ghalib*, Albany: State University of New York Press, 1987.

Fārūqī, Shams ur-Raḥmān, *et al.*, *Dars-i Balāghat*, New Delhi: Taraqqi-i Urdu Bureau, 1981.

______, *Tafhīm-i Ghālib*, New Delhi: Ghalib Institute, 1989.

______, *Andāz-i Guftagū Kyā Hai*, New Delhi: Maktaba Jami'a, 1993.

______, *Urdū Ghazal ke Aham Moṛ: Īhām, Ri'āyat, Munāsibat*, New Delhi: Maktaba Jami'a, 1997.

Ḥālī, Khvāja Alṭāf Ḥusain, *Yādgār-i Ghālib*, New Delhi: Ghalib Institute, 1986 [1897].

Ḥasrat Mohānī, Fazl ul-Ḥasan, *Sharḥ-i Dīvān-i Ghālib*, Karachi: Al-Kitab, 1965 [1905].

Josh Malsiyānī, Labbhū Rām, *Dīvān-i Ghālib ma' Sharḥ*, Delhi: Atma Ram and Sons, 1950.

Khalīq Anjum (ed.), *Ghālib ke Khuṭūṭ*, New Delhi: Ghalib Institute, vols 1–4 (1984–93).

Najm ul-Ghanī Rāmpūrī, Maulvī, *Baḥr ul-Faṣāḥat*, Lucknow: Raja Ram Kumar Book Depot, 1925 [1885/86].

Nazm Ṭabāṭabā'ī Lakhnavī, 'Ali Ḥaidar, *Sharḥ-i Dīvān-i Urdū-i Ghālib*, Hyderabad: Matba' Mufid ul-Islam, n.d. [1900].

Platts, John T., *A Dictionary of Urdu, Classical Hindi, and English*, Oxford: Oxford University Press, 1930.

Pritchett, Frances W., *Nets of Awareness: Urdu Poetry and Its Critics*, Berkeley: University of California Press, 1994.

Pritchett, Frances W., in association with S.R. Faruqi (trans. and ed.), *Āb-e ḥayāt: Shaping the Canon of Urdu Poetry*, New Delhi: Oxford University Press, 2001.

Razā, Kālīdās Gupta, *Dīvān-i Ghālib Kāmil, Tārīkhī Tartīb se*, Bombay: Sakar Publishers Pvt. Ltd., 1988.

Russell, Ralph, and Khurshidul Islam (trans. and ed.), *Ghalib 1797–1869; Volume I: Life and Letters*, London: George Allen and Unwin, 1969.

Shaukat Merathī, Ḥāfiz Aḥmad Ḥasan, *Ḥal-i Kulliyāt-i Urdū-i Mirzā Ghālib Dihlavī*, Meerut: Matba' Shaukat ul-Mataba', 1899.

Vājid, Muḥammad 'Abd ul-Vājid, *Vijdān-i Taḥqīq*, Hyderabad: Matba' Fakhr-i Nizami, 1902.

Vālah Dakanī, 'Abd ul-'Alī, *Sharḥ-i Dīvān-i Ghālib Vuṣūq-i Ṣarāḥat*, Hyderabad: Matba' Nami Fakhr ul-Nizami, 1893.

To You Your Cremation, To Me My Burial: The Ideals of Inter-Communal Harmony in Premchand's *Karbalā*

Syed Akbar Hyder

> Literature is not merely for entertainment. Its supremacy is presently gauged by the extent of emotions it produces to stir our imagination.
>
> (Premchand)

South Asian literary establishments rightly take pride in Dhanpat Rai Shrivastava (1880–1936), popularly known as Premchand, as a visionary and reformer who contributed much to twentieth-century Hindi-Urdu aesthetic sensibilities. As a leading figure who shaped what is perhaps the most consequential strain of twentieth-century South Asian literature, the Progressive movement or *taraqqī pasand adab*, Premchand committed himself to pursuing a utilitarian ethics of literature. Literature is valuable insofar as it acts as a medium through which the socio-economic well-being of a society is enhanced. Such an enhancement entails a reassessment of existing literary standards, including a thorough re-evaluation of notions of beauty. 'We must change the standard of beauty', proclaimed Premchand, and the Progressive Urdu movement subsequently invoked these words as the most important clarion call resonating from the subcontinent's literary circles (Ja'frī 1994: 46).

The task of this essay is to explore the text and context of one of Premchand's dramas, *Karbalā*. The central research question to be addressed in this study is how Premchand's *Karbalā* constitutes a utilitarian nationalist allegory, a source of trans-communal edification, above and beyond simplistic syncretist-separatist polarities. I shall discuss how history is re-enacted in relation to Premchand's nation-building project and how this nation-building project is in turn overlaid with a religio-historical narrative. To this end, I shall attend to two interdependent problematics: one primarily concerning the text of *Karbalā* itself, the other dealing with the context in which this drama was written, published, and read.

The 1920s, when *Karbalā* was published, was a tumultuous decade in north India as far as Hindu-Muslim relations were concerned. The decade saw the acceleration of communal tensions at an unprecedented rate. Some of the major events that hastened the rapid decline of inter-communal relations dealt with the irreverent objectification of the Prophet Muhammad. Relying on the age-old suspicions of many a European that cast the Prophet of Islam as a vicious entity, Paṇḍit Kālīcharan Sharmā, one of the leaders of the Arya Samaj, wrote *Vichitra Jīvan* (Strange Life) in 1923, a book in which the Prophet was depicted as being under an epileptic rather than a divine spell. Within a year of *Vichitra Jīvan*, a Lahore book-store proprietor, Raj Pal, published *Raṅgīlā Rasūl* (The Merry Prophet), one of the most inflammatory works written in South Asia to date. The book further drove a wedge between religious communities, insofar as many Muslims found the treatment accorded to the Prophet as well as his household simply insulting. *Raṅgīlā Rasūl* received the Arya Samaj endorsement in 1924 just as *Vichitra Jīvan* had the previous year (Thursby 1975: 40–3). In addition to what Muslims perceived as character assassination of the noblest of God's messengers in the form of the aforementioned books, other catalysts for Hindu-Muslim conflicts of the early 1920s included the 1923 agitation in Saharanpur over the *ta'ziya* processions of Muharram (in which standards commemorating the martyred family members of the Prophet Muhammad in Karbala are carried in public places) and the *shuddhi* movement calling for Muslim re-conversion to Hinduism (Thursby 1975: 33–4; Barrier 1974: 99–101). In such a rapidly deteriorating communal situation, Muslim fears that a systematic assault on the pillars of Islam was under way only grew. Premchand brooded about these growing anti-Muslim attitudes and actions that were, at least in his opinion, rapidly undercutting threads of national unity. In order to mount a successful campaign against communalism and 'to cement the bonds of Hindu-Muslim unity', Premchand wrote *Karbalā* (Gopal 1964: 235).

The culturally ensconced status of the event of Karbala had enriched literature and art for centuries in South Asia and other parts of the Islamicate world. Karbala for many a Muslim and non-Muslim stands as the signifier of the age-old struggle between virtue and vice, poignantly concretized in 680 CE, when the grandson of the Prophet Muhammad, Husayn b. Ali, refused to pay allegiance to the supreme political authority of his time, Yazid b. Muawiya. The result of this refusal was that Husayn, his family and companions were mercilessly killed on the desert plain known as Karbala. The remembrance of this event in the subsequent decades and centuries was such that Husayn and his followers became martyrs par excellence, figuring prominently in trans-communal literature, visual arts and discourses of devotion and piety. Although Husayn is religiously marked as 'Muslim' in the socio-historical terrain of South Asia, the martyr of Karbala on account of his courage, piety, and steadfastness is revered by plenty of non-Muslims. Hence Premchand's decision to honour Husayn and his comrades was hardly an aberration.

The primary desired audiences for Premchand's *Karbalā* were Hindus: 'The aim of this drama, and of the principal character's portrayal, is to make the Hindus pay a tribute to Hazrat Hussain. That is why this drama which, apart from being religious, is political also' (Gopal 1964: 236). The writing of *Karbalā* was a twofold utilitarian gesture on Premchand's part: first, he hoped to provide a unifying communal impulse; second, through the play, Premchand could express his own devotion to the martyrs of Karbala by paying a 'tribute' to them.

Karbalā appeared in two modes: first in Hindi and then in Urdu. These signifiers of linguistic modes were given to the play by Premchand himself. Although the narrative framework and the plot are identical in both versions of the play, a few differences are worth pointing out. The Hindi play was written in the Devanagari script and contained more Sanskrit words than the Urdu play, which was written in the Perso-Arabic script. The amount of Sanskritized Hindi is tied to the nominal religious markings of the characters—the Muslim characters use fewer Sanskitized words than the Hindu characters. Premchand asserts in the preface to his Hindi version that in order to be faithful to realism, he could not put too many Sanskritized words in the mouths of Muslims, so he has tried to keep the language of the play a 'shared' communal language that both Hindus and Muslims speak (Premchand 1985: 8). In making this linguistic point Premchand suggests, first of all, that religious identity in South Asia is linked to the linguistic one. Owing to this arbitrary distinction, both identities are polarized. Such a polarization is readily at the service of the nationalist discourse of the time that was bent upon creating neat categories and minimizing obfuscation among these categories.

The 1920s were also a time that witnessed bitter Hindi-Urdu language rivalries as both languages were being religiously charged. Given the Muslim claims to Urdu as a privileged lingua franca of Islamic socio-religious reformist discourse of the late nineteenth and early twentieth centuries, and the Hindu proclivities to see Urdu as a language harbouring the foreign Perso-Arabic script, the language of Urdu now inhabited a Muslim space (Faruqi 2001: 45–62).

Premchand, by first publishing *Karbalā* in Hindi (and not in Urdu) in 1924,[1] although validating the Hindi-Urdu polarization at one level, at another re-engages this space through articulating an Islamic allegory, already held in reverence by many Hindus, in Hindi. Through the Hindi *Karbalā*, Premchand postulates the plausibility of an affectionate nexus between Hindi and Islam, Islamic history and the history of Hinduism, thereby attempting to enervate Urdu's hold on Islam, Islam's hold on Urdu, Hinduism's hold on Hindi or Hindi's hold on Hinduism. In the preface to the play, Premchand describes the battle of Karbala as the Islamic counterpart of the epic struggles of the Mahabharata and the Ramayana (Premchand 1985: 5). Through invoking such an analogy at the very outset, Karbala is domesticated, stripped of its foreignness so as to make it more comprehensible and appealing to Hindus.

That the conceptualization of history no longer entails a shared spirit, Premchand would say, precipitates Hindu-Muslim conflict: 'Whenever a Muslim king is remembered, we evoke Aurangzeb' (Premchand 1985: 5). For Premchand, the Indian Muslim by and large existed within the continual state of prejudiced assumptions of Hindus recorded through the Aurangzebian idiom: this fiction had to be countered. Premchand archives the Hindu-Muslim relationship in mutually respectful terms that move beyond Aurangzeb and his times into a temporal zone reflecting a more pluralistic Islam. In archiving the Hindu-Muslim relationship in such a way, what Premchand also does highlight is the attitudinal differences within a religious community: he identifies himself as a Hindu yet disagrees with many a Hindu who fails to find virtue in Islam; he provides no apologies for Aurangzeb's alleged religious intolerance yet refuses to see the Mughal emperor as the ideal follower of Indian Islam. By ideologically fracturing religious communities, he undermines the antagonistic communal bifurcation within the colonial milieu that posited Hindus and Muslims as age-old enemies whose scriptures determined their mode of thinking and living.

Karbalā opens with a description of the disquieting revelry and debauchery at Yazid's court. The caliph Yazid, in the first scene, is flanked by his advisors/sycophants, most notable of whom is Zahhak. To those who are familiar with the topoi of Indo-Persian literature, the very mention of Zahhak is an instant reminder of the legendary Iranian tyrant who shouldered two snakes that were constantly nourished by human brains. The rein of Zahhak was thus a time of mayhem wherein the utility of the human brain was consumed by the dreadful snakes. It took the brave Faridun to defeat Zahhak and restore justice to the land of Iran. So in this opening scene, one ignoble caliph, Yazid, is in the company of another beast of bygone days. When Yazid, concerned as he was with securing the allegiance of the grandson of the Prophet, the Imam Husayn, asks for Zahhak's advice, the latter suggests the most forceful means to accomplish such a goal. Yazid's wife, Hindah, who according to certain sources had once served the Prophet's family, warns her husband against such actions lest he is welcomed by the fire of hell for being irreverent towards the grandson of the Prophet of Islam. Yazid dismisses his wife by explaining away his adherence to Islam:

Hindah, this talk of religion is [only] for religion; not for the world. My grandfather accepted Islam so that he would receive wealth and honour. He did not accept Islam in order to be redeemed. Nor do I think of Islam as a means of redemption today (Premchand 1985: 38–9).

Thus, unconvinced by his pious wife, Yazid sets out to assure his own victory over Husayn. The frame text of the rest of the play corresponds closely to the popular understanding of the Karbala story: Husayn is forced to pay allegiance to Yazid in Medinah; Husayn leaves Medinah because of the pressure in that city to accept Yazid's authority; Husayn's cousin, Muslim, arrives in Kufah to gauge the support and build a base for the Prophet's grandson; Muslim is betrayed by the Kufans, and Yazid's governor, Ibn Ziyad, manages to do away with Muslim; Hurr, in a place called Karbala, blocks Husayn and his companions, who are on their way to Kufah; Husayn's family is deprived of the Euphrates water; Husayn is provided with a night's respite to rethink his determination to oppose Yazid; Hurr, having reconsidered his previous stance, repents and joins Husayn, becoming the first martyr for Husayn's cause; Hurr is followed by the rest of Husayn's companions and family members—Abbas, Ali Akbar, Ali Asghar, Zaynab's sons and so on; Husayn is the last one to attain martyrdom.

Few of Premchand's readers would have qualms about the linear progression and artistic extrapolation of this oft-recited frame text. Premchand takes narrative liberty with the interpolations within this text, relying upon the tradition of *maẓmūn āfirīnī* ('proposition creation') that had historically given writers considerable leeway and poetic licence in the semantic structuring of their works (Pritchett 1994: 91–105). Unlike the writers of *Raṅgīlā Rasūl* or *Vichitra Jīvan*, Premchand relies on established scholarly authorities of Islam, the likes of Amir Ali, and also on the works of elegist-poets whose *marṣiyas* (elegies/threnodies) were oft recited in Muharram gatherings. For instance, Premchand depicts Husayn's farewell to his sister Zaynab by interweaving the verses of Urdu's greatest *marṣiya* writer, Mir Anis, with the prose text of the play:

hamshīra kā gham hai kisī bhā'ī ko gavārā
majbūr hai lekin asadullāh kā pyārā
rañj aur muṣībat se kaleja hai do pārā
kis se kahūñ jaisā mujhe ṣadma hai tumhārā
is ghar kī tabāhī ke li'e rotā hai shabbīr
tum chhuṭṭī nahīñ māñ se judā hotā hai shabbīr
Can any brother bear the sorrow of his sister!
This darling of Asadullah (Husayn), however, is helpless,
His heart shattered by sorrow and hardships,
Whom can I tell, how much I grieve for you,
Shabbir (Husayn) cries at the destruction of this house,
It's not you he parts from, he parts from his mother.

(Premchand 1985: 264–5)

It is worth pointing out here that the drama features several female characters who are inscribed as they had been inscribed in much nationalist literature: as active supplements to the male presence. For instance, one occasion within the play on which women surface as coexistent with the struggle of the Imam is when Husayn asks his family members to abandon him so as to not incur the wrath of Yazid's army. At such a juncture, Sakina, Husayn's daughter, expresses her own determination as well as that of other women of her family to incur suffering for the sake of Islam:

We will never take such disgrace upon ourselves—disgrace that would be generated if Rasul's [the Prophet Muhammad's] sons have sacrificed for the cause of Islam while his daughters remained seated in the house (Premchand 1985: 102).

So the women also contribute to the project of the ideal community/nation by spurning complacency and embracing suffering. Women like Zaynab give impetus to the cause of Islam by happily sending their scions to the battlefront, thereby linking temporary suffering with permanent redemption. Such a discourse that positions women as men's spiritual and ideological comrades had not only become the staple of colonial Urdu literature (e.g., Nazir Ahmad), but also made itself visible within the *marṡiya* traditions of Lucknow and Delhi, where the likes of Sauda and Anis had complemented Husayn's struggle with that of his female relatives: Zaynab, Kulsum, Sakina, Shehrbano, etc. (Husayn 1973).

However, Premchand parts company with the popular *marṡiya* narrative of his time when he inserts a subplot that is intended to enhance his agenda of 'cementing' communal harmony by depicting Husayn as a universal hero who transcends the boundaries of any particular tradition. Thus presented is the story about the mingling of the Hindu and Muslim understandings of truth, personified by Sahas Rai and Husayn. Living in an Arabian village are Sahas Rai and his family, devoted Hindus originally from India. It should be noted here that Premchand, in all likelihood, drew the Sahas Rai interpolation from the legend, popular among a few pockets of Hindus, that a community of Brahmins (the Dutt Brahmins or Mohiyals) existed in Arabia, contemporaneously with Husayn. These Brahmins supposedly came to the assistance of Husayn's cause in Karbala. Several of these Brahmins are said to have lost their lives and the remaining ones, along with their families, moved back to India. At times, these Brahmins are also referred to as the Husayni Brahmins since they still remain devoted to Husayn in spite of considering themselves Hindu.[2]

Disturbed by the news of Yazid's accession to the caliphate, Sahas Rai and a small band of his family members set out to help Husayn. They arrive at Karbala, pay tribute to Husayn, and take up arms against Yazid's army. They first protect Husayn and his companions from the arrows of the adversaries while the former group is busy in ritual prayers. Husayn, in return, blesses these Hindus for protecting him and his followers:

> Friends! My beloved sympathizers! These ritual prayers will be memorable in the history of Islam. If these brave slaves of God had not guarded our backs against the enemy's arrows, our prayers would have never been completed. O Truth Worshippers! We salute you. You are not believers [in Islam], but a religion that has followers who are Truth-worshipping and willing to die for justice, followers who understand life to be insignificant [in the struggle for justice], and followers who are willing to have their heads cut off in the support of the oppressed, is certainly a true and righteous religion. May that religion always remain in the world. With the light of Islam, may its light also spread in all four directions (Premchand 1985: 249).

When Sahas Rai asks for Husayn's permission to confront the forces of Yazid, Husayn insists that the newly arrived guests should not be embroiled in the battle. The conversation that then ensues is worth noting:

> **Sahas Rai:** Sir, we are not your guests but we are your servants. The main principle of our life is to die for truth and justice. This is our duty; not a favour to anyone.
>
> **Husayn:** How can I possibly tell you to go [to the battlefield]. God willing, the foundation that is being laid on this ground by your and our blood will always be protected from time's evil eye and this [foundation] shall never be ruined. May the sounds of joyful songs always rise from it and may the rays of the sun always shine on it. (All seven brothers, while singing praises of India [Bharat], enter the battlefield.)
>
> **Abbas [Husayn's brother]:** Amazingly strong warriors! Now the truth has dawned upon me that Islam also exists outside the realm of Islam. These are true Muslims and it is not possible that the Holy Messenger will not intercede on their behalf.

Hence, all seven brothers from the family of Sahas Rai attain martyrdom, having gallantly defended Husayn's cause. Husayn now has the funeral pyre prepared for his Hindu comrades and delivers a moving eulogy in their honour:

These people are from that pure country wherein the declaration of God's unity (*tawḥīd*) was first raised. I pray to God that they receive a lofty station among the martyrs. Those flames rise from the pyre. O God! May this fire never be extinguished from the heart of Islam. May our brave ones always spill their blood for this [Hindu] community. May this seed, which has been sown in fire today, blossom till the Day of Judgement (Premchand 1985: 252–3).

Husayn speaks in laudatory tones of Hindus as those who are suffused with a determination to vindicate the cause of truth and justice in the face of immense obstacles. As the words of Abbas testify, the Hindus are metamorphosed into ideal Muslims without the effacement of their Hindu identity. Premchand fosters a sensitivity that would accommodate the confluence of the two religions—allowing both to cherish, if not embrace, the differences between them. The Hindu brothers do not perform the ritual prayers with Husayn's band, but they nevertheless ensure the safety of this group while it is praying. The King of Martyrs, the Prophet's grandson, oversees the rites of cremation—rites not endorsed, at least by scriptural Islam. The rigidly binary modelling of communalism is unsettled in the same vein as it had been in much of Perso-Indian poetry. After all, Premchand was a devotee of Ghalib, the unsurpassed destroyer of many such binaries:

vafādārī bā sharṭ-i ustavārī aṣl-i īmān hai
mare butk͟hāne meṅ to ka'be meṅ gāṛo barheman ko ('Arshī 1992: 251).
Fidelity with the strength of determination is the core of faith
If the Brahman dies in the house of idols, bury him in the Kaba.

The Hindi version of *Karbalā* was followed by the Urdu version, serialized from July 1926 to April 1928 in a popular and critically acclaimed Urdu journal of the time, *Zamāna* (started in 1903). It is important to notice here that the publisher of *Zamāna*, Munshi Daya Narain Nigam (1882–1942), had established a reputation for cultivating Hindu-Muslim dialogue and remaining true to Premchand's ideals that saw India's well-being in inter-communal harmony. Nigam found a grounding in his journal to shake off the effects of galling communal tensions by compellingly illustrating that Urdu is a language that belongs to India's Hindus as well as Muslims. Commenting upon *Zamāna*'s contribution to South Asian culture, K͟hwāja Ḥasan Niẓāmī, a prominent scholar of Islam, wrote in a 1928 issue of *Zamāna*:

I don't know of any journal in India in which Hindu and Muslim writers have jointly written in every single issue, year after year, and it is this distinction of *Zamāna* that ought to be written at the highest level of the history of the Urdu language (Niẕāmī 1981: 19).

In praising this journal further, Niẕāmī cites Premchand, right after the Urdu serialization of *Karbalā* was complete, as 'an unprejudiced Hindu, who, having drawn the sword of his pen, rose on the field of action, in order to save his community from literary prejudices' (Niẕāmī 1981: 20).

Although Premchand was the object of Niẕāmī's praise after the serialization of *Karbalā*, Premchand encountered doubts about the merits of publishing *Karbalā* as a 'drama' before the serialization began, from the likes of Syed Ahsan Ali Sambhi (a staff member/critic working for *Zamāna*). Sambhi felt that the theme of the Karbala narrative was so sombre that any attempt to mould it into a medium of trivial entertainment (and the very word 'drama' was widely associated with such entertainment) was bound to upset the Muslim community. Premchand seemed especially sensitive to criticism levelled against him for any aspect of *Karbalā* and he retorted to the editors before the publication of this Urdu drama went into effect:

It'd be better if you don't publish *Karbalā*. There's nothing that I stand to lose, and I am not prepared to undergo these unnecessary pinpricks. I read the life of Hazrat Hussain. His zest for martyrdom moved me and I felt like paying a tribute. The result was this drama. If Muslims do not concede to Hindus even the right to pay tribute to Muslim caliphs and *imams*, I am not keen either. It is no use, therefore, to reply to the letters which have been advising you against publishing the drama. I do wish, however, to say a few things about Ahsan Sambhi's letter. He says that Shi'a Muslims would not like a drama being written about their religious leaders. If Shi'a Muslims avidly read or hear *Mathnavis*, stories and elegies on the life of their religious leaders, why should they have any objection to a drama being written on the subject? Or, is it because this one, *Karbalā*, is written by a Hindu.... History and historical drama, you would agree, are two different things. None can introduce changes in regard to the principal characters of a historical drama.... Drama is not history. It does not affect the principal historical characters. The aim of the drama, and of the principal character's portrayal, is to make the Hindus pay a tribute to Hazrat Hussain. That's why this drama which, apart from being religious, is political also....Khwaja Ḥassan Nizami, incidentally, wrote a biography of Lord Krishna. Just because a Muslim divine had paid his tribute to Lord Krishna, Hindu critics lauded the attempt. My purpose was identical. If, however, Hassan Nizami can have the freedom to pay his tribute to one of another religion but the same is denied to me, then all that I can say is that I am sorry. Kindly return the manuscript.[3]

The manuscript was not returned. I quote Premchand at length here so as to expose readers to the literary integrity and cultural sensitivity of this prophet of communal harmony. Simultaneously, we see the attachment that Premchand felt to this particular facet of Islamic history. Husayn's battle in Karbala had an ethically inspirational value for a Hindu, who utilized it aesthetically for the enhancement of a more unified Indian national community, while the larger subcontinental community was wracked by communal tensions.

Such an ideal community, at least in its imaginary incarnation, was given further impetus by the intertwined discourses of suffering and sacrifice that had permeated the Indian nationalist rhetoric. That Karbala is a story of martyrdom, sacrifice, and suffering makes it an apt refrain in numerous resistance movements. And for Indian nationalists, this is a fitting story with which they can regale their nation. Premchand's friend and inspiration, Mohandas Gandhi, invoked Karbala in the service of his nationalist vision when he embarked on his first salt march in 1930 which, like Imam Husayn's band at Karbala, had approximately seventy-two people in it (Nārang 1986: 121). According to the Mahatma, the incident of Karbala had 'arrested' him, while he was still young. He claimed to have studied the life of the 'hero of Karbala' and came to the conclusion that the people of India must act on the principles of Husayn in order to attain true liberation. The historical progress of Islam, according to Gandhi, is not the legacy of the Muslim sword but a result of the sacrifices of Muslim saints like Husayn (Vazīrābādī n.d.: 43). The themes of comradely inter-communal sacrifice and suffering had consumed the Gandhian rhetoric of birthing the Indian nation much in the same way as they would consume Premchand's *Karbalā*.

Premchand's allegory, *Karbalā*, empowers a nationalist reading springing from the sentiments of sacrifice, suffering, and trans-religious ideal formation. Such readings of Islamic history and the Indian nation are constituted by images from Islam's sacred history and the Hindu community that participates in making this history. The Hindu community is inscribed within Islamic history as a protected, respected, and needed minority in order to set an example for the treatment of India's Muslim minority. Premchand thus allegorically correlates the imaginary minority status of Hindus in seventh-century Arabia with that of Muslims in an ideal, perhaps just as imaginary, unified Indian nation, in order to synthesize the moral tenor of nation building. This Indian nation, interestingly enough, not only locates its prototype in the distant past (as, Anderson argues, modern nations do) but also in the geographical space that accommodates the Euphrates rather than the Indus or the Ganges.

Karbala becomes a device whereby the discourses tying geography, religion, and community into any neat nexus are inflected, not to mention complicated. Islam exists beyond Islamdom just as Hinduism exists outside India. Both religions become ideals free from geographical shackles. Although the Hindu-Muslim religious communities are reified in opposition to each other, their marked significations overflow the signifiers. Hindus become Muslims through their determination to safeguard Islamic ideals, while Muslims are tied to the land of India since it is here that monotheism first flourished. Modern religious communities are represented as the heirs of Husayn and Sahas Rai but each one, in spite of its uniqueness, is encompassing of and necessary for the other without effacing the identity of the self or of the other. Respect for minority rights is championed as the basis of nation building, and the numerical strength of this minority becomes irrelevant. It is as though the nation loses its ethical value when its minority's concerns go unheeded. Although cultural and national spaces remain shared, Premchand does not propagate the idea of a shared or syncretic culture as an alibi for addressing serious minority concerns on their own terms. A work like *Karbalā* supplants the greater nationalist exclusionary imaginings about which Partha Chatterjee writes:

> The idea of the singularity of national history has inevitably led to a single source of Indian tradition, namely, ancient Hindu civilization. Islam here is either the history of foreign conquest or a domesticated element of everyday popular life. The classical heritage of Islam remains external to Indian history (Chatterjee 1993: 113).

By disrupting such a play of nationalist imaginings through his drama, Premchand goes beyond the simplified polarities of syncretism and separatism to locate the nation in the abstract theatre, sacred and solemn, capable of shifting its spatial foci from Arabia to India, as long as it can constitute a site upon which mutual respect, especially the sensitivities towards minorities, plays itself out. This free-floating theatrical space enables each reader-listener to enact *Karbalā* on his or her own terms while the concrete theatricality of *Karbalā* is disavowed, partly in consideration of the pejorative connotations that the theatre/stage has had at times and partly as a distancing strategy. Since visual representation remains a vexed question in Islamicate societies, Premchand eliminates the question of staging this play (at least in its current form) lest attention be deflected from the moral of the play and its utility be disrupted in its staged manifestation.[4] The imminent telos of the play, to hasten the triumph of a people united in diversity, would also be compromised if the playwright's ultimate destination for his work were the stage: the staging might offend segments of readers otherwise sympathetic to the play's spirit. Dis-anchoring *Karbalā* from the hold of the stage by marking the play 'only to be read; not to be performed'[5] is also a solemn distancing mimetic strategy used by Premchand, similar to the one used in Iran whereby actors in the *ta'ziyeh* performance (ironically the only 'serious' theatre in the Islamic world according to Peter Chelkowski) have a script in front of them even when they have the lines memorized, so as to avoid any comparison between themselves and the noble martyrs of Karbala (Chelkowski 1979: 4–5).

Premchand was instrumental in the growth of reformist literature and the fledgling Progressive movement. His call for a re-evaluation of the existing aesthetic standards set the trend for Urdu literature of the subsequent decades. 'The writer's aim,' wrote Premchand, 'is not to cheer the audience and not to provide material for entertainment. Don't degrade him to such a level! He is not even that truth which follows behind patriotism and politics; instead, he is the standard-bearer who shows the path' (Coppola 1975: 152).

In the few concluding words, I register Premchand's *Karbalā* as the singing nightingale of Ghalib's poetic universe, soaring in search of its abode:

> *hūn garmī-i nishāṯ-i taṣavvur se naghma sanj*
> *main 'andalīb-i gulshan-i nā āfrīda hūn* ('Arshī 1992: 66).
> The joyful heat of imagination causes me to sing,
> I am a nightingale of a garden, that awaits its creation.

Similar to the Ghalibian *'andalīb* that awaits the creation of its ideal garden, Premchand's *Karbalā* conjures up possibilities that might appear too idealistic at a particular point in time, perhaps even overwhelming their originary moment itself, but nevertheless inspirational.

Premchand's own frame of reference calls for a reconceptualization of the nation from an undifferentiated unity to a harmonious diversity, and a reconceptualization of polarized religious identities from historically antagonistic relations to mutually beneficial ones. While admiring Premchand's utilitarian ideals, we should also be wary of the potential pitfalls in the socio-literary landscape in which religious identities hold primacy—pitfalls that have become all too obvious in post-colonial South Asia. The fraught relationship between religious communities and the nation dictates that the only way that communities can come together is through 'belonging' to a religious category. Recognizing the double-edgedness of such a discourse and considering how much Premchand himself relied upon imagination and creativity when penning *Karbalā*, there is no need for his readers over time to foreclose the possibility of alternative frames of references. The time is ripe for us to call for a reassessment of religion as a privileged identity marker at the expense of other identities, such as class and gender. We should beware of notions that lock us into the posture of creating religion's hegemony over the secular and instead read *Karbalā* as a creative text that helps us usher in new and different ways of thinking and coexisting.

Notes

[1] The Hindi *Karbalā* was first published in the Devanagari script in November 1924 by Ganga Pustak Mala of Lucknow.

[2] As far as the historicity of this narrative is concerned, Premchand is not interested in the truth behind the 'Hindu' presence at Karbala. He claims that he was exposed to this story by reading *Ā'īna*, a journal that was published in Allahabad (Premchand 1995: 211). For a fascinating although poorly documented account of the Husayni-Dutt Brahmins, *see* Abū Tālib 1984.

[3] Premchand's letter from Hindi-Urdu has been translated in Gopal 1964: 235–7. For the original letter, *see* Premchand 1978, 1: 146–8.

[4] Premchand 1985: 6; Premchand 1995: 212.

[5] Although he makes this clear in his Hindi version, he suggests that the play could be staged with some modifications. What exactly these modifications are, we are never told. However, by the time his Urdu version is ready to go to press, he insists that the play is 'only to be read'. The Urdu play would give Muslims a wider access, and it is possible that Premchand did not want controversy over the staging of the play to hurt his agenda of bringing religious communities together. As Premchand himself points out, there are two types of dramas: one written for the stage, the other for reading only.

Bibliography

Abū Tālib, 'Dut Brahmin Imām Husayn se Rabṯ-o-Zabṯ', in Mahdī Naẕmī (ed.), *Reg-i Surkh*, New Delhi: Abu Talib Academy, 1984.

Anderson, Benedict, *Imagined Communities*, London: Verso, 1991.

'Arshī, Imtiyāz (ed.), *Dīvān-i Ghālib Urdū: Nuskha-i* 'Arshī, Lahore: Majlis Taraqqi-i Adab, 1992.

Barrier, N. Gerald, *Banned: Controversial Literature and Political Control in British India, 1907–1947*, Columbia, Missouri: University of Missouri Press, 1974.

Chatterjee, Partha, *The Nation and its Fragments*, Princeton: Princeton University Press, 1993.

Chelkowski, Peter (ed.), *Ta'ziyeh: Ritual and Drama in Iran*, New York: New York University Press, 1979.

Coppola, Carlo, *Urdu Poetry, 1935–1970: The Progressive Episode*, Unpublished PhD dissertation, University of Chicago, 1975.

Faruqi, Shamsur Rahman, *Early Urdu Literary Culture and History*, New Delhi: Oxford University Press, 2001.

Gopal, Madan, *Munshi Premchand: A Literary Biography*, New York: Asia Publishing House, 1964.

Ḥusain, Ṣāliḥa, *Khavātīn-i Karbalā, Kalām-i Anīs ke Ā'īne meṅ*, New Delhi: Maktaba-i Jami'a, 1973.

Ja'frī, 'Alī Sardār. 'Taḥrīk-i Jamāliyat aur Siyāsat', in Qamar Ra'īs and Sayyid 'Āshūr Kāẓmī (eds.), *Taraqqī Pasand Adab, Pachās Sāla Safar*, Delhi: Educational Publishing House, 1994.

Nārang, Gopīchand, *Sāniḥa-i Karbalā Baṭaur Shi'rī Isti'āra: Urdū Shā'irī kā ek Takhlīqī Rujḥān*, Delhi: Educational Publishing House, 1986.

Niẓāmī, Khwāja Ḥasan, 'Urdū Hindī aur Risāla-i Zamāna', in Srī Nārā'in Nigam (ed.), *Yādgār-i Jashn-i Ṣad Sāla Munshī Dayā Nārā'in Nigam*, Lucknow: Sri Narain Nigam, 1981.

Pandey, Geetanjali, *Between Two Worlds: An Intellectual Biography of Premchand*, New Delhi: Manohar, 1989.

Premchand, Munshi, *Karbalā* (Urdu), Delhi: Lajpat Rai & Sons, 1960.

———, *Chiṭṭhī Patr* (Correspondence), vol. 1, Allahabad: Hamsa Prakashan, 1978.

———, *Karbalā* (Hindi), Delhi: Saraswati Press, 1985.

———, *Premchand: A Miscellany, Selections from the Monthly Zamana (Kanpur) 1903–1942*, Patna: Khuda Bakhsh Oriental Public Library, 1995.

Pritchett, Frances, *Nets of Awareness: Urdu Poetry and Its Critics*, Berkeley: University of California Press, 1994.

Swan, Robert, *Munshi Premchand of Lamhi Village*, Durham: Duke University Press, 1969.

Thursby, Gene, *Hindu-Muslim Relations in British India: A Study of Controversy, Conflict, and Communal Movements in Northern India, 1923–1928*, Leiden: E.J. Brill, 1975.

Vazīrābādī, Anjum, *Ḥusayn Dūsroṅ kī Naẓar meṅ*, Lahore: Maktaba-i Ahbab, n.d.

Bibliography

C.M. Naim

Books

Twenty-five Verses of Ghalib, trans. C. M. Naim. Calcutta: Writers Workshop, 1970.

Faiz Ahmad Faiz, *Eleven Poems and Introduction*, trans. C. M. Naim and Carlo Coppola, Calcutta: Dialogue Calcutta (19), 1971.

Ghalib's Lighter Verses, trans. C. M. Naim. Calcutta: Writers Workshop, 1972.

Five+One (short stories), New Delhi: Bhasha Prakashan, 1976.

Naim, C. M. (ed.), *Iqbal Jinnah and Pakistan: The Vision and the Reality*, Syracuse: Maxwell School of Citizenship and Public Affairs, Syracuse University, 1979.

Parasi, Harishankar, *Inspector Matadeen on the Moon: Selected Satires*, trans. C. M. Naim. New Delhi: Manas, 1994; 2nd ed., New Delhi: Katha, 2003.

Rai, Narain Vibhuti, *Curfew in the City*, trans. C. M. Naim. New Delhi: Roli Books, 1998.

Hyder, Qurratulain, *A Season of Betrayals: A Short Story and Two Novellas*, trans. C. M. Naim. New Delhi: Kali for Women, 1999.

Ambiguities of Heritage: Fictions and Polemics. Karachi: City Press, 1999.

Zikr-i Mir: The Autobiography of the Eighteenth Century Mughal Poet: Mir Muhammad Taqi 'Mir', 1723–1810. New Delhi: Oxford University Press, 1999.

Ahmad, Nazir, *The Repentance of Nussooh (Taubat-al-Nasûh): The Tale of a Muslim Family a Hundred Years Ago*, trans. M. Kempson, ed. C. M. Naim. Delhi: Permanent Black, 2004.

Urdu Texts and Contexts: The Selected Essays of C. M. *Naim*. Delhi: Permanent Black, 2004.

Pedagogical Materials

Urdu Reader (with John Gumperz, June Romery, and A. B. Singh), Berkeley: Center for South Asia Studies, University of California, 1960.

Conversational Hindi–Urdu (with John Gumperz and June Romery), 2 vols, Berkeley: ASUC Store, University of California, 1963.

Readings in Urdu: Prose and Poetry. Honolulu: East–West Center Press, University of Hawaii, 1965. Available at *http://dsal.uchicago.edu*.

Introductory Urdu, 2 vols, Chicago: Committee on Southern Asian Studies, University of Chicago, 1975. 2nd ed., Chicago, 1980. 3rd ed., Chicago, 1999. Also published New Delhi, 2000. Available at *http://dsal.uchicago.edu*.

Articles

'Formal and Informal Standards in the Hindi Regional Language Area' (with John J. Gumperz), *International Journal of American Linguistics* 26:3 (1960), 92–118.

'Faiz Ahmad Faiz: A Biographical Sketch' (with Carlo Coppola), *Mahfil* 1:1 (1964), 2–3.

'Sadat Hasan Manto: A Biographical Sketch', *Mahfil* 1:1 (1964), 12–13.

'Traditional Symbolism in the Modern Urdu Ghazal', in *Languages and Areas; Studies Presented to George V. Bobrinskoy*, ed. Milton Singer (Chicago: Committee on Southern Asian Studies, University of Chicago, 1967), 105–11.

'The Consequences of Indo-Pakistani War for Urdu Language and Literature', *Journal of Asian Studies* 38:2 (Feb. 1969), 269–83.

'Arabic Orthography and Some Non-Semitic Languages', in *Islam and Its Cultural Divergence (Studies in Honor of Gustave E. von Grunebaum)*, ed. G. L. Tikku (Urbana: University of Illinois Press, 1971), 113–44.

'Yes, The Poem Itself', *Literature East and West* 15:1 (March 1971), 7–16.

'The "Muslim Problem" in India', *Quest* (Bombay), 75 (March–April 1972), 51–63.

'A Program for Partial Automation in Comparative Reconstruction', *Anthropological Linguistics* 4:9 (Dec. 1972), 1–10.

'Muslim Contribution to Literature in India: The Medieval Period', *Encyclopaedia Britannica*, 15th ed., in 'Art of South Asian People' (Chicago, 1974), 144–46.

'Ghazal and Taghazzul', in *The Literatures of India: An Introduction*, ed. Edward C. Dimock (Chicago: University of Chicago Press, 1974), 185–97.

'Muslim Press in India and the Bangladesh Crisis', *Quest* (Bombay), 94 (March–April 1975), 27–37.

'The "Pseudo-dramatic" Poems of Iqbal', *Journal of South Asian and Middle Eastern Studies* 1:2 (Dec. 1977), 58–67.

'The Theme of Homosexual (Pederastic) Love in Pre-modern Urdu Poetry', in *Studies in the Urdu Gazal and Prose Fiction*, ed. Muhammad U. Memon (Madison: South Asian Studies Publication Series 5, 1979), 120–42.

'The Art of the Urdu Marsiya', in *Islamic Society and Culture: Essays in Honor of Professor Aziz Ahmad*, ed. Milton Israel and N. K. Wagle (New Delhi: Manohar, 1983), 101–16.

'Prize-Winning Adab: A Study of Five Books Written in Response to the Allahabad Government Gazette Notification', in *Moral Conduct and Authority: The Place of Adab in South Asian Islam*, ed. Barbara D. Metcalf (Berkeley: University of California Press, 1984), 290–314.

'Urdu in the Pre-Modern Period: Synthesis or Particularism?', *New Quest* (Bombay), 6 (Feb. 1987), 5–12.

'How Bibi Ashraf Learned to Read and Write', *Annual of Urdu Studies* 6 (1987), 99–115.

'Being a Muslim in India: The Challenge and the Opportunity', in *Contemporary Indian Tradition: Voices on Culture, Nature, and the Challenge of Change*, ed. Carla M. Borden (Washington, D.C.: Smithsonian Institution Press, 1989), 57–65.

'Poet–Audience Interaction at Urdu Mushairas', in *Urdu and Muslim South Asia (Studies in Honor of Ralph Russell)*, ed. Christopher Shackle (London: School of Oriental and African Studies, University of London, 1989), 167–73.

'In the Eye of the Intifada' (2 parts), *The Message International*, August 1989, 11–18; September 1989, 21–36.

'Urdu', in *The Cambridge Encyclopedia of India, Pakistan, Bangladesh, Sri Lanka*, 'Literature: Regional Languages', ed. Francis Robinson (Cambridge: Cambridge University Press, 1989), 424–27.

'The Outrage of Bernard Lewis', *Social Text* 30 (1992), 114–20.

'The Ghazal Itself: Translating Ghalib', *The Yale Journal of Criticism* 5:3 (Fall 1992), 219–32.

'Minority Rights or Human Rights?', *South Asia Bulletin* 12:2 (Fall 1992), 35–8.

'Mughal and English Patronage of Urdu Poetry: A Comparison', in *The Powers of Art: Patronage in Indian Culture*, ed. Barbara Stoler Miller (Delhi: Oxford University Press, 1992), 259–76.

'Exile, Displacement, Hijrat: What's in a Name!', *The Toronto South Asian Review* 11:2 (Winter 1993), 74–8.

'The Situation of the Urdu Writer: A Letter from Bara Banki, December 1993/February 1994', *World Literature Today* 68:2 (Spring 1994), 245–6. Reprinted in *Annual of Urdu Studies* 10 (1995), 121–5.

'The Second Tyranny of Religious Majorities', *South Asia Bulletin* 14:2 (1994), 104–7.

'Ambiguities of Heritage.' *The Toronto Review* 14:1 (Summer 1995), 1–5.

'Urdu Education in India: Some Observations', *Annual of Urdu Studies* 10 (1995), 153–9.

'Popular Jokes and Political History: The Case of Akbar, Birbal and Mulla Do-Piyaza', *Economic and Political Weekly* 30:24 (June 17, 1995), 1456–64.

'Getting Real About Christian–Muslim Dialogue', *First Things* 57 (Nov. 1995), 10–12. Reprinted in *Word and World* 16:2 (Spring 1996), 179–83; *Salaam* (New Delhi) and *ISIM Newsletter* (Leiden).

'Urdu Shikasta' (with Frances Pritchett), in *Reading Nasta'liq: Persian and Urdu Hands from 1500 to the Present*, ed. William L. Hanaway and Brian Spooner (Costa Mesa, CA: Mazda Publishers, 1995), 227–69.

'Mir and His Patrons', *Annual of Urdu Studies* 14 (1999), 85–95.

'A Dissent on "Fire"', *The Toronto Review*, 18:1 (Fall 1999), 11–19.

'The Earliest Extant Review of *Umra'o Jan Ada*', *Annual of Urdu Studies* 15:1 (2000), 287–91.

'Transvestic Words? The *Rekhtī* in Urdu', *Annual of Urdu Studies* 16 (2001), 3–26.

Response to the forum, 'Tracking "Same-Sex Love" from Antiquity to the Present in South Asia', in *Gender and History*, 14:1 (April 2002), 14–17.

'Dahe' and 'Marsiya', in *South Asian Folklore: An Encyclopedia*, ed. Margaret A. Mills, Peter J. Claus, Sarah Diamond (New York: Routledge, 2003), 134, 185.

'Ghalib's Delhi: A Shamelessly Revisionist Look at Two Metaphors', *Annual of Urdu Studies* 18 (2003), 3–24.

Translations

'Twelve Poems and an Introduction' (trans. of poems and preface by Faiz Ahmad Faiz), *Mahfil* 1:1 (1964), 3–10.

'Cold, Like Ice' (trans. of a story by Sadat Hasan Manto, with Ruth L. Schmidt), *Mahfil* 1:1 (1964), 14–19.

'Metamorphosis' (trans. of a story by Intizar Husain), *Mahfil* 1:1 (1964), 22–9.

'The Smell of Adam's Son' (trans. of poem by N. M. Rashid, with A. K. Ramanujan), *Mahfil* 2:2 (1965), 2.

'Sheba in Ruins' (trans. of poem by N. M. Rashid, with A. K. Ramanujan), *Mahfil* 2:2 (1965), 5.

'The Tale of the Old Fisherman' (trans. of chapter from *Udās Nasleṅ* by Abdullah Husain, with Gordon Roadarmel), *Mahfil* 2:2 (1965), 7–16.

'Three Poems' (trans. of poems by Faiz Ahmad Faiz, with Carlo Coppola), *Mahfil* 2:2 (1965), 39–41.

'Waasokht' (trans. of poem by Faiz Ahmad Faiz, with Burton Raffel), *Mahfil* 2:2 (1965), 42.

'The Old Bookseller' (trans. of poem by Jilani Kamran), *Mahfil* 2:2 (1965), 51.

'Come Snake, Bite My Heel...' (trans. of poem by Gauhar Naushahi), *Mahfil* 2:2 (1965), 52.

'Thatha' (trans. of poem by Mukhtar Siddiqi), *Mahfil* 2:2 (1965), 63–6.

'Urinal' (trans. of short story by Sadat Hasan Manto), *Mahfil* 4:2 (1968), 21–2.

'The Poem (Ghalib's) Itself' (trans. of poems by Ghalib), *Mahfil* 5:4 (1969), 97–114.

'Two Men, Slightly Wet' (trans. of short story by Iqbal Majid), *Edebiyat* 1:2 (1976), 199–205.

'And Now the Pen Brings Forth Some Jokes' (trans. of anecdotes by Mir Taqi Mir, with introduction), *Annual of Urdu Studies* 2 (1982), 49–51.

'Mozelle' (trans. of short story by Sadat Hasan Manto), in *Selected Short Stories from Pakistan*, ed. Ahmed Ali (Islamabad: Pakistan Academy of Letters, 1983), 191–213.

'The Wounded Cat in an Empty Sack' (trans. of poem by Saqi Faruqi), *Annual of Urdu Studies* 3 (1983), 44.

'Fancy Haircutting Saloon' (trans. of short story by Ghulam Abbas), *Annual of Urdu Studies* 3 (1983), 65–73.

'The Prisoner(s)' (trans. of short story by Intizar Husain), *Journal of South Asian Literature* 18:2 (1983), 115–20.

'To Be or Not To Be' (trans. of short story by Zahidah Hina), *Annual of Urdu Studies* 4 (1984), 69–73.

'Three Poems' (trans. of poems by Kishvar Nahid), *Annual of Urdu Studies* 4 (1984), 75–7.

'Two Poems' (trans. of poems by Zahidah Zaidi), *Annual of Urdu Studies* 4 (1984), 78.

'Four Poems' (trans. of poems by Fahmidah Riyaz), *Annual of Urdu Studies* 4 (1984), 79–80.

'Six Poems' (trans. of poems by Parvin Shakir), *Annual of Urdu Studies* 4 (1984), 81–2.

'Three Poems' (trans. of poems by Tanvir Anjum), *Annual of Urdu Studies* 4 (1984), 83–4.

'Travelogue' (trans. of poem by N. M. Rashid), *Annual of Urdu Studies* 5 (1985), 21–2.

'Sheba in Ruins' (trans. of poem by N. M. Rashid, with A. K. Ramanujan), *Annual of Urdu Studies* 5 (1985), 35–6.

'Poems from *Māvarā*' (trans. of poems by N. M. Rashid), *Annual of Urdu Studies* 5 (1985), 49–50.

'Poems from *Īrān meṅ ajnabī*' (trans. of poems by N. M. Rashid), *Annual of Urdu Studies* 5 (1985), 51–2.

'A Woman' (trans. of short story by Rajindar Singh Bedi), *Annual of Urdu Studies* 5 (1985), 77–80.

'Prabodh and Maitriya' (trans. of short story by Rajindar Singh Bedi), *Annual of Urdu Studies* 5 (1985), 98–100.

'Evening', 'The Color of My Heart', 'A Scene' (trans. of poems by Faiz Ahmad Faiz with Carlo Coppola), *Annual of Urdu Studies* 5 (1985), 113–15.

'Wazir Agha: Eleven Poems' (trans. of poems by Wazir Agha, with introduction), *Annual of Urdu Studies* 6 (1987), 33–41.

'Their Fear' (trans. of Hindi short story by Asghar Vajahat), *Namaste* 9:3 (1989), 25–9.

'Six Poems' (trans. of poems by Azra Abbas), *Annual of Urdu Studies* 7 (1990), 45–8.

'Autobiography' (trans. of essay by Surendra Prakash), *Annual of Urdu Studies* 7 (1990), 62–6.

'The Grave' (trans. of short story by Ram Lal), *Namaste* 11:4 (1991), 24–8.

'Some Other Man's Home' (trans. of short story by Jilani Bano), in *Domains of Fear and Desire: Urdu Stories*, ed. Muhammad Umar Memon (Toronto: TSAR Publications, 1992), 142–54.

'Introducing Mirza Zahirdar Beg' (trans. from the novel *Taubat un-Nuṣūḥ* by Nazir

Ahmad), in *Modern Indian Literature: An Anthology*, vol. 2: Fiction (New Delhi: Sahitya Akademi, 1992), 1127–31.

'A Lover's Predicament' (trans. from the novel *Umrao Jan Ada* by Mirza Muhammad Hadi Rusva), in *Modern Indian Literature: An Anthology*, vol. 2: Fiction (New Delhi: Sahitya Akademi, 1992), 1191–213.

'Parveen Shakir: A Note and Twelve Poems', *Annual of Urdu Studies* 8 (1993), 181–91.

'Dawn' (trans. of short story by Muhsin Khan), *World Literature Today* 68:2 (Spring 1994), 247–9.

'Seven Poems' (trans. of poems by Afzal Ahmad Sayyid), *Toronto Review* 16:1 (Fall 1997), 52–8.

'Five Poems' (trans. of poems by Iftikhar Nasim), *Annual of Urdu Studies* 13 (1998), 287–9.

'Mir On His Patrons' (trans. of excerpts from *Zikr-i Mir*), *Annual of Urdu Studies* 14 (1999), 97–102.

Index